A history of Dagenham
in the County of Essex

A history of Dagenham in the County of Essex

John Peter Shawcross

Facsimile reprint of the 2nd edition (1908)

Scans prepared by Derek Alexander

VALENCE HOUSE

a place of discovery

Valence House Publications

Published in 2016 by Valence House Publications
Valence House, Becontree Avenue
Dagenham, Essex RM8 3HT

www.valencehousecollections.co.uk

ISBN 978-1-911391-03-6

Introduction and all editorial material copyright ©Valence
House Publications 2016

Cover image: Crown Street, Dagenham c1900 by A.T. Bates,
1987 Valence House Museum (LDVAL 3035)

INTRODUCTION

When the Reverend John Peter Shawcross began work on this book in the late 1890s, Dagenham was already in the grip of change. Census figures show that in the 40 years between 1861 and 1901 its population had risen by 125%, from 2,708 to 6,091. This was mainly due to the opening of railway stations at Chadwell Heath (1864) and Dagenham (1885) followed by the inevitable growth in commuter housing.

He knew the pace of change would accelerate: "In a few years Dagenham will lose its rural individuality, and be drawn into the relentless vortex of Greater London, and the fields, lanes, woodlands and green swards will disappear never to return".

Most of his research was done using old documents, but he often refers to stories from 'old inhabitants" whose memories stretched back to the middle of the 19th century – allowing us glimpses of a now-vanished landscape and way of life.

We are grateful, too, for his account on pages 116 to 122 of memorial inscriptions in Dagenham parish churchyard, many of which are now illegible or have disappeared altogether. The illustration on page 103 of the brass on Sir Thomas Urswick's tomb inside the church is also of vital importance – the section depicting the Urswick sons has since disappeared, so the is drawing is our record of what is now lost.

Some of Shawcross's statements are not accepted by modern historians. For example, on page 266 he writes that "In regard to its derivation, Chadwell Heath means the heath adjoining St Chad's Well". It's now believed that the name Chadwell derives from Chaudewell, meaning cold spring.

Unfortunately Shawcross's research notes and original manuscript have not survived, despite efforts by John Gerard O'Leary to track them down when researching his own history, *The Book of Dagenham*.

THE AUTHOR

John Peter Shawcross was born in 1863 in the town of Hanley in the Staffordshire Potteries, and baptised at Holy Trinity, Northwood on August 9th. His father William was a schoolmaster who would later make a change of career, becoming a Church of England vicar.

John gained a first-class degree in theology at Oxford University in 1886. He was ordained the following year and appointed Curate of Holt with Little Witley, Worcestershire. In 1890 he obtained his MA degree and was runner-up in the Ellerton Theological Essay prize competition.

In October 1893 John was appointed Vicar-designate of Chadwell Heath. St Chad's Church had been opened in 1886 on land donated by retired corn merchant Richard Payze of Broomfield House. It was initially a chapel-of-ease within the parish of Dagenham, but was promoted to parish church status when Chadwell Heath became a separate parish in 1895. The Reverend Shawcross was formally instituted by the Bishop of St Albans on 3 October 1895. His home was a vicarage in the High Road (at the junction with what is now Farrance Road), built on land donated by the Romford brewers Ind Coope.

On 30 November 1893 John married Henrietta Maria Sale at Trinity Church, Paddington. His bride was the daughter of Colonel Thomas Henry Sale of the Bengal Engineers. Their first child, Mildred, followed in 1895 but sadly died before her second birthday. On 28 March 1898 their son Leonard was born.

In 1904 the first edition of Shawcross's *A History of Dagenham* was published. Later that year he resigned from St Chad's, preaching his final sermon on Thursday 13 October. His new post was Chaplain to the Winchester Union. He issued a second edition of his *A History of Dagenham* in 1908.

In 1917 Shawcross was appointed Vicar of Bengeworth, near Evesham in Worcestershire. He plunged into researching the history of his new parish. Sadly, failing eyesight forced him to retire in January 1926 and move to a Home for the Blind in Portland Place, Brighton. His history of Bengeworth was published the following year.

On 2 June 1929 John Peter Shawcross died at Brighton aged 65. His body was taken back to Bengeworth where he was buried on 7 June. Arthur Lewis, his successor as Vicar of Bengeworth, described him as "a student to the end" who "had little regard for outward things".

Probate records reveal that Mr Shawcross's estate was valued at £10,195. His widow Henrietta reached the age of 90 before passing away in January 1948 at Wood End House asylum in Hayes, Middlesex. Their only surviving child, Leonard, died unmarried at Eastbourne in October 1977 aged 79.

Linda Rhodes
Local Studies Librarian for Barking and Dagenham

Valence House is the home of the London Borough of Barking and Dagenham's Museum and Archives and Local Studies Centre. It is a focus for local community heritage projects in which professional staff encourage enthusiastic volunteers to use their natural talents and learnt skills for mutual benefit.

Previous titles from Valence House Publications:

- H.C. Fanshawe: The life of Sir Richard Fanshawe 1608-1666 (chapter from his History of the Fanshawe family, originally published 1927)

- Sebastopol to Dagenham: Crimean War letters of Captain Thomas Basil Fanshawe

Note on the text and illustrations:

The illustrations in the original book are on glossy paper tipped in to the text. For this edition, we have reproduced the illustrations but have not included the blank page on the back of each. Because the illustrations are not paginated, the odd and even page numbers sometimes appear on the "wrong" side of the text.

The Rev. John Peter Shawcross
with his son Leonard

(from his book *Bengeworth: being some account of the history
of church and parish* (1927), plate X, page 75)

A HISTORY OF DAGENHAM

IN

THE COUNTY OF ESSEX

BY THE REV.

J. P. SHAWCROSS, M.A.,

FORMERLY VICAR OF CHADWELL HEATH, AND
CHAPLAIN TO THE WEST HAM COUNTY BOROUGH ASYLUM

SECOND AND CHEAPER EDITION

London

SKEFFINGTON AND SON

34, SOUTHAMPTON STREET, STRAND, W.C.

Publishers to His Majesty the King

1908

PREFACE

THE present work owes its origin to a list of the vicars of Dagenham, which I compiled and printed several years ago in the *Chadwell Heath Church Monthly*. The list had not long been published before some fresh names and facts came to my knowledge which caused me to revise it, with various additions and corrections. While engaged in this research, I consulted, *inter alia*, the various county histories of Essex (Morant, Salmon, Muilman, etc.), where I came across references to or succinct descriptions of the manors which formerly existed in this parish. These several accounts were, from the nature of the case, of an abbreviated character, and therefore capable of expansion with more fulness of detail, both in regard to the manors themselves and their lords and tenants. With this accumulation of notes relating to the vicars and to the manors of Dagenham, I found that I had sufficient material on hand for a brief history of Dagenham. A perusal of the parish registers considerably augmented this nucleus, which some of my friends advised me to publish. An intimation to this effect to the local public brought in additional matter—the result being this present volume, the compilation of which has proved an agreeable relaxation in the round of parochial work in a growing district of London-over-the-Border.

A parochial history may be regarded from three points of view at least. First, as the history of a little world in itself. Secondly, as a local history considered as part of the history of our country generally. Thirdly, as a combination of the two former—the history of the annals of a local, circumscribed district with a

portion of the larger history of the nation absorbed in it. In
some cases, from the nature and character of the place, the history
of a parish is that of a limited area and little more. But in the
present instance we have a narrative which will be found to throw
light upon and include, though obliquely, part of the history of
our country at large. This is due to the proximity of the parish
of Dagenham to the city of London. It is this which chiefly
gives our present local history its interest and its value. It will
be seen from the following pages that some seven or eight Lord
Mayors of London, as well as several judges, had some connection
by residence or otherwise with Dagenham, and that a few of these
were buried in the churchyard here. Next to the history of
London is, perhaps, in point of interest, that of the villages round
London. The marvellous and steady growth of the metropolis,
whereby the suburbs and outlying villages are being incorporated
within its borders, tends to deepen that interest. In a few years
Dagenham will lose its rural individuality, and be drawn into the
relentless vortex of Greater London, and the fields, lanes, woodlands, and green swards will disappear, never to return.

I desire to express my best thanks to the Rev. Dr. Moore,
vicar of Dagenham, for granting me free access to the parish
registers and minute books, and to the Revs. C. C. Harrison and
W. H. Shawcross, and W. W. Glenny, Esq., for useful hints and
suggestions. My grateful acknowledgments are also due to
E. J. Sage, Esq., for allowing me to consult his large collection
of MSS. and wills relating to Dagenham and the surrounding
parishes, the Barking Manor Court Rolls, extracts from the parish
registers, and for much oral information ; also for allowing me to
reproduce maps and engravings ; to C. Avery, Esq., for some
archæological notes ; to Mrs. Ridout for notes on the Fanshawe
family ; and to A. Bennett Bamford, Esq., for the great pains he
has taken in preparing the illustrations, maps, and plates of arms
for this book, and in correcting the proof-sheets.

I am indebted also to E. A. Fitch, Esq., for the loan of two
blocks illustrating Dagenham Breach ; to the author of "Ilford

Past and Present," for that of St. Chad's Well; to Mr. R. T. Aldous for several excellent photographs, and to Mr. Robt. Farrance for permission to reproduce the painting of the Three Mills of Chadwell Heath.

I would add that, although it has been my endeavour to secure accuracy as far as possible, this work makes no claim to infallibility. I shall be glad, therefore, of any corrections and additions to this book, should it ever be republished.

J. P. S.

September, 1904.

PREFACE TO THE SECOND EDITION

IN publishing the second edition of the " History of Dagenham," I desire to express my gratitude to the general public for their favourable reception of this work. The press notices and reviews were of an appreciative character, and in some cases contained many useful suggestions and helpful criticisms. I am indebted to various friends and readers for kindly pointing out slips and errors, and for supplying additional notes; particularly would I thank Sydney Maddocks, Esq., S. Pepys Cockerell, Esq., A. M. W. Fuller, Esq., and C. H. Firth, Esq. (Regius Professor of Modern History at Oxford).

J. P. S.

St. Cross, Winchester,
November, 1908.

The corrections and additions will be found at the end of the book. They have reference to the following pages: 5, 6, 17, 20, 22, 23, 30, 34, 38, 39, 40, 54, 57, 58, 67, 70, 74, 75, 76, 78, 81, 87, 90, 109, 110, 111, 119, 127, 133, 140, 141, 143, 154, 172, 182, 184, 185, 188, 196, 199, 204, 205, 210, 211, 212, 214, 218, 263, 265, 267, 268 280 284, 300.

TABLE OF CONTENTS

x   Table of Contents

LIST OF ILLUSTRATIONS

  1. MERTTINS OF VALENCE.—Azure, two bars or; in chief a Catherine
     wheel between two bugle horns garnished and stringed argent.
  2. HENSHAWE OF VALENCE.—Argent; a chevron ermines between three
     Cornish choughs sable, beaked and membered gules.
  3. TIMOTHY LUCY OF VALENCE.—Gules; semée with crosses Botonée, three
     luces hauriant argent; over all, Fanshawe of Jenkins.
  4. OSBORNE OF PARSLOES.—Quarterly ermine and azure; a cross or.
  5. BONHAM OF VALENCE.—Gules; a chevron wavy between three crosses;
     patée fitchée argent charged with a crescent gules.
  6. COOTE OF VALENCE.—Argent; a chevron between three cootes sable.
  7. FANSHAWE OF PARSLOES.—Or; a chevron between three fleure-de-lis
     sable.

  1. HERVEY OF MARKS.—Gules; on a bend argent, three trefoils slipped vert;
     a crescent of the second for difference.
  2. URSWICK OF MARKS.—Argent; on a bend sable, three lozenges of the
     first, on each a saltier gules.
  3. MILDMAY OF MARKS.—Argent; three lions rampant azure, armed and
     langued gules.
  4. HARVEY OF WANGEY.—Or; a chevron between three lions or leopards'
     faces gules.
  5. UPHILL OF DAGENHAM.—Sable; a pale between four trefoils slipped
     argent.
  6. ALIBON OF DAGENHAM.—Vert; on a bend argent, three crosses formée
     fitchée azure.
  7. COMYNS OF DAGENHAM AND ROMFORD. — Azure; a chevron ermine
     between three garbs or.

"There is not an acre, I think I may say, in England, certainly there is not a parish or manor, that has not its place in English history, either as the scene of some considerable act, or as the home of some considerable man ; and there is not, I think, an intelligent person in England who is not in one way or another a sharer in such interests of tradition, if he would or could realize it. By grasping your own personal connection with these, you realize your historical relation to the progress of the country, and by working out the details of the local or personal history in which you are so interested, you may yourselves largely contribute to the ascertaining of historical truth in details. Every parish must have a history, every parish has a register, every person has a parish. Every manor has a lord, and every lord has had a share in the struggles by which our national life has become what it is, and every lord has had a following of his tenants, whose blood, shed for him, as it may have been, quite as certainly as for the cause in which he was enlisted, may constitute for us, who are not descended from lords of manors, our personal link with the past. Of course, some parts of England have been the scenes of more bloody battles and keener political conflicts than others, but it is very rare to find any district which has not its own special traditions and local affections" (Bishop Stubbs's "Lectures," 3rd edition, p. 473).

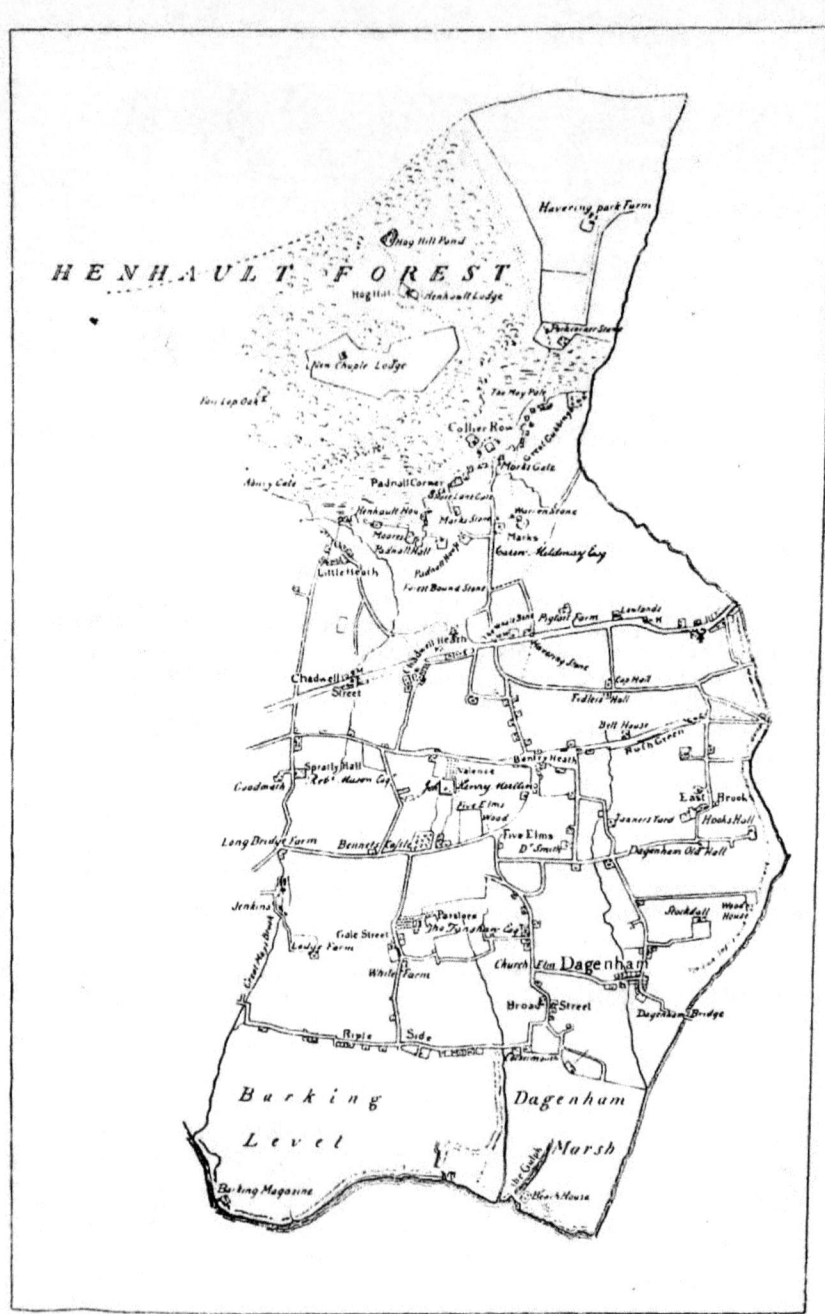

MAP OF DAGENHAM.   [*To face p. 1.*]

A HISTORY OF DAGENHAM

CHAPTER I

THE PARISH OF DAGENHAM

> "I love thee,—when I trace thy tale
>   To the dim point where records fail ;
>   Thy deeds of old renown inspire
>   My bosom with our fathers' fire ;
>   A proud inheritance I claim
>   In all their sufferings, all their fame,
>   Nor less delighted, when I stray
>   Down History's lengthening, widening way."
>
> MONTGOMERY.

THE parish of Dagenham is one of several which lie at the south-east extremity of the county of Essex. It consists of a strip of land nearly oblong in shape stretching from the river Thames on the south to Hainault Forest on the north. On the west it is bounded by the ancient parish of Barking, of which it was formerly a part, and also by the modern parish of Great Ilford. On the east it is separated from the parishes of Romford and Hornchurch by the Beam, a tributary of the river Rom. The parish is about seven miles long and one and a half miles wide, and contains an area of 6650 acres.[1]

The general features of Dagenham are of a diversified and comprehensive character, as it comprises river, lake, forest, coppice, heath, marsh, arable land, and pasture. Its general situation is low. At its southern extremity the land level is only four feet above that of the sea ; this rises gradually to seventy feet, its highest point at Marks Gate on the north. The river and gulf cover some 200 acres, and the foreshore and marshes 300 acres more. The soil is London clay, gravel, and sand, with a stratum of moor-logg and peat near the river.

---

[1] It is not to be confounded with Dagenhams or Dagnams, an estate lying three miles to the north-east of Romford.

B

Territorially the parish of Dagenham is in the metropolitan county of Essex, in the half-Hundred[1] of Becontree, and with eleven other parishes makes the Romford Union. Ecclesiastically it is in the diocese of St. Albans, in the archdeaconry of Essex, and in the rural deanery of Chafford. In two instances it is included in the South Barking deanery, and in one case in Barstable.

Judging from the contents of the parish registers, and from the large number of Londoners buried in the churchyard, this parish was well known in London. Many of the citizens knew it as a quiet, retired village, fertile and well-wooded, distant some thirteen miles by river from London Bridge and twelve by road from Aldgate. It had the distinction of containing more manors than any other parish round London on its east side, occupied by people of wealth and position. The importance of the parish may also be inferred from the fact that it contributed at one time to the king's taxes more than what came from " Bednal Green," " Westhamme," or " Easthamme " The more than ordinary gratification with which the news of the adhesion of Dagenham to the Royalist cause was received by Charles I. supports this inference.

The earliest mention of Dagenham is in the Charter of Hodelred, which contains the names of certain lands granted to the Abbess of Barking for the endowment of the abbey there. Most of the places mentioned in that deed cannot be recognized ; but Deccanhaam is certainly Dagenham. Hodelred was the father of Sebbi,[2] king of the East Saxons, consequently the date of this grant would be about 692-93. The document is the oldest of its kind in England. It is in Latin.[3] The following is a translation of that part of it which refers to Dagenham and its immediate locality—

I, Hodelredus, father of Sebbi, in the province of East Saxons, with his consent, by my own will, and being of a sound mind and of a sober judgment, give in perpetuity to thee, Hedilburga the Abbess, to increase the monastery which is called Beddanhaan. And I, with full legal right, transfer to thy possession certain lands called Ricingahaam, Budinhaam, Daecanhaam, Angenlabeshaam, and what is called Unidmundesfelt in the heath by the wood.[4]

[1] It is called a half-Hundred because the Royal Liberty of Havering-atte-Bower was taken out of it.

[2] Sebbi is mentioned elsewhere as a generous contributor to the fund for building the original St. Paul's Cathedral.

[3] A facsimile is given in Lyson's " History," and a Latin recension is quoted at length in Dugdale's " Monasticon."

[4] Possibly the heath afterwards known as Chadwell Heath.

This is done in the month of March, and I have requested witnesses to bear testimony to this my deed of gift.

If any one shall attempt to oppose this charter of gift, or render it null and void, let him know, before Almighty God and Jesus Christ His Son and the Holy Spirit, that is, the Undivided Trinity, that he is condemned and cut off from all Christian communion.

. . . Now these are the boundaries of the land . . . on the east, Writola Burora ; on the north, the Centincertbrogh ; on the south, the river Thames.

Should any one desire to increase this benefaction, may God increase his goods in the land of the living with His saints, now and always. Amen.

I, Sebbi, king of East Saxons, have subscribed, for confirmation.

I, Oedelraedus, the donor, have subscribed:

I, Ercenuualdus,[1] bishop, have assented and subscribed.

I, Unilfrid,[2] bishop, have assented and subscribed, and I, Haedde,[2] bishop, have agreed and subscribed.

I, Ouda, priest and abbot, have subscribed in agreement.

I, Egebaldus, priest and abbot, have agreed and subscribed.

I Hagona, priest and abbot, have agreed and subscribed.

I, Hooc, priest and abbot, have agreed and subscribed.

Seal ✠ of the hand of King Sebbi.

Seal ✠ of the hand of King Sigihearde.

Seal ✠ of the hand of King Suebredus.

The document is endorsed—" De Terra quam donavit Odilraedus."[3] It is also mentioned in Bishop Ercenwald's grant of privileges and confirmation of lands to the monastery of Bercingas, or Barking.[4]

The derivation of Dagenham is obscure. " Ham " means, of course, a village or town,[5] and Dagen may be a corruption of " Daecan," or " Dekken," or " Daken," the name of some Saxon inhabitant or early colonist. Probably the name meant at first no more than a piece of land belonging to one " Deccan," situated where the village proper now stands, and which afterwards came to

---

[1] Bishop of London and founder of Barking Abbey.

[2] A Unilfrid (Wilfrid) was Bishop of Mercia (Worcester) 717-43. Haeddi was Bishop of the West Saxons (Winchester) in 676.

[3] See " Cartularium Saxonicum," vol. i., edited by Mr. W. de Gray Birch.

[4] In Domesday Book, Barking is called Burchingas. Salmon derives it from *berg*, a hill, and *ing*, a meadow, *i.e.* a hill in a meadow. Morant derives it from the Saxon *beorce*, birch-trees, and *ing*, *i.e.* a meadow planted with birch-trees. Others suppose *burg* to mean a fortification.

[5] Generally speaking, the names of our parishes are Saxon ; as the old rhyme says—

> " In ford, in ham, in ley, in tun,
> The most of English surnames run."

be used in an extended sense, to describe the southern portion of the present parish. It is thought by some that the name meant, originally, "the village of the Danes," but against this theory is the fact that the name Deccanham is found, as already stated, prior to the Danish invasion. It is variously spelt—Daecanhaam, Deckenham, Dakenham, Dagnham, and Daggenham. Norden, in his "History of Essex" (printed about 1594), marks it "Dagnhams." It is not mentioned in Domesday, as it was then included in the parish of Barking.

In the *Taxatio Ecclesiastica*, or *Valor Ecclesiasticus*, of Pope Nicholas, made about 1291, the Ecclesia de Dakenham (which is included in the hundred of Berkyng) is assessed at £13 6s. 8d. The object of this taxation was to ascertain the total amount of the first-fruits which the Pope had granted to the king to carry on the Holy Wars with the Saracens. In 1293 a valuation of all livings in the county of Essex was made by command of Edward I. This valuation is that which all the ancient statutes refer to, being that by which all the first-fruits to the Pope were settled until the new survey was made by Henry VIII. in 1523. Dagenham comes under the "Decanatus de Berkyng," and is valued at twenty marks.[1] From this it would seem that the parish, as an ecclesiastical *cure*, dates from the thirteenth century at least, and possibly from the beginning of that century. Out of this grew the civil parish of Dagenham, the order of progress being, first the church, then the area it was more immediately meant to serve, and finally the parish, having its unit in the church for assessments and taxations of whatsoever kind.

We read of an order being made on May 7, 1274, in the king's name, at Westminster, to the escheator, to cause Peter de Bezile, nephew and heir of Emery de Bezile, tenant-in-chief, to have seisin of a messuage and a carucate[2] of land in Dakenham, whereof Emery was seised in demesne as of fee at his death, and which he held of the Abbess of Barking.

The earliest designation of Dagenham as a *parochia* occurs in a Latin document dated 1312–13. It is a "release by John and Richard Godefroy, of Berkyngg, to John . . . and Agnes his wife, of land, 'in villa de Berkyngg in parochia de Dakenham, formerly the dower land (*i.e.* marriage portion) of Amicia Godefreyes,

---

[1] A mark was a silver coin, of the value of 13s. 4d.

[2] Carucate is the term describing the team employed on land, and thus describing the land actually in cultivation. It varied in extent, from sixty to eighty acres.

sometime wife of Robert Godefreyes. Witnesses—Thomas de Dakenham, Richard le May, Stephen Bysshopp,[1] and others.' Given at Berkyngge the Tuesday after the Feast of the Nativity of St. John Baptist, in the sixth year of Edward the Second."

An interesting glimpse into the state of the parish in the fourteenth century is afforded us in a valuable subsidy roll, unfortunately undecipherable in places. It is an assessment of Dakenham, made in the thirteenth year of Edward II. (1320-21) by John de Lyston and Henry Grigge. Fifty-six names are given under Dakenham, not including those (about twenty) which cannot be deciphered, as against twenty-two in a subsidy for Layton, of the same date, and seventeen for " Wanstede and Hilleforde." It is as follows :—

VILL. OF DAKENHAM.

	s.	d.				s.	d.
John de Cokermowe	9	1½	Henry Attwoode	..	..		—
Gilbert de Ridere	3	6¾	Gerald Cor	..	..		—
Godfrey de Frislinge	3	0¼	Willm de Newry	..	..		—
William Coto	2	1½	Gilbert Hunfrie'	..	..		—
William Alfrid	2	2	John de Coke	..	..		—
John Hack	2	3	Henry de Cornshaw	..	..		—
Hugh le Tork	2	3	Willm Hugh	..	..		—
John Hunfrey	2	3	Will. Nulock	..	..	1	2
Godebold ..	3	3	John Godbald	..	..	1	0
Rich. le May	3	5¼	* * *		*		
John Mathew	2	0¼	John Cripe	..	..	1	0¾
Ralph de Lord	1	11	Robert Purl	..	..	2	3
Henry Beese	2	0	de Domino of Valence	..		3	4½
John Hankyn	1	0	John de Estbroke..	..		2	3
John de Lakenham		—	Margaret de Willowby	..		4	6
Simon Spurling	..	—	Will. at Glan	..	..		—
John Chigboke	..	—	De Reginald de Ree	..			—
John Nolesh	..	—	John de Estbroke..	..			—
John	..	—	Henry Allred	..	..		—

Here the membrane has been torn off.

In the *Inquisitiones Nonarum* (dated 14 Edward III. *i.e.* 1340-41) there is a list of the assessments of various parishes in Essex. That of Dagenham is as follows :—

Dakenham. Tax, £13 6s. 8d. By the present assessment these are charged, John de Beyntree, William Peet, William Nolot, John Galent (to

---

[1] See Appendix B for his will.

pay), £13 6s. 8d. And afterwards it was found by the jurors that the amount paid is not more than £8. So the assessment is less by £5 6s. 8d., as it appears to the same jurors.

It would appear from this "inquiry into the ninths" that even in those early days the taxpayers of Dagenham were either unable or unwilling to discharge their liabilities to the national revenue.[1]

On March 25, 1428, the House of Commons made a grant of tonnage and poundage to the King (Henry VI.). This was raised by a tax on parishes and towns graduated in proportion to the sums by which their respective churches were taxed for ecclesiastical tenths. Thus no parish of fewer than ten persons was to be taxed. In cases where the value of the church was under ten marks, the parish was assessed at 6s. 8d. In this assessment it was ordered that the parish of Dagenham should pay £1 6s. 8d. towards the king's revenue. The entry on the "Feudal Aids" runs thus— "Ecclesia de Dagenham taxatur ab antiquo xx marcas, subsidium xxvis. vllld." ("Feudal Aids," vol. xi.).

It is worthy of note that Dagenham is not here included in the hundred of Chafford. The "ab antiquo" probably goes back as far as 1284, when John de Kirkby and Nicholas de Castello published their "Inquisition."

The following rent roll throws light on the geography of the parish in the fifteenth century.

RENTALS AND SURVEYS.

31 Hen. VI.

The rental of the tenements of John Norton in Barkyng and Dakenham by the cognizance of Thomas Pike and others, made in the month of December in the 31st year of the reign of King Henry the sixth (1452).

William Say, Master of Saint Anthony, for a certain field containing twenty acres late belonging to Alan Mercar, formerly Hervey Hardegray's senior and afterwards John Kent's, and lately belonging to Henry Hardegray, son and heir of Henry Hardegray, senior, which same field of land lies between the lane called Gestes lane on the west side, and the land late John Alleyn's, now (Thomas) Stapelton's on the east side, and abuts at one end upon the land of the aforesaid Thomas Stapelton on the north side,

---

[1] In 1290-91 the citizens and burgesses of England granted to Edward I. a fifteenth of all their goods and movables. And the king granted to the said citizens and burgesses that the robes of them and their wives, and certain of their jocalia, should not be taxed to the said fifteenth. In 1297 the first none, or ninth, was levied. See T. Madox, "History of the Exchequer," p. 503.

and at the other end upon the high road leading from Hornchurch towards London on the south side, paying yearly for the same at the feasts of Easter and Michaelmas by equal portions .. .. 9s. 7d.

Of the same Master of Saint Anthony for the same field yearly at the Feast of Saint Andrew for gravel .. .. 10d. one ploughshare.

Of Hugh Niche for one croft of land containing eight acres sometime John Jamvyll's and late Thomas Jamvyll's, which lies between the land called sextenfredon on the east side and the footpath which leads from Smalwelcrouch towards Berkyng on the west side, one end abutting upon the high street[1] called Northstrete near Smalwelcrouch on the north side, the other end extending to the high way which leads from London towards Hendon on the south side, paying yearly for the same at the Feasts of Easter and Michaelmas by equal portions .. .. .. 2s. od.

Of the aforesaid Hugh Wiche for one croft of land next Smalwelcrouch containing three acres, sometime Roger Longe's and late George Belsby's, which lies between the lane leading from Smalwelcrouch towards the land of William Leveson by the green lane on the north side, and abuts upon the lands of Thomas Janvyle on the west side, paying yearly for the same at the Feasts of Easter and Michaelmas .. .. .. 12d.

Of Walter Bure for one parcel of land lying in Longlonde which was formerly Robert Malmayn's and late John Malmayn's, and the said parcel contains four acres, paying yearly for the same at the feasts aforesaid 12d.

Of Alice Wyote for a tenement in Estrete in Barkyng sometime John Gambon's and late Peter Mawer's, which is situated next the high street leading towards Romford on the north side, and next to Spitell there on the west side, and the curtilage late John Broune's on the east side, paying yearly for the same .. .. 15d.

Of Robert Gayton for a certain grange there with a curtilage, sometime John Brown's and late Nicholas Keen's, which lies next the said tenement of Alice Wyote in Estrete on the west side, and the curtilage of John Smalwell, senior, on the east side, and the aforesaid high way on the north side, paying yearly .. .. 18d.

Of John Sparowe of Longbrych for one messuage and three acres of land sometime Thomas Lewer's and late William Thershe's, lying next Busshecrouch on the north side and the messuage of Joan Cokkelys on the south side, and abuts upon the street called Bushstrete on the east side and upon the lands of William in the lane on the west side, paying yearly at the terms aforesaid .. .. 2s.

Of John Horell for one acre of land sometime John Bush's, lying between the said lands of Thomas Lewer on either side, and abuts upon Bushstrete on the north side, and upon the lands of the aforesaid Joan Cokkel on the south side, paying yearly for the same .. .. 1d.

Of Robert Croucheman for the tenements which lie in Rippell late

---

[1] The old meaning of street implied a highway or lane; from the Latin *strata via*, a "spread-out way."

William Canoun's and afterwards Thomas Vincent's for term of the life of his wife, and late Stephen Alborgh's, and abuts upon the tenement late John Lithcock's on the east side, and upon the high way leading from Dagenham towards Barkyng on the north side, paying yearly for the same ..   ..   6d.

Of the cellarer of Barkyng for a tenement called Tewyng lying in Northstrete next Saint Nicholas' Helme, paying yearly ..   ..   12d.

Of the Abbess of Barkyng for a garden sometime William Holman's, which lies in Eastrete in Berkyng, paying yearly for the same ..   2s.

Of Thomas Nattok for a garden in Rippell, lying upon the land late called Osthynland, upon the land late Thomas Pike's, and abuts upon the high way leading from Dagenham towards Barkyng, paying yearly 16d.

Of John Sparowe of Longbryche for a croft late John Nattok's, and late Thomas Lewer's, which lies next Porter's, paying yearly   2s. 4d.

Of William Peryman for land in Estmarsh late Richard Gaale's, and late John Purlevaunt's and Alice his wife's in right of the same Alice, paying yearly for the same   ..   ..   6d.

Of William Nattok for a croft of land containing 1½ acres and 1 rood, which lies next the lane which leads towards Rippell on the east side, and the lands of John Mile and John Outhred, sometime John Hatheman's, on the west side, and abuts upon the land of John Purlevaunt on the south side, and upon the high road leading from Barkyng towards Byntreheth on the north side, and pays yearly   ..   ..   3d.

Of William Nattok of Galesstrete for 4 acres of land sometime John Edrich's, and late Gilbert Sparowe's of Dakenham, which lies next the street at "Castell" on the north side, and the land of John Purlevant on the south side, and abuts upon the land of John Bush on the west side, and upon the land of William Ravenyng on the east side, and pays yearly   ..   ..   20d.

Of Agnes Busch of "Rippell" for a parcel of land containing 8 acres late John Brooke's of Rippell, lying in Ripplemersh next Hyelmeswalle, and the lands late Richard Cooke's on the east side and abuts upon the land of the Convent of Barkyng on the south side, and upon the land called Mabill' on the north side, paying yearly for the same at the terms aforesaid ..   ..   2s. 6d.

Of the Abbess and Convent of Barkyng for a parcel of land called Godland, containing 5 acres, which lie in Estmersch of Rippell, between the land late Richard Cooke's and John Bray's on the south side, and the land of John Brooke on the north side, and abuts upon the wall called Hyelmeswalle on the east side, and upon the land of John Purlevant on the west side, paying yearly for the same   ..   ..   ..   12d.

The land of the abbess.

Of John Sparowe of Cokermouth for a parcel called Mabill' Godland, containing 8 acres, lying in le Estmersch of Rippell next Hielmsewalle on the east side, and upon the land of Agnes Brooke on the south side, and upon the land called Litill Brooke on the north side, paying yearly   12d.

Of John Sawkyng for a croft containing 2 acres of land sometime Stephen Alborgh's, lying in Estberymersch, and abuts upon the land of John Camise late William Canoun's on the north side, and upon the land of the Abbess of Barkyng called Cowlase on the south side, and the land of John Busch on the east side, and the common way leading to the marsh on the west side, paying yearly .. .. 8*d*.

Of Thomas Nattok for a messuage and curtilage built upon, and 9 [Endorsed acres of land lying in Rippeldon between Dionysia Jacob on the west Mark side, and the land of Agnes Gale on the east side, and abuts upon the Fuller. high way leading from Dagenam towards Barkyng on the south side, and upon the land late Walter Gante's on the north side, paying yearly 2*s*.

From the sixteenth century onwards there are some ten extant subsidies of Dagenham. One made in the sixteenth year of Henry VIII. has come down to us in an excellent state of preservation. Not only are the various assessments given, but also the amounts to be paid severally by the king's taxpayers in Dagenham. The money was required to defray the cost of a little war which had broken out between England and France several years previously. The roll is in rough Latin, and may be rendered thus—

This first payment indented of the subsidy granted to the King and Parliament held at London and adjourned to Westminster was in the fourteenth year of our sovereign King delivered to William Wyott, gentleman, and John Eden, esquire, chief Collectors, of the aforesaid subsidy in the towns hereafter mentioned.

Under Dagenham occur the following names—

						(Tax to be paid.)
John Wodeland (assessment)	..	..	..	£7	..	.. 3/6
John Asgeld, in goods ..	..	..	..	£8	..	.. 4/-
Thomas Lymington, labourer	..	..	..	20*s*.	..	.. -/4
Thomas Denengs, in goods	..	..	..	£15	..	.. 8/-
William Smyth, labourer	..	..	..	20*s*.	..	.. -/4
John Tiler, labourer ..	..	..	..	20*s*.	..	.. -/4
Henry Clerk, in goods ..	..	..	..	30*s*.	..	.. 1/2
Thomas Eyre, in goods ..	..	..	..	£7	..	.. 3/6
William Peere	..	..	..	40*s*.	..	.. 1/-
John Sympsun, in goods	..	..	..	£5	..	.. 3/6
William Trulove, labourer	..	..	..	20*s*.	..	.. -/4
Hught Dennys, labourer ..	..	..	..	20*s*.	..	.. -/4
John Ashe, labourer ..	..	..	..	20*s*.	..	.. -/4
Robert Denys, labourer ..	..	..	..	20*s*.	..	.. -/4
William Clerk, in goods ..	..	..	..	£5	..	.. 2/6

		(Tax to be paid.)
Henry Rychardsun, in goods	20s.	-/4
Richard Pronges, in goods	£4	2/-
William Wyld, labourer	20s.	-/4
Richard Pecok, in goods	£8	4/-
John Potter, labourer	20s.	-/4
William Dellysbye, labourer	20s.	-/4
William Kynge, in goods	£5	1/-
John Kynge, in goods	£5 8s.	1/2
William Potter, his serv\. for his wages	40s.	-/8
Thomas Yonge, labourer	20s.	-/4
William Woodeland, in goods	£10	15/-
Paid John his servant for his wages	£5	1/-
Richard Gylby, serv\. to Henry Clerk	20s.	-/4
Richard Woodeland	20s.	-/4
Richard Wyne, in goods	£5	1/-
Robert Hoke, in goods	£3	1/6
Richard Stephyn, in goods	20s.	-/4
Richard Hoke	£5	2/6
Richard Purland, in goods	£30	30/-
William Estbrok, labourer	20s.	-/4
Richard Hatton, in goods	£20	20/-
John Baylye, labourer	20s.	-/4
William Dale, in goods	£3	1/6
Peter Wodeland, in goods	£3	1/6
Richard Sawkyn, in goods	40s.	-/8
Richard Brewer	£3	1/6
William Upnye, labourer	20s.	-/4
William Barber, in goods	£3 10s. 0d.	1/9
John Barber ,, ,,	£3	1/6
Thomas Huntinge, in goods	£30	30/-
William Crane, his servant for his wages	40/-	1/-
Henry Gyll, labourer	20/-	·4
Thomas Hoke, in goods	£6	5/-
Thomas Hoke junr.	£3	1/6
John Gar, in goods	£5	5/-
John Skerrwode, in goods	£5	5/-
Thomas Dene, labourer	20s.	-/4
James Abyson, in goods	£5	5/-
William Aslepe	40s.	1/-
William Eddolde, labourer	20s.	-/4
John Hoke, labourer	20s.	-/4
William Hoke, servt to Thomas Hoke for his wages	40s.	1/-
William Perryman, in goods	£3	1/6
Thomas Trulove ,, ,,	£7	3/6

John Upny, in goods ..	..	..	..	£7	..	..	3/6
Thomas Mille, in goods	..	..	..	£5 6s. 8d.	..	4/6
John Merylowe, labourer	..	..	..	20s.	..	..	-/4
Thomas Coke „	..	..	..	20s.	..	..	-/4
Thomas Canon „	..	..	..	20s.	..	..	-/4
Thomas Clerk, in goods ..	..	..	..	40s.	..	..	1/-
William Person, in goods ..	..	.	..	40s.	..	..	1/-
Thomas Jewell, labourer ..	..	..	..	20s.	..	..	-/4
John Gyles, in goods	..	..	..	..	£5	..	5/-
John Busthar „	..	..	..	..	£5 6s. 8d.	..	4/6
Robert Estbrok, labourer ..	..	..	..	20s.	..	..	-/4
John Lynt, in goods	..	..	..	..	20s.	..	..	-/4
William Estbrok, at the well	..	..	..	£20	..	..	20/-
John Stace, labourer	..	..	..	..	20s.	..	..	-/4
Harry Purlond, in goods ..	..	..	..	£7	..	..	5/6
Robert Gyll „	..	..	..	..	40s.	..	..	1/-
Thomas Purland „	..	..	..	..	£5	..	..	5/-
Thomas Estbrok, servt to Thomas Purland	..	20s.	..	..	-/4
Thomas Estbrok jun. servant to Harrye Purlond	20s.	..	..	-/4
John Hoke, labourer	..	..	..	..	20s.	..	..	-/4
Robert Norwyshe, servant to the sergt at the law	£6 13s. 4d.	..	5/6
Thomas Hellett, his servt.	..	..	..	20s.	..	..	-/4
William Cowpar, his servᵗ	..	..	..	20s.	..	..	-/4
One Muche for his servᵗ for his wages	..	..	20s.	..	..	-/4
One Pattmore for his wages	..	..	..	20s.	..	..	-/4
Richard Estbrok, in goods	..	..	..	£5 6s. 8d.	..	4/6

The total number of inhabitants liable to the King's tax is eighty-five. The aggregate assessment is £330 1s. 4d.—equal to £3500 in modern money.

A later subsidy, made in the first year of Edward VI. gives under Dagenham the following—

Dame Julian Norwich, widow	40/-
John Campe, yeoman, in all places (i.e. in all places where he held property	20/-
Henry Clark, husbandman	20/-
Andrew Dowsett, husbandman	15/-
Richard Horne the elder, husbandman	10/-
John Money, shipwright	10/-
Peter Clarke, husbandman	10/-
William Grasby, husbandman	10/-
William Purlond, husbandman	10/-
William Upney, husbandman	10/-

All being the King's natural subjects within his grace's realm.   Also

John Pechye, the smith	..	..	..	10/-
John Brown, husbandman	..	..	..	10/-
Thomas Estbroke, at Feld, husbandman in all places			..	10/-
			Total ..	.. £9 5s. od.

This subsidy is issued in the King's name and authority, and is signed by his commissioners.

JOHN GALE, Knight.
ANTHONY BROWN, Esquire.

Several subsidies were made during the reign of Queen Elizabeth. The earliest runs thus—

This extract indented made the fifth day of Marche in the ninth yeare of the reigne of our Sovereign Ladie Elizabeth by the grace of God of England, ffrance and Irelande Queene, defender of the faith, witnesseth that we Anthony Cooke, Knight, Richard Cooke, Thomas Powle, Edwarde Barret and Henry ffanshawe, Esquires, Commissioners among others assigned in the said County of Essex, and by Levysion have appointed for the setting, taxing and assessing of all persons dwelling within the Hundred of Becontree in the said Countie, as well by their land tenements, annuities, fees, and other yearly revenues and profits as by their goods and chattels and other moveables being chargable to and for the said paying of the Subsidie lately granted to the Quene's majestie, her heirs and successors by Parliament holden at Westminster in the eighth year of her Majestie's reign, have done in all things by virtue of the said commission by act in manor and farme as herein may appere.

And the same do certifie accordingly and we also have appointed Willm Stedman of the parish of Barkynge to be high collector of the same Hundred to leavie and gather the said severall taxations and assessments appointed for the said first payment of the said subsidie. And of the same to make payment in the receipt of the Quene's majestie's exchequer, according to the same act before the first day of April next to come. To whom our said collector we have delivered the counterpane of this extract indented, and also have taken bonde of hym for the sure payment of the somes therein contayned which bond annexed to this our extract we do certifie according to the tenor of the said acte of Plam^t in witness whereof we the said Commysioners to this present extract indented have set our hands and seales the daye and yeare first above written.

BARKYNGE TOWN.

						s.	d.
Wm Nutbrowne ..	..	..	£20	..		26	8
Robt Richmond	..	..	£20	..		26	8
Robt Stanton ..	..	..	£3	..		4	0
Thom. Baron Esquire of Ilforde Magna	..		£50	..	£3	6	8

DAGNAM.

Land	Richard Estbrooke	..	..	20/-	..	16*d.*
	John Eddall	..	..	20/-	..	16*d.*
	John Sokes	..	..	20/-	..	16*d.*
	James Rayman ..	..	..	20/-	..	16*d.*
	Humfrey Tilons..	..	..	20/-	..	16*d.*
	Richard Sandwith	..	..	£8	..	8*s.* 0*d.*
	John Purlond	..	..	£6	..	8*s.* 0*d.*
	James Lyttle	..	..	£4	..	5*s.* 4*d.*
	John Peache	..	..	40/-	..	2*s.* 8*d.*

						s.	*d.*
Goodes	Joan Lyttle, widow	..	..	£10	..	15	0
	Thom. Humphrey	..	..	£8	..	8	0
	Joan Truelove, widow	..	..	£5	..	5	0
	John Champney	..	..	£3	..	3	0
	Joan Harmond, widow	..	..	£3	..	3	0
	Willm Stockdale ..	..	..	£4	..	4	0
	Francis Elmer	..	..	£6	..	5	0
	John Asheley	..	..	£3	..	3	0
	John Browne	..	..	£3	..	3	0
	Thom. Blaslock ..	..	..	£3	..	3	0
	Thom. Cooke	..	..	£4	..	4	0
	Henrie Wyelde ..	..	..	£4	..	4	0
	John Estbroke	..	..	£3	..	3	0
	John Dowset	..	..	£3	..	3	0
	Robt. Dore	..	..	£3	..	3	0
	Willm. Stretton ..	..	..	£3	..	3	0

The following list is found in the subsidy roll of the Libertie of Havering, made on September 5 in the eighth year of the reign of James the First, the High Commissioners being Nich. Coote, Thos. Fanshawe, and Willm. Heigham, who appointed Thos. Barnes to be high collector of the " subsedie." [1]

DAGENHAM TOWNE WARD.

						s.	*d.*
Landes	Hunting More	..	..	..	.. £5	..	13	4
	Anne Osborne, widowe	..	..	£3	..	8	4
	Robert Skinner	..	..	..	1 (20/-)	..	2	8
	John Holmes	..	..	..	40/-	..	5	4
	Richard Turner ..	..	..	..	40/-	..	5	4
	William Crane	..	..	..	20/-	..	2	8
	George Radsdale	..	..	..	20/-	..	2	8
	Thomas Gill	..	..	..	20/-	..	2	8
	John Stockdale ..	..	..	..	20/-	..	2	8

[1] For additional subsidies see Appendix B. Some interesting information will also be found there in the " Inquisitiones post mortem."

Dagenham Towne Ward—*continued.*

							s.	d.
	Nathaniel Tracy, Gent.	..	..	..	£8	..	13	4
	Roger Sither	..	..	..	£5	..	13	4
	Richard Wittam	..	..	..	£5	..	8	4
	Paul Pearson	..	..	..	£5	..	8	4
Goodes	Richard Francis	..	..	..	£4	..	6	8
	William Poole	..	..	..	£3	..	5	0
	Edward Foster	..	..	..	£3	..	5	0
	Lawrence Wickes	..	..	..	£3	..	5	0
	Henry Speller	..	..	..	£3	..	5	0
	Francis Green	..	..	..	£3	..	5	0
	Thomas Baker	..	..	..	£3	..	5	0
Goodes	Julio Scott	..	..	..	£3	..	5	0
	Robert Commynes	..	..	..	£3	..	5	0
	William Baldon	..	..	..	£3	..	5	0
	Robert Scott, in terr.	..	..	..	£6	..	16	0
Assessors	William Comyns, in terr.	..	..	£5	..	13	4
	John Truelove, in terr.	..	..	£3	..	8	0
	Thomas Esbrook, in terr.	..	..	£2	..	5	4

It is interesting to note, as showing how the people here have clung to the soil, that about 30 per cent. of the names in the foregoing subsidies still linger in the neighbourhood, especially among the poor. One is reminded of the old Scotch saying : " The puirest man has as lang a pedigree as the greatest, only he knows less about it, that's a'."

The village proper, or " towne," consists of two roads running at right angles to each other, and each about a quarter of a mile in length. Of these, one—now called Church Road—was known as High Street, and the other as Broad Street or Bridge Street, because it led to the bridge over the dyke. In these two streets were the few shops, the tan-yard, and village smithy. This corner of the village is picturesque and quaint. In the High Street lived, at the end of the seventeenth century, the vicar of the parish, one of his Majesty's judges, a royal standard-bearer, and a wealthy tanner, who was entitled to " arms and gentry." This cannot be said now.

The population of the parish has more or less steadily increased during the last six centuries. Judging from the subsidy rolls the figure stood at 600-700 in the fourteenth century, and at 800-900 in the fifteenth century. In the sixteenth century the parish is returned as containing 300 " howselynge " people, *i.e.* communicants. Roughly speaking, this gives us the number of parishioners who were over three or four years of age ; multiply this by four and we get the approximate population in 1551, when the above-mentioned return was made. The earliest known census was taken in 1821, when the churchwardens and overseers made a house-to-house visitation throughout the parish, the figure being 1864. In 1851 the population of Dagenham was 2448 ; in 1881, 3402 ; in 1901, 6064.

The assessment or value of the parish of Dagenham for the king's taxes has fluctuated greatly. It stood charged to pay £13 6s. 8d. in 1340, a sum to be multiplied by fifteen to give its present value. In 1523 the assessment was £300—equal to ten times its value ; but in 1567 it dropped to less than £100, unless this subsidy was an imperfect or a limited one. In 1781 it was estimated at £3000 ; in 1881, at £27,000. It is now £42,000.

CHAPTER II

THE SOCIAL AND POLITICAL LIFE OF DAGENHAM

" There gleams my native village, dear to me,
Though higher change's waves each day are seen,
Whelming fields famed in boyhood's history,
Sanding with houses the diminished green ;
There, in red brick, which softening time defies,
Stand square and stiff, the muses' factories,—
How with my life knit up is every well-known scene."
LOWELL.

THE parish of Dagenham contained within its borders three " principal " manors, viz. Cokermouth, Parsloes, and Valence, and three " reputed " manors, viz. Dagenham, Great Porters and Frislings. Besides these, the manors of Jenkins, Marks and Wangey adjoined it, and were, indeed, sometimes included under Dagenham. The presence of all these manors naturally gave the parish considerable importance and influence in the neighbourhood.

The modern idea and conception of manors is that of their being charming country residences. This is just what they were not ; at least, not primarily. They were official residences, occupied, not merely by people of wealth, but by those who, in virtue of holding them, stood in a certain relation to the king. The derivation of the word from the Latin *manerium* (a staying-place) implies that it was the abode of a person of substance. There is evidence that manors existed in this country in the time of our Saxon forefathers, and it is quite possible that there were one or two in this parish at that early period. The Saxon suffixes, "ham " and "tun," though generally understood to mean a village community, meant originally the " estate of a lord," that is to say, an estate with a village upon it ; in one word, a manor.[1] We learn from Domesday, or Survey of England, that there were, at the Norman Conquest, 1422 manors

[1] See Seebohm's " Village Community," chapters i.-ii.

and 5,000,000 acres of land under cultivation. The greater part of the manors were seized by William the Conqueror, and distributed among his nobles and retainers, who held them from him as the head (caput). The Abbey of Barking was left untouched, and allowed to retain the status of a capital or principal manor, with the abbess as its lord. Each manor throughout the country was invested with certain rights, privileges, and duties, whereby it was constituted a centre of local authority and government. Sometimes the lord of a principal manor divided it into two or three smaller manors, called titular, "reputed," or quasi-manors, and held by "mesne" lords. Such probably were the manors of Dagenham, and more particularly Great Porters and Frislings. But the lord always kept the capital manor and certain "demesne"[1] lands for his family; probably Cokermouth was the manor retained by the Abbess of Barking for the special needs of the abbey, as the monks were famous for their success in agriculture. Added to this, the lord had the right to certain specified services from his tenants, and it was the great variety and diversity of these services which made the conditions and form of land tenure so varied.[2] Such was the case here; the abbess was entitled to certain services, as well as to rents (in money or in kind) from the tenants of the manors belonging to the abbey (on this, see the chapters on the manors).

The lord of a "principal" manor enjoyed the right of holding two courts, of which one was termed the "Court Leet and View of Frankpledge," and the other the "Court Baron." The former was the court of the "township," at which the constables were chosen for the year, and the ale-conners, watchman, and town crier appointed. At this court the rights and customs appertaining to the manor (*i.e.* the manorial estate *plus* the community of dependants or serfs attached to it) were enumerated, the misuse and repair of roads and bypaths were inquired into, and disturbances, encroachments, and land and labour grievances discussed. At the Court Baron of the manor, matters relating to reliefs, fines, leasings and forfeiture of leases, the cutting of timber, the granting of "heriots,"[3] the letting of waste land, the provision of a common

---

[1] From the Latin *dominium* and the Norman *de mayne*. It implied that part of a manor which the lord retained in his own hands for his family.

[2] To check the growing influence of the principal lords through the multiplication of small manors, a statute of Edward I. (1272–1307) forbade any further subinfeudations. It was known as the "Quia Emptores"—Because Buyers.

[3] Provisions or personal service to be rendered to the lord in time of war; also a tribute or fine payable on the decease of a vassal or tenant.

pound for strayed animals, and of stocks for drunkards and other delinquents were gone into and settled. Cases also were sifted and decided relating to trespass and damage by cattle and pigs, neglect of ditches and fences, loss and injury caused by assaults, accidents, and carelessness, and through work being imperfectly done or wilfully neglected. At this court all "free tenants" (*i.e.* the villani proper) who held allotments from their "lord" had the right to be present and give their vote.

The lord, on taking possession of a manor, would inquire into the buildings within and without the moat, the number and condition of the dovecotes, and also of the fishponds, the extent of arable land and of pasture, what pasture land he shared with his tenants in right of ancient custom, what parks and *demesne* woods there were, and whether there was a wood outside the demesne. He would also inquire into the pannage (the fruits of the forest, *e.g.* acorns, nuts, etc.), the herbage, the honey, and all products and issues of the forest and the mills belonging to the manor. He would inquire as to the pleas, privileges, heriots, fairs, tolls, markets, roads, customs, gifts, and services, and lastly, what churches belonging to the advowson were attached to the manor. In regard to his *tenants*, he would ascertain how many had been born on the estate, or had lived twenty and more years on it, and how many were newcomers, what lands they held of him, and what of others, and what services they rendered to him, and what to others ; whether by "socage" and military service ; what were fee farms and what *in eleemosynam* ; [1] what rents his tenants paid, and what accrued to him at their death ; how many were *villein* tenants, and what dues and payments they could make without being reduced to poverty and ruin ; what was the value and kind of work done by them.

The land of the lord's demesne was usually cultivated by the *villata*—the tenants in villenage. These were allowed to have allotments on their own account in the open fields round the village. Thus arose the small farmers, whose allotments were re-granted from father to son in unbroken regularity by the manorial lord. These small farms "possessed all the unity and indivisibility of an entailed estate, and were sometimes known apparently by the family name of the holders" (Seebohm). The *villani*, moreover, had certain rights of pasturage in the open fields after the crops were gathered, as well as on the green commons of the manor or township.

---

[1] For a charitable purpose, the relief of the poor, etc.

Dagenham.
From the Map of Barking-Manor
made in 1653
For Thomas Fanshawe Esq.

Truelove

Truelove
2 . 1 . 5

5 . 0 . 14

Wyhill
2 . 1 . 25

Baker
1 . 3 . 7

Truelove
2 . 1 . 0

Truelove
1 . 3 . 10

Baker
5 . 5 . 0

Goacocke
4 . 1 . 38

Cummins
2 . 3 . 24

Truelove
2 . 0 . 28

Baker
2 . 1 . 36

Baker
1 . 3 . 32

Wilton 0 . 3 . 0

Jaskott
1 . 1 . 20

Wilton
1 . 0 . 2 . 36

Cummins
3 . 2 . 37

Neary

Cummins
1 . 1 . 0

Cummins
1 . 1 . 20

1 . 1 . 20

Parsonage
2 . 1 . 26

Great   Busfield
Cummins
14 . 3 . 16

Truelove
1 . 1 . 16

0 . 2 . 23

[To face p. 19.

Next to the above class came the cottieri, or bordarii.   These were tillers of the soil, and very rarely held land.   They corresponded to the agricultural labourers as they were, say, fifty years ago.

The next class was that of the serfs, or slaves, who were reckoned as part of the lord's household, and could be dealt with (short of being put to death) as he thought fit.

The chief men on the estate were (1) the seneschal, or steward, whose duty it was to arrange all the details of the manor courts, receive his lord's rents, see to the proper discharge of the services due to him, the holding of the markets, the ploughing of the fields, and the supply of oxen needed for the general cultivation of the soil.   Added to this, it was his business to report to his lord every instance of a horse or an ox being sold to a purchaser outside the manor, or of any of the *villani* taking their corn to be ground at a mill other than that of his lord.   With a few additions, his work was pretty much the same as that undertaken at the present day by the agent on a nobleman's estate.   (2) The *præpositus*, or bailiff, literally, the husbandman, who was not so much over as *in front* of the others—our "foreman," who superintended their labour.[1]

We come now to the manor-house itself.   It was a simple structure, consisting of a hall (thirty to fifty feet long), with a large room on one side of it and a kitchen on the other.   Under the large room was a vaulted cellar.   Round the house was a wall or palisade, or moat, or the last two combined.   The space within the moat was regarded as almost sacred.   The hall was usually built of stone, but the rest of the house of wood, with a preference for oak.   After the Norman invasion, the manors were less simple in design.   On the further side of the court, or square, were built the bakery, brewery, laundry, with outhouses and stables.   The large room was reduced, and a chapel and lady's bower added, while to the kitchen was joined a buttery.   The hall was the living room for the most part. It had no fireplace, but an open fire was lit, when required, on the hearth.   In the hall the court was held ; here the family dined in state, and sometimes slept.   The general bareness of the walls was relieved by tapestry.   At the end of the hall (opposite the main entrance) was a raised platform or daïs, on which was the lord's table ; while all round the hall were benches and boards, which were laid on tressels, when wanted for meals.

---

[1] This account is from "Fleta," an anonymous work meant to be "the landlord's handbook in the management of an estate."   It was written in the time of Edward I.

The household of a manor would consist of the lord of the manor, and his lady, his children, pages, squires, maidens, and servants. The pages would be the children of noble families, sent to be prepared for high places and important offices, whether at home or abroad. Their education would be mainly in the hands of the priest of the family, who would teach him gentlemanly accomplishments. The maidens (who were also of high birth) would learn weaving, spinning, and tapestry work. The servants, male and female, ten or more in number, made up the manorial household.

The proceedings of the day began with prayers in the private chapel, at five in the summer and six in the winter. This was followed by breakfast, which was a light meal, and occupied only about half an hour. The business of the day was then transacted, and took up the morning till eleven, when dinner was served. The lord and his family sat at a high table on the daïs, and the household at the tables or boards arranged in two or more rows down the hall. After grace had been said, huge joints of meat were brought in (boiled rather than roasted), with a certain amount of ceremony and musical accompaniment, and were delicately carved by the pages, not by the servants, this being part of their education. The plates were of silver (for the high table), and of lattyn and pewter for the household ; so, too, the drinking vessels. There was no glass, nor yet forks. The *menu* comprised meat and bread, without vegetables ; sweets and dessert, butter, and several kinds of cheese, with ale, mead, wine, and spices. In the hall were cats, dogs, and hawks, which were fed during the meal. To drown the unmelodious noise they made, and also to give an air of leisure to this, the principal meal of the day, minstrels were engaged to play patriotic music. After dinner, the company listened to old ballads, or heard, with breathless interest, the detailed and dramatic description of some chance pilgrim from the East ; or, if these were not then to be had, the afternoon was spent in hunting, chess, dice, and cards. At five or six o'clock came supper, which was like the previous meal, but on a smaller scale. This was followed by singing, dancing, and carousing. Tea, coffee, and smoking were then unknown luxuries. At eight the household retired to rest, not, however, in their several chambers, but in beds placed all round the hall.

The manors were but scantily supplied with furniture, judging from ancient wills wherein various household effects are bequeathed to relatives and others mentioned.

The decline of the manors set in, roughly speaking, after the Wars of the Roses. Their official status had been steadily declining during the previous century, but it was with the accession of the Tudors that the manors noticeably lost their prestige. The manor-houses were now transformed into more convenient and comfortable residences, beautifully decorated, and were more adequately and richly furnished by the wealthy London merchants who from this period generally owned or inhabited them.

In the parish registers we frequently come across the term "yeoman." Originally it probably meant one who took care of an estate; then one who farmed a small estate, but did not rank as a gentleman. The yeomen were created by the sale of the abbey lands, on the dissolution of the abbey, by the Crown, or by their new owners, to the tenants who at that time held them, and who subsequently built larger farmhouses. Hence the yeoman was regarded as a prosperous member of the community. "Not so wealthy as an English yeoman" (Shakespeare). As the lords of the manors declined in influence the yeomen steadily forged their way until they became the backbone of the parish. It was the yeomen who controlled the affairs of this parish from the time of the later Stuarts, who levied the rates, repaired the old parish church, rebuilt the present one, founded a free school for poor children, administered with charitable liberality the Poor Laws of Queen Elizabeth, provided and superintended the workhouse, and bequeathed the greater part of the parochial charities.

The description occurs for the last time in the following entry, since when the usual term is "farmer"—"Thomas Noble, yeoman, buried July 5, 1848."

Next to the yeomen came the tradesmen of the parish—the tanner, the miller, the carpenter, the tailor, the weaver, the black-smith, and the shoemaker.[1] The tanner in the later years of Queen Elizabeth was a Robert Comyns, who lived in a large house near the church. Of the other tradespeople there is but scant information, beyond the fact that the several trades remained in the same families for generations. It is worthy of note that people of quality did not hesitate to put their sons to trade. Bishop Cartwright, of Chester (1688), had sons in trade; so, too, had Justice Mathewes, of Gobions, Romford (1650). The professions were then but few.

---

[1] The registers mention "Huggit the weaver;" "Pechye the tayler;" "Tendell the bucher;" "Waylett the tanner;" "Soles the carpinter;" "Money the shipwright;" "Meekin the smyth," etc.

There was no "Church" or Army or Navy or Civil Service into which parents could enter their boys, nor were there colonies to which they could send them. Occupation in trade meant, therefore, no loss of caste. So long as a man was by birth or merit entitled to "arms and gentry," he was received in society in the best families of the county.

The innkeepers of the parish formed a class to themselves, yet neither·large nor important. As some of them ended their days in the workhouse, or in receipt of parish relief, they do not seem to have been very prosperous either. "Mine host" usually brewed his own beer and baked bread for his customers. In two or three instances he was the village carrier as well. His house was open to all comers for food and shelter. Sometimes one or more soldiers would be billeted on him, or a sailor on his way to his ship, or a "discharged prisoner going back to his settlement," or a "travayling woeman" would be sent to the inn by the parish authorities for her "lying-in," in default of a hospital. The parish records occasionally tell of the death at the alehouse of a "stranger lad," or "wandering youth," or "poor wench," and of the "corinner's orders" for their "buryalls." The various needs which the Dagenham inns had to supply were largely due to the suppression of Barking Abbey, which for six centuries had afforded shelter, food, drink, lodging, and medical care to those who went there for aid.

The village inns were—1. The Cross Keys. This was opposite the church, and was west of the larger house now bearing this sign. It existed prior to 1680. The sign is thought to represent the arms of the Papal see; it appears in the coats of arms of the sees of York, Exeter, Gloucester, and Peterborough. Mr. Miller Christy says there are only five houses with this sign in Essex.

2. The Chequers. This is on the west side of Dagenham, and near the manor of Cokermouth. The village pound adjoined it. This sign is an ancient one, and common in the county.[1]

3. The Bull Inn. This is in the village. Probably built in the time of the Stuarts.

---

[1] Mr. Christy remarks—"It is said to represent the coat of arms of the Earls of Warrenne and Surrey, who bore *chequy*, or and azure, and in the reign of Edward IV. possessed the privilege of licensing alehouses. The old money-changers used boards divided up into squares, like a chess board; and the sign of the chequers may have originated in these "exchequers," as they were called, being hung up outside their places of business. Not improbably the sign also represents the "chequer," or board, divided into squares, and still used in some country inns for keeping a tally or record of the amount drunk by each regular customer. As the sign is now painted, it is almost as often *lozengy* as chequy" ("Trade Signs of Essex").

DAGENHAM HIGH STREET (LOOKING EAST)

(The stone inscribed F.B.D. 1658 is on the house on the right; the letters are probably the initials of the man and his wife who built the house, as on the tradesmen's tokens of that period.)

4. The Rose and Crown. On Beacontree Heath. Of same date probably as the Bull.

5. The Three Travellers. Also on Beacontree Heath. This existed prior to 1780.

6. The White Horse.[1] At Chadwell Heath. Mentioned as existing in 1650.

7. The Crooked Billet.[2] This was the inn for the Forest of Hainault. A rare sign, with doubtful derivation ; probably it was the mark made on cattle belonging to parishioners of Barking before they were turned into the forest. Or was it originally a pastoral staff?

8. The Harrow.[3] Also in the forest.

9. The Ship and Shovel. This was at Rippleside, and is said to have been named after Admiral Sir Cloudesley Shovel. It dates from 1740, or thereabouts. Possibly it stands on the site of an older inn, known perhaps as the Pyx and Housel.

10. The White Hart was in the Chadwell ward of Barking. It is an old house, dating at least from 1650. The sign is probably derived from heraldry, and is very common in Essex.

11. The Greyhound was also in the Chadwell ward on the main road to London. It existed prior to 1700. In the old coaching days it was the usual stopping place, some sixty or seventy coaches halting there during the day. It is a mammalian sign, like the Bull, etc.

There were very few shops in the village. The corn grown in the parish was ground into flour at the Three Mills on Chadwell Heath, and was baked into bread at home. For vegetables and fruit the villagers relied on their own gardens and orchards. Tea, coffee, cocoa, sugar, etc., were, till the eighteenth century, luxuries enjoyed only by the rich. The poor drank beer, mead, and a decoction of barley and ginger. Meat they rarely tasted, excepting

---

[1] "It is in many cases impossible to draw a line of demarcation between signs borrowed from the animal kingdom and those taken from heraldry ; we cannot now determine, *e.g.* whether by the White Horse is meant simply an *equus caballus* or the White Horse of the Saxons and that of the House of Hanover" (Messrs. Larwood and Holten's "History of Sign Boards ").

[2] "I am inclined to think," says the late Mr. H. W. King, "that the Crooked Billet was originally a *fess dancetté*, or a *chevron*—more probably the former—and that it is, therefore, an heraldic sign."

[3] This represents, doubtless, the *portcullis crowned*, which Henry VII. and other sovereigns used as a badge. When the knowledge of heraldry declined, the common people called the sign by the name of the harrow, not knowing of anything else which resembled the device displayed. It thus became an agricultural sign, like, *e.g.* the plough " (Christy's " Trade Signs of Essex ").

pork and bacon. For shopping generally the villagers went to Romford and Barking. At the former town a market was held every Tuesday for hogs and calves, and on Wednesday for corn and leather, by a royal charter of Henry III., granted in 1247. At the latter place a market was held every Saturday. The market began with the ringing of a bell. There was also a fair, or wakes, held every summer in connection with the patronal festival of the church (SS. Peter and Paul, June 29). The travelling pedlar was a favourite too, not only on account of the miscellaneous wares and trinkets he sold, but also on account of the small commissions he executed for them, and the news he brought of events in the outer world. The registers mention the village "taylour," "y*e* smith," "y*e* carpinter," "y*e* butcher" (at Chadwell Heath), "y*e* weaver." There was no post-office. Letters to London were despatched by water or by the mail-coach, and could be franked for fivepence each ; those for the provinces were sent away in the first instance by the mail-coach, the transit, *e.g.* to York, occupying four days. The letters were delivered at the various principal houses in the village by sturdy, weather-beaten dames.

The staple industry of the parish was, as we have seen, farming. Three thousand acres of land were under cultivation, producing splendid crops of corn, which, until the repeal of the Corn Laws in 1832, brought large profits to the growers. Bands of Irishmen used to come over every year for the hay and corn harvest. The parochial records refer to them occasionally—"A strange Irishman killed by a stroke (sunstroke ?) buryed ; " "An Irishman killed by a blow." Haymaking was supposed to begin on the Monday after St. Barnabas' Day (June 11), and lasted a month or more, when the corn harvest began. The latter was ushered in with a " letting supper," consisting of boiled pork and broad beans, and closed with a " settling supper " of roast beef and plum-pudding.

The wages of a Dagenham labourer until the thirteenth century were *nil*. He received from his lord food, clothing, and shelter for himself and family, and as he lived rent-free and paid no rates, he did not really need spending money. By the time of Edward I. (1272) the labour of a ploughman or herdman had acquired a value over and above its equivalent in kind, and was now worth three farthings a day in money. In the fourteenth century wages stood at sevenpence per week, with the addition of meat to the labourer's rations. Money was a scarce article with our forefathers of that period, and people of reputed wealth were often at their wits' end to raise even five pounds on an emergency.   But what was lacking in money was made up by a liberal allowance of meat and drink to the labourer.   The value of money can be better gauged when we remember that at this period a sheep could be bought for five shillings and an ox for ten.   The next two centuries saw little improvement in the labour market, owing to the disturbing effects caused by the Wars of the Roses and the dissolution of the monasteries; but in the seventeenth century wages went up to eightpence *per diem*, without meat and drink, which were now generally stopped, or, if allowed, were reckoned at threepence a day.   A hundred years later they averaged eight shillings per week, with a "prittle (a sack) of potatoes" for a week's overtime.   Women who went out charing or washing earned ninepence a day, in addition to their food, and children, who were sent to work at the tender age of six or seven, received, according to their capability, sixpence a week, with food.

The wages paid to farm labourers in Dagenham compare favourably with those earned by labourers in other parts of Essex, especially in the eighteenth and early part of the nineteenth century.

In addition to the foregoing, some forty or fifty men found employment on the river Thames, either in the eel fishery or in repairing the dykes, marsh walls, and embankment, or in conveying goods and passengers to and from London and Dagenham.   The "Carrier's Cosmography," published in 1637, informs the public that "at the Lion Key boats are to be had that doth carry goods and passengers betwixt London and Raynham (passing Dagenham), Purfleet, and Grayes."

The most prevalent diseases in the parish were the ague, small-pox, and consumption.   These were caused mainly by the effluvium from the marshes and dykes, the ill-draining of the roads, and the damp and unhealthy dwellings in which the poor lived.   The burial register tells a sad tale of almost whole families carried off by some virulent disease—ague, typhoid, and small-pox.   The close proximity of the parish to London exposed it to fearful visitations of the plague, which, for some reason or other, counted far more victims among women than among men.   Small-pox was held in the greatest horror.   Miss Bridget Noel, who was a frequent visitor to the manor of Jenkins, in describing her interview with Madame la Croy, the great fortune-teller, in London, in the latter part of the seventeenth century, says, "One thing she told me which pleased me very mutch, was that I never should have the 'small-pox.'" The well-to-do in the parish who were able to indulge in sumptuous living died, for the most part, from gout.

The healing art was not until the last century in the ascendant, and had but few representatives in the neighbourhood. We hear of " Thomas Comyns, of Dagenham, a Doctor of Physicke," who died in 1656 ; of " Roger Vaughan, of Barking, Barber and Chirurgeon," who practised in 1730, and of a " skillful apothecary " at Romford. Apothecaries and quacks, without degree or diploma, roamed the country at will with their own special panacea. At Bethnal Greene one " Burrel and his wife professed to cure cancers," a profession which brought them plenty of patients, rich and poor (1790–1810). The register mentions one " John Allen, a vagrant cheirurgion, buryed the 28 of Aprill, 1597." Cupping and leeching were the usual methods of treatment resorted to by the medical faculty. For ague, " communion wine," or old port, quinine, or Jesuits' bark, were prescribed. One quaint remedy which was suggested was to swallow a table-spoonful of gunpowder, and immediately afterwards take a sharp walk or run, to get into a complete perspiration, and so " exude the ague." Whether this cure was ever tried we cannot positively prove. The family doctor always advised his patients in Dagenham to avoid going out after sunset as far as possible, and to close all windows at that time, so as to escape the odours of the marshes. Bad cases were sent either to the Charity House at Barking (the local cottage hospital), kept, 1670–80, by one James Clements, or to the various hospitals in London, especially those of St. Thomas, St. Bartholomew, and Guy's. Surgical operations were performed but rarely.

The recreations and amusements of the people of Dagenham were of a varied character. The rich drove in their coach and four to London to see the plays then on the stage. It is not unlikely that the earliest production of Shakespeare's plays was witnessed, among others, by some from this parish. The Fanshawes are known to have patronized the drama in London, going to the theatres there two or three times a week. There was much social intercourse between the families at the various manors, when dice and cards were indulged in, and played for high stakes. Now and then the young gentlemen would play practical jokes on their guests and friends by masquerading as highwaymen, a dangerous diversion, as they not only took their chance of being shot by those whom they challenged, but also of being apprehended by the king's

DAGENHAM HIGH STREET (LOOKING WEST)

officers, and suffering the extreme penalty of the law. Until the last century, fox-hunting was not in vogue, but we hear of Sir Gawin Hervey, of Marks, hunting with a pack of beagles, the company including the Bishop of Norwich (Dr. Harsnett), to whom he bequeathed his " kennell of hounds." The lower orders amused themselves with cock-fighting, bowls, pitch-and-toss, hustle, and morris-dancing. The annual " wakes" was a popular institution, with its booths, the fortune-tellers, and the competitions for prizes, such as ploughing for a smock frock, bowling for a tea-kettle, boys racing for a kerchief, or climbing the greasy pole, and girls competing for a scarlet cloak. Unfortunately the wakes occasioned much disorder and drunkenness, and the sober-minded parishioners sought to have it abolished. This was in 1630. Other adjoining parishes also made the same complaint. These complaints were, however, misunderstood and disregarded. The " Book of Sports," issued by Charles I. in 1634, says—

Wee find that under pretence of taking away abuses, there hath been a general forbidding not only of ordinary meetings but of the Feasts of the Dedication of the churches, commonly called Wakes. Now our express will and pleasure is that these Feasts with others be observed, and that our Justices of the Peace in their several divisions shall look to it.

Until a generation ago May-day was a general holiday in the parish. The children went round the village carrying a gay garland suspended on a pole, and sang a short ditty. This custom is still observed, but scantily. A few days later, the leading parishioners perambulated the parish beating the ancient bounds. The proceedings of the day concluded with a dinner, provided at the charges of the parish.

The internal affairs of the parish were under the entire management and control of the churchwardens and overseers, aided by the vestry, which met on or about March 25, which, till 1752, was the first day of the year (O.S.). These comprised the making and the repair of the roads,[1] the setting up of boundary marks, the relief of the poor, and the keeping of the fabric of the church in good order, and also of the churchyard wall. The money required for these various purposes was provided by the rates—poor, or church, or special—which were collected by the overseers themselves, without any charge to the parish. This task, however, became so

---

[1] In 1585, an Act was passed requiring the churchwardens and constables of each parish to call a meeting on Easter Tuesday or Wednesday, and elect a surveyor and an orderer for one year, to supervise the highways.

irksome and costly, that it was decided, in 1832, to appoint an assistant-overseer at a salary of £60 per annum, the said over-seer to discharge also for that salary the duties of road surveyor. This decision, however, was not carried out, as Mr. Thos. Twyford offered to take the office of surveyor without salary (1834). In the following year Mr. Geo. Winmill was asked to take this post at a salary of £20 a year, which he consented to do. In 1838, Mr. William Haws was appointed assistant-overseer at a salary of 12s. per week. With a view to saving the rates, the principal ratepayers agreed to haul the stone for the highways free of charge. Besides this, they entered into a compact to refrain from using heavy waggons in wet weather, when the roads were soft. We find mention of an Act of Parliament in force in 1774, forbidding more than three horses being used in green lanes and byways, under a penalty of £5.

The parish constable was an important functionary in the village. Originally he was chosen at the Court Leet and View of Frankpledge held at the manor. Latterly, he was sometimes elected at the vestry. He was then duly sworn and invested with authority by a local justice at Barking or Ilford. He ranked higher than the policeman of to-day, inasmuch as he was elected. In theory all the parishioners were personally bound in "peacepledge," but he was the acting executor, and held office usually for one year.[1] His duties were to take cognizance of vagrants and unlicensed hawkers, to lodge complaints against persons committing vicious and criminal acts, to billet soldiers, to commit unruly, riotous, and drunken persons in the stock or watchhouse,[2] near the churchyard gate ; or, if the confinement exceeded a day, to take them to the gaol or house of correction at Barking, and to impound strayed animals either in the pound near the Chequers or in that near the Whalebone. By an ordinance of Parliament passed in 1642, the parish constable was ordered to see that no drinking or trading or work was done on the Sabbath during Divine service. Also at the "Monthly Fast to walk through their said Liberties to search for persons who either by following the work of their calling or sitting in Taverns, Victualling or Ale-houses, or any other ways do not duly observe the same."

In addition to discharging these duties the parish constable

---

[1] In 1797, four constables were elected—James Fenner, Abraham Hunswood, Wm. Smith, Robt. Brittain.

[2] The watchhouse—" the village cage "—was a small enclosure, 8 feet square, surrounded with high iron railings, without roof or covering.

served also as relieving officer. It was his work to ascertain the "settlement" of applicants for relief and report to the church-wardens, to set men in search of work to "clean the towne," paying them as he thought fit, to relieve sailors "on pass" with money or food, and pass them on to the next parish, to give certificates to travelling women, and bring necessitous cases before the notice of the churchwardens and overseers.

The parish constable was an unpaid official, but was allowed his expenses, an account of which he rendered quarterly.   They include a variety of items—"Takeing a sumons ; " "going to the sessions at Chelmsforde ; " "proveing a settlement ; " "mending the stockes ; " "pursuing goose-stealers on the heath ; " "rejistring a voter at ye court ; " "attending coronner's orders ; " "goeing to the Justice's at Ilford" (Angel Inn Court) ; "charitable use money ; " "releeving saylers out by pass " ; "releeving poor woemen " ; "fetching back an apprentis who had run away," etc.

Owing to repeated complaints from the parish constables of Dagenham, Barking, and Havering of their inability to cope with the increasing crime of the neighbourhood, the farmers and other leading inhabitants formed, in 1835, an "association for the prosecu-cution of felons."   It consisted of sixty members.

From the absence of evidence to the contrary, it would seem that the moral tone of the parish was good and satisfactory.   No offences of a serious character stain the annals of the past until we come to the murder of a police-constable at Eastbrook End in 1846.   The earliest offence in the criminal calendar was a transgression of the regulations of the Thames Fishery Board by some fishermen of Dagenham.   The record[1] of this states, that on "the Feast of St. Alphege (April 19, 1329), Estmar Coker and John Wychard, citizens of London, charged Alexander of Dagenham and Edmond Dode and Alan le Spenser of Reynham, and others, all fishermen, for that they had been found fishing in the Thames with twelve nets, known as *tromekeresnet*, and are a kind of 'kidel,' the meshes of which nets ought to be one and a half inch in size, whereas they were hardly an inch, so that they caught small fish or fry which were unable to escape to the great damage of the people of the city.   It was ordered by the mayor and aldermen that the nets be burnt at the cross in Chepe, and the said fishermen committed to prison until they should have made fine, etc.   They were accordingly taken by the sheriff to Newgate.   On the Saturday next after the Invention of the Cross

[1] Riley's "Memorials of London Life."

(May 3) they were brought to the Guildhall[1] and set free, their fines being remitted."

An old MS. makes mention of one Thomas de Dakenham being charged with theft at Maidstone in 1331, but gives no details, so that we cannot say whether he was convicted or left the court without a stain on his character.

At the Chelmsford assizes, held in July, 1740, "Thomas Fuller, late of the parish of Dagenham, was indicted for privately stealing 14s. in money numbered, the property of Thomas King." The prisoner denied the theft, but was convicted, and sentenced to be burnt in the hand.

There were, of course, other offences of a minor order, which were dealt with on the spot, such as drunkenness and goose-stealing.[2] The latter misdemeanour meant not only a loss to the owners, but an annoyance to the churchwardens, as the parish constable regarded "the pursuit of goose-stealers" as an extra, and charged accordingly, 2s., 4s., 5s. Goose-stealers and other delinquents were punished by being clapped in the stocks for two or more hours, the maximum being fourteen; second and subsequent offences were dealt with at the Ilford sessions (held at the Angel Inn), and punished with short terms of imprisonment at the Barking House of Correction. This stood nearly opposite the abbey gateway, and was pulled down before 1760, being replaced subsequently by a gaol built at Little Ilford in 1829. With his imprisonment the offender lost his right to parish relief when destitute or unable to work, a right which meant a great deal in days when vagrancy was severely punished, and the parish authorities refused to help those who were not parishioners or did not bear a fairly good character. Besides all this, the delinquent found it more difficult to obtain work than before, as the farmers and other employers of labour did not care to have men about their farms who had the reputation of being intemperate, quarrelsome, or dishonest. So far as we can read between the lines of the parish minutes, it would seem that the employers of labour in Dagenham occasionally formed a ring not to employ some "ne'er-do-well" in order to get him out of the parish altogether.

Farm lads who neglected their work or did it badly were corrected by their masters with a sound thrashing, or sometimes tied with a

---

[1] The clerk to the Chamber of the Guildhall was one John de Ilford. The Lord Mayor was Simon Swanlond, who had been preceded by Hams de Chiggewelle.

[2] Appendix A, Chapter II.

stout cord to a gate-post for several hours until they showed signs of contrition. An old inhabitant remembers as a child seeing his father release one such who had been, either by barbarous forgetfulness or cruel intention, left out all night by his harsh master, and was found half-dead with exhaustion and exposure to the cold.

An ancient writer in describing his experiences of Essex and the rough uncouth manners of the people there, says of Dagenham, Plaistow, and Barking—" But for them who live in the hundreds, as they call that part of the county which lying more low and flat and near to the sea is full of marshes and bogs, they are persons of so abject and sordid a temper that they seem almost to have undergone poor Nebuchadnezzar's fate, and by conversing continually with the beasts to have learned their manners." [1]

The " education question " does not appear to have been a disturbing factor with our Dagenham forefathers. Until the dissolution of Barking Abbey, a small proportion of the children dwelling on the abbey lands received an elementary education there, sufficient for their requirements. On its suppression, one or two schools were opened in the village, through the influence of the lords of the manors and the vicars of Dagenham. We read of bequests being made in 1720 to the " charity school " by various individuals. There was a school, probably for boys, under a schoolmaster, and another for girls under a " dame," or schoolmistress, in 1690–1700. The boys were taught reading, writing, and elementary arithmetic ; the girls, knitting, sewing, and spinning. In 1815, the Rev. T. L. Fanshawe built a school on part of his glebe for the children of " indigent parents ; " a few years later he started a Sunday school in a room which he rented opposite to the church, in which he took a keen interest. These supplied the needs of the parish until Ford's bequest in 1851, which by its munificence covered a much larger area than formerly. In 1844, a Mr. Glenny built a school at Chadwell Heath, for the needs of the northern part of this large parish. Thirty years later, the Dagenham School Board was formed. Under its auspices schools were built at Chadwell Heath, Hainault, Beacontree Heath, Dagenham village, and Marsh Green, providing an aggregate accommodation for 1400 children.

The Political Life of the parish.—From the " Calendar of State Papers," the subsidies, the registers, and other sources, we have been able to glean many details relating to the political life of Dagenham. The subsidies, which are our most ancient source of

[1] Brome's " Travels over England " (1700).

information, tell us who were liable to the special taxes levied in the king's name. In times of war each *villa* was required to furnish one man for the army, or, in default thereof, to make an equivalent composition towards his expenses. The king's taxes, or feudal aids, as they were called, were raised for other purposes as well, *e.g.* providing an adequate dowry for the king's daughter on her marriage, the knighting of the king's eldest son, etc. As compared with other villages in the neighbourhood, such as East Ham or Rainham, it would seem that Dagenham contributed its full share towards these taxes.

The "Calendar of State Papers" throws much light on the parochial history of a troubled and eventful period, viz. the seventeenth century. We hear of an assessment being made in December, 1634, by Robert Parkhurst, Lord Mayor of London, and others, " for setting forth a ship for his Majesty (Charles I.) of 500 tons burthen, to cost £4085 18s. 7d." To raise this sum Dagenham is assessed at £35 11s. 8d., and the Chadwell ward at £15 6s. 5d.[1] In collecting the former amount the overseers of Dagenham assessed one Henry Knight, the under-keeper of Chapell Hainault Walk, who happened to live just within the bounds of the parish. This coming to the ears of Sir Thomas Edmondes, Treasurer of the Household, Lieutenant of the Forest of Essex, and Keeper of Chapell Hainault Walk, he represented to the king that the keeper of Havering Park, and all other keepers of that forest, were ever exempt from the king's tax. The appeal was allowed.

During the unhappy Civil War, 1642–45, the people of Dagenham as a whole seem to have sided with Charles I. The Fanshawes of Parsloes and Jenkins aided him with money, men, and arms, but the Harveys, *alias* Mildmay, of Marks, the Herveys, of Wangey, and the Comyns families, of Dagenham and Romford, supported the Parliamentarians. After the final overthrow of the Royalist cause at Naseby, in 1645, a rigorous inquiry was made by the Roundheads as to who in Dagenham, among other places, had assisted the unfortunate king, and to what extent. On May 30, 1646, John Fanshaw, of Parslow, was summoned to appear " before the committee for compounding cases," to compound on the Barnstaple Articles for delinquency in bearing arms for the king. He admitted being present at the surrender of that town to Sir Thomas Fairfax, and was ordered to pay a fine of £430.

---

[1] It is interesting, by way of comparison, to note that Stratford Langthorn is assessed at £18 13s. 4d., and Lambeth at £46 10s. 2d.

Subsequently he " begged to compound for the lease of Dagenham parsonage for twenty-one years, held of the Master of Brentwood Free School, adjudged void by the Commissioners for charitable uses of county Essex.   Also to compound for the office of auditor for the northern parts of the Duchy of Lancaster."   No notice having been taken of his appeal, Mr. Fanshaw repeated his petition in December, 1647, and stated that he had paid half the fine, and without compounding could not meet his liabilities.   But the committee were not disposed to show mercy to those who had stood faithfully by the now fallen king.   They ordered him to settle within a month the amount due on Dagenham Rectory, though they reduced the fine.   They requested him also to pay the Rev. Thos. Swinnerton, Vicar of West Thurrock, who was one of the " Plundered Ministers," the sum (£40) assigned to him out of the benefice of Dagenham (January, 1648).   Six months later, a writ was issued for Mr. Fanshaw to be apprehended, and his estates sequestered, until he had complied with the order of the committee.

Other members of this family also paid dearly for their active loyalty, in particular, Sir Thos. Fanshaw, who was fined £910 ; Richard Fanshaw, master of the Ilford Hospital, who was required to surrender the hospital to one Richard Wilcox ; and Sir Simon Fanshawe (1654).

At several sessions of the " Compounding Committee," held at Whitehall, various persons belonging to Dagenham were similarly charged with " opposing the Parliament."   One Chambers of Dagenham was reported to be in the king's army (1645), yet his lands had not been sequestered.   Captain Thos. Burgis, the informer, undertakes to pay charges of inquiry if his discovery produce no benefit.   One Trevors of Dagenham was charged with " delinquency," but the case was adjourned.   A John Figgons, of Dagenham, was charged with sending a man and arms to assist Lord Goring in the late insurrection against Parliament (1649). One Antony Eyre of Dagenham and Chapel Hainault pleaded guilty to " delinquency," and his lands were ordered to be sequestered and assigned to Major Henry Wansey, of Dagenham (April, 1652).   One Captain Gregory Baker of Tillingham was also found guilty of " delinquency in arms at Colchester," and sentenced to lose the profits of his farm at Dagenham, which Samuel Wheeley, of Chelmsford, was authorized to receive for his services.

At the Committee of Inquiry, held at Chelmsford and Colchester, the Royalists were more severely dealt with, some being sentenced to be shot and others beheaded. Among the former were Sir Charles Lucas, Sir George Lisle, and Sir Barnard Gascoigne, for the part they had taken in defending Colchester against the Parliamentary troops. This town was fined £14,000 by Sir Thomas Fairfax, one-seventh of which was afterwards remitted (August, 1648).

During Cromwell's military government of this country, England was divided into eleven districts, and placed under the control of major-generals. The county of Essex was included in the East Midland District,[1] which was entrusted to the charge of General Charles Fleetwood. He was assisted by one Hezekiah Haynes, a narrow-minded and vindictive individual, who was constantly in collision with the local magistrates, owing to the rigorous way in which he sought to maintain "moral" order, with which they had little sympathy. This "moral" order of county government comprised the suppression of cakes and ale, the prohibition of young men walking in the fields on the sabbath, the forbidding people to fetch water on that day from wells and springs, and other harmless occupations. The major-general also forbade the observance of Church festivals under heavy penalties. The major-general had power of life and death in all offences, whether criminal, civil, moral, or ecclesiastical. But what was disliked most of all was his power, frequently exercised, of transporting prisoners without trial; this evoked numerous petitions of protest all over the county, signed largely by Cromwellians. Is it to be wondered at that, before Charles I. had been dead twelve months, the country had begun to writhe under the harassing military rule of the Protector? The chief supporters of the latter in this county, the Earl of Manchester, Sir Thomas Fairfax, Sir Thomas Honeywood, Sir Thomas Darcy, and members of the Mildmay, Mathews, and Comyns families (of Dagenham and Romford), petitioned him to disband his army, but without avail. Consequently, they were all prepared, in 1660, to join in the welcome of Charles II., although they had actively opposed his father, yet without going to the extreme of voting for or tacitly assenting to his execution.

The year 1795 was a memorable one on account of the bad harvest, the hard winter, terrible storms, and general depression in trade. Added to these troubles, England stood threatened with an invasion by Napoleon Bonaparte, who was preparing his "Army

[1] It comprised seven counties—Oxford, Bucks, Herts, Cambridge, Essex, Norfolk, and Suffolk.

of England," consisting of half a million men, for the purpose. The parish minutes bear witness to some of these troubles. We read of a "special vestry being held April 2, 1795, at which the Inhabitants of East Ham and Little Ilford[1] were summoned to attend, pursuant to an Act of Parliament entitled an Act for raising a number of men for the service of His Majesty's Navy." It was agreed to raise two men, who should be equipped and supported by the three parishes, and the "churchwardens and overseers of the said parishes were empowered to agree with sutch volunteers as may offer on the best terms they can." The following year (December, 1796) another "special vestry was held to raise two men for the Navy, in accordance with an order just made by the King's Ministers."

Besides the above, special vestry meetings were held during 1795–96 to "consider the privations caused by the unusually high Prices of Wheat and Meat." The clerk reported that the Privy Council had passed a resolution not to eat any fine bread in their families except such as was denominated standard wheaten bread." Resolved that "it is both prudent and highly necessary that strict attention should be given by every master of a Family to prevent unnecessary consumption of either of the above, and particularly of Bread and Flour. Resolved also that we who are present will prohibit in our Families any superfluous mode of using either Bread, Flour, or Meat until they are reduced to reasonable Prices." It was also decided to open a subscription list in aid of the poor. The price of wheat at this time was thirty guineas per load of forty bushels, and the price of a quartern loaf 1s. 1½d. Beef was 1s. 4d. per lb.

[1] The population of East Ham was then 820, of Little Ilford, 300. It is now 80,000 and 45,000 respectively.

CHAPTER III

THE PARISH CHURCH

" Thus of old
Our ancestors, within the still domain
Of vast cathedral or conventnal church,
Their vigils kept ; where tapers day and night
On the dim altar burned continually,
In token that the House was evermore
Watching to God. Religious men were they ;
Nor would their reason, tutored to aspire
Above this transitory world, allow
That there should pass a moment of the year,
When in their land the Almighty's service ceased."

WORDSWORTH.

IN every parish throughout the land, from John o' Groats to Land's End, the most ancient and conspicuous feature in it is, as a rule, the parish church. "As plain as the way to the parish church," says the immortal Shakespeare, referring to the sacred edifice which with massive tower and tapering spire "seems to lift up the soul silently to heaven with all its dreams." While bishops and monks were building the cathedrals and abbeys which are the glory of our country, churches of a smaller type were erected everywhere for the use of the people. It is computed that about eight thousand churches were built within one hundred and fifty years after the Norman Conquest. These were *parish* churches, and were served by secular priests, who subsisted on the endowments provided for them by the wealthy laity. Broadly speaking, each church, as at Dagenham, was the unit of the parish to which it belonged.

It is difficult to give the exact date when the church was built, but judging from the general architecture of the chancel, with its lancet windows, it may be approximately fixed about the end of the twelfth or the beginning of the thirteenth century. It was erected, doubtless, through the efforts and liberality of the Abbess of

Barking,[1] and was intended to provide for the spiritual needs of the tenants of the abbey lands, and of the fishermen, woodmen, tillers of the soil, and other dwellers in the district. We have not come across any evidence of the existence of an earlier church, although some archæologists think it likely, in view of the proximity of the place to the Abbey of Barking, which was founded four centuries before the Norman Conquest. The site was given by the abbey. The Kentish ragstone used in the building of the church would be brought across the river Thames from Kent, and the timber would be supplied from the king's forest at Hainault, four miles due north. The workmen would, for the most part, belong to the abbey estate, at that time one of great importance in the county of Essex.[2]

As originally built, the church consisted of nave, chancel, chantry (on the north of the chancel), north aisle, and tower. The nave was 59 × 38 feet; the chancel, 47 × 15 feet; the chantry, 40 × 15 feet. The south aisle was added later, as it is described in the will of John Valentyne, vicar (d. 1475), as a " newe ile." " My bodie to be beryed in yᵉ newe ile or chapele of Seynt Petry's Church in Dakenham . . . fferthʳ (i.e. furthermore) I woll yᵗ yᵉ gabill windowe of yᵉ saide new chapele be glasid wᵗʰ my godys." It is, of course, possible that this new aisle replaced an older one. The church was built in the Gothic style of architecture, as we learn from a brief of the date George III.: " This church is an antient pile of Gothic building."

There is no extant record of the actual date of the consecration of the church, the patron saints of which are SS. Peter and Paul (June 29),[3] but it may reasonably be inferred that it took place in some year between 1180 and 1220. The bishop who officiated on that auspicious occasion would probably be either Gilbert Folliott, Bishop of London, 1163-89, or Richard de Ely, 1189-99, or William of St. Mary's Church, 1199-1221. The service would include the celebration of the Mass or Holy Communion in the presence of a large congregation consisting of the abbess, nuns, stewards and sub-stewards, the lords of the manors, yeomen,

---

[1] Adelicia, 1180-95 ; Maud, natural daughter of Henry II. ; Christina de Valoniis ; Sarah de Walebar, covering between them the period 1195-1252.

[2] This abbey was founded by Erkenwald, the fourth Bishop of London, after the conversion of the Saxons to Christianity, and dedicated to the honour of Christ and of the Blessed Virgin Mary. He appointed his sister Ethelburga the first abbess. It was a house of the Benedictine Order.

[3] From old wills and MSS. there is ample evidence that this was the dedication.

goodmen, serfs, fishermen, and villains with their wives and families. The bishop would be assisted by the priests of Barking Abbey, and probably also by the newly appointed chantry priest of Dagenham.

In the Public Record Office there is preserved a MS. inventory of the various properties that belonged to the church and parish of Dagenham, made by three commissioners nominated by Edward VI., 1552–53, viz. Lord Rich,[1] Sir Thomas Josselyn, and Edward Mordaunt, Esq., the last-named being the son-in-law of Lord Rich. It is on two folio sheets, in double columns, the writing being faded and illegible, and runs thus—

CHURCH GOODS. ESSEX.

certified iiij^{to} Octobr̄
A^o Vj^{to} R̄ R̄ E. Vj^{ti}

BEKENTRE.
(Hundred)

DAGNAM.

Thynventory of the parryshe of Dagnam made the thyrde day of october In the syxt yere off the Rayne of our soffereyn lorde Kyng Edward the syxt by the grace of god Kyng of England Fraunce and Ireland Deffender of the Fayth and of the churches of England and Ireland next and Inmedyatly vnder Christe supreme and cheffe hede Consernyng the goods of ye church of the parysshe of Dagnam that ys to say of plate money ornaments pewter coper lattyn ande of bell Mettell as well that that Remayneth of the premyces not sold as that whych hath byne sold synnes the Fyrste yere of the Rayne of our sayd Soffereyne lorde and to whome the same was sold when and for how moche And also to what vses the money Rysyng of the sayd sale was Imployede so farre forth as we now knowe and can Remember and also of the yerely charges and expences of the same church frome the forsayd yere and Fynally what Repacyons are to be don nessessarylry at thys present tyme.

PLAT AND MONEY.

[Inprimis] on chailys[3] solde by the cōsent of the pishe Robard Ienyns ande Iohn logson churchwardyns . . . .

   . . . . ngton dwellyng at the menerys[4] In the
   . . . . of the Reyne of our Soffereyn lorde

---

[1] Lord Rich was one of Henry VIII.'s chief agents in suppressing the monasteries, and was made Chancellor of the Court of Augmentations. He was created Baron Rich of Leez, and Lord Chancellor, by Edward VI. He profited considerably through the spoliation he so actively promoted, for at his death he was found to be possessed of over thirty manors or estates, of which one was Passlowes, in Dagenham.

[2] Anno sexto regni regis Edwardi sexti. Edward VI. came to the throne, January 28, 1547.

[3] One chalice.

[4] The Minories.

. . . .   [rece]yved for yᵉ same at that tyme
   V.ℓi. iij.s̄. iiij.d. (£5 3s. 4d.)
. . . . money of exchaunge at the consent
. . . . from Iohn mabbe goldsmyth
. . . . besyde on lyttyll pyx [1] & on lyttyll
. . . . Chalyces of Syluᵉʳ & gylt
weyeng . . . . . . ownces and halfe a quartᵉ receyved
. . . . Com̄unyon Cuppys of Sylver ande
. . . . .weyeng xxvj ownces weyght for
. . . . payeng for thexchaunge xiij.s̄. viij.d. (13s. 8d.)
. . . . money of thys exchaunge Remaynyng
. . . . xlix.s̄. ixd. as doth apere by the
. . . . subscrybed thys was don thys
. . . . thomas estbroke at fylde ande
. . . . now beyeng churchwardyns
. . . . church plate ij Com̄unyon
. . . . sayd wᵗ a . . . n off a
. . . . [estimacyon] ij ownces.
[money] in our hands at thys   V.ℓi. vj.d. (£5 0s. 6d.)

ORNAMENTES.

. . son ande thomas . . . . [churchwardyns]
. . the thyrde yere . . . . lord
. . . . . mystrys . . . .
. . . .

LATTYN.[2]

Iℓm sold by Iohn logson and thomas Hoke the thyrde yere of our
Sofferayne lord the Kyng by the cōsent off the pishe iiij. canstyckes &
a lectorn wᵗ other small canstyckes & a holywater pott of lattyn weyeng
iiij.ᶜ⁽ʷᵗ⁾ & a halfe & vijˡˡ at xx.s̄. the c(wt) sumʷᵗ

   iiij.ℓi. xj.s̄. iiij.d. (£4 11s. 4d.)

BELLMETTEL.

Iℓm Remeynyng in our church iiij bells wyth a lyttyll Sancebell [3] and a cloke
stryckyng vpon the grett bell the gret bell weyeng by estymacyon   xijᶜ
the thyrdbell weyeng by estymacyon   ..   ..   xᶜ
the secundbell weyeng by estymacyon   ..   .. viijᶜ
the treble bell weyeng by estymacyon   ..   .. vjᶜ
the lyttyll sance bell weyeng about   ..   .. xxxˡˡ

[1] A brass, cup-shaped vessel, with a cover, to contain the reserved consecrated Host.
Sometimes it was used merely for unconsecrated altar breads.

[2] A hard, mixed brass-like metal, much used for sepulchral memorials.

[3] The sanctus bell, rung at the consecration at High Mass. It was usually in a small
turret at the east end of the nave. There was also an Agnus bell, or sacring bell, which
was rung at the elevation of the Host. This was a hand-bell.

Charges & exspences don by Iohn logson & Robard genyns the secunde yere of our Soffereyne lord the Kyng vpon the church on the south syde

Itm pᵈ for tymber lede & shyngle wᵗ the workmanshyp [*of*] the same to the plumᵉʳ shyngler & the carpenter vi.ℓi.

Charges and exspences don the thyrd y[ere] of our Soffereyne lord the Kyng by Iohn logson & thomas Hoke by cōsent of the pishe wythyn the [church].

Itm pᵈ for lyme & Redocar¹ & for wasshyng [*the*] church and for the Rodelofte clo[th ?]² wyth [other] exspences.

Itm sold by Iohn logson and . . . .

. . . . of Dornix³ ande ij tunecles⁴ for deacon

. . . . the pᶦce xxxvj.ŝ viii.d. (£1 16s. 8d.)

. . . . london a cope . . [*ve*]stment of

. . . . at wyth iij old v[estments] and a

. . . . crosses⁵ iiij torche wᵗ ther seuᵉʳall

                        viii.ŝ. iiij.d. (8s. 4d.)

. . . . [*Henry*] clarke Iohn p[echy] Richard sakes

. . . . other of yᵉ pishe as meny olde albys alter

. . . . paynted clothes⁶ as cometh to vjᶦ

. . . . . [*Sold*] [to] Sʳ Iohn Sander & to Iohn Vayle and

. . . Sakes a vayle wᵗ other clothes staynede for vjᶦ vii.d.

                        (6s. 7d.)

. . . . thys present yere at the cōsent offe

. . . . by thomas estbroke at fyld & thomas

. . . . . [*estbroke at*] well now beyeng churchwardyns to

. . . . the curat on olde vestment of fustyan in

. . . . corporaces wᵗ cases iiij old towells & ij olde

. . . . [*clo*]thes pᶦce⁷ ..   ..   .. xᶦ (10s. 0d.).

---

¹ Red ochre.

² The veil or cloth in which the crucifix upon the rood-beam was shrouded during the season of Lent in token of mourning. The rood-loft was a strong beam stretching across the chancel arch, ten feet from the floor and two or three feet wide. From this loft, or gallery, the Gospel was sometimes read in the Communion Office. In the centre there was usually the figure of Christ crucified, attended by the Blessed Virgin Mary and St. John. Access to the rood-loft was by a winding stair in the wall of the chancel. Under the rood-beam a screen was sometimes erected, partly to conceal the altar, and partly to relieve its own heavy appearance. These screens were known as *cancelli*, hence the word chancel.

³ Dornex, an inferior kind of damask originally manufactured at Doornick in Flanders.

⁴ These were the dalmatic and smaller tunicle, worn by the deacon and subdeacon respectively. The former was a short and wide tunic, slit up the sides, with short, wide sleeves.

⁵ Probably two; one for processions, the other (the "cross for the dead") to be laid on the body when brought into church.

⁶ Ornamental altar-cloths or frontals.

⁷ The towels were small linen cloths or corporals, used at celebrations.

[*Itm*] sold to paxtons wyffe a towell p^ce .. .. .. xij^d (1s.)
[*Itm*] sold to ij vndercum^er ij cortaynes of Sendall^1 .. xij^d (1s.)
Itm sold to Richard Sakes Iohn Sakes Harry clarke ande wyllm estbroke
an old vestment of blew damaske & on alter cloth & ij albys p^ce^2

iiij^s v^d (4s. 5d.)

Itm sold to Rychard Sakes & thomas estbroke at fyld a front & a cover of
sattyn of bryges and on old alter cloth p^ce .. .. ix^s vj^d (9s. 6d.)

ORNAMENTS REMAYNG.

Itm ornaments Remayng to the church not sold.
Itm a byble^3 & a papharasys^4 ij salters^5 a syrplysse
Itm a Cope & a vestment of Red velvet
Itm a Cope & a vestment & a herscloth of blake velvett
Itm a Whyt vestment of velvet
  and an olde cope of blew damaske
Itm a table for the Comunyon & iij table clothes
Itm a payer of small orgayns^6

PEWTER.

Itm sold to on of london xliiij^u of pewter the pryce xxv^s (£1 5s. 0d.)
  Charges & expences don . . . .
  of our Soffereyne lorde the Kyng . . . .
  Hoke & Iohn Bayley by co[*sent*] . . . .
Itm p^d for glasyng of iij wyndowes & mendyng the . . . .
  for a Comunyon table . . . .
  Charges & exspences don . . . .
  our Soffereyne lord the Kyng by [*Iohn*] . . . .
  & thomas estbroke at well in the [church]
Itm p^d for takyng down the alters & fortrymyng . . . .
  & the pulpett & for makyng ij new stiles in the chyrch yarde for
  pavyng tyle lyme and the layeng of the pavyng in the chauncell & in
  the church .. .. xs

---

^1 A fine silk texture made in India.

^2 The alb is a white tunic of linen, woollen, or silk material, worn with girdle (with other vestments) at celebrations.

^3 The Great Bible, printed in 1540, in London, with Archbishop Cranmer's preface, and on the title-page, "appointed to be read in churches." Its pages are 15 × 19 inches.

^4 The Paraphrase of Erasmus on the New Testament, which, together with the Book of Homilies, was ordered to be placed in every church (August, 1547).

^5 Psalters—books containing the Psalms divided into certain portions for the service of the Hours.

^6 Organs were introduced into English churches at the close of the tenth century. Latterly there were two kinds : (1) the *regals*, a small portable organ, with a single row of treble pipes, and a small bellows worked by the left hand ; (2) "a pair of organs," that is, an organ with two rows of pipes. It stood usually in the chancel ; if very large, at the west end of the church. After the Restoration, the organ was sometimes placed on the rood-screen.

Charges & exspences don thys present yere by thomas es[*tbroke*
at] fylde & thomas estbroke at [*well*] by cosent of the pish[*oners*]

Itm pᵈ for a new byble & a paphrasys . . . .

Itm pᵈ for mendyng our church wall & for nayly[*ng*] a shet of lede that
the wynde blew of & for m[*akyng*] a cope & makyng a syrplyce & for
a bell Rope . . . .

Itm pᵈ for ij busshels of lyme & for wrytyng . . . .
& for ij papars of te deū (Te Deum) in song . . . .

Itm pᵈ for mendyng of a baldrycke ¹ . . . .

Itm spent at vycytracyon at barkyng . . . .

Itm spent at yengarton ² & at our metyng . . . .
at the makyng of our bokes . . . .

Itm for wrytyng of our bokes at thys tyme . . . .

Repacyons to be don at thys tyme

Itm our church ys at thys time present on gl . . . .
sore by the gret wynde for the whych gla[*ss*] . . . .
ded byd a glasyer iiij nobles ³ to have yt d[*on*] . . . .
colde not have yt don vnder V nobles . . . .
decay in dyvers places for shynglyng . . . .
ys decayed in ledyng [Itm] Welake [a shyngler?] . . . .

Itm our chauncell ys in gret decay . . . .
ande a wendow broken by theves . . . .
vpon the sowth syde & the west syde . . . .
down the whych church ye[*rd*] . . . .
don by our Soffereyne lord . . . .

God Sa[*ve the Kyng*]

Thomas estbroke at fylde } churchwardyns.
Thomas estbroke at well }

Iohn logson)
Wyllm pyckman } parrysheners.
Iohn pechy)

[*Endorsed*]

Appoynted to the Church Gardians there for . . . .
. . wᵗin . . . . Coope and vestment of blak veluet the heerse
Cloth and . . . . the Residue cōmytted to the Custodie
of Thomˢ Eastbroke of the F[*yld and Thomˢs*] Eastbroke of the
Well salfelie to kepe to such vses as shall ple[*ase our lord the Kyng*]

This inventory is of historical value on account of the information
it gives us about the condition of Dagenham church, its ornaments,

¹ Baudryk, baudrick, or baldrock was a leather strap by which the bell-clapper was suspended from the staple inside the bell.

² Is this another word for "visitation" in previous line?

³ The noble was a gold coin, value 6s. 8d., struck in the reign of Edward III., which increased in value to 10s.

DAGENHAM OLD CHURCH
(From an old painting made about 1770)

the ministerial vestments of its clergy, and its goods and properties in general, in the middle of the sixteenth century, while the Reformation was in progress. The costly articles which are mentioned were very likely pious gifts made from time to time to the church by the various abbesses of Barking, and by the lords and ladies of the manors in the parish. The vicars, too, sometimes made bequests to the church. Our parish church was certainly richer, far richer then in its furniture and general appointments, than it has ever been since. The chalice, which was sold for £5 3s. 4d., equal to £60—£70 of present money, was probably richly studded with jewels. The small chalice, silver-gilt, would be that which was used at private communions for the sick ; the cup of silver would be that used on ordinary occasions. The vestments worn at celebrations were of rich quality and beautifully embroidered. They comprised a cope of blue damask, another of red velvet, another of white velvet, two white linen albs, and a cotton surplice. They were never replaced, the result being that at Dagenham, as in many other parishes for the same reason, vestments fell into disuse. The altar vestings included three or four embroidered frontals, three white linen cloths, corporals or housing cloths, and napkins or small "towels."

The inventory mentions, *inter alia*, the "taking down of altars." These were the high altar and the altar in the chantry, both probably of stone, with a marble slab on the top of each. One of these slabs was dug up during the excavations that were made when the present church was restored in 1878–79, and replaced on the oak altar table. It is of fine Purbeck marble, and is 5½ feet long, 3 feet wide, and 1⅓ inch in thickness. At each of the four corners and in the centre is a cross engraven, symbolical of the five sacred wounds of the Divine Redeemer. No trace or part of the second altar has been found as yet. It seems pretty certain that the chantry altar was never replaced after being taken down in 1548, and also that no holy table was substituted for it afterwards. This latter fact is not surprising when we reflect that, by an Act of Parliament passed in 1546–47, and another in the year following, all chantry endowments were alienated from their original purpose and transferred to the king. With this disendowment of the chantry priests came about the suppression of chantries and the disappearance of the altars in them.

The inventory contains no reference to the font. This, too, was of Purbeck marble, and with its pedestal stood about 4 feet high, without its cover, which was forest oak, elaborately carved. Unfortunately the font has disappeared ; it was probably destroyed, supposing that it then existed, when the tower collapsed in 1800. Some portion of the base still remains, and is now in the vicarage garden.

Within the massive western tower there was a peal of five bells, including the *sanctus* bell. There was also a clock and hour bell. The tower was of the type commonly found in Essex, with a turret at its south-east corner ; the spire was not added till 1804.

Under ordinary circumstances no exception whatever could have been taken to the royal order to the Commissioners to make the inventory *per se.* On the contrary, inventories are always useful, and, not infrequently, interesting and instructive.[1] But in this case it was an unworthy proceeding. For its *real* object was to ascertain the extent and value of church properties and effects with a view to taking possession of whatsoever articles appeared valuable, the proceeds of the sale of these goods presently finding their way partly into the pockets of the Commissioners and partly into the royal coffers. As the parish was only allowed to retain the "cope and vestment of black velvett and the herse-cloth," a considerable sum must have been realized out of this proceeding. The theory suggested by an eminent Essex antiquary—the late Mr. H. W. King— that possibly these goods were not actually sold, because Queen Mary, who came to the throne in 1553, strictly forbade these transactions, is unfortunately without support, as, with one exception, the present church goods date no further back than 1678. It is, of course, true that some of the money was spent in necessary repairs, such as relaying the tiles, mending the windows and the roof, and cleaning and colouring the interior of the church, but the cost of these repairs would fall very far below the total sum realized by the sale of the various articles mentioned in the inventory. It is significant that Bishop Bonner offered a vigorous opposition to the inquiry here and elsewhere in his diocese, and was imprisoned in the name of the young king. When he was released, he found that one-third of the churches in the diocese of London had been plundered of their goods under the guise of inventories being made of them.[2] To make matters worse, the legalized spoliation of Dagenham church was probably followed by a general looting

---

[1] The longest inventory of church goods in this locality is that of South Weald, near Brentwood.

[2] His successor, Nicholas Ridley, translated from Rochester, favoured the inquiry.

by "theves" and unscrupulous persons of whatever valuables still remained there.

After the disastrous results of the inventory had passed away an effort was made by the parishioners to put the chancel in a thorough state of repair. Aided with the generous interest of the Fanshawe family, and of other influential residents, they were able, between 1580 and 1630, to carry out the partial restoration of the church, which was imperatively needed. The chancel was put in a thorough state of repair, and the east wall strengthened on the outside with a stone buttress. Inside the chancel, the bay between it and the chantry was filled in with a brick wall, 8 feet high, which was extended to the small west bay of the chantry. The latter was now converted into a vestry, but was called the "rector's chancel," out of deference to the patron who claimed it as his own property. The rest of the church fabric was carefully restored at the same time, as we find no subsequent mention in the church accounts of any extensive or important repairs beyond "shingling," and "glassing the windows," for a considerable period. It was not till 1770, or thereabouts, that the church was seen to be in a dangerous condition, owing to the foundations of the tower having crumbled away, causing it to press heavily upon the west and south portions of the nave. To remedy this, large sums of money were spent from time to time, amounting in all to over £1000. The cracks and fissures in the walls were filled in with ragstone and cement; the tower was girded with strong iron clamps, and a buttress set up against the south wall of the church. Unfortunately, the efforts made by the parishioners to save their church were all in vain, though they averted its collapse for a time. Eventually the vestry decided, in 1797, to accept the estimate of a Mr. Samuel Cleare to "take down and rebuild the tower for £1176 5s. 0d., exclusive of the old materials." It was also agreed to obtain a brief, and the Rev. Mr. Downs (curate), and Messrs. Hunsdon and Grigg (churchwardens), together with Messrs. Ford and Cleare, were deputed to apply for it at the Chelmsford Quarter Sessions (January, 1798). This was granted in the following July, and runs as follows :—

BRIEF.[1]

"GEORGE III., by the grace of God, of Great Britain, ffrance,[2] & Ireland, King, Defender of the Faith, and so forth, to all & singular Archbishops, bishops, Archdeacons, Deans, and their officials, Parsons, Vicars, curates, and all other spiritual persons & to all Teachers & Preachers of every separate congregation, & also to all Justices of the Peace, Mayors, Sheriffs, Bailiffs, Constables, Churchwardens, Chapel-wardens, Headboroughs, Collectors for the poor & their overseers & also to all officers of cities, boroughs, & towns corporate & to all other our officers, ministers and subjects, whomsoever they be, as well within liberties as without to whom these presents shall come,—

" Greeting,—Whereas it hath been represented unto us as well as upon the humble petition of the Minister, Churchwardens & principal inhabitants of the Parish of Dagenham in the County of Essex as by certificate under the hands of our trusty & well-beloved Justices of the Peace for our said County of Essex assembled at their general Quarter Sessions of the Peace held at Chelmsford in & for our said county on Tuesday, the Ninth Day of January in the thirty-eighth year of our Reign That the parish church of Dagenham aforesaid is a very ancient pile of Gothic building and by length of time is become so ruinous in many parts that it hath been with extreme danger to themselves for some months past that the Parishioners have ventured to assemble therein for Divine worship. That the north and south sides of the Tower in particular are split from top to bottom and were obliged some years ago to be ramped with iron bars at a great expense those of late owing to the total decay of the foundation having given way the Tower is in great danger of dividing assunder & falling upon the Church the south east angle being considerably thrown out of its perpendicular presses so heavily upon the south aile of the church as to occasion a fracture throughout the whole side. Therefore it is deemed necessary to be totally taken down and rebuilt for sixty feet in height from the ground or thereabouts exclusive of the foundation and twenty-four feet square that the east and west end walls of the south aile are also so much out of repair as to be thought necessary as to be also taken down & totally rebuilt. That the Lead over the roof of part of the Church & of the Gutters thereon must be recast & relaid and the tiling on other part of the roof and places of the

---

[1] *Briefs* originally were official letters issued by the Pope of Rome, and sealed with the seal of the Fisherman's ring. They were written in Roman characters, and signed by the secretary of Briefs, usually a cardinal. After the Reformation, Papal briefs were forbidden, but, instead of them were issued, as occasion required, "letters patent from the sovereign," authorizing collections for various charitable objects, *e.g.* the building or restoring of churches, the relief of sufferers from public calamities, etc.

In 1653, one Thomas Baker was committed for trial at the Wiltshire Quarter Sessions for collecting money with false briefs.

[2] George III. was the last English monarch who bore the title of " King of France."

Church must be also taken off & relaid and the whole of the ceiling in the Church must be new and the Church in many other parts being very much decayed is adjudged in need of new timber, stone bricks and other works substantially & repair and support the same. That the parishioners have from time to time laid out & expended the sum of eleven hundred and twenty pounds and also several other sums of money within the last twenty years for temporary repairs to various parts to keep up the Church which are found to be no longer sufficient for the purpose but that the whole Church is now adjudged necessary to undergo a thorough repair. That the truth of the premises hath been made appear to our Justices assembled at their Quarter Sessions of the peace aforesaid, not only by the inhabitants but also upon the oaths of the Reverend Ralph Downes, Minister, Henry Hunsden and Phœbus Grigg, Churchwardens and Samuel Cleere an able & experienced Architect & Surveyor who hath carefully viewed & made an estimate of the charge of rebuilding the Tower and repairing the Church, which together upon a moderate computation amounts to the sum of one thousand one hundred & seventy-six pounds five shillings exclusive of the old materials which sum the Inhabitants are unable to raise among themselves being considerably burthened with a numerous poor and are therefore unable to undertake so very great a work without the charitable assistance of well-disposed Christians. They have therefore humbly besought us to grant unto them our most gracious Letters patent . Licence & Protection under our great seal of Great Britain to empower them to ask, collect & receive the alms benevolent & charitable contributions of all our loving subjects throughout England & Town of Berwick upon Tweed & our Counties of Fflint, Denbigh, & Radnor in Wales & from house to house throughout our Counties of Essex, Herts, Kent, Suffolk, Middlesex, Surrey, Hants, Berks & Bucks & all Cities, Boroughs & Market Towns to enable them to rebuild their said Tower & repair their said Church unto which their humble request We have graciously condescended, not doubting but that when these presents shall be known by our loving subjects they will readily and cheerfully contribute their endeavours for accomplishing the same.

KNOW YE THEREFORE that of our special grace and favour we have given and granted and by these our Letters patent under our great seal of Great Britain We do give and grant unto the said parishioners and inhabitants and to their deputy and deputies the Bearer and bearers hereof authorised as is hereinafter directed full power, licence and authority to ask, collect and receive the alms or benevolent and charitable contributions of all our loving subjects within all and every our counties, cities, boroughs, towns, priviledged places, hamlets, cinque ports, districts, parishes, and all other places whatsoever throughout England our town of Berwick upon Tweed and our counties of Fflint, Denbigh and Radnor in Wales and from house to house throughout our counties of Essex, Herts,

Kent, Suffolk, Middlesex, Surrey, Hants, Berks and Bucks and all cities, boroughs, market towns for the purpose aforesaid. AND THEREFORE in pursuance of the tenor of an Act of Parliament made in the fourth year of the reign of the late Queen Anne entitled an Act for the better collecting charity money on Briefs by letters patent and preventing abuses in relation to such Charities our will and pleasure is and we do hereby for the better advancement of these our pious intentions require and command all Ministers, Teachers and Preachers, Churchwardens, Chapel-wardens and the Collectors of this Brief and all others concerned that they and every of them observe the directions in the said Act contained and do in all things conform themselves thereunto and that when the printed Copies of these presents shall be tendered unto you the respective Ministers and Curates, Churchwardens and Chapelwardens and to the respective Teachers and Preachers of every separate congregation and to any person who teaches or preaches in any meeting of the people called Quakers that you and every of you under the penalties inflicted by the said Act do receive the same and you the respective Ministers and Curates, Teachers and Preachers and persons called Quakers are by all persuasive motives and arguments earnestly to exhort your respective congregations and assemblies to a liberal contribution of their charity for the good intent and purpose aforesaid. And you the Churchwardens and Chapelwardens together with the Ministers or some of the substantial inhabitants of the several parishes and Chapelries and all other places within our counties aforesaid and all cities, boroughs and market towns are hereby required to go from house to house in the week-days next following the publication of these presents to ask and receive of the Parishioners and Inhabitants and all other persons their Christian and charitable contributions and to take the names in writing of such as shall contribute thereunto the sum and sums by them respectively given and indorse the whole sums upon the said printed Briefs in words at length and subscribe the same with your own proper hands together with the name of the parish and place where and the time when collected and to enter the same in the Public Books of account kept for each parish and chapelry respectively and the sum and sums collected together with the printed Briefs so indorsed you are to deliver to the Deputys and Agents authorized to receive the same. AND WE DO by these presents nominate, constitute and appoint John G. Ffanshaw, John Tyler, H. M. Bird and Christopher Tyler, Esquires, William Ford, James Armstrong, Joseph Osburn, Robert Brittain, Reginald Heath, William Bentley, John Biggs, John Hunsdon, Samuel Seabrook, William Stevenson and John Steven-son, gentlemen and the Minister and Churchwardens for the time being Trustees and Receivers of the Charity to be collected by virtue of these Presents with power to them or any three or more of them to give deputa-tions to such Collectors as shall be chosen by the Petitioners or the major part of them and the said Trustees or any three or more of them are to

make and sign all necessary orders for the due and regular collection of
this Brief and advancement of the said Charity and to see that the
money when collected be applied according to the true intent and meaning of these presents. AND LASTLY our will and pleasure is that no
person or persons shall receive the said printed Briefs or monies collected
thereon but such only as shall be deputed and made the bearer and
bearers of the presents and duplicates hereof. IN WITNESS whereof
we have caused these our Letters to be made patent and to continue in
force for one whole Year from Michaelmas Day next and no longer.

WITNESS ourself at Westminster, the 23rd day of July in the thirty-
eighth year of our reign.

PHILIPPS.

The above brief is written on a sheet of parchment about two
feet square. The royal arms are at the top, with a vignette of
George III. and Queen Charlotte on each side. It is stamped with
a forty-shilling stamp.

The response to this sovereign mandate was disappointing,
only £68 10s. 8d. being collected from the "king's loving subjects."
Building operations were for a while suspended, partly from lack of
funds and partly because Mr. Wm. Bentley refused to carry out his
contract for Mr. Cleare to take down the tower. This delay was
most untimely. Matters went from bad to worse, until at last the
tower fell with a tremendous crash upon the nave, utterly destroying
the south-west porch, the roof, the singing gallery, the font and pews,
and damaging the chancel arch. This calamity occurred on the
Second Sunday in Advent, 1800. No lives were lost, as the congregation were waiting in the churchyard for the vicar, who was
fortunately late that morning. With this collapse the old church
ceased to exist. Only a new church could repair this disaster, and
it reflects credit on the parishioners that they redoubled their
energies, without delay, to make good the loss they had sustained
and rebuild their house of prayer.

CHAPTER IV

DAGENHAM NEW CHURCH

" Now shall the sanctuary
And the house of the Most High be newly built.
The ancient honours due unto the church,
Buried within the ruined monasteries,
Shall lift their stately heads, and rise again
To astonish the destroyer's wondering eyes,
Zeal shall be decked in gold ; religion,
Not like a virgin robbed of all her pomp,
But bravely shining in her gems of state,
Like a fair bride be offered to the Lord."
WEBSTER.

FOUR days after the collapse of the old church, the vestry decided to rebuild their parish church without delay. They had in hand £400 in Exchequer Bills, as well as £90 for some old lead sold to Messrs. Barrow and Healey, of Bromley, £26 2s. 0d. for old iron bought by Mr. James Knight, and £4 17s. 0d. for old tiles. To these sums they added a further sum of £400, raised by two rates and invested in Exchequer Bills. Their first act was to obtain a faculty from the Bishop's Court, after which they entered into negotiations with Mr. Wm. Mason to rebuild the tower, spire, and nave for £2431 9s. 4d., exclusive of such old materials as had not already been sold. The foundation-stone was laid on Easter Tuesday, 1801. In the parish register the ceremony is described as follows :—

Be it Remembered
that the first stone of the New Church of Dagenham
was laid the 13ᵗʰ day of April, 1801,
by Mr. Henry Fanshaw,
Proxy for John Gascoigne Fanshawe, Esq.,
and Henry Merttins Bird, Esq.

When a suitable prayer was composed and Delivered on the solemn occasion by the Reverend Ralph Downes, Curate of the Parish.

John Biggs } Churchwardens.
John Burley }

Thomas Twyford } Overseers.
James Fenner }

Mr. William Mason, Architect to the new Church.

In the Presence of

John Biggs, Churchwarden; H. M. Bird; Ralph Downes, Minister; H. Fanshaw; T. Fanshaw, aetatis 8; John Tyler, Willm. Ford; H. M. Bird; H. Bird; James Armstrong, James Stafford, J. Evans his mark ×, Lanct. Tuck, Thomas Boulton, J. Bustard, William Mason, John Symonds, W. Bentley, Phoe. Grigg, Henry Hunsdon.

The new church was built according to a plan made by Mr. Sam. Cleare, which he had handed over to Mr. Mason. It was to be "1½ feet narrower in the body and 1½ feet narrower in each of the side aisles, making the whole 4½ feet narrower than the old church; the pews to be laid out on a modern plan like some of the new-built churches." The "modern plan" was that of the high-backed, square pews, with doors, roomy and comfortable, perhaps, but ill-calculated to promote reverence during Divine service. A large new gallery was to be erected at the·west end in place of the former smaller one, to bring up the total accommodation to three hundred and fifty.

For a time all went well with the building of the church, and the committee had no reason to be unduly uneasy as to the dis-charge of their liabilities, until the end of the year, when it was reported that the cost of pulling down the old church and of providing new materials for the new one had exceeded Mr. Mason's expectations by £700. He was advised, therefore, to suspend operations for a few months. Meanwhile the committee consulted Dr. Maurice Swabey, surrogate and registrar for the diocese of London, as to the best method of raising the necessary funds. On his advice, they decided to apply for a second brief, which was granted on July 7, 1802. Unfortunately, it met with no better success than its predecessor, only £70 being sent in obedience to it. The heavy taxes caused by the war with Napoleon, the hard winters and the succession of bad harvests, had made money scarce, and the rebuilding of the church proceeded but slowly in consequence. To make matters worse, the treasurer (Mr. Bird) announced, at a special vestry (July, 1802), that although he had expended £1795 17s. 6d., a further sum of at least £3000 would have to be spent before the church could possibly satisfy the requirements of the Archdeacon of Essex (the Ven. Wm. Gretton), who had written to him on the subject. This grave piece of news so alarmed the committee that they determined as a last resource to raise the amount needed by special loans. Mr. Wasey Sterry,[1] a Romford solicitor, was accordingly instructed to take the necessary steps to get a special Act of Parliament passed for the raising of £3500 to complete the work. The Fanshaw family interested themselves, and it speaks much for their influence that the Act was procured in less than three months from the time it was first suggested. Mr. Sterry proved himself an able adviser, and Mr. Trower, who was retained as counsel, "conducted his case efficiently" in drawing up the special Act.

It is entitled "An Act for the more effectual repairing of the Parish Church of Dagenham in the County of Essex; 43 George III." Under its terms the following trustees are appointed :—John Gascoigne Fanshawe, John Hopkins Dare, John Tyler, Christopher Tyler, Wm. Ford, Jas. Armstrong, Robt. Brittain, John Burley, Phœbus Griggs, Hen. Hunsdon, Thos. Twyford, John Biggs, Lanc. Tuck, together with the vicar and churchwardens for the time being. These are empowered to raise money by annuities, no annuity to exceed £12 for every £100 borrowed, to be paid out of the rates and assessments on the first Tuesday in December. The interest on bonds of £50 each is to be 5 per cent. The trustees are to rate land and householders at 1s. 6d. in the £, and levy distress warrants in case of non-payment. They are to meet at least quarterly. It is also enacted that no more interments shall take place in the church unless the graves are built with brick and arched over, and at a distance of 6 feet from the walls and pillars. Lastly, it directs that, on the completion of the church, the vicar and churchwardens shall allot the pews to the parishioners of Dagenham.

No time was lost in carrying out this Act. Loans were obtained in due course from a Mr. Buckland and Miss Berkley of £1000 each, and from Miss Barley of £1500, the committee entering upon a legal agreement to pay them life annuities of £33, £27 10s. 0d., and £45 respectively. These were on the security of the church rates.

The rebuilding of the church seems to have proved a long and tedious affair, as the edifice was not ready for consecration till the summer of 1805. On July 8 of that year, the Lord Bishop of

[1] He was also the steward of Barking Manor, in which office he was succeeded by Mr. Edward Sage, the last to hold it.

London[1] (Dr. Porteus) drove down in his coach and four, accompanied by his chaplain, the Rev. Edward Hodgson, the Diocesan Registrar (Dr. M. Swabey), and Mr. Joseph Walker, the Notary Public and Deputy Registrar of the Consistory Court of London. The bishop robed in the vicarage, and wore a wig, in addition to the usual episcopal attire. The service was at 11 a.m. The petition for consecration having been read, the service of consecration was proceeded with according to the usual form. This was followed by the Holy Communion, during which, after the Nicene Creed had been sung, the bishop preached a sermon suitable to the occasion. After the service his lordship consecrated an addition to the churchyard, a tent having been erected for his convenience. It is a significant sign of the times that, beyond the vicar (Rev. H. Morice), no local clergy were present. A very large number of parishioners attended, and the solemn proceedings were impressive and edifying. There is no mention of the dedication of the six new bells which had been hung in the tower; this detail was, doubtless, considered to be included in the general consecration of the church.[2]

It was unfortunate that the old church should have collapsed when it did. Had it held itself together for another fifty years, until the Victorian Renaissance, which began with the Oxford Movement, it would have stood a chance of being rebuilt in a manner more worthy of its sacred object. Neither Mr. S. Cleare, nor Mr. W. Mason, possessed the qualifications for their task. To make matters worse, Mr. Mason set to work with ruthless hand, and treated the *débris* of the fallen edifice as a mass of rubbish. Instead of removing it, he utilized it for the floor of the nave, and made the latter fifteen inches higher than the level of the chancel floor. The insertion of his name over the west arch of the tower was another and less excusable mistake on his part.

[1] Beilly Porteus was Bishop of London, 1787–1809, during which period he administered his diocese with more diligence than was usual with Georgian bishops. He abolished the fraudulent sale of advowsons then customary, stoutly upheld the sanctity of the Lord's day, espoused the cause of the slaves in the West India Islands, and refused to allow Lady Huntingdon's chaplain, though in holy orders, to officiate in London churches because he was the head of a Dissenting seminary. He encouraged the establishment of Sunday schools, and was the first vice-president of the British and Foreign Bible Society. He was a strong evangelical, and a most eloquent preacher.

[2] The service consisted of Psalm xxiv., the prayers of Consecration, Matins (the special Psalms being lxxxiv., cxxii., and cxxxii., and the Lessons 1 Kings viii. 22–62 and Hebrews x. 19-26), the Communion Office to the end of the Nicene Creed, which was followed by the *Jubilate* and sermon (the Epistle was 2 Cor. vi. 14-17 ; the Gospel St. John ii. 13-18).

In 1844 an organ was placed in the church by voluntary contributions. It was put on the gallery, or "singing-loft," where the village orchestra had formerly been.

In 1877 a vestry was held to discuss the question of reseating and restoring the church, and it was resolved to apply for a faculty to remove the high pews, to lower the floor of the nave 15 inches so as to make it below the level of the chancel floor, to substitute a new pulpit and lectern in place of the "two-decker," to remove the organ from the west gallery to the chancel, to reseat the entire church with low deal benches, and do away with the north gallery, which had been erected in 1835. All these propositions were agreed to, except the last one, which was stoutly resisted by some parishioners, and had to be settled by a poll, which was taken in March, 1878, the result being as follows :—For the removal of the north gallery, 144 ; against, 92.

During the excavations made during the work of restoration, some interesting discoveries were brought to light by Mr. J. Hammond, who had the work in hand. These were the altar slab, already referred to, the skeleton of a man in armour, and the jawbone and teeth of a horse, which were all found in the nave, just outside the chancel. It is, of course, impossible to say whose remains they were, beyond the fact that they were probably those of some warrior who had a fancy that his charger should be buried with him. A piscina of Purbeck marble was also discovered, plastered up.

The restoration was completed by October, 1878, and on the 17th of that month the reopening service was held, the Venerable Archdeacon Blomfield being the preacher. A memorial window— the east window—inserted by public subscription to the memory of the Rev. T. L. Fanshawe, was unveiled at this service. A public luncheon followed, at which Mr. John Fanshawe presided.

Several improvements have been made in the church during the last few years. The ceiling of the nave and chancel has been curiously painted with a modern florid pattern of trefoil ; a fine iron screen has been placed in the chancel, and a handsome stained-glass window, both to the memory of Mr. G. Currie ; and two similar windows to the memory of Mr. T. L. Coppen and Mr. G. Stevens respectively.

DAGENHAM CHURCH
(Prior to its restoration of 1878)

THE COMMUNION PLATE.[1]

This consists of—1. a silver flagon, with the date, 1755, marked on it, and also the letters "J. S.," for John Smith. On the rim is the inscription, "A gift to the Parrish Church of Dagenham, Essex." It stands 13½ inches high, has rather a large bowl, and an ornamental handle. It was given by the Rev. Dr. Blackbourne, vicar.

2. A silver chalice, or cup, with the date mark, 1678 ; also a maker's mark, "W. M.," with a cinquefoil and two pellets on either side and one below, inscribed on a plain shield. On the bowl is the inscription, "The Communion plate for ye parish of Dagenham in Essex. I. N. I. R. Churchwardens 1678."[2] The weight is also stated, 19 ozs. 7 dwts. This cup is 10¾ inches high, and the bowl is 4¾ inches across.

3. A small silver cup, with the York mark and date mark for 1598. Also another, probably the maker's mark, which is undecipherable. Round the rim is the inscription, "Private Communion plate for ye parish of Dagenhā to be kept by ye minister." It stands 5 inches high, and the diameter of the bow is 3 inches.

This cup is extremely interesting on account of its rarity.

4. A silver paten, with diameter of 5½ inches, with marks and inscription similar to those on the chalice (3), with the addition, "IN . IR Churchwardens 1678."

5. A silver alms dish, with the date mark for 1727, and mark of maker, "M.," in a circular die, and the inscription, "The gift of Mrs. Mary Tyler, 1729."[3] Its diameter is 11½ inches.

6. One metal alms dish, not earlier, probably, than 1840. Diameter, 9 inches.

7. Another similar alms dish.

8. A silver alms bason or plate, with scalloped sides, with inscription, "The gift of Mr. Thomas Waters." The other marks are very much worn, but "appear to be those of J. Bodington, B.O with a mitre above in a shaped stamp, repeated three times."

THE BELLS.

The church belfry contains a peal of six bells, all of which were cast in the early part of the nineteenth century by the old firm of

[1] *Vide* Freshfield's "Communion Plate of Essex."
[2] John Nevell and John Ramsden.
[3] In memory of her husband, Christopher Tyler, who died in 1724.

Messrs. Mears (now Mears and Stainbank), Whitechapel. They were placed in the belfry in 1804, when the church was rebuilt, and are very well hung. The tenor bell weighs 15 cwt., and the others, except number five, which weighs 13 cwt., about half a ton each. On the tenor bell is the following inscription :—

James Armstrong, Phœbus Grigg, Rev. Henry Morice, Vicar, John Gascoyne Fanshaw, John Tyler, Esqᵐ, Messrs. William Ford, Thomas Twyford, Lancelot Tuck, John Biggs, John Dangerfield, Churchwardens, Robert Brittain, John Burley, Hy Hunsdon, Treasurers, Trustees appointed by an Act of 43ʳᵈ George III, John Hopkins Dare, Christopher Tyler, Esqᵐ· more effectually repairing the Parish Church of Dagenham, Essex. W. Sterry, Solicitor, T. Meres, Fecit, 1804.

On the fourth and fifth bells is the brief inscription : " Thomas Meares of London, Fecit, 1804."

The bells are hung at the top of the tower, immediately under the spire proper.

THE PARISH MAP.

This is in an oak case in the vestry, and is mounted on a roller. It is mounted on glazed canvas, and measures 16 × 8 feet. It is in an excellent condition. At the foot of it is inscribed—

We the undersigned tithe Commissioners for England & Wales do hereby certify this to be a correct copy of the map on the plan referred to in the apportionment of the Rent Charge in lieu of tithes in the district comprising the whole of the Parish of Dagenham in the County of Essex, except part of the Forest of Hainault. In testimony whereof we have hereunder subscribed our respective names and caused our official seal to be affixed this 26ᵗʰ Day of November in A.D. 1844.

William Blamire,
Wm. Towne.

Scale, 2⅓ chains to an inch.
Signed, F. J. Martin,
     Assistant Tithe Commissioner.

There is also, in the vestry, a strong iron-bound chest, in which are deposited the parish registers and archives. In the choir vestry, at the west end of the church, there are two fine hatchments belonging to the Comyns and Fanshawe families.

CHAPTER V

THE PATRONAGE OF THE BENEFICE

> " Some honour I would have,
> Not from great deeds, but good alone ;
> The unknown are better, than ill-known."
>   COWLEY.

UNTIL the dissolution of the monasteries by Henry VIII. in 1537–39, the right of presentation to the vicarage of Dagenham belonged to Barking Abbey. This right was exercised in virtue of the abbess and convent of the said abbey being the Lord of the Manor of Cokermouth, a portion of which estate had been granted in 1330 by John de Cokermuth for the endowment of the benefice of Dagenham.[1] So far as we can judge, the patronage was conscientiously and judiciously administered by the various abbesses, and regarded as a sacred trust. At the dissolution of the monasteries in 1538–39, Barking Abbey, with all its estates, was confiscated by Henry VIII., by an arbitrary exercise of the royal prerogative, and vested for a time in the Crown. While thus vested, the right of nomination to the benefice of Dagenham was granted to William Powsnett, the last steward of Barking Abbey, who nominated to the benefice four times (1540–50). He lived at Loxford Hall. In the subsequent distribution of Church property by the king, among the royal favourites and courtiers, the great tithes of Barking and Dagenham were bestowed upon Sir Anthony Browne. In 1550 this Sir Anthony set apart a considerable portion of the tithes of Dagenham to endow a grammar school which he had built at Brentwood. This explains why the trustees of that school receive the rectorial or greater tithes of Dagenham. The vicarage was then endowed by Sir Anthony with tithes amounting to £40 per annum. On his death, the advowson passed to his nephew, Wistan Browne, Esq., but was shortly afterwards sold

[1] See Appendix A.

to a Mr. John Bullock, who resold it to Mr. William Nutbrowne. For some years the patronage was in the Swinnerton family, but subsequently, for some unknown reason, it fell to the Bishop of London, who had three successive presentations. During the Rebellion the patronage came into the possession of the Darcy family, but was purchased in 1700 by the Rev. Samuel Kekewich, vicar of Rainham. It soon changed hands again, as we read that "John Brett, clerk, of Dagenham, bequeathed the advowson of Dagenham to Mr. William Blackborne, in 1715." From Mr. Blackborne the patronage passed into the hands of the Fanshawe family, for whom Mrs. Bonynge presented four times. In 1854 the Rev. Robert Bewick purchased the advowson, and seven years later sold it to his successor in the benefice, the Rev. John Farmer. The present patron is Stewart Stevenson Moore, Esq. (eldest son of the vicar), of the Middle Temple, and Sub-Deemster of the Isle of Man.

It should be mentioned that the patron sometimes presented to the benefice by deputy, or allowed a friend to present for him. This will explain any discrepancy in the list of the patrons and those who nominated to the vicarage.

THE VALUE OF THE BENEFICE.

Although certain lands were granted by John de Cokermuth for the permanent endowment of the church of Dagenham, the vicar did not receive the rent of those lands, but was paid the tithes on lands allotted to the new benefice. What their value was prior to the spoliation of Barking Abbey we cannot say exactly, but it was probably not less than £500 per annum of present money. The earliest reference to its value is found in the *Taxatio Eccles.* of Pope Nicholas, made about 1291, where the Ecclesia de Dakenham is assessed at £13 6s. 8d. It is also referred to in the "Feudal Aids" (1428), where we learn that the Ecclesia de Dagenham is taxed "from ancient time" at twenty marks, with a subsidy of 26s. 8d.

In the Certificate of Colleges and Chantries, 1 Edward VI., it is stated that the "yerly valewe of the seid church of Dagenh'm doythe amount to the sum of 66s. 8d.

> " Rent resolute   ..   ..   null.
> " Goods, chattells, etc.   ..   ..   ..   null."

In 1646 the vicarage was stated in a return to the House of Commons to be worth £80 a year.

Newcourt, in his " Repertorium " (published 1708), sets the value

down thus—" First-fruits, £19 10s. 0d. ; Tenths, £1 19s. 0d. ; Episcopal Procurations from the Rector, £0 10s. 0d. ; Episcopal Procurations from the Vicar, £0 1s. 6d. ; Archdeacon's Procurations,
£0 8s. 8d. ; Synodalia, £0 1s. 0d."

In 1838 the tithes of the benefice, hitherto paid in kind, were
commuted at £851 2s. 6d. An old bill of sale, date 1854, adver-
tises the sale by auction at Garraway's Coffee Rooms, London, of
the Advowson and Next Presentation of the Vicarage of Dagenham,
together with 4 acres.   It states that the value is £850 per
annum, the age of the present incumbent (Rev. T. L. Fanshawe)
62, and the population of the parish 2000.

The following is a copy of a terrier and inventory of all the
" Buildings, Glebe-lands, Tythes & other profits & rights belong-
ing to the Parish of Dagenham in the Diocese of London," made
June 27, 1818.

Imprimis,—A Vicarage House, lath & Plaister with Tiles, out-
buildings, a stable cover'd with tiles, a coach-house cover'd with thatch.
With a garden adjoining the House, situate in the Village of Dagenham
aforesaid, opposite the Church & occupying about ½ acre.

Item,—Glebe land consisting of one field called Lads Piece adjoining
the Village & containing about 2½ acres & one small Field adjoining Mr.
Joyner's orchard containing about one acre.

Item,—The Endowment of the Vicarage.   Neither the Vicar or the
Churchwardens have any knowledge of or know where it is & therefore are
not enabl'd to specify the particulars.

The Repairs of the Church and fence belongs to the Parishioners &
the Repairs of the Chancel to the Holders of the Great Tithe.

A Baptismal Font of Marble with a cover of wood.

A purple cloth cover for the altar table & two cushions.

A velvet cushion for the Pulpit with hangings.

A large Book of Common Prayer.

A Bible in good condition for the Vicar & a large Book of Common
Prayer for the Clerk.

Communion Plate,—One Silver Plate, One Silver Salver, One Flagon,
a large Silver Cup, A smaller Do, A small salver.

Signed by T. L. Fanshawe, vicar.

Geo. Winmill & Henry Gray, Churchwardens ; and H. Fanshawe, Esq.,
Jas. Biggs, Willm Smith, John Hanson, Thos. Twyford, Willm Seabrook,—
Inhabitants.

THE RECTORY OF DAGENHAM.

Sir Anthony Browne, by his will, dated December 20, 1565, and proved June 5, 1567, bequeathed to the master and guardians of the Free School, Brentwood, the parsonage of Dagenham with the appurtenances, except the patronage of the vicarage, for twenty years, for the maintenance of the aforesaid school. The rent of the parsonage was then £24 a year. By two deeds, executed in 1573, his heir, Wistan Browne, Esq., conveyed this parsonage or rectory, together with other specified properties (not in Dagenham), as directed by the will of Sir Anthony. In July, 1622, a body of statutes was published by the Bishop of London (Dr. George Abbot), the Dean of St. Paul's (Dr. John Donne), and Sir Anthony Browne, patron of the school, relating to the management of this charity.

In 1667 the right of patronage, together with other appurtenances, was conveyed by the then heir of the founder to Sir William Scroggs, afterwards Chief Justice of the Court of King's Bench. From Sir William it passed to Thomas Tower, Esq, who also inherited the mansion and estate of South Weald, in which family it has been ever since.

The rectorial tithes of Dagenham were, in 1802, leased for twenty-one years to John Gascoigne Fanshawe, Esq., of Parsloes, at the yearly rent of £1115. The lease was renewed to his son Henry, and expired in 1823.

Previous to 1802 these tithes had been let upon leases renewable every seven years on payment of fines. For a long time they belonged to the Fanshawe family. From 1700 to 1764 the reserved rent was £40, when it was increased to £100, and later on to £140. In 1803 this system of leases was abolished, and a lease was granted at a rack-rent. The rectorial tithes were then valued at £1363 per annum, if let to several occupiers, or £1138 if let to a stranger. As Mr. Henry Fanshawe was also the lessee of the vicarial tithes, he disputed the claim of Anthony Browne's Charity to the tithe of reed and wood as rectorial tithe, and a reduction of rent was allowed in consequence, but was afterwards withdrawn.

In 1785 one Captain Chas. Cumbers filed a petition in the Court of Chancery, to establish his claim—as the heir of the founder, Sir Anthony Browne—to the patronage of the Brentwood Free School, on the ground that the patronage could not be alienated by the founder's heirs. The petition was, however, dismissed, in consequence, as Captain Cumbers stated, of his not being able to meet the pecuniary liability of the suit.

The parish book of Dagenham contains brief references to this threatened litigation and the payment of the rectorial tithes. The Rev. Edw. Edwards writes to the Rev. T. L. Fanshawe, vicar (October, 1825), that having been appointed by the lawful heir of Sir Anthony Browne, master of the Brentwood Grammar School, in the room of the Rev. Chas. Tower; & Lawrence T. J. Richardson, M.D., & Thos. Wright Brewer, of South Weald, having been appointed guardians of the school, the payers of the great tithes of Dagenham should be careful to pay their tithes to the right person. The Bishop of London, on being appealed to in the matter, supported Mr. Edwards's claim. Meanwhile, however, a few of the tithe-payers made an attempt to evade their liability altogether, but this was frustrated by the "corporate body of the school" instructing their agent, Mr. T. W. Twyford, to duly inform all such objectors that "the High Court of Chancery have not given any decision adverse to Tithe being paid to Brentwood."

CHAPTER VI

THE VICARS OF DAGENHAM

" Bishops and priests, blessed are ye ; if deep
(As yours above all offices is high)
Deep in your hearts the sense of duty lie ;
Charged as ye are by Christ to feed and keep
From wolves your portion of His chosen sheep.
Labouring as ever in your Master's sight ;
Making your hardest task your best delight,
What perfect glory ye in heaven shall reap !
But, in the solemn office which ye sought
And undertook premonished, if unsound
Your practice prove, faithless though but in thought,
Bishops and priests, think what a gulf profound
Awaits you there, if they were rightly taught
Who formed the ordinance by your lives disowned."

WORDSWORTH.

THE parish of Dagenham has had fifty vicars. The following list
has been compiled from Newcourt's " Repertorium " (published in
1708), the Institutions for the Dioceses of London and Rochester,
the parochial registers, and various MSS. and wills.

Name.	Date of Institution.	Patron.
I. William de Walleyton	16 Kal. Iune, 1335	Abbess and Convent of Barking
II. Sir Iohn Ufford	Prob. Sept., 1383–84	,, ,,
III. Thomas Westurne	Oct. 7, 1390 (or 1394)	,, ,,
IV. Thomas Lyllington	Prob. Feb., 1394–95	,, ,,
V. William Leaster	Nov. 8, 1408	,, ,,
VI. Robert Haynton	Prob. April, 1422	,, ,,
VII. Iohn Besewyke	Nov. 12, 1422	,, ,,
VIII. William Boteler	Feb. 15, 1422	,, ,,
IX. Robert Couper, M.A.	Sept. 19, 1440	,, ,,
X. William Redenesse	April 8, 1455	,, ,,
XI. Henry Walfrey	Feb. 25, 1461	,, ,,
XII. Iohn Valentyne	Aug. 8, 1471	,, ,,

Name.	Date of Institution.	Patrons.
XIII. George Davie, A.M.	April 23, 1476	{ Abbess and Convent of Barking
XIV. Iohn Lowe	May 14, 1485	„ „
XV. Iohn Long, A.M.	April 5, 1499	„ „
XVI. Richard Nicholson	Prob. Iune, 1506	„ „
XVII. William Barlee	May 19, 1530	„ „
XVIII. Henry Purtennte	1532–33	`„ „
XIX. George Bolles	Ian. 10, 1533	„ „
XX. Thomas Duke, A.M.	Feb. 1, 1538	{ Edward North and George Hadley, Gentlemen
XXI. William Southy, A.M.	Oct. 9, 1540	{ William Pouncet, Gent.
XXII. Thomas Wagstaffe	Nov. 16, 1544	? „ „
XXIII. Hugh Talbote	1548–49	? „ „
XXIV. William Smith	April 28, 1549–50	? „ „
XXV. Iohn Velstede	Dec. 12, 1554	{ Philip and Mary, King and Queen of England
XXVI. Iohn Finnymore	Nov. 12, 1557	„ „
XXVII. Iohn Berryman, A.M.	Oct. 29, 1579	{ Willm Nutbrowne, Gent.
XXVIII. Thomas Manninge, A.M.	Nov. 6, 1617	{ Mr. Ralph Ward (pro hac vice)
XXIX. Percival Hill	Dec. 6, 1637	Bishop of London
XXX. Rodolf Richards, A.M.	Mar. 14, 1640	„ „
XXXI. Charles Trew, A.M.	Nov. 22, 1641	„ „
XXXII. Thomas Coleman, A.M.	1644	{ House of Commons Committee

[John Bowyer, A.M., a Presbyterian, was appointed first lecturer and then vicar of Dagenham, 1643–50.]

XXXIII. George Walker, B.D.	1650	{ House of Commons Committee
XXXIV. Jonathan Lloyd, A.M.	1651	„ „
XXXV. Frederick Tilney	March, 1652–53	„ „
XXXVI. Isaac Smythies, A.M.	Oct. 2, 1663	{ Sir Thos. Darcy, Bart.
XXXVII. Isaac Harrison, S.T.P.	Oct. 23, 1674	{ Sir Willm. Darcy, Bart.
XXXVIII. William Lamplugh, A.M.	Jan. 21, 1682	{ Sir Thos. Darcy, Bart.
XXXIX. James Symonds, M.A.	May, 1704	{ Rev. Samuel Kekewich
XL. William Butler, L.L.B.	Jan. 16, 1719	{ Willm Blackborne, Esq.

Name.	Date of Institution.	Patrons.
XLI. Francis Stanley, M.A.	Mar. 18, 1736–37	Willm Blackborne, Esq.
XLII. Abraham Blackborne, D.D.	April, 1739	„ „
XLIII. Edward Chaplin, M.A.	June 8, 1798	Thomas Thorston, Esq.
XLIV. Henry Morice, M.A.	June 11, 1801	Mrs. Sarah Bonnynge
XLV. Tempest Slinger, M.A.	Aug., 1807	„ „
XLVI. Richard Glover, M.A.	June 13, 1811	„ „
XLVII. Thomas Lewis Fanshaw, M.A.	Nov. 5, 1816	„ „
XLVIII. Robert Bewick, M.A.	April, 1857	Rev. Robt. Bewick
XLIX. John Farmer, M.A.	Nov., 1861	Rev. John Farmer
L. John James Stevenson Moore, LL.D.	April, 1876	Thomas C. Moore, Esq.

From the above list it will be seen that few vicars stayed here for any length of time, and that, with two or three exceptions, none of them attained any high degree of celebrity outside their own parish. We have been able to glean a few biographical notes about the majority of them, which may interest the reader, from the light they throw on the lives and times of the clergy of past ages. Of the 27 vicars who are known to have been graduates, 10 belonged to the University of Oxford and 16 to that of Cambridge, and of the latter no less than 7 came from St. John's College.

I. WILLIAM DE WALLEYTON was in all probability appointed vicar of Dagenham not long after the consecration of the church in 1330. Originally, when churches were built, they were served by the priests of the monastery on whose estate they were built. For a time this system worked well, but as the wealth of the monasteries increased, there was a growing desire on the part of the laity to have a resident priest permanently attached to each particular church. Added to this, the bishops generally were averse to monks having any parochial charge, and tried as far as possible to confine them to cloister life and rule. Too often the secular priests who were nominated to the cure of souls were miserably paid, and were removed on trifling pretexts. To check such abuses, and to secure perpetual vicars, adequately endowed and properly instituted, the Synod of Westminster had, in 1200, decreed " that in any church appropriated by any of the religious, a vicar be instituted by the care of the bishop, who is to receive a decent competency out of the goods of the church."

The enforcement of this decree caused, in process of time, the establishment of the vicarial system all over the country. Possibly the services at Dagenham church were undertaken for a few years by a secular priest (sometimes termed chaplain or vicar) belonging to Barking Abbey. But after John de Cokermuth had obtained royal licence to grant certain lands in Dagenham to the Abbess and Convent of Barking, with a view, doubtless, to providing a " decent competency " for a resident priest at Dagenham, the first vicar was appointed in the person of William de Walleyton. Nothing is known of him, though from his name we may conjecture that he was of Norman extraction. Nor do we know precisely how long he was vicar here, except that from a reference to him in the will of one Hugh Smyth his resignation or death must have occurred before 1385.

II. Sir IOHN UFFORD,[1] or UFFOURDE, is described in the will above mentioned as vicar of Dagenham. His name is one of the few not included in Newcourt's " Repertorium." He died in 1390. His will, in Latin, is as follows :—

I, Iohn Uffourd vicar of the parish church bequeath my soul to God & will that my body be buried in the cemetery of Saint Ethelburga, Barking.

Item, I give to the monastery of Barking xx*d*. to pray for my soul. To the priest for the execution of this will, 12*d*. I desire the Abbess of Barking to be my executor and Iohn Ewere to whom I leave the residue of my goods, and power reserved for the Abbess of Barking when necessary. Proved 9th October, 1390.

It is uncertain whether he was identical with or related to the John de Offord who was rector of St. Dionis Backchurch—which stood in Lyme Street until the Great Fire of 1666—from 1332-50, and also Dean of the Arches.

III. THOMAS WESTURNE was presented October 7, 1390. According to Newcourt, he held the benefice until 1408, when he was appointed rector of Ingatestone by the Abbess and Convent of Barking. There is, however, an ancient record which mentions one Thomas Lullington as vicar of Dakenham in 1395. This MS. describes a grant made by Henry Geffrey and Amice his wife, of the village of Berkyng and of the parish of Dakenham to Dom., *i.e.* Sir, Thomas Lullington vicar of Dakenham, Dom. Ralph Matsale, Chaplain, Dom. Nicholas Harpour, Chaplain, and others, of Land in

---

[1] Until the Reformation, parish priests were called "sir ;" afterwards, till the middle of the eighteenth century, " master or Mr.," when the present prefix, " Reverend," came into use.

Dakenham. Witnesses, Iohn Durward, Steward, Thomas Pragul, Iohn Taylour. Given at Dakenham, Thursday in the Feast of St. Catherine the Virgin, in the 19th year of the reign of Richard II. (1395).

The discrepancy is solved by the theory that Thomas Westurne had resigned the benefice of Dagenham before 1395, and held some other cure of souls until 1408, when he was presented to Ingatestone (November 12), where he died in 1409.

IV. Sir THOMAS LULLINGTON is mentioned as being vicar of Dagenham in 1395 in the will referred to above.[1] The date of his institution is uncertain, as Newcourt makes no reference to him. No details of a personal character are known of him. One would fain hope that he answered to the description which Chaucer, his illustrious contemporary, gives of the faithful pastor of his day—

> "A good man of religion did I see,
> And a poor Parson of a Town was he.
>
>   *   *   *   *   *   *
>
> "Wide was his parish—houses far asunder,
> But he neglected nought for rain or thunder ;
> In sickness and in grief to visit all,
> The farthest in his parish, great and small ;
> Always on foot, and in his hand a stave,
> This noble example to his flock he gave :
> That first he wrought and afterwards he taught.
>
>   *   *   *   *   *   *
>
> "He was a shepherd, and no mercenary,
> And though he holy was and virtuous,
> He was to sinful men full piteous ;
> His words were strong but not with anger fraught—
> A love benignant he discreetly taught,
> To draw mankind to heaven by gentleness
> And good example was his business."
>
>   CANTERBURY TALES.

V. WILLIAM LEASTER was instituted November 8, 1408. We do not know how long he held the benefice or whether he vacated it by cession, resignation, or death.

VI. ROBERT HAYNTON. Beyond his name we know nothing of him. Newcourt merely says that he succeeded William Leaster, and resigned in 1422.

VII. IOHN BESEWYKE was vicar for three months only, dating from November 12, 1422.[2]

---

[1] A William de Lullington was rector of St. Dunstan's in the East, 1396-99, and afterwards Dean of Chichester.

[2] A Thomas de Besewick was rector of Farnham and Hornsey in 1357 ; subsequently of Wickford (Essex) and Lusby (Lincolnshire).

VIII. WILLIAM BOTELER was instituted February 15, 1422, and retained the incumbency until his death in September, 1440. From an old will we learn that he was granted, in 1433, probate of the will of Iohn Widmerpole, vicar of Berkyng.

IX. ROBERT COUPER was vicar from September 19, 1440, till his death on April 12, 1454. He was of good family, and graduated at Oxford in or about 1433. In his will he desires to be buried "ante ostium cancelli" (in front of the chancel gate). He is mentioned in the *Inquisition post mortem* Thomas Ursewyk (1479), as having been "vicar of the church of Dagenham."

X. WILLIAM REDENESSE was presented April 8, 1455. After holding the benefice six years, he effected an exchange with the then vicar of Fulham, but resigned this latter position after holding it one year only.[1]

XI. HENRY WALFREY was instituted to the vicarage of Fulham February 16, 1453–54, and resigned in 1461, on his acceptance of the vicarage of Dagenham. He died in June, 1471.

XII. IOHN VALENTINE, or VALENTYNE, was presented to the benefice on August 8, 1471. Four years later he resigned, presumably on account of feeble health, as he died in November, 1475. His will (in which he describes himself as "late vicary of Dakenham") contains the following :—

My body to be beryed in yᵉ newe ile or chappel of Seynt Petrys church in Dakenham aforesaid ; also I woll yʳ all my on 'shelonde be sold to yᵉ most a waile and wᵗ yᵉ mony yʳ of an antiphon to be bowth to yᵉ use of yᵉ saide churche, by sides ij bokys wiche I have gefe yʳ to by my lyve. fferthʳ I woll yʳ yᵉ gabill wyndowe of yᵉ saide new chappell be glasid wᵗ my godys.

The will continues—

Also yef Iohn Sturmyn yᵉ young scoler of Oxforde, woll be a prest, I woll he have my secunde best portose,[2] wich was William Dauys wᵗ ij bokys or queyers of morall matʳ whereof on is Seynt Gregoryes workys and els mat[3] (d. November 9 ; pr. November 23, 1475. C.C.L.).

The "newe ile" was the south aisle of the church ; it was demolished when the tower and west portion collapsed in 1800.

[1] Hennessy, in his "Novum Repertorium," makes Walfrey succeed Couper, and exchange with Redenesse.
[2] The Portiforium, or Portuary, or Breviary. It contained the antiphonal service, with musical notation sometimes.
[3] And other matter.

XIII. GEORGE DAVIE, or DAVY, was an M.A. of Oxford, where he graduated in 1457. He was instituted to the rectory of Ingatestone, in the gift of Barking Abbey, May 8, 1470. Six years later he resigned this benefice and accepted that of Dagenham, which he held till his death in February, 1484. In his will he desires to be buried "in medio cancellariæ coram summo altari" (in the middle of the chancel before the high altar).

XIV. IOHN LOWE was instituted May 14, 1485, and died at Dagenham in March, 1499.

XV. IOHN LONG took his B.A. at Oxford in 1469, and his M.A. several years afterwards. He was presented to the rectory of Much Warley in 1484, where he remained seven years. From 1487 to 1491 he was vicar of Wormingford also. In 1494 he was appointed rector of Ingatestone, and five years later vicar of Dagenham. He remained at the latter place till 1506, when he was appointed vicar of the mother parish of Barking, where he died in August, 1524.

XVI. RICHARD NICHOLSON was instituted in 1506, and held the benefice till his death in 1530.

XVII. WILLIAM BARLEE, or BARLEY, L.B. (Cambridge), was presented by Dorothy Barley, the last Abbess of Barking Abbey, May 19, 1530. He resigned the benefice in 1533.[1]

XVIII. THOMAS PURTENNTE. A vicar bearing this name is mentioned as a witness to the will of one John Bisshope, who died 1533. Beyond his name and attribution nothing is known of him. He is not mentioned by Newcourt.

XIX. GEORGE BOLLES, or BOWLYS, was instituted January 10, 1533. He was the last vicar appointed by the Abbess and Convent of Barking. He died in February, 1538. In his will he desires to be buried in the parish church of Dagenham, "in the pase between bothe sides of the quere." He bequeaths to the cathedral of Saint Paul for "an oblation to the Blessed Sacrament, 7d.," and adds—

I woll at the daye of my buriall *Dirige* and masse be solemply songe in the honour of God moor specially & for my soul and all other souls which I had specially cause to pray and for all other soules, to the present fyve prests besides the high masse prest every of them to say the holy masse of the fyve wounds of our Saviour Iesus Christ, to each, 8d. The

---

[1] A William Barlee was vicar of Wicken Bonant, and Archdeacon of Northampton. So Newcourt. A John Barlee, D.D., vicar of Matesale, Norfolk, was, in 1483, elected master of Gonville Hall, Cambridge. He may have been father of the above, or of our William Barlee.

clerkes beside the parish clerke and three childer that canne singe perfectly the versicles to attend the *obite* to be kept in the church for 7 yeares. To Elyn Ednam my sister's daughter £10. Item, to the same all my pewter & lattyn & all my Cobberds, tongs, fyve panne spitts & all other stuff in my larder houses, Kectuyn & Brew house & my bed sted standing in the p'lor. And the best ffether bed saving my own my best covering saving my own paire of woollen blankets, two paires of shets that were last bought, one pair of shets, two pellovers (pillow-covers?) & the best basin. To my cosin Iohn Nevall a velvett sagg, and xx*s.* to my sister Margaret wife of the said Iohn Nevall my side gowne lyned before with saint Thomas wosted tawnye. To Sir Thomas Wackestaffe now stipendiary in the said parish, my sarcenett typett, my typpett furry'd with blak conye & my best bonnett. The Residue to my cosin Laur. Leyrav my unkle's sonne & maister Iohn Clerk, exor, of Merton towne in the countie of Surrey, gent., overseer.

Mem. That George Bolles willed to be buryed in saint Pancras churchyard with as little cost as might be. He gave unto Maister Harfe his ambeling nagge. He willed unto the woman that kept him 6/8, to his aunt ffoster 7/6.

This last memorandum was probably dictated by the testator on his death-bed.

XX. THOMAS DUKE was born at Hedington, Wilts. He graduated B.A. at New College, Oxford, in 1522, M.A. 1526, and B.D. 1530. He was fellow of his college 1519–32, and proctor in 1529. In 1531 he was appointed chaplain of Hornchurch ; seven years later he was presented to the vicarage of Dagenham by the new patrons, Edward North and George Hadley, Gentlemen. He died September, 1540.

XXI. WILLIAM SOUTHY, A.M. (Oxford, 1533), was instituted to the benefice on the presentation of Wm. Pouncett, Gent., the last steward of Barking Abbey. Mr. Southy resigned in 1544, afte· holding the benefice three years.

XXII. THOMAS WAGSTAFFE, or WACKESTAFFE, was institute September 16, 36th Henry VIII., R.A. (Rex Angliæ), having pre viously been curate of the parish. In a subsidy, 38th Henry VIII., he is assessed (under Dagenham) at XIX£., and required to pay a contribution of 6/4 "towards the cost of the late war" between England and France. In the will of G. Bolles mention is made of "Sir Thomas Wackestaffe, now Stipendary in the said Parish." Mr. Wagstaffe died in April, 1549. He was the last of the pre-Reformation vicars.

XXIII. SIR HUGH TALBOTE is mentioned as the incumbent of

Dagenham in the certificate of colleges and chantries made in 1547–48. Probably he was appointed during the lifetime of Mr. Wagstaffe, in which case there were for a short time two vicars of the parish. He is thus referred to—

One Sir Hugh Talbote of th' age of LV yeres, havinge no'n other p'mo 'con (*i.e.* promotion or preferment) and of goode conversac'on and usage (*i.e.* manners) and l'rate (*i.e.* literate or learned) is now incumbent of the town of Dagenh'm.

In all probability Mr. Talbot began his public ministrations with the first Prayer-book, which was ordered to be used on and after Whitsunday, 1549.[1] It is uncertain how long he retained the incumbency. He is not included in Newcourt's list of the vicars of Dagenham.

XXIV. WILLIAM SMITH was instituted April 28, or, according to the *London Register*, May 4, 3 Edward VI. 1549-50. He was ejected in February or March, 1552, by order of Philip and Mary, Rex et Regina Angliæ.[2]

XXV. IOHN VELSTED, or VELSTEDE, was instituted by Bishop Bonner of London, March 27, 1553, and resigned in the autumn of 1557. During his vicariate, one of his parishioners, Christopher Lyster, a husbandman, a blind man, was burnt with five others at the stake at Colchester for heresy (April 28, 1556).[3]

XXVI. IOHN FINNYMORE was instituted November 12, 1557. In the following year (September 21, 1558) he was presented to the rectory of Loughton, and held the benefices jointly till his death (at the latter place) in October, 1576.

A Iohn Finnymore is mentioned (*Alumni Oxon.*), "who had also read at Cambridge," as a suppliant for the B.A. at Oxford in 1538; probably the same.

XXVII. IOHN BERRYMAN, or BERRIMAN, A.M. (Cambridge), was presented by William Nutbrowne, Gent., on October 29, 1579, the benefice having been vacant three years. From 1568 to 1574, Mr. Berryman was rector of Shelly; from 1572, till his death in October, 1617, he was rector of Rochford, where he resided for the most part,

---

[1] The Act of Uniformity ordered this book to be used by all ministers "in any cathedrale or parishe churche, or other place within this Realme of England, Wales, Calyce, and Marches of the same or other the Kinges Dominions."

[2] One hundred beneficed clergy in Essex were ejected at this period, almost solely because they were married.

[3] See Foxe's "Book of Martyrs," vol. viii., where this pitiable affair is placed as stated, and not at Stratford-le-Bow, as commonly supposed, from the "Martyrs' memorial" there.

and where he died. An old county record says that when Lord Rich and Robert Wright were apprehended at Rochford for "dispraising the Book of Common Prayer and speaking evil words against the Church and the Queen" (Elizabeth), one of the witnesses against the latter was (1576) Iohn Berryman, rector of Rochford. This piece of activity on Berryman's part was not forgotten by his enemies, for when Archbishop Whitgift caused an inquiry or "survey" to be made in 1600 into the state and discipline of the clergy, they caused Berryman to be reported to the Bishop of London (Dr. Bancroft) as "an ignorant and unpreaching minister," and a "double-beneficed man."[1] Notwithstanding these charges, no attempt seems to have been made to disturb him.

During Mr. Berryman's tenure at Dagenham the oldest extant parish register was procured, though unfortunately it does not contain his signature, and possibly not even his handwriting at all.

XXVIII. THOMAS MANNINGE belonged to an old Essex family; an ancestor of his, of the same name, having been vicar of West Thurrock, Gingrave, and West Horndon, 1440-56. He graduated M.A. at Cambridge 1608-9, and was instituted to the vicarage of Dagenham on November 21, 1617, on the presentation of Mr. R. Ward, who probably presented for the Swinnerton family. He had previously served as curate to Mr. Berryman, as he signs himself from 1611 to 1617 as "minister" and "clerk," but from 1617 and onwards as "vicar," "vicarius," "vicʳ Dagenhamiæ," and "vicʳ Dagenhamiensis." Mr. Manninge stands out among the vicars of this parish as having been a much married man, as he had no less than four wives in succession. His first wife, Joane, was buried January 26, 1618. In November, 1619, he married Mary Worseleye, a widow, who died in February, 1626, "beloved by all and much lamented." His third wife, Alice, died in December, 1631, and his fourth wife, Elizabeth, in July, 1637. Mr. Manninge died shortly afterwards, and was buried in Dagenham church, in accordance with his wish. He was held in much esteem by his flock, as he was a diligent parish priest and also a "painfull" (*i.e.* painstaking) preacher. His handwriting is remarkably elegant and legible, and fortunately there is a good deal of it in the parish register. He left six sons and three daughters, viz. Thomas, Samuel, John, Joseph, Benjamin, and Robert; and Dennis, who married (November, 1619) Edward Thickens, Ann, who married (July, 1627) William

---

[1] The county of Essex was returned as "containing 300 benefices, of which 173 were held by ignorant and unpreaching ministers, and of whom 61 have two benefices apiece."

Geast, clerk (*i.e* curate), ffrances, who married Thomas Petchye (October, 1631).

Mr. Manninge bequeathed in his will 20/- to the poor of Dagenham, to be given on the day of his burial (September 28). He directs his executors to educate his sons Joseph and Benjamin out of the rents of certain properties, after which they are to revert to his son and heir, Thomas. Also to sell 11 acres of marsh land, and out of the proceeds pay £30 to Joseph when 21, to Benjamin £100, to "my servant, Joane Green, £30," to Anne Guest, 20/- for a ring,[1] to Mr. John Morse, the minister of Romford, 20/-, "praying him to preach my funerall sermon."[2] There are also bequests to "my sexton, 20/-," and 10/- to John Betts; the residue to "my loveing friends, Robert Cliffe, citizen and merchant taylor, and Arthur Taylor, citizen and fishmonger, whom I appoint my exors. Also I entreat my loving friends and neighbours, Mr. John Harvey, Mr. Thomas ffreshwater and Mr. Thomas Truelove to be overseers; to each 20/- for rings. 10 Sept., 1637."

Mr. Manninge was fortunate in his times, as he was the contemporary of some of the greatest men this country has produced—Shakespeare, Bacon, Ben Jonson, Milton, Spenser, Beaumont, Fletcher, Richard Hooker, William Laud, George Herbert, Thomas Fuller, and Lord Herbert of Cherbury, not to mention others, all flourished at this period.

XXIX. PERCIVAL HILL was instituted to the vicarage December 23, 1637, on the presentation of the Bishop of London (Dr. Wm. Juxon). In 1640 he was appointed rector of St. Katherine Coleman. He exercised his ministerial office at Dagenham for the last time on March 1, 1640, when he read the Burial Office over one Edward Joyce. The entry of this "buryall" ends with the words—"Sic desinit Per: Hill, vic." (So ends Per. Hill, vic.). His lot was cast in troublous times, and his loyalty to his Church and king exposed him to much persecution at the hands of the inexorable Presbyterians. Walker remarks—"Mr. Hill was not formally sequestered from the rectory of St. Katherine Coleman, but forced to resign in order to prevent it. His parishioners having articled against him."[3] He is supposed to have died before the Restoration.

XXX. RODOLF, or RALPHE RICHARDS was a native of Bradbrook, Northamptonshire, and was matriculated as a poor scholar at

---

[1] A mourning ring; sometimes it bore an inscription.

[2] Vicar of Romford, 1615–48. On account of his sympathies being with the Puritans, he was appointed "approved preacher" for Romford.

[3] "Sufferings of the Clergy," by John Walker (1714).

University College, Oxford, in 1630, taking his B.A. in 1631 and
M.A. in 1634. He was instituted to the vicarage of Dagenham by
the Bishop of London immediately after the resignation of Mr.
Hill. An entry in the register says—"March 14th, 1640. Hic
incipit Rodolphus Richards" (Here begins Rodolph Richards).
After holding the benefice eighteen months he was appointed
rector of Helmdon, Northants, where he died, and was buried,
September, 1668, in his fifty-sixth year.

XXXI. CHARLES TREW, or TRUE, graduated B.A. at
Magdalen College, Oxford, in 1619, and M.A. in 1622. In 1628 he
was appointed rector of Abington, Northants, where he remained
thirteen years, when Archbishop Laud recommended him to the
vacant benefice of Dagenham.

As Mr. Trew was reputed to be an ardent Royalist, the Presbyterians presented a petition to Parliament complaining of this
nomination, and asking for his immediate ejection, on the ground of
his " malignancy." But the House of Commons was in no mood to
obey the behests of the Presbyterians, much as it disliked the
policy of the king and the energetic measures of Archbishop Laud
to restore discipline and order in the Church. In response to
another petition, Parliament issued, however, a mandate permitting
Mr. True to retain the benefice of Dagenham, but requesting him
"to permit John Bowyer to have the free use of the pulpit of
Dagenham church every Lord's day in the forenoon." In other
words, Mr. Bowyer was appointed morning lecturer at Dagenham.
(September, 1642). By this arrangement the pulpit of Dagenham
" spoke Geneva in the morning and Canterbury in the afternoon."
Even thus the Puritans were not satisfied, and as they were gaining
the ascendency in the country, they succeeded, a year later, in
sequestering Mr. Trew (October, 1643). Under the terms of the
sequestration, Mr. Trew was to receive one-fifth of the value of the
benefice, if the local committee thought proper to grant it to him.
But this allowance does not appear to have been paid with any sort
of regularity, as Mr. True complained to the House of Commons of
" arrears of fifths" being due to him from the benefice (February,
1644). We do not know anything further of this ill-used clergyman, but as we read of a Mrs. Trew complaining that she could not
obtain her fifths, and was in a state of destitution, it may be inferred
that he died early in 1645. It is gratifying to know that the House
of Commons made an order for her case to be settled (May, 1645).

The ejection of Mr. Trew was brought about by his refusal to sign " The Solemn League and Covenant." This document was drawn up by the Scotch Presbyterians in revenge for the attempt made by Charles I. to introduce the English Liturgy into Scotland, in July, 1637. All who signed it solemnly pledged themselves to uproot and destroy ¦Church government by bishops, deans, archdeacons, etc., not only in Scotland, but in England and Ireland also. In 1643 the Westminster Assembly adopted the covenant, and persuaded the House of Commons to require every person in England, above the age of eighteen, to subscribe to it. This proceeding proved a short and easy way of convicting and punishing all those, whether laity or clergy, who were favourable to the Church and king. The former had to pay heavy fines, and sometimes to compound their estates; while the latter were ousted from their benefices and plundered of their goods, for their "delinquency" or "malignancy," as the refusal to take the covenant was termed. Local committees were appointed by Parliament to administer the covenant; and so thoroughly did they do their work, that no less than two thousand clergy were sequestered in the various counties of England and Wales. The most vindictive of these committees were those nominated by the " fighting Earl of Manchester," as he was termed, to whom the eastern counties were entrusted for " purgation." These committees were empowered to nominate any persons they thought fit to the vacant benefices. In less than one year, over four hundred Presbyterian ministers were appointed to benefices in the eastern counties alone, from which " ill-affected and scandalous clergy" had been ejected.

In January, 1645, the Directory for Public Worship was ordered by Parliament to be used in all churches, instead of the Book of Common Prayer. In the following August this order was renewed, with prescribed penalties. Any one using the Prayer-book, either privately or publicly, was to be fined £5 for the first offence, £10 for the second, and for the third suffer a year's imprisonment. Any minister not using the Directory was to be fined forty shillings for each offence.

In order to establish themselves permanently in the former position of the now suppressed Church of England, and also to lessen the dissatisfaction expressed on all sides at their harsh proceedings, the Presbyterians determined to set up their own form of Church government throughout the land. *Inter alia*, the county of Essex was divided into fourteen *classes* or divisions, described as " The Division of the County of Essex into several *Classes*, together with the names of the ministers & others fit to be of such class, certified by the standing committee of that county, and approved of by the committee of Lords and Commons appointed by ordinances for the judging of scandall & approving the classes in the severall counties of England." The first *classis* of Essex consisted of the Liberty of Havering and Chafford *classis*, together with the following parishes :—West and East Ham, Walthamstow, Wanstead, Horn-church, Romford, Havering, Layton, Barking, Ilford parva, Dagen-ham, and Woodford.

The sequestration of Mr. Trew was followed by an order granted October 9, 1643, "to sequester the Rents & Profits of the vicarage of Dagenham to the use of Mr. John Bowyer, M.A. An orthodox & godly divine." [1] Owing, however, to the opposition this proposal met with in that parish, the local Puritan committee, which met "at the Crowne in Rumford," deemed it advisable to retain the lectureship only for Mr. Bowyer, and to sanction the institution by the Bishop of London of a Mr. Coleman to the benefice.

XXXII. THOMAS COLEMAN took his B.A. at Magdalen Hall, Oxford, in 1618. He was known as "Rabbi Coleman," from being a ripe Hebrew scholar. He sat in the Westminster assembly. In 1632 he was nominated to the rectory of St. Peter's, Cornhill, where, from the nature of his preaching, he was accounted a "severe Puritan." In 1644 he became vicar of Dagenham ; nothing further is known of him, except that he held that position in July, 1646.

A few of his sermons are extant, viz.—

1. "The Christian's Course & Complaint," preached to the House of Commons at their monthly fast, August 30, 1643. The text is Jer. viii. 20, and the subject falls under three heads—the Text, the Introduction, the Coherence.

2. "The Heart's Ingagement," a sermon preached at St. Margaret's, Westminster, at the Publique Entering into the Covenant by (i.) some of the Nobilitie, Knighthood and Gentry ; (ii.) Divers Colonels, Officers and Souldiers ; (iii.) Those of the Scottish Nation about the Citie ; (iv.) Many reverend Divines here residing. The thanks of the Commons Honourable House of Parliament are prefixed to this discourse, which was delivered on September 29, 1643. The sermon, based on Jer. xxx. 21, occupies thirty-nine pages, and is divided into "foure generall heads"—

(1) The Opening of the Phrases.

(2) The Propounding of the Point.

---

[1] "House of Commons Journal," 1643–45.

(3) The Viewing of the Duties.

(4) The Encouragement to the Practice.

3. " Hopes Deferred & Dashed observed in a sermon to the House of Commons in Margaret's, Westminster, on July 30, 1645, being the monethly Fast," based on Job xi. 20.   The sermons are characterized with much verbiage, laboured and uncritical argument, and ultra analysis of each word of the text, not to mention forced applications of passages of Holy Writ.   From the number of quotations from the original Hebrew and Rabbinical writings, it would seem that the members of the House had a wider and more . accurate knowledge of the Hebrew Bible than their modern successors would pretend to.

On the cession, whether by ejection or death, of Mr. Coleman, Sir Thomas Honeywood, Knight (guardian of the patron, Thomas Darcy, Esq.), appointed Mr. JOHN BOWYER, lecturer, to the vicarage of Dagenham, then valued at £80 per annum.   In the following year he was appointed to the vicarage of Hillingdon, Middlesex, but continued to reside at Dagenham.   The register contains entries of the baptism and burial of several of his children ; the former being a clear proof that Mr. Bowyer was not an Anabaptist.   In 1648 he signed the " Testimony of the ministers in the Province of Essex to the Trueth of Jesus Christ & to the Solemn League & Covenant as also against the Errors, Heresies & Blasphemies of these times & the toleration of them."[1]   During his tenure of office here, a serious outbreak of the plague occurred in the parish. Mr. Bowyer died in October, 1650, and was buried, strange to relate, under the communion-table in the church.

XXXIII. Mr. Bowyer was succeeded by Mr. GEORGE WALKER, a priest of the Church of England, who held very strong Puritan views.   He was educated at St. John's College, Cambridge, where he graduated M.A. and B.D.   In 1615 he was appointed chaplain to Dr. Felton, Bishop of Exeter, and in the year following to the " Pastorate of St. John the Evangelist, Watling Street, London."

---

[1] It declares that the " Confession of Faith, Direction of Worship, and Humble Advice for Church Government, presented by the Reverend (Westminster) Assembly of Divines to the Honourable Parliament are so agreeable to the Word that we cannot but bless the Name of our God for His presence with that assembly. . . . That we look upon our Solemn League and Covenant as a most choice blessing from God . . . & that from our soules we doe utterly detest as all former cursed doctrines of Popery, Arminianisme & Socinianism ; So likewise all the damnable Heresies, Errors & Blasphemies of these present evill times, whether of anti-Scripturists, Familists, Antinomians, anti-Trinitarians, Arrians, ana-Baptists, or whatsoever is found contrary to sound Doctrine." It contains one hundred and thirty signatures.

According to Neal ("History of the Puritans") he "was an Oriental scholar, a Logician & theologist," and these qualifications being allied to a rigid, Calvinistic mind, caused him to be held in repute by all those, whether Presbyterians, Independents, or Churchmen, who saw in Archbishop Laud's efforts to reform the English Church a desire to bring it into subjection to Rome. In October, 1638, he preached a series of vigorous discourses against the "Sabbatarian sacrilege" of Charles I. To silence this fearless preacher, Laud caused him to be imprisoned for a brief period, and on his release required him to enter into a bond of £1000 to confine himself in his brother's house at Chiswick. As usually happens in such cases, these severe measures failed in their object, as the censured sermons were printed at Amsterdam, under the title, "Divers Sermons on the Sabbath," and were widely circulated in this country. It is worthy of note, however, that, though his views on the Sabbath are inflexible, Mr. Walker is sound on matters of Church doctrine. Take, *e.g.* the following extract—

Publick Baptisme is most fit to bee administered on the Lord's Day in the publicke assembly. 1. Because it is joyned with preaching, Mathew 28 . 16. Secondly it is the receiving of the Baptized into the true Visible Church. Thirdly, in publick it may be better performed by the joynt prayers of the whole congregation. Fourthly, it may much profit the whole publick congregation of God's people by putting them in minde of the covenant made in Baptisme.

Mr. Walker was rewarded for his hostility to the king and primate by being nominated a member of the Westminster Assembly, which met in St. Margaret's Church, Westminster, where "he gain'd great Reputation by his munificent and publick Behaviour." He also had the honour of preaching the sermon before "the Honourable House of Commons at their solemne monthly Fast, January 29, 1644." This sermon, which took three hours in delivery, was ordered to be published with the thanks of the House of Commons affixed."[1] In his preface he "thanks God for enabling him to frustrate and bring to naught the counsells and purposes of the proud persecuting Prelate of Canterburie who six yeares before brought me to answer in the Star Chamber with full intent to lay a heavy censure on me and not allow me to preach any more." The sermon is based on Ps. lviii. 9, which he translates thus, "Before

---

[1] A collection was made at the close on behalf of the "Plundered clergy"—those clergy who had been ejected for their disloyalty to Charles I.

they shall feele your sharp pricks, O Bramble,[1] he will take away everie one of them as with a Tempest or whirlwinde, as well the greene as the drie." The discourse simply bristles with Hebrew quotations, and is, of course, highly polemical and full of supposed scriptural references to the misguided Charles I. and his "evil counsellor," the primate.

Mr. Walker is mentioned in Laud's " Tryal and Troubles " (under the seventeenth day) as one of the witnesses who charged the archbishop with Arminianism, a system of theology which was meant to overthrow Calvinism. Five years after the archbishop's martyrdom, he was appointed vicar of Dagenham, but he only held this preferment a few months, and died in December, 1651, at the age of seventy. He was buried at Dagenham.

XXXIV. Mr. Walker was succeeded by his son-in-law, Mr. JONATHAN LLOYD, a priest of the Church of England. Mr. Lloyd was the son of a rich alderman of Shrewsbury, and graduated B.A. at Emmanuel College, Cambridge, about 1630. He was a man of some erudition, and possessed an excellent library. His wife died on the 3rd, his daughter on the 8th, and he himself on the 18th of December, 1654. There is a marble tablet in the chantry to his memory, with a fulsome Latin inscription. The register contains no entry of his burial.

In his will Mr. Lloyd desires to be "buried in a Christian way in the chancell of the parish church of Dagenham neare the body of my wife." He requests his executors to erect a monument of marble with a suitable inscription to his memory. He bequeaths to the library of the Free Schools in Shrewsbury his Hebrew Bible, " commonly called the Kinge of Spaine's Bible in eight severall faire volumes & my Bomberg's concordance in Hebrew in folio." To Emmanuel College, Cambridge, he bequeaths "two faire books upon the Pentateuch, and one faire book to the Library of Zion College, London." The will proceeds—

To my fellow-labourer in God's Vineyard, Mr. Edmund Calamy, B.D. & preacher at Mary Aldermanbury, London, one Hebrew Bible, in 8 small volumes with strings ; And to my loving Uncle Mr. James Walton one other Hebrew Bible & having green silk strings ; To Mr. Sam[l] Fisher one faire Greeke testament in folio & my library ; To Mr. John Walls, pastor of Olave's in the Jewry Doctor Wheloker's works in folio ; To my loving friend Mr. frederic Tilney late fellow of Jesus College, Cambridge, my Eusebius' Works in two faire volumes in Greek. The residue of books to

[1] The " Bramble " was Archbishop Laud ; the " Tempest " Oliver Cromwell.

my brother-in-law, Mr. George Walker's children or any of mine own brother's children that shall be members of the Church of England or any other reformed Church. To my ever-esteemed cosine Faith Taylor & Ann Kendall & Elizabeth Lawrence 20/- each for rings. To my sister Mrs. Joane Ludford my best paire of curtaines. To my brother Mr. Thomas Lloyd all my wearing apparell and plate. To my cosin Mr. Theophilus Walker £5. To my cosin Mr. Joseph Woolnough £5. To my brother-in-law, George Walker of Lincoln's Inn, £5. Among my own brothers & brothers-in-law, £400, viz. Mr. Sam¹ Lloyd, Mr. John Ludford & Thomas Ludford, on condition that they pay to my mother-in-law, Mrs. Catherine Walker, widow of George Walker, Rector of St. John Evangelist, London, £24 per annum for life. Residue to my Exors. Witnessed by Robert Commyns & others, 19 December, 1654.

XXXV. On the death of Mr. Lloyd, the patron, Mr. Darcy, recommended Mr. FREDERICK TILNEY, a clergyman of the English Church, for the vacant benefice, to the Romford Committee. His qualifications and appointment are thus recorded in the " Acts of the Commissioners " (Book iii.)—

" Know all men by these presents That the seventh day of ffebruary, one thousand six hundred fifty and foure there was exhibited to the Comifsioners for approbation of Publique Preachers a presentation of ffredericke Tilney Clerke to yᵉ Vicarage of daggenham in yᵉ County of Essex made to him by Thomas Darcy, Esqʳ the Patron thereof Together with a Testimony in the behalfe of the said ffredericke Tilney of his holy & good conversation. Upon perusall & due consideration of the premisses & finding him to be a person qualified as in & by the Ordinance for which approbation is required. The Comifsⁿ above menconed have adjudged & approved the said ffredericke Tilney to be a fit person to preach the Gospell & have graunted him admission & doe admitt the said ffredericke Tilney to the Viccarage of daggenham aforesaid to be full and perfect possessor & Incumbent thereof, and doe hereby signify to all persons concerned therein, that he is hereby intituled to yᵉ Profitts & perquisites & all Rights & Dues incident and belonging to the said Vicarage as fully and effectually as if he had been instituted and inducted according to any such Laws & Customs as have in this Case formerly been made, had or used in this Realme. In witness whereof they have caused the Comon Seale to be hereunto affixed and the same to be attested by the hand of the Regʳ by His Highness in that behalfe appointed. Dated at Whitehall the 7th day of ffebruarye one thousand six hundred fifty and foure." [1]

This declaration, which is headed ffredᵏᵉ Tilney, No. 687, is—

[1] In the " London Inſtitutiones " he is entered as " Frederick Filney, 2 December, 1656."

"certifyed as aforesaid by William Whitaker, He. Huerth, Wm Peache,
. John Yardly, Edw. ffoord, of Great Warley, Wm Powell of little Warley,
Tho. Goodwin, of South Weald."

The nomination of Mr. Tilney to the vicarage of Dagenham was
a bold stroke on the part of the patron, inasmuch as he had been
ejected in 1644 from his fellowship at Jesus College, Cambridge,
for "recusancy." This harsh proceeding was the result of the
campaign ·against the Church led by the Earl of Manchester, who
had ejected nearly all the heads and fellows of the colleges at
Cambridge.[1] The earl had, however, married a daughter of Sir
Thomas Cheke, of Pirgo,[2] near Romford, who was on intimate terms
with Mr. Darcy, and it was due, doubtless, to this fact that the
nomination of Mr. Tilney was accepted. Added to this, Mr. Tilney
had been the "loving friend" of the last vicar, and leaned in his
views, doubtless, to Puritanism. The parish records are silent about
him, except in regard to his death, which is thus entered—"Mr.
fredrick Tillney, minister of dadginham, was buried August 1, 1663."

During this vicar's tenure of office, the Commonwealth came to
an end. On September 3, 1658, Oliver Cromwell died, and on
May 29, 1660, Charles II. entered London amid the applause of
the people. With the return of the monarchy came the restoration
of the Church and the reinstalment of all surviving incumbents who
had been expelled during the Rebellion. The Prayer-book came
into use again, and Churchmen were able to breathe once more the
air of freedom.

---

[1] Notwithstanding his zeal in this direction, he was opposed to the execution of
Charles I., and stayed away from Parliament during Cromwell's Protectorate. At the
Restoration he became a loyal subject of Charles II.

[2] Sir Thomas died March, 1659. He mentions in his will "Carew Mildmay, of
Marks, my good ffriend." Another daughter of his married the Earl of Warwick. Sir
Thomas is praised in Fairfax's despatches as having rendered valuable aid in crushing the
Royalists in Essex.

DAGENHAM VICARAGE

CHAPTER VII

VICARS OF DAGENHAM—*continued*

XXXVI. Isaac Smythies was an M.A. of Cambridge (St. John's College). He was appointed rector of Bradwell-juxta-Coggeshall in 1654, and seven years later rector of Broomeley. In October, 1663, he was instituted to the vicarage of Dagenham on the presentation of Sir Thomas Darcy, Bart., when he paid £19 9s. 7d. as first-fruits to the Crown. His institution is twice referred to in the register—"Isaacus Smythies vica' de Dagnam Incipit curam Gregis on 2d Octobris, 1663." There is also an entry of the baptism of his son Joseph on "November the 22th, 1661, at Bradwell next Coggshall." During the early part of his vicariate Dagenham was visited with the plague, with many fatal results, and it doubtless fell to his lot to officiate at these burials. In 1666 occurred the Great Fire of London, which caused various homeless families to take up their abode in the village, as we find mention of children being baptized of parents "burnt out of house and home." Yet another feature of his ministry was the building of the present vicarage house. Mr. Smythies died at Stisted, but was buried at Dagenham, May 30, 1674. The record of his burial says that "he was minister of this place tenn and a halfe yeares and died aged too and fifty."

In his will, dated June 30, 25 Charles II. (1674), Mr. Smythies bequeaths to Elizabeth his wife, his property in Stisted, and apportions certain lands among his sons. He directs his executors to give his only daughter Elizabeth £100 when twenty-one, or on her marriage. Also to "Richard my sonne £40 to bring him up till he comence Bachelour of Arts, and all my books except Mr. Swinick's works." He charges his children "to be loving to their mother and live in the Feare of God & in the practice of the truth held forth in the Doctrinoll articles of our English Church & be obedient to authority." He desires Mr. Blackmore and Mr. Meadowes of Barkingberry to "assist his wife in retaining her

G

Dues," and gives them each 10s. for rings and 20s. for the poor. The will is attested by Stephen Dore, Richard Kemp, and Mary Chandler.

XXXVII. ISAAC HARRISON was instituted October 23, 1674, on the presentation of Sir William Darcy, Bart. He took his M.A. at Cambridge, and proceeded in 1679 to the degree of Doctor in Divinity. He resigned or died in 1680–81.

XXXVIII. WILLIAM LAMPLUGH was the son of Thomas, Bishop of Exeter, and afterwards (1688–91) Archbishop of York. He took his B.A. degree at St. John's College, Cambridge, in 1668, in which year he was ordained deacon. In 1673 he was appointed vicar of Hatfield Peverel (Essex), where he perhaps remained two years at the most. Newcourt says he was vicar till 1682, but this statement is not borne out by the register of that parish. From the absence of any evidence to the contrary, it would seem that Mr. Lamplugh was without any parochial charge from 1674 to 1681, when he was presented by Sir Thomas Darcy, Bart., to the vicarage of Dagenham. He died in the latter part of 1704, at the age of sixty, having survived his wife four months only. " January 21, 1704, Wil^m Lamplugh, vicar, who was vicar of Dagenham 23 years, was buried."

In his will Mr. Lamplugh leaves to his son Edward £200, and two freehold messuages in Collier Gate Street, in the parish of Christ Church in York city ; to his cousin Elizabeth Price, £50 ; to "my good friend Samuel Kekewich," £20 ; to his cousin the Rev. Wm. Lamplugh and Mr. Francis Hilliyard, bookseller, of York, " one guiney each." The rest of his estate to his son Edward and his daughter Mary, but if both died before the age of twenty-one, it was to be disposed for the benefit of the poor of Dagenham. The will was proved by Samuel Kekewich, clerk, of Romford (vicar of Raynham), July, 1705.

From the register we learn that Mary Lamplugh married one Edward Osborne, of Dagenham, in 1705.

XXXIX. JAMES SYMONDS was an M.A. of St. John's College, Cambridge. He was ordained deacon by the Bishop of London in 1672, and priest by the Bishop of Gloucester in 1674. A few years later he was appointed chaplain to the Earl of Westmoreland, and in 1691 became rector of Stapleford Abbotts, near Romford. In May, 1704, Mr. Symonds was presented to the vicarage of Dagenham by the patron, the Rev. Samuel Kekewich, vicar of Rainham. Not wishing, however, to resign his rectory, he applied to the Bishop of London for licence to hold the two livings jointly, on the ground that they were not more than eight miles apart. The application being considered reasonable, and being supported moreover by the Lord Bishop of Norwich, leave was granted by *fiat*, February 26, 1704. Mr. Symonds retained these eligible benefices till his death, which took place in October or November, 1719, and probably at Stapleford Abbotts.[1]

XL. WILLIAM BUTLER was an LL.B. of St. John's College, Cambridge, where he graduated in 1713–14. In the year of his ordination he was appointed chaplain to the Marquis of Annandale. On March 29, 1716, he was instituted to the rectory of SS. Anne and Agnes,[2] London, with that of St. John Zachary. Two or three years later he was appointed lecturer of St. Clement, East-cheap. His institution to the vicarage of Dagenham took place on January 16, 1719, on the presentation of William Blackborne, Esq., P. Jur. (*i.e. pleno jure*, " in full right "). Two years later he was appointed chaplain to the Earl of Burlington. On the Feast of the Epiphany, 1728–29, Mr. Butler was collated to the prebendal stall of Eald-street in St. Paul's Cathedral. Yet another honour bestowed upon him was that of being elected a proctor in the Lower House of the Convocation of Canterbury. Besides being a man of learning, he was diligent in his calling, if we may judge from the large number of *adult* baptisms that took place during his vicariate here. Mr. Butler died on October 9, 1736, and was buried in the church. A gravestone, with a suitable Latin inscription, was placed to his memory by his " most beloved daughter Margaret." [3]

Mr. Butler was unquestionably the most distinguished of all the vicars of Dagenham, and had a high reputation as a preacher, which he well deserved, judging from the sermons he published by request. These are—

1. " A Sermon preached before the Rt. Hon. Sir Robert Beach-croft, Knight, Lord Mayor of London, the Aldermen & Citizens of London at the Cathedral Church of St. Paul, on Wednesday, Jan. 16, 17$\frac{11}{12}$, being the Day appointed by Her Majesty (Queen

---

[1] His successor at Stapleford Abbotts was the Rev. Zachariah Pearce, who was consecrated Bishop of Rochester in 1756.

[2] " This church stood on the north side of Pope Lane, and was anciently called St. Anne in the Willows, from trees that grew about there ; the patronage formerly belonged to St. Martin's-le-Grand, till Henry VII. annexed that church with all its possessions to Westminster Abbey, which now became patron, till Queen Mary, by Letters Patent, March, 1553-54, bestowed it on the Bishops of London for ever." (Hennessy's " Novum Repertorium," London).

[3] In 1743 his son, Edward, was brought from London to be buried at Dagenham.

Anne) for a Publick Fast." On the inner title-page is the vote of thanks of the Court to Mr. Butler (chaplain to the Lord Mayor) for his sermon. This discourse, which was based on Prov. xxi. 30, and covers nineteen pages printed matter, was delivered during the War of the Spanish Succession between England, Holland, and Austria on the one side, and France on the other. The following extract is a good specimen of his style, while the *matter* might have been heard only the other day.

Far be it from us that we should be of that brutal Temper as to delight in War; a Thing so cruel & odious in the sight of God that He expresly forbids His servant David to build His Temple because he was a man of blood. And yet those wars he was engaged in are said to be the Lord's Battles. As the Lord whom we serve is the God of Peace so is it a Duty to be the children of Peace, to account the Life of Man as it is a sacred Thing & not to be play'd off lightly. But tho' these are great and true characters of Peace in general; yet every sort of Peace is not more eligible than War. If it was so, it would follow that all war was unlawfull, that we never ought to enter into it upon no consideration. We must not take up arms to defend our selves but sit still & become the Prey of every bold Invader. Our Lives and Liberties, Our Religion & Properties, Our Wives & Children must be all sacrific'd and tamely given up for the Sake of Peace, without any Remedy to save our selves, except Miracles. Had we acted by this Principle I dread to think what would become of us by this Time. When therefore we pray for Peace we pray for such a Peace as is more eligible than War. Our prayers this day are for a Blessing on the Forces of her most Gracious Majesty and her Allies till those who are her and their Enemies shall submit to such a Peace.

2. "A sermon preached to the Societies for Reformation of Manners," at St. Mary-le-Bow, on Monday, January 1, 1721, from Eph. v. 11 [1] (twenty-three pages). The peroration is rather fine—

Lastly, some may be tempted, each to say within himself, let every man take care of himself. But there be those who cannot look to themselves; They are mad & raving, the Fumes of Wine or Lust or some other predominant Passion has got the better of them; they are intoxicated & have no Understanding. Is it not then great kindness to them & Charity in us to confine such Persons and endeavour tho' by harsh means, to recover their Senses? This certainly is a Work and labour of Love & in this work are you engaged, who go about to reclaim men, & bring

---

[1] The operations of this society were twofold—(1) "the propagation of wholesome literature," (2) "the prosecution of persons guilty of immorality, drunkenness, profane swearing, and trading on the Lord's day." The number prosecuted from 1690-1721 was 77,469 persons.

them to a sober mind. Go on then in God's Name. And may the God of Heaven who looks down & sees how you are employ'd Prosper the work of your Hands. Be as watchful & zealous to enlarge His Kingdom as the Devil & his Agents are to lay it waste.

3. "A Sermon preached at the Visitation at Romford on April 19, 1723, & dedicated to the Reverend Doctor Gooch,[1] Arch Deacon of Essex with great respect by your very humble servant." It is based on Exod. xx. 7, and is a plea for loyalty to the king (George I.), with a repudiation of the old "Popish Pretender" (James, the son of James II.) This sermon, which took two hours in delivery, is as full of political and controversial matter as it is devoid of Christian doctrine.

4. "A Sermon on Exod. xviii. 21, preached before the Lord Mayor of London & Liveries of the several Companies of this City, at St. Laurence, Jewry on Sept. 29, 1729." The vote of thanks of the Court is prefixed to it. The concluding passage of this discourse is so instructive and worthy of perusal by the "City Fathers" that we here reproduce it.

Thus you have heard the Character of a good Magistrate, as described in the words of my Text by these Four Qualifications. He must be an able Man, a Man of Capacity & Understanding, for fear he should do Wrong, when he means perhaps and designs to do Right, but does not, because he knows no better. He must fear God, have Him always before his Eyes, or he will hardly fear any one else, nor scruple to pursue his own Interest, to the neglect of the Publick, by any means that he can. He must be a Man of Truth, a Lover of Justice & Equity to that Degree, as to be swayed by no other Consideration ; neither by Pity to the Poor, nor Favour to the Rich ; but steady & impartial between them both. And lastly, he must hate Covetousness, the most ruinous to government, especially in Magistrates, of all Vices. Leave out any of these Ingredients, then the End and Design of the Law will soon be defeated at least, if not perverted. And the Magistrate who is not adorned with all these Badges, is but the Figure & Image of himself, dressed up indeed & decked with the Robes of his office, which, without those ornaments of Virtue & Wisdom, may as well become his Statue. But there is no need for me to multiply Words on this Subject before an Audience of Magistrates who know & by Experience too, a much better Master than Books, what it is to govern well. Witness this great & populous City,[2] so well regulated & ordered ; whose Fame hath been long ago proclaimed far & wide & so much admired above other Cities, that by universal Consent, she

---

[1] The Ven. Thomas Gooch was Archdeacon 1714-37.
[2] The population of London was then just under a million.

has ever had the preference for wise, pious, just & generous Magistrates. In a word, she has gained such a name abroad & appears in grandeur so magnificent, that it will be very difficult to find her Equal. May she ever continue thus to flourish & abound. May she always find such Magistrates, able men, fearing God, Men of Truth & hating covetousness. May the succeeding generation of Magistrates learn to tread in the Steps & follow the bright Example of their wise Predecessors who have raised this City to such a Pitch of Glory, that to keep it up in the same Lustre for the Time to come, will be their sufficient Commendation.

It was not, however, only in London that Mr. Butler's rhetorical gifts were appreciated ; he was in great request at Dagenham as a preacher of " funeral " sermons. More saints and worthies departed this life during his vicariate than at any other period in the annals of our parish—in one single year fourteen persons were honoured with sermons of this character. Whether this was a mere coincidence, or whether Mr. Butler had the rare faculty of detecting the hidden virtues of his flock, we cannot at this point of time determine.

XLI. FRANCIS STANLEY was the son of the Rev. Dr. William Stanley, Archdeacon of London, and graduated M.A. at Corpus Christi College, Cambridge, of which he was taxor. He was ordained deacon in 1719, and priest the following year by the Bishop of London. In 1721 he was nominated by his father to the vicarage of St. Leonard, Shoreditch. This benefice he held till October, 1723, when he was instituted to the valuable living of Much Hadham, Herts, which his father had resigned on his preferment. to the Deanery of St. Asaph. In 1730-31 he was appointed chaplain to the Earl of Abercorn, and Prebendary of Twyford in St. Paul's Cathedral. On the decease of Mr. Butler in 1736, Mr. Stanley was chosen to succeed him by the patron, William Blackborne, Esq. At his institution, an application was made on his behalf, after the custom of those "good old times," when pluralities were episcopally sanctioned, to his Grace the Bishop of London, for a dispensation to hold both benefices jointly, " they being not more than twenty-five miles apart," which was granted by the usual order (March 18, 1736-37, Thos. Parry, N.P.). His stay at Dagenham was, however, but brief, as he resigned this benefice in 1739, and resided wholly at Much Hadham, where he died in 1776. The burial entry runs thus—" 1776, Sept. 18. The Revd. Francis Stanley, M.A. Rector of this Parish for the space of 53 years."

XLII. ABRAHAM BLACKBORNE was instituted in 1739 on the

presentation of his father.   He took his B.A. at Peterhouse, Cambridge, in 1736, his M.A. in 1740, and his D.D. in 1746.   He married Frances, the daughter of Thomas Fanshawe, Esq., of Parsloes and Wyresdale.[1]   He is said to have been an active parish priest, generous, courtly, and of remarkably fine presence.   In 1763 he accepted the vicarage of Hampton-on-Thames, which is by water only seventeen miles from Dagenham.   From a comparison of the registers of these parishes, it would seem that he resided in each for six months every year, and had a curate in each place. The venerable doctor died on Sunday, November 26, 1797, at Hampton, at the age of eighty-two, and was buried in a vault in Richmond churchyard.   His incumbency at Dagenham of fifty-eight years is the longest of all the vicars of this parish.

It was coterminous, it is interesting to note, with the ministerial career of John Wesley.   Wesley began his ambitious and self-authorized but much-needed mission in 1737, and died in 1791. There is no record in his *Journal* of any visit to Dagenham, but he must have frequently passed through it on his journeys to Colchester, where he often preached, and this with the permission of the Bishop of London.   He mentions, however, a visit to Barking—"Tuesday, January 6, 1784.   At noon I preached at Barking and in the evening at Purfleet, to a people that were all alive.   The next day I went on to Colchester and on Friday, 9, returned to London."

XLIII.   EDWARD CHAPLIN graduated B.A. at Trinity College, Cambridge, in 1793, from which he migrated to Merton College, Oxford.   He was instituted to the vicarage of Dagenham, June 8, 1798, on the presentation of Thomas Thorston, Esq.   The entry of his institution describes Dagenham as being in *Barstable* Deanery ; probably this was an error for Barking (in which deanery Dagenham was till 1858) on the part of the registrar's clerk.   He resigned the living in the early part of 1801, probably on account of ill-health. His curate, the Rev. Ralph Downes, B.A. (St. John's College, Cambridge), remained in charge of the parish till his successor was instituted, and for some time afterwards served as curate.

XLIV.   HENRY MORICE was presented to the benefice by Mrs. Sarah Bonnynge, and instituted on St. Barnabas' Day, 1801.   He took his B.A. degree at Oxford (St. John's College) in 1798. Shortly after his institution he was placed on the Commission of

---

[1] A burial entry says that her mother, "Ann Fanshawe died in child-bed and was buried in Barking Church, August 9th, 1762."

the Peace for the county of Essex.   In his time the present new church of Dagenham was built on the site of the old one, which had unfortunately collapsed in 1800.   Unhappily, his moral character was not in accordance with his sacred vocation, and conscious that his influence was not for the good of his parishioners, he resigned the living in 1807, and retired into private life at Abbotswick.   In the parish minutes there is a letter from the vestry, thanking him "for the way he discharged his duties as a minister and a magistrate, and also for the honourable motives that induced him to resign the living of this parish."   Two children were born to him at the vicarage, viz. Mary and Henry William. Among those who occasionally officiated for him were his father, the Rev. William Morice, B.D., rector of Wennington, and the Rev. John Fanshawe, vicar of Frodsham.

XLV. TEMPEST SLINGER, an M.A. of Cambridge (St. John's College), was instituted in October, 1807, on the presentation of Mrs. Bonnynge, widow.   A man of gentle, unassuming disposition, assiduous in the discharge of his pastoral duties, he was held in high esteem by his flock, and his early death on May 22, 1811, from an accident in Whitechapel, caused deep sorrow to the villagers.   He was buried in the vicar's chancel in the church, being the last incumbent to whom that honour was accorded.   He left a widow and two daughters.

XLVI. RICHARD GLOVER graduated B.A. at St. John's College, Cambridge, in 1767.   He was presented to the living by Mrs. Bonnynge, and instituted June 13, 1811.   He was only here a brief period, as he was appointed chaplain of St. Mary's Hospital, Ilford, in 1814, but by the wish of the patron retained the living of Dagenham till the end of 1816, when he resigned it.

XLVII. THOMAS LEWIS FANSHAW was born on St. Matthew's Day, 1792.   He was educated at Eton and St. Mary Hall, Oxford, where he took his B.A. in 1815, and his M.A. in 1819.   He was ordained deacon in June, 1816, and priest the following September, and served as curate of Tytherton Lucas, Wilts.   He was also chaplain to the seventh Earl of Kintore.   On November 5, 1816 (after less than six months' parochial experience), Mr. Fanshaw was instituted to the vicarage of Dagenham, to which he had been presented by Mrs. Sarah Bonnynge, his aunt, exercising her right of patronage for the fourth time.[1]   He married, in 1821, Catherine

[1] Mrs. Sarah Bonnynge, widow, was sister to Mary, wife of John Fanshawe, Esq., of Parsloes, where she lived the last few years of her life.   She was buried in the Fanshawe

Stephens, eldest daughter of Major-General John Gaspard le Marchant, of Guernsey, a distinguished officer, who was killed at Salamanca in 1812.

Mr. Fanshaw was of small physique, and bore a strong facial resemblance to John Keble, for whom he was sometimes mistaken. He was an energetic parish priest, and built, at his own expense, in 1822, the school which is now the church room. He resigned the benefice in 1857, owing to mental breakdown, and died March 5, 1858, at Kingsbury. He was buried in the family vault on the 17th. His memory is held in much esteem by the old inhabitants. He had issue—(1) John Gaspard, born 1824 (died December, 1903), educated at Eton, clerk in the Board of Trade ; married, 1853, Barbara, third daughter of the Hon. William James Coventry (of Earl's Croome Court, Worcester), son of the seventh Earl, by whom he had three sons and two daughters ; (2) Thomas Basil, Colonel 33rd Regiment ; (3) Richard, late clerk in the House of Commons.

During his vicariate, Mr. Fanshaw lived for many years with his brother at Parsloes Manor, the vicarage being let to a Captain Alexander Moore.

XLVIII. ROBERT BEWICK was instituted in May, 1857, by the then Bishop of Rochester, on the presentation of his sister   He was an M.A. of Queen's College, Cambridge. He was a man of dignified appearance, a good classical scholar, and is remembered as an impressive preacher. A dubiously expressed compliment was paid to his abilities in this respect by one who admired him—" He was a fine preacher to sit under, and I always liked his conclusions."

Mr. Bewick was not here long, as he resigned in 1861. He was unmarried, his sister living at the vicarage with him.

XLIX. JOHN FARMER graduated B.A. at Gonville and Caius College, Cambridge, in 1854, and M.A. in 1857. He was ordained in 1855. His institution to this benefice took place in October, 1861, on his own presentation. He resigned the living in 1876, and retired into private life. He was chairman of the first School board of Dagenham.

L. JOHN JAMES STEVENSON MOORE, the present vicar, was educated at Trinity College, Dublin, where he graduated B.A. in 1853. In 1873 he proceeded to the degrees of LL.B. and LL.D. by accumulation. He was ordained deacon in 1855, and licensed to the curacy of Christ Church, Chester, where he remained three

vault in Dagenham church, on January 20, 1832, at the age of seventy-two. She left £30,000 to her nephews at Parsloes.

years, when he removed to Farnworth, Lancs. In 1860 he was appointed Government chaplain of the Isle of Man. Four years later he accepted the office of chaplain of Missions to Seamen at Swansea, which he held for fourteen years, when he was instituted (Easter, 1876) to the vicarage of Dagenham on the presentation of his father.

Dr. Moore married Louisa, third daughter of Major D. Stewart, of Barassa Place, Perth, and of Maryvoor, Isle of Man. He has three sons and one daughter, viz.—

1. Stewart Stevenson, M.A., Keble College, Oxford; vice-Deemster to his Majesty in the Isle of Man.

2. John Edward Stevenson, M.A., Sidney Sussex College, Cambridge ; head-master of Llandaff Cathedral School.

3. Charles James Stevenson, M.A., Emmanuel College, Cambridge ; Indian Civil Service.

4. Louisa Mary (died 1904).

During the incumbency of the venerable doctor, the church has been twice restored and the churchyard considerably enlarged. The new church of St. Chad, Chadwell Heath, has also been built to meet the spiritual needs of the north portion of the parish. Since 1876 the population of Dagenham has nearly trebled.

CHAPTER VIII

CHANTRY PRIESTS AND CURATES OF DAGENHAM

"Give me the priest whose graces shall possess
Of an ambassador the just address,
A father's tenderness, a shepherd's care,
A leader's courage, which the cross can bear,
A ruler's awe, a watchman's wakeful eye,
A pilot's skill, the helm in storms to ply,
A fisher's patience and a labourer's toil,
A guide's dexterity to disembroil,
A prophet's inspiration from above,
A teacher's knowledge and a Saviour's love."

BISHOP KEN.

IN addition to the foregoing list of vicars this parish had its chantry priests also. Their duty was primarily and chiefly to celebrate mass for the repose of the souls of the deceased founder or founders and benefactors of the church in the private chapel or chantry attached to and usually, though not always, contiguous to it. The chantry was, as a rule, built on the north or south side of the chancel, from which it was separated by a screen of wood or stone ; in Dagenham church it was of oak. Sometimes the chantry priest, or *cantarist*, as he was termed, performed other duties besides that above mentioned, *e.g.* at Little Bentley (Essex) he was required by the will of the founder to assist the vicar in his cure of souls. At Coggeshall (Essex) he served as curate-in-charge of a small hamlet, the chantry being in this case some distance from the parish church. At Dagenham the chantry priest was appointed by Barking Abbey, and probably lived near the chantry.

In 1486, Avery, or Alured, Cornburgh, Esq., of Gooshays Manor, near Romford, and the lord of a manor in Hornchurch, who held office at the Court of Edward IV., Richard III., and Henry VII., founded a chantry at Hornchurch, with an annual endowment of

£200 in modern money.[1]   By direction of his will the chantry priest was also to preach at least two sermons every year in the churches of South Ockendon, Hornchurch, Dagenham, and Barking. Not wishing his bequest to be forgotten by future generations, this Alured Cornburgh prepared, during his lifetime, a tomb for himself, with a description in verse of the various legacies left by him and their purpose.   He specifies the duties to be discharged by the cantarist, and also to the length of holiday (six weeks) to be allowed him.   Weever, in his "Antient Funeral Monuments" (published about 1630), has fortunately preserved this description, which is now quite undecipherable.   The tomb was in Romford church. We quote one stanza—

> "The Chantrie Preest in this Church shall bynd him preching
> And in other when he is disposyed soul helth to avans;
> Namely at South Okendon, Hornchurch, Dagenham & Barking;
> At euery of them twise a yere or moo to Goddy's pleasans,
> And at two times seuerall this is sufficians,
> Forty days in the yere he shall have to disport,
> If his disposition require such comfort."

The following is a list of the chantry priests whose names have come down to us :—

Thomas Smyth, "clericus," 1364.   Mentioned as a witness in a grant of land from John Stylman to John Outhrede, both of Dakenham.

Benjamin Edwold.   Mentioned in a grant of land, 42 Edward III. (1369–70); also as appointed to collect the tithe of corn (with others) of Dakenham for Barking Abbey (1371).

Ralph Matsale, "chaplain," 1394–95.

Dom (i.e. Sir) Nicholas Harpour, "chaplain."

(These are both mentioned in a grant of land made in the nineteenth year of Richard II. (1395–96).)

John Geve, "chaplain," 1508.   Referred to in a deed of sale by "John Coker, of Daggenham."

The dissolution of the chantries commenced in 1529, when an Act was passed forbidding any person receiving money for celebrating mass for the dead.   In 1545 a statute was enacted directing that the revenues of the chantries should be appropriated to the king's use, but as Henry VIII. died shortly afterwards, many were left untouched, but another Act, of 1547-48, gave the remainder to

---

[1] Harl. MS. 27386 records a conveyance of land in Barking by Agnes Lake, wife of Richard Lake, of Haveryng-atte-Bower, to Averidus Cornburgth, "armiger." Date, 1461–62.

the young king, Edward VI., under the pretext of building grammar schools, augmenting the endowments of universities, and making provision for the poor and needy.   Less than half of the confiscated endowments were applied to these purposes ; the bulk of the spoil was expended in defraying the cost of the wars in Scotland and Ireland, and in rewarding royal favourites for their devotion to the Crown.

It should be mentioned that in a few cases, where the chantries were at some distance from the parish church, the inhabitants purchased them from the person to whom they were given, and raised among themselves the endowment for the maintenance of a resident priest ; as *e.g.* at Billericay, Essex, where the chantry became eventually the parish church.

CURATES OF DAGENHAM.

Sᵣ Thomas Wackestaffe, " stipendiary " of Dagenham.
(Mentioned in the will of George Bolles, vicar, 1538.)
John Waddisworth, " clerk "   ..   ..   1598.
(His daughter Alice was buryed the xxvijᵗʰ of June, 1598.)
John Elborowe   ..   ..   1610-15.
(Administration of will granted May 4, 1615, to Mary the relict.)
Thomas Manninge   ..   ..   ..   1615-17.
John Bell, " clerk"   ..   ..   ..   1619.
Gowyn Diar, " clarke "   ..   ..   ..   —
(Married Margaret Haygood, December 28, 1619.)
William Geast, " clerk."   ..   ..   ..   —
(Married Ann, the daughter of Mr. Thomas Manninge, vicar, July, 1627.)
Mr. Thomas ffountaine   ..   ..   ..   1635-37.
John Friday   ..   ..   1675-79.
(A note in the register says that he " came in this year (1675) curate to Dr. Harrison, vicᵣ, being hired for the purpose.")
Edward Partington   ..   ..   ..   1707-10.
John Brett ¹   ..   ..   1710-15.
Henry Westall   ..   ..   1715-17.
Alexander Jephson   ..   ..   ..   1718-32.
William Stead   ..   ..   1733-40.
George Downing ²   ..   ..   ..   1744-45.
(Afterwards vicar of Little Wakering.)

¹ The son of Samuel Brett, a mercer of Romford. The register of that parish has the entry of his burial—" 1715. Julye 11th, the Reverᵈ Mᵣ John Bret, curat of Dagenham, native of yᵉ place was buryed." Bequeathed the advowson to William Blackborne, Esq.

² Mr. Downing officiated at the wedding of Captain Cook, the great circumnavigator. The entry in the Barking register is as follows :—" James Cook of yᵉ parish of St. Paul,

John Fisher	..	..	..	..	1750.
Richard Clarke	..	..	..	..	1756.
Samuel Freeman	..	..	..	..	1761.
John Langhorne [1]	..	..	..	1761–64.

Mr. Langhorne was ordained in 1760, while a master at the Wakefield Free School. In the following year he took the degree of B.D. at Clare College, Cambridge, and came to Dagenham. While here he was noticed by Bishop Warburton, of London, who appointed him lecturer of St. John's, Clerkenwell, whereupon Mr. Langhorne removed to London " for the convenience of his booksellers." In 1765 he was nominated assistant preacher at Lincoln's Inn, and subsequently rector of Blagdon, Somerset, and Prebendary of Wells. Mr. Langhorne was, besides being an accomplished classical scholar and an eloquent preacher, a poet of repute. His poems are chiefly translations from the classical poets (especially Plutarch), sonnets, elegies, and dramatic verses, the best being, " The Death of Adonis," " The Visions of Fancy," " The Tears of Music " (on the death of Handel), " The Country Justice," " Hymn to Hope," and " An Elegy on the Death of Thomas Gray." Mr. Langhorne was twice married, and died in 1779, in his forty-fifth year. A selection from his works is included in Dr. Samuel Johnson's " English Poets," *vide* " Memoirs," by his son, John T. Langhorne, vicar of Harmondsworth and Drayton, Middlesex, who mentions that "Mr. Langhorne, while at Dagenham, was on intimate terms with the Gillmans."

William Pow	..	..	..	..	1765–66.
Richard Sargeant	..	..	..	1767.
Crispin Green	..	..	..	..	1769.
Lewis Powell	..	..	..	..	1770.
Henry Walter	..	..	..	..	1771.
Joseph Digby	..	..	..	..	1772.
Charles Graham	..	..	..	..	1773.
Henry Meen	..	..	..	..	1774.
Giles Powell	..	..	..	..	1774.
Thomas Woodroffe	..	..	..	1775.

Shadwell, in y⁰ county of Middlesex, batchelor, and Elizabeth Batts, of y⁰ parish of Barking, in y⁰ county of Essex, spinster, were married in this church by y⁰ Archbishop of Canterbury's license, this twenty-first day of December, one thousand seven hundred and sixty-two, by George Downing, vicar of Little Wakering, Essex." He was subsequently appointed chaplain of the Ilford Hospital, in the chapel of which he was buried in 1778.

[1] The late Prof. Benj. Jowett claimed descent on his mother's side from the poet Langhorne.

John Thornhill	..	..	..	..	1777–79.
John Fosbrook	..	..	..	..	1779.
John Sherman	..	..	..	..	1780.
Benjamin Symonds		..	..	..	1780.
William Parker	..	..	..	..	1781.
John Jones	..	..	..	..	1781.
Isaac Twycross	..	..	..	..	1782–84.
Frances Massingberd		..	..	..	1784–94.
Edward Cuthbert		..	..	..	1794.
Ralph Downes	..	..	..	..	1796–1806.
W. H. Reynell	..	..	..	..	1806.
Charles Robert Rowlett	..	..	..	1810–15.
D. G. Stacey	..	..	..	..	1832.
George Bailey	..	..	..	..	1851–58.
Henry Stokes	..	..	..	..	1859–62.
David Parker Morgan	..	..	..	1877–78.
William Morris	..	..	..	..	1879–83.
Alban Wylde	..	..	..	..	1880–84.
Clement Charles Harrison		..	..	1888–92.
Stephen Cundy	..	..	..	..	1890–93.
Clement Charles Harrison		..	..	1898.

CHAPTER IX

THE CHURCHWARDENS AND PARISH CLERKS

" Hail to the State of England ! and conjoin
 With this a salutation as devout,
 Made to the spiritual fabric of her Church ;
 Founded in truth ; by blood of martyrdom
 Cemented ; by the hands of wisdom reared
 In beauty of holiness, with ordered pomp,
 Decent and unreproved. The voice that greets
 The majesty of both, shall pray for both ;
 That, mutually protected and sustained,
 They may endure as long as sea surrounds
 The favoured land, or sunshine warms her soil."

WORDSWORTH.

THE office of churchwarden is one of some antiquity, dating
prior to the Conquest. Their primary duty was to take care of
the church, its fabric, furniture, and goods on behalf of the
parishioners. Later, they were required to assist in maintaining
the moral tone of the parish, and present to the bishop or archdeacon, at their visitations, heretics, lax communicants, and
persons of irregular life. It is a joint office, shared equally by
each warden. Until the Parish Councils Act came into operation (1894), the churchwardens were a parochial legal corporation,
and *ex officio* overseers. Unless expressly excluded, they were
usually trustees of the charities of their parish. They are
appointed at the Easter vestry, that date being within a few
days coincident with March 25, which, under the old style, began
the civil and ecclesiastical year. Their duties are specified in the
Canons of 1591.

The following is a list of the churchwardens of this parish, so
far as we have been able to trace them :—

1510 { Thomas Edolf.
       Thomas Trulove.

Mentioned in a grant of land made 2 Henry VIII.

1545–47 {
Robard Genyns.
Iohn Logson.

1549–51 {
Thomas Estbroke at fylde.
Thomas Estbroke at the Welle.

1551–53 {
Iohn Logson.
Thomas Hoke.

These five are mentioned in the Inventory as having sold various properties and goods belonging to the church at the request of the Commissioners.

1595–98. Iohn Umphrey, " buried Maye 21, 1598."

1637. Stephen Dore.

1649–51. William Baldwin.[1]

1672–73 {
Thomas Bonham.[2]
John Emerson.

1674–75 {
William Hadden.
Thomas Elkin.

1676–77 {
John Nevill.
John Soanes.

1678–79 {
John Nevill.
John Ramsden.

1680–81 {
Stephen Dore.
John Ramsden.

1682–84 {
William Eaton.[3]
Robert Woolston.

1692–95 {
Thomas Stevens.
John Willson.

1787 {
William Potter.
Robert Brittain.

1788 {
Robert Brittain.
John Biggs.

1789–90 {
Samuel Stock.
Samuel Waters.

1791–94 {
Samuel Waters.
Stephen Harvey.

1795 {
Stephen Harvey.
Henry Hunsdon.

1796–98 {
Henry Hunsdon.
Phœbus Grigg.[4]

[1] A yeoman ; buried in the church ; occupied land called " Hooks."

[2] Of Valence ; buried in Dagenham church.

[3] Lived at " Wards," near Eastbrook End (so Barking Manor Rent Roll, 1663) ; died 1694.

[4] The Rev. E. Chaplin refused to accept Wm. Ford, who had been elected vicar's warden.

1799–1800 { William Ford.
John Biggs.

1801 { John Biggs.
John Burley.

1802 { John Biggs.
Samuel Seabrook.

1803 { John Biggs.
Lancelot Tuck.[1]

1804 { John Biggs.
John Dangerfield.

1805 { John Biggs.
John Hanson.

1806 { John Baker.
Thomas Boulton.

1807–08 { John Baker.
John Lowers.

1809–12 { John Baker.
M. A. Burke.

1813–14 { Rev. John Fanshawe.
William Smith.

1815 { George Winmill.
William Smith.

1816 { George Winmill.
James Dickson.

1817–19 { George Winmill.
Henry Gray.

1820–22 { George Winmill.
John Kittle.

1823–24 { George Winmill.
George Edward Pollett.

1825–26 { G. E. Pollett.
John Pickering Peacock.

1827–29 { J. P. Peacock.[2]
Samuel Seabrook.

1830–33 { John Clark.
G. E. Pollett.

1834 { G. E. Pollett.
John Hasten.

[1] The Rev. H. Morice nominated Wm. Ford as vicar's warden, but the vestry refused to elect him.

[2] The Rev. T. L. Fanshawe declined to accept Mr. Peacock as his warden, and appointed Mr. Pollett instead (1827). The matter was thereupon referred to Dr. Stephen Lushington (chancellor of the diocese), who replied by quoting the 39th Canon, and stating that the election of the wardens by the vestry was valid, inasmuch as the vicar had allowed two days to elapse before protesting against the person nominated. Mr. Pollett lived at Eastbury House; died 1844. Mr. Peacock lived at Whalebone House.

1835–36 { Ephraim Seabrook.
{ William Warren Boulton.

1837 { G. E. Pollett.
{ Archer Moss.

1838–40 { Thomas Lee.[1]
{ Archer Moss

1841–44 { Henry Fanshawe.
{ Thomas Cowling.

1845–54 { Henry Fanshawe.
{ Thomas Waters Brittain.
{ E. H. Denison.[2]

1855–57 { J. C. Thorogood.
{ T. W. Brittain.

1858–60 { James Miller.[3]
{ T. W. Brittain.

1861 { Charles Otter.
{ J. Miller.

1862 { J. C. Thorogood.
{ J. Miller.

1863 { H. Thompson.
{ J. Lamming.[4]

1864 { C. Freeman.
{ J. Lamming.

1865–74 { Wm. Reeve Mihill.
{ C. Freeman.

1875–78 { George E. L. Currie.
{ C. Freeman.

1879 { William Cathie.
{ George Stevens.

1880–82 { John Tyler.
{ George Stevens.

1883–84 { General Whish.
{ G. E. L. Currie.

1885 { R. E. C. Nichols.
{ G. E. L. Currie.

1886 { Stewart Stevenson Moore.
{ G. E. L. Currie.

1887–88 { H. W. Catchpole.
{ G. E. L. Currie.

1889 { H. W. Catchpole.
{ G. Stevens.

[1] Of the Warren.
[2] Appointed vicar's warden, November, 1854, in the room of Henry Fanshawe, deceased.
[3] Of Chadwell Heath.
[4] Of Padnalls.

1890-96 { Wm. Varco Williams.
          G. Stevens.
          John Smith.[1]

1897-99 { W. Varco Williams.
          John Smith.

1900 { Joseph Currie.
        John Thorogood.

1901 { Samuel Gunary.
        Alfred Howgego.

1902-03 { George Fox.
          Reuben March.

CHURCHWARDENS OF CHADWELL HEATH.

1895-96 { Herbert Archer Moss.
          Thomas Sears.

1896-19— { H. A. Moss.
           William Clark.

PARISH CLERKS.

The parish clerk is an ancient and honourable institution. Every parish was required, from the thirteenth century, possibly earlier, to maintain a clerk to assist the parish priest in his public and private ministrations. Lyndwood (1423-66) says, " The Clerks must not be twice married and they must have no bodily ailment or impediment. They must have sufficient knowledge to read the Epistles and Lessons, to sing Responsals, Grails and other parts of the service, in order to be able to assist at Mass, Matins and Canonical Hours." This office was endowed with certain fees ; sometimes, as *e.g.* at Castleton, Derbyshire, with a piece of land, and was, in consequence, often bestowed on some poor scholar. The parish clerk was also required to accompany the priest when visiting the sick, to carry holy water, and sprinkle the people with it, hence the name given to him, *aquæ bajulus* (water-carrier). He was to attend to the due publication of banns, write out the certificates, and hold the *pallium* over newly married couples. Until the Reformation, he held, as near as possible, the office of sub-deacon ; but subsequently his office was shorn of its dignity, and he became a parish official, who performed various duties in the church and churchyard. A royal injunction of 1548 ordered that he should assist the churchwardens in registering all monies given to the poor. At a later period it often fell to his

[1] Elected parish warden, September 14, 1896, in the room of G. Stevens, deceased.

lot to make the entries of baptisms, marriages, and burials in the
registers. In this capacity, as the parish remembrancer, it lay
within his power to immortalize parishioners and others for good
or ill. Sometimes he adds the words, " vir honestus," " memoria
justi beata," " a woeman much lamented ; " but in three or four
cases he makes a note of an uncomplimentary character, *e.g.*
" Henery soun of Thomas Bonham, Esq'. buried August 14, 1674,
whose burial not paid yet." In one instance he indulges in a little
versifying—

> "As carefull nurses in there cradles lay
> those babes which would too longe wanton play,
> So nature his nurse for to prevent his sins in living crimes
> hath laid him in his bed of dust betimes."

The subject of this pessimistic reflection was his own child !

No wonder that the parish clerk was looked upon as a
"scholard," as distinguished from the parishioners generally, who
were "no scholards." They did not know that he was only able
to read and write after a fashion, but only judged him from the
way he sometimes magnified his office by officiousness and eccen-
tricities of mind and habit.

The parish clerk of Dagenham was nominated by the vicar ;
but, as the office was a freehold, he could only be removed by the
bishop or archdeacon for any misconduct. He received a salary
of 26*s.* a year, paid half-yearly. The washing of the surplice four
times a year was an extra, for which the clerk was paid 2*s*
He would, of course, get his share of the fees, and, if he was one
of the six bell-ringers, he would have his share of what they
received also.

The office of parish clerk was quite distinct from that of the
vestry clerk. The latter was the servant of the vestry in so far as
it had to do with *civil* matters only ; he answered to the clerk of
the modern parish council. The duties of the parish clerk had
reference to the church as a place of worship, a public building,
and the centre of unity for the parish. The two offices at Dagenham were seldom held by the same person, *e.g.* in 1800 the parish
clerk was one Samuel Laizell, a worthy but illiterate man ; the
vestry clerk was Thomas Cutler, schoolmaster and village grocer.

The following is a list of the parish clerks :—

> 1598. John Waddisworth, " clerk " (parish clerk ?).
> 1619. John Bell, " clerk " (parish clerk ?).

1619. George Diar, " clarke."
1652. Richard Gyver.[1]
1670. William Mayes, or Mayers[2] (the poet).
1674. John Davis.
1682. David Church.
1700(?). William Reynolds.[3]
1724. Jonathan Belsham.[4]
1731. Edward Jenner.[5]
1755. Stephen Raines.[6]
1795. John Armstrong.
1800. Samuel Laizell.
1822. Benjamin Holgate.[7]
1853. Benjamin Holgate.
1864. James Palmer.
1878. James Walter Palmer.[8]
1901. Henry Walter Palmer.

[1] Buried September 26, 1852.
[2] " William Mayers, clerk of this place foure yeares, died at Stoke, June 23th, 1674.' '
[3] " William Raynold, yᵉ clark (a sermon), buryed Aprile 1, 1724."
[4] Buried June 4, 1731.
[5] Buried March 13, 1755.
[6] Buried March, 1795, at the age of eighty-four.
[7] The salary then was £5. See parish minutes—" Pd. to Benj. Holgate salary to Micklemas, 1825, £5 0s. 0d."
[8] Resigned 1901 ; succeeded by his son. The last two appointments were made by the present vicar.

THE URSWYCK TOMB.

[To face p. 103

CHAPTER X

THE MONUMENTS IN THE CHURCH

> " It was a marble large and white,
> And he read it by the misty light ;
> It said that virtue's paths he trod,
> And loved his country and his God ;
> That he was mild, sincere, and good,
> With grace and courtesy imbued ;
> Of gallant heart, of steadfast mind—
> A tender son, a husband kind—
> Who never broke the word he gave—
> In friendship staunch, in danger brave."
>
> MACKAY.

THE old parish church of Dagenham contained a large number of monuments and sepulchral stones, as we know from wills, registers, and other sources that a good many vicars and parishioners of influence were buried in the church, chancel, and chantry. The oldest stone to which we have any reference was to the memory of Richard Treswell. It bore the inscription, with coat of arms— " Hic jacet Ricardus Treswell, filius Iohannis Treswell, generosus, qui obiit, 18 die Iul . anno Dm̄i . 1509." Near it was a slab to the memory of one Buteler or Boteler, but with an indecipherable inscription, beyond the date 1519. Another gravestone was inscribed— " Elizabeth Fitzlewes, wife of Sir Ricard Fitzlewes, daughter of Sir Raphe Sheldon ; she died 2nd of Ianuary, 1522 " (with coat of arms). Another one bore the inscription—" Anne Barantine, wife to Sir William Barantine, Knight. She obiit 27th of December, 1522." Unfortunately, all these memorials, with many others also, were completely demolished when the present church was built in 1803-4[1] One solitary monument survives as a witness of the glory of the former church, viz. the altar tomb of Sir Thomas Urswick, Knight.

---

[1] In the centre aisle of the chancel there is a fine gravestone, on which was a brass and inscription, both of which are gone. There was also a coat of arms, now missing.

But not only were these monuments destroyed, others were removed and placed promiscuously in the nave and chancel, with the result that the words "Hic jacet" on the present gravestones are not literally true.

In the vicar's chancel is the following inscription on a stone—

M. S.[1]
Here lieth the body of
Mrs. SUSANNA UPPHILL,
youngest daughter of
Jacob Upphill, Esq.,
and Anne his wife,
Who died 20 January, 1724,
Aged 65.
The last of that family.

Near this is the stone to her brother's memory—

Here lies interred ye Body of
RICHARD UPPHILL, Esq.,
Standard Bearer to their late Majesties King William, Queen Mary and Queen Ann and to his present Majesty King George, who departed this life 26th February, $171\frac{7}{8}$ and left by his will after the decease of his sister Susanna Upphill, Ninety Pounds per annum to the Poor Children of Dagnum Parish (not receiving alms).
Aetatis suæ . 59.

At the head is a coat of arms.

Close by is another gravestone, at the head of which is a coat of arms.

Siste viator
Ne te lateat quis hic situs
Hoc ut scias moræ pretium erit.
THOMAS BONHAMUS, Armiger
Valenciæ Trinobantium [2] Dominus.

Poeta jucundus.
Attamen sublimis
Radiam ingenii jubar
Politioresque literatura
Felixque elegantiæ ornamentum exemplar
Aeternum celebrandus
Nunquam heu satis lugendus
Caelum non capit marmor,
Vi rupes ipsa nisiquod

Die Mai anno . 1676.
Aetate suæ . 73.

---

[1] Memoriæ Sacræ —to the sacred memory.   [2] See Appendix, Chapter X.

Adjoining this is a stone with the following :—

Here lyeth the Body of
THOMAS COMYNS,
Dr. of Physicke, the 7th son of Robert Comyns, of Dagenham in Essex,
Gent., being about the age of 32 years when he dyed, which was on ye
27th August, 1656.   His dying words were—

"I desire to be dissolved and to be with Christ."

On the south wall of the chancel is a well-preserved tablet, with
the following :—

Neare this place are buried the bodies of
JACOB UPHILL,
of this Parish, Gent., and ANN his wife ; he departed this life ye 16th day
of June 1662, in the thirty-sixth yeare of his age ; she on ye 15th day of
Aug. 1667 in ye 42nd yeare of her age, by whome he had eleaven children.

Antony the eldest was killed on board ye Royall Katherine with the
Earle of Sandwich.

Jacob dyed a-coming from the East Indies where he had lived 22
yeares a merchant.

Richard is standard-bearer to her most sacred Majesty Ann, Queen
of Greate Brittaine.

John died a-going to the East Indies.

Philadelphia, ye eldest daughter was first marryed to William Sandys of
Misserden in Glocestershire, Esq.   Her second husband was William
Duncombe, B.D., sometimes Rector of Astead in Surry.

Ann marryed Sr Oliver Buteler, of Testen in the County of Kent,
Bart.

Mary marryed Sr Robert Howard, a son of the Earle of Barkshire.

Susannah is unmarried.

The other three dyed younge.

This monument was erected by Philadelphia Duncombe.   Anno
Dominy, 1707.

On the north wall of the vicar's chancel, at the north-east
corner, there is a mural tablet inscribed as follows :—

To the happy memory of
JONATHAN LLOYD,
son of John Lloyd, Citizen and Alderman of Shrewsbury, Master of Arts
and Faithful pastor of Dagenham, who departed this life, ye 18th day of
December, 1652, and ANNE his wife, ye daughter of George Walker, who
preceded him in that charge on the 3rd December 1652, and ANNE their
daughter, who died ye 8th of the said December.

Viator, siste gradus hoc sub marmore,
Jacent sepulta nobilis prosapia.
Decora forma, litteræ ad mirandum
Quidquid terrenam sapit excellentiam
At altiora hujus Pastoris munera
Ortus caelestis et piæ mentis decus,
Et quæ expandit abdita evangelia
Monumentum provisere stant perennius.[1]

Catherine Walker, their dear mother, hath caused this monument to
be erected.

On the south wall of the chancel, near the sanctuary, is a white
marble tablet, partly covered with drapery, with the inscription—

In Memory of
MARIA MASSINGBERD,
Wife of Francis Burrell Massingberd
Merchant of London
Brother of William Burrell Massingberd, of South Ormesby
in the County of Lincoln, Esq.
She was daughter of Thomas Fanshaw
of Parsloes in this Parish, Esq.
Died April VIII. MDCCLXXVII
Aged LII years.
Three of her children lie buried with her
Who died in their infancy and she left
one surviving son Francis.

Close by the north door, leading to the vicar's chancel, is a
white marble gravestone, which says—

Here lyeth interr'd the body of
Mrs. ANNE LAMBE
who dyed the 5 day of January, 1752.
Aged 74 years.
This is next to that of Mrs. Uphill.

On the north side of the chancel is an altar tomb (the only one
of its kind in the church) to the memory of Sir Thomas Urswick,
Knight. On the top of it are brass effigies of the knight, his lady,

[1] Traveller, stay thy steps beneath this monument,
Here lies buried one of noble family.
Comely in person, marvellous in learning
Whatever savours of earthly excellence.
But yet higher were this Pastor's gifts,—
A heavenly birth, the grace of an holy mind
Which reveals the Gospel's hidden treasure,—
Such endure a monument more lasting than any brass.

and their four sons. Originally there were brasses of their nine daughters also, but these have disappeared, having been torn out, however, since 1815, as a sketch of all of them is given in Ogborne's "History of Essex,"[1] published in that year, with coat of arms. The inscription is also wanting. Sir Thomas was Recorder of London, and was influential in persuading the citizens to receive Edward IV. in 1471 as their rightful king.[2]

To the west of the altar tomb is a gravestone with a Latin epitaph, to the memory of the Rev. Dr. Butler, a former vicar.

GUILELMUS BUTLER, L.L.B.
(hujus ecclesiæ) vicarius necnon S.S. Annæ et
Agnetis apud Londinenses Rector,
Eccles. Cathedral, Divi Pauli
Prebendarius et proclero Dioc.
Lond. in inferiori domo convocationis
Prov. Cantuar procuratorium
Unus variis laboribus attritus
Hic tandem requiescit anno ætatis
65 et salutis . 1736.
Paulo prius moriturus est et quasi mortis
præsciens hos jecit versiculos.

Me non invitum Deus evocat, ite labores,
Ite procul curæ, cætera pacis erunt,
Quod vidi in terris animus magis
Horruit omni morte, quod expectem,
Tu mihi Christe dabis.

Margaretta Butler, filia dilectissima
in piam patris memoriam hoc posuit.

Adjoining this is a stone inscribed thus—

Here lyeth the Body of
Mr. JAMES WHITE,
Corn Chandler of Romford, who departed this life April the 15th in the year of our Lord Anno Domini . 1777. Aged 59 years.
One whom God has blest all his life long.

Also here lyeth interred the Body of
Mrs. CATHERINE WHITE,
Wife of the above James White,
who departed this life March 31 . 1778. Aged 68 years.

Behold God is my salvation I will trust and not be affraid for the Lord Jehovah is my strength and my song He Who is become my salvation.

[1] See Appendix A, Chapter X.
[2] See Chapter XXI.—on Marks.

On a line with this is another similar stone—

Here lyeth buried ye body of
JOHN WHITE
of this Parish Gen^t
who decesed Febr ye 2nd 1673.
Aged 68 yeares.
He hath given to 7 poore
widdowes one dozen of bread
weekly for ever.

Blessed is he that considereth the poor, etc.
Psalms ye 41st and ye first.

And also the Body of
JAMES WHITE
of this Parish who died the 2^d of Nov^{br} 1725.
Aged 48 yeares.
Likewise the body of
MARY WHITE
his wife who died Oct^{br} ye 8th 1759.
Aged 74 yeares.

Adjoining this is a stone inscribed—

Neare this place lies the body of
RICHARD ALIBONE, Kn^t.
Requiescit in pace.

There is a handsome mural stone of alabaster on the south side of the east window in the vestry or chantry. It contains two epitaphs, the upper one being encircled with rich floral carving. The inscription runs thus—

Were here, no epitaph nor monument
Nor line nor marble to declare the intent,
Yet goodnes hath a lasting memory
The just are like to kings that never die
Theire death a Passage or Translation is
An end of woes an Orient to Bliss
Thrice happy Couple that do now possess
The fruits of theire good workes and Holines
Now God rewards theire Allmes & Charitie
Their strict observinge Saboath's Pietie
Here were they wont to spend their seaventh daye
Here was theire Love theire life theire Heavens way
Here did they praye but now they praise & singe
And God accepts their soules sweete offeringe
Only theire Bodyes heere remain in ground
Waiting the surge at the last Trumpets sound.

Under this quaint eulogy we read—

Here lyeth

JAMES HARVY, Esqr.

second sonne of Sr James Harvy Knight sometyme [1581] Lord Mayor of London. He took to wife Elizabeth second daughter of Antony Radcliffe sometyme Alderman of London and lived with her in Wedlocke above six and thirty yeares & had by her eight sons and nine daughters. He departed this life the 6th of Aprill. Anno Dmi 1627. Ætatis suae 67.

And the said ELIZABETH she survived him one yeare and odd dayes and departed this life the 8th of June, Anno Dmi . 1628. Ætatis suæ 55. Whose bodies are both here interred waitinge for the glorious coming of our Blessed Saviour.[1]

A coat of arms, almost obliterated, is underneath this inscription.

By the fireplace in the vestry is a broken tombstone, which is covered by the fender and the carpet, with the words—

of   THOMPSON of London who departed this life 21st febr. 168$\frac{7}{8}$ being eighteen months old.

Under the organ are the tombstones of John Hopkins Dare, died January 9, 1805, aged twenty-three, from a fall off his horse ; and of the Rev. Tempest Slinger, a vicar of the parish, who died May 22, 1811, aged seventy-four, from an accident in Whitechapel.

But the most handsome and conspicuous monument in the church is that to the memory of Sir Richard Alibon. He is represented life-size, wearing his judicial robes and holding in his right hand a roll of parchment. His wife stands holding a clasped book. On the top of the monument, which is of fine white marble, is an urn ornamented with the sword and scales of Justice. At the foot is a skull with cross-bones. There are two tablets, with inscriptions, the upper one being in Latin and the lower one, which is a more or less free translation of it, in English, as follows :—

H. S. E.[2]

D. RICHARDUS ALIBON, Eques Auratus.
Vir ingenio cæterisque animo dotibus egregius.
Nec minus optimarum artium institutis excultus.
Juris Anglicani prudentiâ simul et praxi
In Hospitio Legum Graiensi florentissimus.
Solâ meritorum Laude Jacobo R. II^{do} Notus.
Primo in Ejusdem Advocatum, deiude in Banci Regii

---

[1] See the chapter on Wangye Manor, where the Harvey family lived
[2] Hic sepultus est.

Justitiarum ab eodem est cooptatus.
Primus Romanæ Fidei Cultor
Qui a centum fere et Quinquaginta Annis
Tanto Tribunatu Præsiderat
Qui dum hoc munere fungeretur
Eâ Justitiæ et Integritates Famâ Inclarius,
Adversus Potentes fortis et intrepidus,
Erga reos et pauperes affabilis
Ut Hostes Ejus Infensissimi nihil in eo reprehenderent.
Præter Religionem.
Dum Patris Regioque Juri Assuendo
His animi Dotibus Instructus incumbet,
Morte ereptus est
Mensis Augusti die XXII.
Salutis nostræ MDCLXXXVIII.
Ætatis suæ LIII.
Et requiescit in pace.
Dilectissimo Conjugi pariter dilecta Conjux
Dᵐᵃ Barbara filia Dⁿⁱ Joannis Blakestone,
Neptis Dⁿⁱ Gulielmi Blakestone Equitis Aurati
de Gibside in Comitatu Dunelmensi
Hoc Pietatis Suæ Monumentum
M.P.

Here lies interred the body of
Sir RICHARD ALIBON, Knt.,

a person of extraordinary, both natural & acquired, parts; eminent in
the knowledge and practice of the law; of the honourable society of Grey's
Inn; recommended only by his merit to the favour of James II., to whom
he was of counsel, learned in the laws & advanced to be one of the
justices of the Court of King's Bench, being the first of yᵉ Romish faith,
these 150 years, who being called to a place of such high rank, which he
discharged with so eminent justice & integrity, as gained him a general
love & applause; whilst his great abilities were thus applyed in a faithful
service of his king and country, He happily ended this transitory life,
August 22 . 1688, the year of his age 53.   May he rest in peace!   In
honour to the memory of her dearest husband was this monument of grief
& conjugal affection erected, by his no less dear relict, dame Barbara
Alibon, who was daughter to John Blackstone, Esq., and grand-daughter
to Sir William Blackstone, of Gibside, in the County of Durham.

The subject of this laudatory inscription was the eldest son of
Job Alibone, a Roman Catholic, who had a place in the London
Post-office, of Fair Rytes, Hornchurch, and Dagenham, by Mar-
garet, daughter of Dr. Richard Chamber, minister of St. Andrew's,

Hubbard Gardens, London. He studied law at Grey's Inn, and was made a judge in 1687, in which year he bought a house on the north side of Dagenham "towne," opposite to where the Comyns family lived. This house, which was known as the "Camms," was approached through an avenue of trees. It was pulled down early in the nineteenth century. On the accession of William III., Sir Richard Alibone went to reside at a house near Red Lion Square, in London, where he shortly afterwards died. It is thought that his death was from fright at current rumours that a charge of treason was to be brought against him for having accepted an office which he was disqualified from holding on account of his religious faith.

In regard to his "extraordinary parts" and "great abilities," it would seem that his reputation as writ in marble does not agree with his fame as recorded in history. For, as it happened, the abilities of the learned judge were put to a severe test in the famous trial, which stands unique in our national history, viz. that of the Seven Bishops. The reader will recollect that this trial arose out of the ill-advised policy of James II. in issuing the Declaration of Liberty of Conscience in 1687, and again still more emphatically in the following year. His object was to further the cause of Roman Catholicism by persuading his disaffected subjects that he was not the tyrant they supposed him to be. A royal mandate was issued to the Bishops to instruct their clergy to read the king's Declaration during Divine service, in London, on May 20, and in the country on the following Sunday, May 27. But the Bishops, after consulting together, resolved—

"That the clergy could not read the Declaration, either in prudence or in conscience ; not in *prudence*, for three reasons, because it was contrary to the interest of the Church, because it would be taken as a proof of their approbation or their cowardice, and because it would lead to the reading hereafter of other and perhaps still more offensive papers ; nor could they read it in *conscience*, because it contained illegal matter, as it presupposed not merely a dispensing, but even a disannulling power in the Crown " (Lingard's "History of England," vol. x. chap. iii.).

To the Bishops who passed this resolution, viz. Dr. Sancroft, Archbishop of Canterbury, Dr. Turner of Ely, and Dr. White of Peterborough, four more joined themselves, viz. Dr. Lloyd of St. Asaph, Dr. Ken of Bath and Wells, Dr. Lake of Chichester, and Dr. Trelawney of Bristol. The seven Bishops drew up a respectful letter to the king, asking for the clergy to be excused from reading the Declaration, on account of the latter being wanting in legality and constitutional procedure.   The king, taken by surprise at the turn matters had taken, replied warmly that he had not expected such treatment from the Church of England, that they were (wittingly or unwittingly) seeking to over-throw both the throne and Church, and that the Declaration was perfectly reasonable and just.   Finding, moreover, that the Bishops would not change their minds, he determined to prosecute them for a civil misdemeanour, and thus vindicate and confirm his own royal authority.   The trial took place at Westminster Hall on June 29, 1688, amid intense excitement and frequent demon-strations of sympathy with the Bishops.   The counsel for the prosecution charged them with publishing a seditious libel against the king.   The judges were Wright, the Lord Chief Justice, Halloway, Powell, and our Richard Alibone, the first and last of whom summed up against the Bishops.   Speaking of the qualifica-tions of the several judges, Macaulay, with his usual pungency and incisiveness, says—

" The new Chief Justice, Sir Robert Wright, was ignorant to a proverb ; yet ignorance was not his worse fault.   His vices had ruined him.   He had resorted to infamous ways of raising money, and had, on one occasion, made a false affidavit in order to obtain possession of five hundred pounds. Poor, dissolute, and shameless, he had become one of the parasites of Jeffreys, who promoted him, and insulted him.   Such was the man who was now selected by James to be Lord Chief Justice of England.   One Richard Alibone, who was even more ignorant of law than Wright, and who, as a Roman Catholic, was incapable of holding office, was appointed a puisne judge of the King's Bench " (Chapter VIII.).

The trial ended in the acquittal of the Bishops, who received the gratitude of the whole country for the stand they had made to vindicate the rights and liberties of the people.

On the north side of the chancel, and near the chancel screen, is a mural tablet inscribed thus—

In the family vault under this tablet are reposed the remains of the late SARAH BONYNGE, widow, who departed this life January 10, 1832, aged 73 years.

Also the remains of JOHN GASCOIGNE FANSHAWE, Esq., late of Parsloes in this parish, who departed this life December 23, 1803, aged 57 years.

Also the remains of MARY FANSHAW, widow of the above J. G. Fanshawe, who departed this life March 22, 1811, aged 63 years.

Also MARY, third daughter of the Rev. Thomas Lewis Fanshaw, M.A. vicar of this parish, fourth son of the above named John Gascoigne Fanshaw and Catherine Stephens his wife who died on the 19th of July, 1827, aged two months.

Also CATHERINE SOPHIA, the eldest daughter of the above named Thomas L. Fanshawe and Catherine S. his wife who died at Parsloes on the 27th of April 1841 in the 19th year of her age.

Also of JOHN FANSHAW, Clerk, M.A., vicar of Frodsham, Cheshire and for many years student of Christ Church College, Oxford, who died 27th of October 1843, aged 70.

Also the remains of HENRY, second son of the above John Gascoigne Fanshaw, and Mary his wife, died 13th of October, 1854, aged 80.

Also THOMAS LEWIS FANSHAW, Clerk, fourth son of the above named John G. Fanshaw and Mary his wife, of Parsloes and for forty-one years vicar of this Parish. Born 21 Sept., 1792, died 5 March, 1858, in the sixty-sixth year of his age.

In the nave of the church are the following mural tablets. On the south-east wall—

Sacred to the memory of
NATHANIEL and JAMES ROGERS
sons of James & Mary Rogers
& descendants of John Rogers the first Protestant martyr
in the reign of Queen Mary.   They were born in this Parish
July 19, 1738 & November 6, 1741 respectively
and died in London
the former Febr. 10, 1810, aged 72 & the latter Aug. 16, 1811 aged 70
Nathaniel Rogers M.D. grandson of James
caused this tablet to be erected.

Below the inscription is a handsome coat of arms, with the motto, *Nos nostraque Deo.*

Under this we read—

In a vault near this spot repose the mortal remains of
JONATHAN ARNOLD, Esq'.
formerly of Whalebone Cottage in this Parish.
A devout man & one that feared God.
He died at Bow in Middlesex on the 14th Febr. 1857
in the 78th year of his age.   His sorrowing widow
has erected this tablet to the memory
of an affectionate & beloved husband.
Also MERCY ARNOLD
widow of the above
who died November 9th 1864.

Next to this is a much smaller slab—

Sacred to the memory of
ALEXANDER MILNER
whose death was caused by an accident
on board the ship Boyne off Vizigapatam
on the 2nd of August 1846.
He died at Waltair on the 8th of the same month.
Aged 30 years.

I became dumb & opened not my mouth for it was Thy doing.

Also to the beloved memory of
ALFRED LOUIS MILNER
who departed this life at Pater, South Wales,
on the 19th October 1846 aged 23 years.

Every man's judgment cometh from the Lord.

They were the second & youngest sons of John Milner, Esqr. of Chadwell
Heath in this parish.[1]

On another tablet, with coat of arms—

Sacred to the memory of
JOHN GUILLEMARD, Esqr.
late of Gower Street, London.
Fellow of the Royal & of several other Scientific Societies
who died on the 22nd of November 1844,
in the 81st year of his age.[2]
His remains are laid with those of his
maternal grandfather and grandmother
Mr. and Mrs. Pilon in the adjoining cemetery.

Next to this is another one, with figure of a young widow
weeping over an urn—

Sacred to the memory of
Mr. WILLIAM STONE
of this Parish, farmer,
who died the 23rd day of July 1839
in the 76th year of his age.
Also sacred to the memory of
Mrs. SARAH STONE
who died November 5th, 1852
in the 86th year of her age.
Wife of the above
And niece of the late William Ford.

They rest in peace.

---

[1] He lived at Heath House, facing the "Three Mills."

[2] An occasional visitor to Beansland (Whalebone) House, where his grandparents
lived. He and John Sabetier, Esq., of Christ Church, Newgate, inherited their estate.

On the north wall of the nave is a tablet thus inscribed—

Underneath is interred the Body of
Mr. THOMAS WATERS
of this Parish, who departed this life March 6ᵗʰ, 1756, aged 73 years.
He charitably left the Interest of one
Hundred pounds South Sea Annuities to
place out att school yᵉ Poor children
of the Poor decayed Parishioners
of this Parish.

A friend so true there are but few
And difficult to find
A man more just and true to trust
There are but few behind.

Next to this is another one—

Sacred to the memory of
JOHN TYLER, Esqʳ.
late of Mawneys in the County of Essex.
He died the 24ᵗʰ September 1807
Aged 69 years.

Beloved.   Lamented.

And another one, well worthy of its position, with a scroll held
by two cherubs, on which is the text, " Take heed that ye despise
not one of these little ones."

In the year 1825
WILLM. FORD, farmer
by his will gave
the munificent sum of
Ten thousand Pounds
to found a free school
in this Parish
to be conducted upon the
principles of the
Established Church of England
and the Interest of the sum of
One Thousand pounds
to supply warm clothing
to the aged poor
yearly for ever.

Go and do thou likewise.

CHAPTER XI

THE CHURCHYARD

"' I like that ancient Saxon phrase, which calls
The burial-ground God's acre ! It is just;
It consecrates each grave within its walls,
And breathes a benison o'er the sleeping dust."
LONGFELLOW.

THE old churchyard consisted originally of an acre of land, in the form of a square. It was enclosed by a wall five feet high, built of brick and flintstone. In the Book of Parish Accounts (1660–85) we find here and there mention of repairs to the wall—"For 12 hundred of barens for yᵉ church wall, £03 . 00 . 00;" and, "For carrying yᵉ materialls to yᵉ wall, £01 . 10 . 00." Weeding is also mentioned as another incidental expense, thus—"Pd for cutting weeds in yᵉ churchyard, £00 . 01 . 00 ;" and, "Outting the weeds, £00 . 01 . 06." There is almost an entire absence of yew-trees, the typical churchyard tree of England ; perhaps the soil does not suit them. There is no churchyard cross either, and, indeed, no trace of one having ever existed here.

In all probability the churchyard was set apart for the burial of the dead from the time the church was consecrated, 1180–1220. Taking the number of burials in it as averaging twenty a year (exclusive of those in the church itself, which perhaps averaged two or three per annum) until the enlargement of the churchyard in 1804, the total number of bodies lying in the ancient portion of "God's acre" would be over eleven thousand. These are spread over a period of some six hundred years, but are all destined to meet at "that great day, when we shall all of us be contemporaries and make our appearance together."

Originally the churchyard extended on its south side to the first pathway which runs parallel with the church, east to west. In 1804 it was proposed at a vestry meeting to enlarge it, and subsequently agreed that Mr. Cuff, the owner of the land adjoining the churchyard on the south side, be asked to meet the vicar, the churchwardens, and Mr. Wasey Sterry (a solicitor from Romford) on Sunday, June 17, to discuss the matter after morning service. The result of this conference was, however, disappointing, inasmuch as Mr. Cuff named £100 as his price for the acre of land required for the enlargement. At the present day this sum would be considered small, but to the vestry it appeared exorbitant, and he was asked to reduce his figure, but in vain. Annoyed at his utter want of sympathy with their scheme, the vestry at last determined to bring him to reason by lodging a complaint against him with the archdeacon, on account of the dilapidated condition of the fence between his land and the churchyard. This counter-move had the desired effect; for Mr. Cuff, fearing that he might be condemned in costs at the Archdeacon's Court for breach of contract, and, further, be required to repair the wall at his own expense, now made an offer of eleven and a half rods of land adjoining the churchyard on condition that the parish properly fenced the same and kept it in repair for ever. This offer was accepted, and Mr. Kittle was instructed to make a stout oak fence at a cost not exceeding £1 11s. 6d. per rod. Benj. Holgate, the village carpenter, was ordered at the same time (August, 1804) to make a new pair of gates for the west entrance to the churchyard. The addition to the churchyard was consecrated by the Bishop of London (Dr. Beilby Porteus) on July 8, 1805, immediately after the consecration of the new church. A tent was provided for the bishop in the churchyard, and a large congregation witnessed the impressive ceremony. The form of service used was that which is now in use at similar services.

A further enlargement of the churchyard was proposed by the Rev. T. L. Fanshaw, in 1832, when he offered a plot of land adjoining the churchyard on the east, and facing the vicarage gate, on condition that the parish enclosed it with a brick wall. But the vestry, having considered the offer, declined it, a decision that was subsequently a matter of considerable regret.

The churchyard was again enlarged in 1876, with the addition of half an acre of land on the south side, which was duly consecrated in that year by Bishop Claughton, of Rochester.

The churchyard contains a large number of tombstones. The majority of these are plain marble crosses, which speak of Christian hope; others are simple upright stones; and others again, not many, are merely pedestals supporting urns, suggestive of pagan despair. There are about twenty stones which belong to the seventeenth century, but the inscriptions on them are almost obliterated. A fair proportion of altar tombs, flat stones, and grave spaces are enclosed with iron railings, though this was not due to the churchyard being depastured by sheep and oxen, as there is no evidence that this irreverent custom ever prevailed here. The oldest and finest tombs are on the north and south sides, and are quite close to the walls of the church. It is rather remarkable that there is not a single tombstone in the churchyard which marks the resting-place of a vicar of Dagenham, although there are several within the church itself. Under the chancel are several vaults, the largest of which belonged to the Fanshawe family.

A brief summary of the memorials in stone contained in the old churchyard is here given—

At the west end—

1. Anne, second daughter of Lieutenant-Colonel Harrison, 57th Foot, and wife of Thomas Cutler ; Thomas Cutler, who died December 14, 1845, aged 72.

2. Thomas Boulton, died October 8, 1823 ; his wife Elizabeth, died May 16, 1812. (The inscription much defaced.)

3. William Warren, died February 9, 1837, aged 66.

4. Edward Jenner, late cooper in H.M. magazine *Poorclett*, died March 7, 1812, aged 83.

5. The Bird family.

6. The Little family.

7. The Rogers family.

8. William Helmore, died 1771. (Very indecipherable.)

9. Altar tomb of brick with stone top, to Mr. Samuel Yull and family.

10. Samuel Stoor, died November 29, 1791.

11. George Coppen, died November 1769. Another one to Thomas Coppen and Silena Coppen.

12. William Garner, late farmer of Bentrey Heath, "died in this parish"[1]

13. The Flint family.

14. The Fish family.   Plumber and glasier, died   1852.

15.   Farrow.

16.   Harper.

17. Benjn. Holgate, died   1852.

18. The Kittle family (three stones).

[1] This detail is mentioned on some other stones also.

19. Pulleyn of Pentonville, London, died October, 1815.
20. The Harding family.
21. The Wackett family.
22. The Hunsdon family.
23. Mr. Fortescue, of St. Andrew's Holborn, died   1819.
24. Three large stones, side by side, all enclosed with high iron railing.
The first to the memory of William Ford, died December 16, 1825, with
the lines—

> " Long time on earth I tilled the ground ;
> Now in it here a resting-place have found.
> And as the purest wheat do spring from dust
> I trust through Christ to rise among the just."

The middle stone is to the memory of Joseph Ford, Mrs. Stonar, the
mother-in-law of one of his daughters, and Joseph Sutton, of Eastbrook
End and Southwark, with the suitable conclusion, "Requiescat in pace."
The third stone is to the memory of another Joseph Ford, who died in
1762.

25. Mr. Benjamin Wallis, of Furze Cottage, in this parish, died   1831.
26. Mr. Archer Moss and family.   An altar tomb.
27. Theodosia Ann, wife of Thomas, Lord Denman, Chief Justice of
England ; born November 21, 1779, died June 26, 1852.   Also her grand-
daughter, Theodosia Ann, daughter of the Hon. Richard and Emma
Denman.[1]

" The stone which records their death may tell the virtues of which the
one gave early proof, and by which the other was through a long life
endeared to all.   Innocent, pious, gentle, and affectionate, well-prepared
for that bliss which their bereaved friends humbly trust they are now enjoy-
ing together.

> " Of such is the kingdom of God."

28. Three stones to the memory of the Monk, Hanson, and Draper
families, respectively.
29. Altar tomb, with iron railing, to the Freeman family.
30. Three stones to the Gray family.
31. To the Sockett and Wade families, respectively.
33. Four stones to the Holmes, Cowling, Higgs, and Pritlove families,
respectively.
34. Two stones to the Seabrook family.
35. To the Blackwell family.

Proceeding to the north side of the churchyard, we come
across the following stones, the inscriptions on which are rapidly
vanishing :—

[1] Lord Denman was then residing at Parsloes, having taken it on a short lease.   He
was made Lord Chief Justice in 1830.   He and Stephen Lushington were counsel for
Queen Caroline, wife of George IV., in the famous trial at Westminster (1820).

36. A handsome altar tomb to John Chessey, of London, died May, 1750.

37. To Captain Willis, of the Royal Artillery, died August, 1828.

38. William Johnson, 1760.

39. Three stones to the Tyler family. Of these, one is enclosed with iron palisades, and another is a tall pedestal stone with urn. Under them is the vault.

40. To the Robinson family.

41. Two altar tombs (one with coat of arms) to Thomas Witham and family, of London, died 1640.

42. Three stones to the Pollett, Chase, and Boyton families, respectively.

43. Four stones to the Bridgman (of Romford), Mitchell, White, and Thorogood families, respectively.

44. To William Higgins, of London, died 1787.

45. Two solid stones, cylindrical in shape; inscription gone.

46. An altar tomb, scalloped at the sides, and with coat of arms on the top, inscribed thus—

"Here lyeth interred yᵉ Body of Capt. Richard Comyns, who died yᵉ 10 of February, 1700, in the 45ᵗʰ year of his age.

"Also Dorothy Comyns, his wife, who dyed July 13ᵗʰ, 1731.

"Also John Comyns, Gent., who died March 15ᵗʰ, 1743.

"Also Sarah the wife of the above; died July 31, 1748."

47. Stone to the Willis family.

On the east side are stones as follows :—

48. To the Palmer family, especially "James, who met with his death by the falling in of a grave, November 16, 1878."

49. To Samuel Thorogood, "killed while harvesting, August 16, 1840." And the appropriate line—

"In the midst of life we are in death."

50. Two tombstones to the Twyford family.

51. An elegant cross of white marble to the memory of Beatrice Mary, the daughter of the Rev. John Farmer, vicar; died July 12, 1868, aged 7 years.

51. Stone to John Winger.

52. Stone under chantry window to the Dean family.

53. To the Coombes family.
To Abigail Waite, died 1694.

54. Six stones to the Brittain and Waters Brittain families.

55. To Daniel Dossiter, died November 1791.
Also Mary Dossitor, spinster, 1819.

56. To Mr. Samuel Waters, yeoman, of this parish, died January 2, 1803, aged 64.

57. Two more stones (south-east) to the Twyford family.

58. To the Haws family.

59. Two altar tombs to the Bennett and Merttins families. The inscriptions say that Thomas Bennett, Esq., the grandson of Henry Merttins, died in June, 1802, aged 80. Also that George Merttins, Esq., grandson of Sir George Merttins, Knt., and son Michael Merttins, died May, 1786, aged 60; also that Henry Merttins, Esq., of Vallence (brother to Sir George), who married Elizabeth, the daughter of Sir Edward Wood, Knt., and niéce of the Rt. Hon. John Roberson, D.D., Lord Privy Seal and Bishop of London, died November 26, 1710, aged 40. Edward, their son, died in 1706, aged 19.

The inscriptions are nearly obliterated.

On the south side of the churchyard are the following tombs :—

60. An altar tomb to the Rev. Mr. Thomas Wright, D.D., late rector of Christ Church, Middlesex, who married Hester, the fourth daughter of Henry and Elizabeth Merttins, of London, jeweller, who died August 15, 1736, aged 44. " Let my last end be like his." Also of Hester, who died April 17, 1762, aged 66. The inscription continues—Also of Alexander Bennett, youngest son of Sir John Bennett, who married Mary, the daughter of Henry and Elizabeth Merttins ; died September 30, 1769. Mary the widow died April   aged 67.

61. An altar tomb, with iron palisades, to Mr. Higgins. (Inscription undecipherable.)

62. An altar tomb, with iron railing—the whole almost hidden by evergreens—to the memory of Lieutenant-Colonel Graves, died 1847.

63. Three stones to the Spooner family.

64. Six stones to the Cleeve, Gilbey, Biggs, Martin, Hunsdon, and Moys families, respectively.

65. An altar tomb with epitaph completely effaced.

66. Altar tomb to Daniel Pilon, of Christ Church, Middlesex, goldsmith and citizen, of London, and an inhabitant of this parish ; died April   .
Also Francis Pilon, wife of Mr. Nicholas Peter Pilon, of Norfolk Street, Strand.

67. Altar tomb to John Henry Merttins, the only son of John Henry Merttins, Esq., who died April, 1710. Also the father of J. H. M. Also Henry Merttins Bird, Esq., of Barton House, Warwickshire, and late of Vallence, died 1818.

68. Two stones to the Boyton family.

69. Obelisk tomb to Police-constable George Clark, murdered at Eastbrook End on June 29, 1846. Erected by his comrades of the " K " (Metropolitan) Division.

70. Two stones to members of the Palmer family.

71. Three stones to the Stafford family, one of whom was "a victualler and bricklayer."

72. Two tombs (one an altar tomb) to the Cannon family.

73. Altar tomb (iron-railed) to the Higgins, Glasbrook, and Lightwood families.

74. Three stones to the Hasten, Smith, and Bloice families, respectively.

75. Three stones to the Carter, Smith, and Chalk families, respectively.

76. Two stones to the Tuck family, and one to the Mitchell family.

77. Stone (iron-railed) to Sarah Hannah, the widow of Alfred Gray, of Wonts Farm ; died 1857.

78. Eight stones to the Collier, Linsell, Mudd, Spurrier, Archer, Edwards, Gray, and Smith families, respectively.

79. Five stones to the White, Smoothy, Tanner, Morgan, and Burke families.

80. An altar tomb to Robert Hunsdson, died 1858.

81. Stones to the Coppen family, of Whalebone Farm.

82. Stone to William Bennett, killed at Chadwell Heath Station, November 27, 1867, aged 55.

CHAPTER XII

THE PARISH REGISTERS (BAPTISMS)

"How blest if through this world of strife
And sin and selfish care,
Our snow-white robe of righteousness
We undefiled wear."

PARISH registers owe their origin primarily to the Act of Supremacy, passed in 1535 at the command of Henry VIII. It declares that the king desires to exert his supremacy for the good of the Church, and being unable to attend personally to the work, he therefore appoints his well-beloved Thomas Crumwell " to treat and examine all causes ecclesiastical, and to exercise, provide, and exert all and all manner of jurisdiction, authority, or power ecclesiastical, which belongs to him as supreme head, and to visit, reform, order, and amend such things as might be lawfully reformed." Under this Act, Thomas Crumwell was, in July, 1535, appointed his Majesty's vice-general, and it was in this capacity that he issued " Royal Injunctions " to the bishops and clergy (September 28, 1538) of which one was—

That every Parson, Vicar or Curate . . . shall for every church keep one Book or Register, wherein he shall write the day and year of every Wedding, Christening and Burying made within the parish . . . and also there insert every Person's name that shall be so wedded, christened and buried . . . which book he shall every Sunday take forth and in the presence of the wardens or one of them write and record in the same all the weddings, christenings and buryings made the whole week before and for every time that the same shall be omitted, shall forfeit to the said church iiis. iiiid.

These Injunctions were sent by Bishop Bonner, of London, to his archdeacons,[1] to be by them brought before the notice of the clergy of the diocese. We do not, however, know whether the

---

[1] The Archdeacon of Essex at that time was Richard Rawson (1503–43), who had succeeded Francis, Archbishop of Byzantium.

then vicar of Dagenham procured parish registers or not ; he *may* have done so, but as those for the mother parish of Barking only date from 1558, and they are the oldest in the neighbourhood, there is a presumption that he did not obey the Injunctions. Possibly the recent spoliation of Barking Abbey, in which Crumwell had proved himself a willing tool in the hands of the king, had produced a feeling of bitter resentment against that "vicegeneral's" mandates. Be this as it may, there is no evidence that either Dagenham or Barking had a parish register dating from 1538, as is the case with many parishes of less antiquity and importance.[1]

On the accession of Queen Elizabeth (1558), a fresh mandate was issued to the clergy, to procure registers for their parishes. It was in obedience to this, doubtless, that Mr. Iohn Finnymore, at that time vicar of Dagenham, procured the first parish register. Unfortunately this has perished, but how long it has been missing it is impossible to say. No one ever knew of its existence until November, 1882, when Mr. W. J. Harvey, an enthusiastic antiquary, picked up in the church belfry a sheet of paper written upon both sides, which turned out to be a leaf of an old register dating from 1558, if not from 1538. The membrane was mutilated, but Mr. Harvey succeeded in deciphering some thirty entries of marriages that had been solemnized during the space of three years—1568-71. These are given at length in the next chapter.

Owing to the general disregard of the Royal Injunctions to procure parish registers, with the result that the great majority of parishes were without them, the Convocation of Canterbury issued an ordinance in 1597, with the approval of the Queen and signed by the Great Seal, that parchment register books should be purchased at the charge of each parish.[2] In compliance with this ordinance, the vicar (Mr. Iohn Berryman) and churchwardens (Iohn Humphry and   ) of Dagenham procured "yᵉ vellum regester book." It is a handsome folio volume, bound in calf and in good condition, excepting that some half-dozen pages have been cut out. It bears the title—"Dagenham, Essex. Register of Baptisms, Marriages and Burials, 1598 to 1667." At the top of its third page is the declaration that "James the ffirst of England, Scotland and ffrance and Irelande, kinge, defender of yᵉ ffayth began

---

[1] The Romford register dates from 1561, Hornchurch from 1576, and Havering-atte-Bower from 1677.

[2] This ordinance was incorporated as Canon lxx. in the Canons of 1603 ; agreed upon in the Synod of London, and issued by the authority of James I.

his reigne the xxth day of March, 1602." The writing is bold and clear on the whole, though from 1640 to 1656 it is very indecipherable, and the different years are mixed up in a confusing manner. Where the vicar probably took the trouble to make the entries himself, the writing is of a lithographic character, the spelling correct, and the expressions used flavoured with a dash of Latinity here and there. But where the entries were made by the parish clerk, the writing is indifferent and blurred, and the spelling based strictly on phonetic principles. Hence we find that, either for the sake of variety, or to ensure accuracy in one case at least, the same name is spelt in several different ways on the same page. Notwithstanding the directions in the Canon, only the name of *one* parent is given, and *nowhere* do we find the churchwardens affixing their signatures at the foot of any of the pages, as required by the Canon. The vicar alone signed his name. Now and then we come across an entry of a baptism at a church other than Dagenham. Thus—"William, son of Thomas Witham, baptized in London, 20th June, 1650."

Down to 1642, the name of the father of the child only is given ; after that year the Christian names of both parents are frequently found. Sometimes the vicar, or clerk, omitted them, but left space for them to be inserted after they had been ascertained. Thus—"Sarah, daughter of   Stallin of Chadwell Heath baptized 4th of Decemb. 1656;" and " Elizabeth daughter of   Meekins yᵉ Smyth of Chardwell, in Barking parish, baptized 17 October, 1666." It is worthy of note that these omissions have reference to parents living some distance from the church and "towne." Where the father was a person of substance, the clerk could evade the difficulty by writing " Mr." or "Yeoman." Thus—"Sarah daughter of Mr. Blythman of Chappell Henault in this parish, bap. June 6, 1667 ; " and " Joseph, son of Goodman Waylett, the tanner, bap. July 11, 1667."

In about twenty cases the date of the *birth* is added to the entry of baptism. This detail is interesting, as showing us that it was the custom for infants to be baptized within ten, and at the most fifteen, days after their birth. Thus—" John Willson son of Edward Willsen bornne 27th of March baptized 11th April 1654."[1]

---

[1] See the rubric in the (private) Baptismal Office—" The curates of every parish shall often admonish the people that they defer not the baptism of their children longer than the first or second Sunday next after their birth, or other holy day falling between, unless upon a great and reasonable cause, to be approved by the curate."

In some registers in this county the names of the godparents of the child baptized are added to the entries. No such addition is, however, found in the Dagenham register. Nor do we find a baptism marked " Private," or with the initials " P. B."

The number of baptisms fluctuated considerably from year to year. Thus in 1598 there were 23, in 1604, 29, but in 1600 only 12, and in 1602 only one. The sexes were, on the whole, equally divided ; where there is a preponderance, it is on the side of the males, *e.g.* in 1612 there were 18 males to 13 females. During the period that quasi-Presbyterian ministers had charge of the parish, the total number dropped to 5 in 1645, 3 in 1646, but went up to 19 in 1648. Probably, as Dagenham was noted for its "recusants" and " malignants," the more strict church-people of those times took their children elsewhere to be baptized by some clergyman of their own Church, or had them baptized at home by one of the numerous ejected clergy, of whose presence in the neighbourhood they were secretly informed, that they might receive the benefit of his ministrations. Such baptisms would, of course, be unregistered. Occasionally, the parents of the children baptized were citizens of London, one or both of whom had perhaps married from Dagenham, or were possibly staying with relatives and friends when the children in question were born. Especially was this so during the Plague of 1665, and after the Great Fire of 1666, when the number of baptisms was 35 and 42 respectively. Thus—

Richard son of Willm. Pusey, a cityzen of London was baptized 25th August 1665.

Ane, daughter of Mr. Hills, the Jeweller, of London, bap. the 2th September, 1665.

Richard, sonne of Mr. John Wiseman of London baptized 9th December, 1665.

Joseph, son of   Russell a London butcher burnt out of house & home, baptized November 1st, 1667.

In regard to the Christian names given to the children, the favourite ones were (for the boys) Thomas,[1] John, Joseph, Peter,

---

[1] " Whether it be that Thomas à Becket was for so long the favourite English saint, or from whatever other cause, it certainly seems to be the fact that the name 'Thomas' is much commoner in England than in any other country. The words 'tom-fool,' 'tom-boy,' etc., though perhaps not complimentary to the 'Toms' of England, certainly shows how large a family they must have been" (Preface to "Tom Brown at Oxford").

For famous Thomases we have Thomas à Kempis, Thomas à Becket, Thomas Aquinas, Thomas Arundel, Thomas Wolsey, Thomas. Cranmer, Thomas Crumwell, Sir Thomas More, Thomas Ken, Thomas Wilson, Thomas Brown, Thomas Guy, Thomas Bodley.

Robert, Richard, Henry, Christopher, and William ; and (for the girls) Elizabeth, Martha, Susannah, Jane, Joan, Mary, Catherine, Sarah, and Ann. Charles and Philadelphia occur three times. Old Testament names are rare, even during the Cromwellian period, when scriptural names and phrases were affected.   In about a dozen instances surnames alone are given as Christian names, the recipients being mostly females, *e.g.* Parnell, Dennis, Silvester, Bennett—all girls.   Double surnames are never found ; and from 1598 to 1740 only *one* Christian name is given.

Children who were born out of wedlock are variously described—"begotten out of wedlock ;" "the base son ;" "the base daughter ;" and "the bastard son or daughter of —— ;" "proles spuria ;" "ignotus and ignota ;" "filius and filia vulgi ;" "spuria proles et incognita."

These constituted 9 per cent. in the seventeenth century, and 14 per cent. in the eighteenth century.

It may not be out of place to mention here that until the year 1757 the civil year began on Lady Day (March 25), and ended on the eve of the following Lady Day.   This explains why the annual parish meeting was, and still is, held a day or two after that day, to elect officers for the ensuing year and transact other business. It also explains why the principal vestry meeting was, and still is, held at Easter, viz. because that festival coincided more or less with the new year's day, according to the old style, and was a suitable time to elect churchwardens, pass church accounts, and discuss all and sundry matters connected with the parish church, charities, etc.

In 1752 an Act was passed whereby the legal year was to be reckoned in 1757 from January 1.   The "old" style (known as the "Julian") had taken the year to be just 365 days 6 hours, being an excess of eleven minutes a year, and giving a difference in eighteen centuries of eleven days.   To rectify this, the Act reckoned September 2 as September 14.   The introduction of the new style (the "Gregorian") evoked some opposition on the part of the ignorant, who imagined that they were being deprived of a portion of their lifetime.   "Give us back our eleven days !" was a cry heard at the hustings at election time, after the Act had come into operation.

The following is a selection of entries in the register :—

Aprill, 1598. Imprimis. William the sonne of William Sebrook was baptized the xxii. day of Aprill anno dm̄, 1598.

Agnes the daughter of Jeffraie Stevens was baptized the xxxth Aprill, 1598.

Anne, the daughter of Albone Cox, gentleman, was baptized the xix day September, 1598.

Richard the sonne of George Wingar was baptized the iv. daie of Februarie, 1598.

Marye the daughter of John Stokdale was baptized the xiii. daie of March, 1598.

Anne the daughter of Widow Newland was baptized the same daie.

1599.   Thomas the sonne of Henry Upney was baptized the v. Aprill, 1599.

Richard the sonne of Wm Whyte in Cnanncerie lane Shoemaker was baptized the xvth daie of Aprill, 1599.

Robete the sonne of John Nicholls baptized the xvth daie of Julie.

Richard the sonne of Thomas ffoeboat baptized ye same daie.

William Ponson the sonn of Andrew baptized the vijth day of August, 1599.

Henry the sonne of Stephen Childe was baptized the xxiii day of Septem, 1599.

Thomas the sonne of John Trulove baptized the xith daie of Novemb, 1599.

Richard the sonne of John Ethersall baptized the xxvijth daie of Novemb.

Henrie the sonn of Humfraye Bursden baptized the xvith of March, 1599.

1600.   Joan the daughter of Thomas Estbrook baptized the iiijth of Maye, 1600.

Stephen the sonne of Henery Hood baptized the xth daye of August.

John the son of James Barnie, gentleman, baptyzed the xviiith of September, 1600.

John the sonne of John Copin baptized the xviiith daye of September, 1603.

Martha the daughter of John Newton pewterer and citizen of London was baptized the viith day of October, 1603.

Agnes the daughter of Edmund Toller baptized the xvij daye of January, 1603.

Parnell the daughter of Wm Porter baptized the iiijth of March, 1603.

1604.   Joanne the daughter of Thomas Whitney was baptized the first of Aprill, 1604.

Gowin the sonne of Willyam Umpfrey was baptized the xxvijth of Maie, 1604.

Marye, the daughter of Roger Scarborough, baptised the vith of Maye, 1605.

Mary the daughter of Rowland Snagges, baptised the xvth of September.

FAC-SIMILES OF ENTRIES IN THE PARISH REGISTERS.

Agnes the Daughter of Jefferaie Struens was baptized the xxxth daie of Aprille anno Dm̄i 1598

John the Sonne of Jamis Basrie gentleman baptized the xviiith of Septemb 1600

Thomas the sone of Thomas Greentree baptized the xith of febra . 1603

William sonne of William Storkdale Bapt undecimo Sep 1608

Robert sonne of Robert Commyns Bapt yᵉ 3ᵗʰ of ffebruarie 1610.

Thomas sonne of William Eastbrooke Bapt 5 of Mar 1612

Thomazin Daughtr of Nathaniell Gilbert Bapt yᵉ 21 of Aprill 166

Jristopper sonne of Cristopher Seabrooke was bap februar 1628.

Sidny Benton Daughter of mr Jeremiah Benton baptized march 10 th 1665 ✱

John Taylor of his parsermiddowes and Eme Backman of aye same parish singlewooman married the 25th of november 1610

John Bell s. c Alice Elkin w. marryed ye 16 of Julye 1621

ffrancis Shaterton and Amy Taylor of Rumford were married februarary the 9th 1659

ffather warrington was buried Aprill yᵉ 9ᵗʰ 1605

[Inset between pp. 128 and 129.

Agnes the daughter of Jeffraie Stevens was baptized the 30th daie of Aprill, A.D. 1598.

John the sonne of James Harvie, gentleman baptized the 18th of Septemb. 1600.

Thomas the sone of Thomas Greentree baptized the 19th of februa. 1603.

William sonne of William Stockdale bapt. 11th Sep. 1608.

Robert sonne of Robert Commyns bapt. ye 3th of februarie 1610.

Thomas sonne of William Eastbrooke bapt. 5 of Mar. 1612.

Thomazin daughter of Nathaniell Gillbert bapt. ye 21 of Aprill 1616.

Christopher sonne of Christopher Seabrooke was bap. februar. 1648.

Sidny Benton Daughter of Mr. Jeremiah Benton baptysed March 10th, 1665.*

John Stapler of this parish, widdower & Eme (Amy) Backman of the same parish singlewoeman married the 25th of November 1610.

John Bell s.[ingle] and Alice Elkin w.[idow] marryed the 16 of Julye 1621.

Francis chaterton and Ann Tayler of Rumford ware marryed february the 9th 1659.

ffather warrington was buried Aprill ye 9th 1605.

---

* Possibly the equivalent of Bentham ; if so, he was an ancestor of the celebrated Jeremy Bentham, whose father had a house in Barking near that " of my neighbour Sir Crisp Gascoigne " (1780-90).

The article "ye" is the contraction of "the," written with a long-tailed "h ;" so "yt" for "that."

Jonathan, filius Thomæ Pheild bapt. 29th December.

Jane & [name omitted, but it must have been a *boy*] Gemini Gideonis Smith, bapt. 8 Janu.

1606. William, sonne of Roger Jenninges, bapt. 27th Aprillis.

1607. Samuell sonne Jacobi Harvie, Armigeri, Bapt. eodem die.

1608. William sonne of Robert Commyns, bapt. xixteenth of October.

George, sonne of John Peachye, Bapt. xxix. of October.

1609. George, sonne of Julio Scott. Gen. Bap. 30th of Aprill.

John sonne of Adam Edlin, bap. primo Octob.

Martha, daughter of Thomas ffrancklin, Bapt. 14 of Januarye.

1610. Jone daughter of Edward Salmon, Bapt. the 19th of Aprill.

John sonne of Michaell Meade, Bapt. the 20th of Maye.

Marye, daughter of John Gadling, Bapt. 28th of October.

Rebecca, daughter of Roger Littler, Gent. Bapt. the 3th of January.

1611. Timothye the sonne of Michaell Throgmorton, Bapt. the 8 of Aug.

Ann, daughter of Robert Gold alias Grow, Bapt. the 19th of Sept.

Martha and Mary, daughters of John Stapler, Bapt. the 8th of Decemb.

Marye daughter of Richard Highhā, Esq. Bapt. 13th of ffebruarye.

1613. ffrancisca-Katharina daughter of James Pike, Bapt. 10th of November.

Susan, daughter of Thomas Lovett, Bapt. 22th of June.

Thomas sonne of John Brooke of Hornechurch, Bapt. yᵉ 4th of ffebruarye.

1616. Sarah daughter of Paul Pearsonne, Bapt. yᵉ 10th of Aprill.

Robert sonne of Vincent ffrancis, Bapt. yᵉ 14th of Aprill.

1618. Grace, daughter of Thomas Griffin, Bapt. yᵉ 2 of ffeb.

1619. John, sonne of John Sage, Bapt yᵉ 23 of Maye.

1620. Thomasin, daughter of Williā Bateman, Bapt. yᵉ 8 of March.

1622. Margarett daughter of Richard Medcalfe, of Hornchurch, was Bapt. yᵉ 7 of Aprill.

1623. Hunting sonne of Hunting More, Gent. was Bapt. yᵉ 21 of Marche.

1625. John, sonne of Maʳ Wilkinson, bapt. yᵉ 8 of Maye.

William, sonne of Maʳ Joh. Worsenum, bapt. yeᵉ 23 of Septem.

1627. Thomas, sonne of William ffanshawe, Esqr. bapt. yᵉ 27 of decembᵉʳ.

1632. John and Thomas, Twins of John Walton, bapt. yᵉ 14 of August.

1634. Thomas sonne of Mr. Thomas Bonnā, bapt. yᵉ 21 of January.

1635. Ann, daughter of a gentileman at beansland bapt. yᵉ 17 of Sept.

1637. Ann, daughter of Adirina Vanderbilt bapt. yᵉ 9 of Octobʳ

K

1641. June 15. Jane the daughter of Tho. Sorrell, gentl. bapt.

1643. Elizabeth daughter of John Rucke of londone bapt. feber. 23.

At the foot of the page containing the entries for 1644 is the note—" These are the names Regestered after the Directorie wass seet forth by Order of parli'ment, 1644."

There are no entries under 1646.

1647. hoope and Charitie Twins of Thom : Turner bap. feb. 24th.

1650. Willia, sonne of Thomas Witham was baptized in london The 20th daie of Gune.

At the foot of this page are the following,—

Goodman Starleg of Bentree heath had a sonne buried ye 27th of ffeb. 1653.

1653. John Walsall the sonne of John Walsall borne the 20th of Jan. baptized the 27th Jan.

1655. Anddru the sun of William Waller, Guly.

Hephzibah daughter of Samuel Roe of chadwell heath baptized Novemb. 16th. 1652.

1656. Thomas son of John Valentine of Ripple Side bapt. Jan 11.

Thomas son of William Niccolls of Dagenham Towne bapt. Jan. 18.

1658. Benjamin sonne of Mr. Benjamin Ayliffe bapt. August 5th.

Mary daughter of Goodman Soanes bapt. ffeb 24th.

1664. Richard son of Armiger Mane bapt. June the 2.

1665. Richard sone of Mr. John Wiseman of london bapt. 9th of Decemb.

1665. John sone of Christr of Pricklowe baptized Janary. 15th.

Sidney Benton daughter of Mr. Jeremiah Benton baptized March 10.

1666. Hanah daughter of Cleare Talbutt, Gent. baptised Sept. 10th.

Mary Daughter of Goodman Robert Osman Septem 11, baptised.

1667. Ralph sone of Ralph son of Goodman Rust baptised Aprill 2th.

Thomas sone of Thomas Hickabotton a seaman bap. Decber 24th.

The entries were continued in another register, which cannot be found, and has not been seen since about 1859. Fortunately for the parish its contents had been carefully transcribed by Mr. E. J. Sage, by whose kind permission they are here reproduced.

It began in 1668, and ended 1722, and was thus described— "The Register Book for the Parish of Dagenham in the County of Essex for the Baptizings, Marriages and Burials. Begun March 25, 1668. Isaac Smythies, Vicar." It was a "vellum book" similar to its predecessor.

Margery þe daughter of George Wright buryed þe 23 þe 14 of
Aug 1605.

John copin Buried ye 4th of October 1618

John wreight an offer of them yt were drowned Buryed ye 15 of
January 1621.

Judith daughter of John clorke of London Buryed ye 21 of ffebruary 1621.

Margery weife of Henry Dowset Buryed ye 5 of October 1624.

Mother wittham ye 8 of may 1626.

The widdow Turke Buryed ye first of maye 1627.

William baldwine the Churchwarden buried Dec 1 of 1651.

1653 { Goodman Bowdoll of Chadwell heath buried }
     { a fonn a cald Abraham þe 22th Dec }

Goodman Starley of Bentree of oak gada fonne buried
ye 27° of ffeb. 1653.

Tho Manninge Vicarius

Per: Hill vic

Jsaacus Smythies vicar

Willm Lamplugh : vic :

For modernized rendering see next page.

[Inset between pp. 130 and 131.

Margery the daughter of George Wright buryed the 28th of Aug. 1605.

John Copin Buried ye 4th of Octob'r 1616.

John Wreight another of them that were drowned Buryed the 15 of January 1621.

Judith daughter of John Clerke, etc.

Margery weife of Henry Dowset, etc.

Mother Wittham, etc.

William baldwine the churchwarden buried October, 1651.

Goodman Bowdell of Chadwell Heath buried a sonne cal'd Abraham the 22th dec. 1653.

Goodman Starleg of Bentree heath had a sonne buried the 27 of Feb. 1653.

Elzabeth y° daught' of John Walker, baptiz'd April y° 23th, 1668.

Edward sone of Edward Osborne baptyzed June y° 12 and dyed soon after.

A sone of Samuell Row, Decemb' 20.

Mary, daughter of Willm Brewster was baptized Octob' y° 26, 1669.

Bathsheba daughter of Mr. John Blythman Decemb' 6, 1669.

ffrancis sone of William Eaton & Dorothy his wife was baptiz'd June y° 27th, 1670.

Smyth, Mary y° daughter of Simon the Taner baptiz'd March y° 28, 1671.

James sonn of Mr. Blytheman, May y° 30, 1671.

Susan daughter of William Brewster, August 20, 1671.

Harris sonn of Mr. Thomas Salter was baptized Septemb. y° 7, 1671.

Thomas and Susanna twinns of Mr. Thomas Berry, Novemb' 19.

William sone of William Eaton, August 28, 1673.

Susanna daughter of Thomas Berry, May 19.

Elizabeth daughter of Willm Brewster was baptized June 1, 1674.

William sonn of Willm Eaton, Octob 26, 1674.

Jeane y° daughter of Willm Brewster was baptis'd y° 20th of Julye, 1677.

William sonn of Willm Eaton, Decemb' y° 2th.

Matthew, daughter (*sic*) of Willm Bruster was baptiz'd January 17, 1678.

John y° sonn of John Emerton, Jun' Septemb' y° 10th, 1678.

William y° son of Meyles Tyler was baptyzed y° 7 off Novemb'.

William sone of Mr. Thomas Bonham baptized Septemb' ye 23th, 1679.

William y° sone of Edward gillett, 17 off Octob', 1680.

Robert y° sone of John Emerton, Jun' March 31, 1681.

Elzabeth the Daughter of Thomas Bonham, Esqier and Elizabeth his wife was baptized April y° 3, 1681.

Grace y° Daughter of Willm Bruster, 26 off Septemb, 1682.

John sonn of John Hammond was baptized March 8, 1682.

Rebekah Daughter of Thomas Bonham, Esq. and Elizabeth his wife baptized y° 21 of June, 1683.

John sone of Miles Tilor & Dorthy his wife 14 of Septemb'.

Mary Daughter of Mr. Hug. Banks and ffrances his wife, Octob' y° 7, 1682.

Dorothy y° Daughter of Mr. Richard Comyns and Dorothy his wife baptized y° 18 of August, 1688.

Ann daughter of Richerd & Mary Taylour was baptiz'd y° 29 of Decemb', 1690.

Elzabeth Daughter of John & ffrances Emerton July y° 6, 1693.

Here follows a blank space sufficient for a dozen names, when

the entries commence again.   These were, however, copied from
1694 into the parish book of accounts.

In 1694–95 Parliament passed an Act of a singular and novel
character, to raise money for the cost of the war then waged by
William III. against France.   This was the Taxation Act, which
imposed duties on births, marriages, and burials.   The clergy were
required, under a penalty of £100, to keep a register of all births
in their parishes, whether the children were baptized or not.   This
explains why the birth is noted as well as the baptism ; and also
why local Dissenting ministers sent entries of children baptized by
them for insertion in the parish register.   The tax for births varied
from 2s. to £30 ; for marriages, 2s. 6d. to £50 ; for burials, 4s. to £50,
according to the social position of the person born, married, or buried.
The Taxation Act was still more peculiar, in that it imposed a
duty, varying from 1s. to £12 10s., upon bachelors above twenty-five
years of age, and upon widowers of any age.   The Act was only in
force five years.   Strange to say, there is no reference to it in the
parish book of accounts, which served as the parish register from
1693 to 1722.   A selection of baptismal entries in it is here
appended—

Hinery & Margrate twins of Robert Billings & Sarah his wife bapd.
yᵉ 11 of December, 1694.

Mary daughter of John Clarke & Mary his wife bapt. 5ᵗʰ of May 1695,
born yᵉ latter end of Aprill.

Christofer son of John Cook who was born yᵉ 25 of September,
1695.   Prefixed to this entry are the words, "I know nothing of yᵉ baptᵐ,"
in another hand.

Mary daught. of John Prentice & Margaret his wife was baptised yᵉ
6ᵗʰ of October, 1695, born upon yᵉ first day of yᵉ same month.

Francis son of Mr. Francis Eaton & Ann his wife baptised the 21 of
February 1695 born upon yᵉ same day.

Mary daughter of Francis Belshaw was baptised the 17 of May 1696,
was born upon the 15 of yᵉ same month.

Elizabeth daughter of Mr. Peter Cooze & Jude his wife was baptised
yᵉ 2ᵈ of June 1696 ; born upon yᵉ first day of the same month.

Thomas son of John Fanshaw, Esq. & Mary his wife was born yᵉ 18
of September 1696 ; baptised yᵉ 27 of yᵉ same month.

Elizabeth daught. of Frances Finch, widd. & posthum. child of
Thomas Finch, late of Dagenham deceased, was born the 29 of May, bapt.
yᵉ 12 of June 1698.

Elizabeth daughter of Edward Claget, Citizen of London in yᵉ parish of
Sᵗ. Michael Royal & Elizabeth his wife born yᵉ 27 of June 1702, baptized
yᵉ 10 of July following.

James son of Abraham Kent of Dosington in Glostershire & Ann his wife, born y° 5ᵗʰ of March 1702, bapt. y° 14.

William son of Robert Hills of Luton in Bedfordshire and Susanna his wife born y° 28 of March 1703, bapt y° 11 of April.

Mary daught. of John & Elizabeth Warren, born 16 of May, bapt. 20, 1703.

Mary daught. of John Tarlin of North Uckindon & Hanna his wife born 27 of Febr. bapt. y° 12 of March, 1703.

The register makes mention of an Act (the Stamp Act) coming into force on October 1, 1783. The recent wars between this country and America, and also with France, had completely drained the National Exchequer, and the succession of bad harvests had caused general distress. To meet the deficit on the revenue, a duty was fixed upon every entry in the register. Legal authority was given to the parson of each parish to demand the sum of 3d. from the parents of every child brought to be baptized, and from the parties married, and from the person in charge of each funeral. The penalty for non-payment was £5. This tax placed the clergy in a truly invidious position, not only as the ostensible collectors of a war tax, but also as guilty of a form of simony, in appearing to charge a fee for the Sacrament of Holy Baptism. Perhaps this accounts for the idea which still lingers in some parts, that a charge is made for the administration of this Christian rite.

The only apparent results of this Act were the extension of the interval between the birth and the baptism from the usual ten or fifteen days to three or four months, and the more frequent occurrence of double Christian names. This latter may, of course, have been a coincidence with and not a consequence of the Act. The tax was regularly paid to the collector on June 21 and December 24. Parish paupers (P. P.) were excused the duty, which was allowed out of the rates.

A few selections are appended—

Dinah, daughter of John & Sarah Alester, born Nov. 19, 1783, baptized P. P. Nov. 30th.

James the son of William & Mary Denham, from Mrs. Birch's, Chadwell Heath, was baptized Jan 13, 1785.

Kezia & Martha, twins of John & Sarah Baker, baptized by a Dissenting minister, Dec. 14, 1787.

Henry Randel Burgess was baptized at the Whalebone House, June 23, 1788.

Isaac, son of Isaac & Esther Smithyman, baptized Jan 27, 1794,

Registered by certificate from Thomas Straham, Dissenting minister of the Romford congregation by whom the child was baptized.

The Stamp Act was repealed in 1794. In 1812 Lord Rose's Act was passed, requiring the use of separate printed books, similar to those now used, for baptisms, marriages, and burials. With the introduction of these books, the old, simple, and sometimes quaint entries, with their touch of local colouring, became a thing of the past.

The following entries, taken from the Barking register, refer to persons belonging to Dagenham, Chadwell, and Little Heath.

Richard the sonne of Robert Hawkeswell of Dagenham p'ish baptized here the 10th of August, 1572.

Elizabeth daughter of John Reade of Chawdwell baptized the 17th of August, 1572.

William sonne of Thomas Harris of Little Heath baptized the 14th of Septem. 1572.

Thomas the sonne of Thomas Miller of Chawdwell baptized the 7th of Septem, 1578.

William the sonne of Robert Darton of Chawdwell baptized the 26th of December, 1585.

Martha, daughter of Goodman Jeames of Chawdwell bap. the 7th of March, 1590.

John the sonne of Robt Hariot of Litt. Heath bap. 28 March, 1592.

Henry the supposed sonne of Richard ffisher of London, from the Grayhound, bap. the 17th of Octob, 1592.

Margarett the daughter of [no Christian name] Osborne of Dagenham, baptized the 4th of Septem, 1597.

There are frequent entries of infants belonging to "the fforest," _e.g._ "Francis Linett, bap. the 7 March, 1563, of the fforest."

Two more run thus—

Winefrede Skinner from Padnall Corner, baptized the 7th of June, 1593.

Two children born at the Crown at Illford bap. 12 Octob, 1595.

CHAPTER XIII

THE PARISH REGISTERS (MARRIAGES)

"Now sign your names, which shall be read,
  Mute symbols of a joyful morn,
  By village eyes as yet unborn ;
  The names are signed, and overhead
  Begins the clash and clang that tells
  The joy to every wandering breeze."
                                    TENNYSON.

THE marriage entries are the oldest parochial records extant, inasmuch as the fragment discovered in 1882 of the register of 1558 or 1538 happened to contain entries of marriages from 1568 to 1571. They are brief and simple, but few details being given of the parentage or condition of the benedict and bride.

Mēsis Maij Anno Dni. 1568. Rycherde gollding and alis Denning was maryed the xxx^{ti} daye.

Mensis Augusti an° Dni. 1568. Iohn webe & Elzebeth peache wydowe was maried ye xxx^{ti} Daie.

Mensis Septembris an° Dni 1568. Iohn Stace & Ann Wilkinson widowe was maried ye xijth daye.

Mensis Octobris an° Dni 1568. Robert Winchela & ales hede wydowe was maried the forthe Daye.

. . . . Iohn Sparrowe & Raberges fyshare was maried ye xiiijth Daye.

Mēsis Novebris anno Dni 1568. Iohn Greme & Iayne harrower, widowe, was maried ye xxv^{ti} Daie.

Mensis Maij an° dni 1569. Iohn Aliff getillman & Ione hasarde ye daught^r of . . . . hasarde was maryed the xxi Daie.

Mensis Maij anno Dni 1569. Steven fynche & merget brayser wydowe was maried the xxvi^{ti} Daye.

Mensis Iunij a° 1569. Iohn gervys and . . . . was maryed ye xxvijth day.

Mensis Iulij a° 1569. Robard Whytton & agnes sparrowe were maryed ye thyrd daye.

Iohn palmʳ & Ione falbotte wydowe were maryed yᵉ 5th daye.

hūfry malpas & alys wylyas wedowe were maryed yᵉ xijᵗˡ daye.

Mensis octobris. wylyā matheson & margery dearyng were maryed yᵉ xijᵗʰ daye.

henry dowset & agnes bryges were maryed yᵉ xvi day.

Mensis novēbris. edward arden & margaret harwode yᵉ 14ᵗʰ daye.

Mensis Ianuarij. Iohn stace & Ione dowcett maryed yᵉ xxᵗʰ day.

Mensis Iulij aᵒ 1570. henry porter & Ione gynnoy yᵉ xx . . .

Mensis novēbris.

thomas stace & mary swynborō yᵉ xijᵗʰ d . . .

Iohn Grene & elzabeth devenysh yᵉ xiiijᵗʰ . . .

Mensis Ianuarij.

andrew wadyngton & margery skynnʳ yᵉ . . .

Mensis februarij.

thomas coke & agnes hūfrye yᵉ iii day.

wylyā stokedall & Alys edoll yᵉ xxvij day.

Mensis . . . aᵒ 1571.

Iohn stace & catheren palmer yᵉ fyrst daye.

henry clarke & Ione brasyer yᵉ vi day.

wyllyā chapnay & alyce pache wedow yᵉ xij day Iulij.

Iohn gyllom & eme halls yᵉ xvᵗʰ day.

henry wylcoke & elzabeth essbroke yᵉ xxxᵗʰ

. . . . Septebris.

. . . . . fyld & agnes sylvestʳ

. . lyn & Iane seebroke yᵉ xxiij day.

. . octobris.

. . . . agnes Iayle wedowe yᵉ xviij day.

. . . . . . and elen coke yᵉ xxviij day.

. . novebris .

. . . . . and . . . Rodyahl yᵉ xiᵗ day.

The marriage entries are continued in the register which dates from 1598. In this we notice, instead of the modern descriptions, "bachelor" and "spinster," the terms "single man," "single woman," and "single persons." The occupation of the bridegroom is, as a rule, only given when it conveys the idea of a *status*, as, *e.g.*, farmer. About 85 per cent. of the weddings were after banns, and the remainder by licence, this latter proportion being rather higher than is usually the case in villages. Until 1764 there was no signing of the registers by the happy pair or by the witnesses to the ceremony, or even by the officiating minister. It sufficed to put on record the fact that such and such persons were married on such and such a date. In a few entries the vicar or clerk, not being quite certain on the point, omitted the surnames, but left spaces for them, which he unfortunately forgot to fill in afterwards.

There was far less intermarriage between the families in this parish than is usual in villages. Widows constituted about one-fourth of the total number of brides, while nearly the same proportion of the fair maidens of Dagenham were woo'd and wed by lovers who lived outside the parish—a fact which supports the tradition that the women here were extremely handsome, personable, and eligible.

During the seventeenth and eighteenth centuries the weddings averaged eleven per annum, the highest number being sixteen in 1635, and the lowest being *one* in 1648. One other point deserves mention, viz. that very few weddings took place during the season of Lent; for, taking one year with another, there is an entire absence of marriage entries between February 10 and April 24, the period which includes, with more or less margin, the forty days of Lent. The total number for two hundred years—1598–1798—is four only. From this period they are less rare, though by no means frequent.

A selection from the marriage entries is given—

Imprimis,—Iohn Smyth and Ione Cooper were maried the iiij[th] daie of maie, 1598.

Thomas Peachie widower of Styfford and margaret lytle of this p'ish, widowe, were maried the xxiith daie of maie, 1598.

Thomas Boxer Servaunt to Mr. Harvie of Marks in this p'ish and Katherin Wortley were maried the Second day of Iulie, 1598.

William Poole Singleman and ffrancis Stephens widow were maried the xvijth daie of September, 1598.

Thomas English and Alice Parish were married the iiijth Iune, 1599.

Bartholomew Tedden citizen & Taylour of London and Elizabeth Wood cytizen also of London were by a Lycence from the Archbishopp of Canterburie [1] married wth consent of theyr parentes the xth daie of Iune, 1599.

William Brewer and Ioane Prior were married the xvth daye of Iune, 1600.

Thomas Greentree and Iane Lewis were marryed the xixth of October, 1600.

Henry Cooke and Mary Courtney Single p'sons were marryed y[e] xxth of Aprille, 1601.

Thomas Woodburne, haberdasher of the Cyty of London and

---

[1] John Whitgift was archbishop 1583–1604.

Constance ffrancis, widowe, of the said Cytye were marryed xxvth daie of June, 1601, having a Lycence from my L. of Canterburye.

Edmund Walter widower & Agnes Nevill Singlewoman were marryed the first of ffebruarie, 1601.

Thomas Peachye singleman and Wynefred upney widow were maryed the vth of Aprill, 1602, having a lycence from Mr. Do^ter Stanhope.

Hannyball Horsey of Witchington in the countye of Warw^k gent & Alice Onyon daughter of James Onyon of the pishe of Whyte Chappell in the Countye of Midd. Brewer, were marryed the xxth of Aprill 1602, having a lycence from the Archbishopp of Canterburye.

Arthur Locker singleman & Agnes Peacock, Singlewoman were married the xxvth of maye, 1603.

John Neave singleman & Rose Howel widow were marryed by a lycence from my L. of Canterburie the xviith day of October, 1603.

Tymothy Pearson and Joane Clarcke single psons were married the xxvij of October, 1604.

Adam Edlin widower of Barkinge and Joane Silvestre widowe were marryed the xviijth of November, 1604.

Robet Spuce (or Spirce ?) of Wennington widower and Dorethye Campe widow were marryed the xxixth of November, 1604.

John Hayes of Alveley singleman and Elizabeth Osborne widow were marryed the 4th Daye of ffebruarie.

Julius Scott, Gen.[1] et margaret moore were married the 3th of March, 1605.

Stephen Warwick of Barking widdower and Marian Sigins of Dagenham singlewoeman were married the 5th of June, 1606.

Humfreye Cook of Orsett Widdower & Joane Brewer single woeman married the 2 of October, 1606.

George Berryman of Romfford singleman et Margarett Eden of Dagenham single woeman married October 7, 1606.

William Berryman of much Baddow singleman and Jane Dowsett, virgo, nupt. 30th Octob^r.

John ffrith of Rainham widdower & Agnes Humphrye of Dagenham, widow married the xth of Septem. 1607.

Robert Comins & Margery Humphrye both of Dagenham married ye same day (i.e. 3 Sep. 1607).

Thomas Wreight widdower & Edith Toller, wid. both of Dagenham married the second of november.

Edward ffoster & Elsabeth Spike both of Dagenhā single married Septims ffebruarij, 1607.

Thomas Potts, Esq. & Anna filia M^rl Mebwoke conjunct, 18 July, 1608.

---

[1] "Julius Scott holdeth one close called Huntings, with house and garth" (Barking Manor Survey, 1616).

Richard Nightingale of High Ongar, singleman & Elsabeth Rand, of Dagenham, single woeman, conjunct. 5 Novemb, 1608.

Hugh Emmerson of Epping singleman & Jane Hayward of Dagenham single woeman married 8th June 1609.

Edmund Kettle of Hadleigh, singleman & Marian Burdye of Dagenham singlewoeman married the 9th of November.

Thomas Sorrell of High Easton, singleman and Susan Truelove of dagenham, singlewoman married the 16th of Aprill, 1610.

William ffawboate and Joane Nutbrowne both of Dagenham single, married the ffirst of Julye.

William Commyns & Elizabeth Carter both single were marryed ye 17 February 1611.

Matthew Todgwell of London, singleman & Ann Commyns of Dagenham singlewoeman were marryed ye eodem.

Jefferey Lawlye & Agnes ffoster single were marryed ye 6 of Sept. 1612.

Thomas Cartwright & Jeane Miskin were marryed ye 29 of Aprill, 1613.

George Outred and Martha Palmer were marryed ye 3 of June.

Edward Osborne, Esq. & ffrancis Daughter of James Harvye Esq.[1] maryed 4th Decem. 1615.

Samuell Sumner Singleman & Margerye Humphrye singlewoeman married 14 of Novem. 1616.

John Bonner & Ann Radsdale were marryed ye 19 of June, 1617.

James Benson & Judith Kittcatt marryed ye 20 of Aprill, 1620.

William Haynesworth & Martha Mackam marryed ye 4 of Maye, 1620.

Robert pettingale S. & Johan Whitnye S. marryed ye 23 of Octob. 1621.

ffrancis Emes & Sindony Carleton, S. marryed ye 30 of June, 1622.

Benjamin Morris S. & Mary Pettit S. both of Hornchurch & servants unto Mar John Rogers of ye same, by licence frō Mar Archdeacon marryed ye 23th of Januarye, 1622.[2]

Richard Norris, of Romford and Mary Webster, of the same, by licence from the Archdeacon, Dec. 29, 1623.

Thomas Moore, of Barking, to Joane Sumners, of the same parish.

Adam Hill, wi. & Margaret Letton of Romford, wid. maryed ye 10 of ffebruarye, 1623.

Roger Thorneton, wid. Esq. & Ann Harvye sing. were marryed ye third of June, 1624.

Thomas Norris, w. & Sisely Kampton S. ye 30 of January, 1625.

William Geast clerk, S. & Ann Manninge Daughter of Tho. Manninge of Dagenham clerk, S. 8 of July 1627.

Anthony Gardner S. and Ann Carew, S. marr. ye 4 of Decem. 1628.

Abrahã plumpton S. & Joane pamplin S. marr. ye 5 of Novem. 1629.

Oliver Wharton, S. & Sarah Wingar S. marr. ye first of November, 1630.

---

[1] Of Wangey.   [2] George Goldman, Archdeacon of Essex, 1609-33.

Thomas Harburne, singlem. & Joane Preston, single were marryed y⁰ 3 day of Apprill, 1631.

Abraham Boundoewell singl. & Mary Clerke marryed ye 12ᵗʰ of Maye, 1633.

Thomas ffitch & Rebecca Barnaby, both singl. marayed ye 3th of Octobe, 1633.

Richard Cogden, wid. & Sisely Gladdin singl. marryed y⁰ 16th of June.

Thomas Audeley, wid. & Elsabeth Presberry, singl. marryed y⁰ 6th of Octob. 1834.

Thomas Bunnyan & Parnell Porter, marryed y⁰ 20 of Octob. 1636.

Matthew Wells & Elizabeth Elwort, sing. marryed y⁰ 18 of Novemb. 1636.

John Brasell & Ann Gadlinne, Sing. marryed y⁰ 24 of September, 1637.

Andrew Willmore & Ellen Weeden marryed Aprill 2th, 1638.

Thomas Gerzey & Ann Gamblinn marryed the 8th day of September, 1639.

1641.   June 14.   phillip Battisford & Elizabeth Griffin, maryed.

1641.   Oct. 9.   John Sawkyn & Elsabeth Butler, maryed.

John Stone and Ann Cradshaw marred november 5th, 1644.

Edward chetham of london & Elizabeth [space] singll. woman wear maried January xith, 1645.

During the Commonwealth there was a considerable falling off in the number of weddings in the parish. This was due chiefly to the unsettled nature of that dismal period, and also to the general dislike to the new form of marriage in the Public Directory, which had come into use by order of Parliament (1644–45). In this service holy matrimony was treated as no more than a solemn legal contract. The Puritans even went so far as to urge that marriages should not be performed on the Lord's day. Added to this, a layman was now substituted for the vicar or curate of the parish, and empowered to perform the marriage ceremony himself or depute some one else by certificate to do it for him. The legal official or registrar of marriages for this district was Justice Joachim Mathewes, who had been a devoted adherent of the Cromwellian cause.[1]

---

[1] Joachim Matthews lived at Great Gobions at Collier Row. He was appointed in 1654–56 a commissioner for the removal of "scandalous and insufficient ministers" in this part of Essex. His name is also in the list of ministers and elders (under Romford) appointed and approved by Parliament during the Presbyterian régime. During the Civil War he served as a colonel under General Fairfax. In 1651 he received the degree of D.C.L. honoris causâ, on the motion of Cromwell, who was then Chancellor of the University of Oxford. He sat as M.P. for Maldon from 1656 till his death in 1659. He was buried, at his own request, in a "decent manner in Rumford Church." His eldest son, Philip, was created a baronet in 1662, for the part he had taken in promoting the Restoration.

The entries at this period are as follows :—

Robert Greene Chelmsffood & Sarah Gosline wear maried the 9th of March, 1651.

Moses Sanders & ffrancis bellfould wear maried April 8th, 1651.

William Norris, ffarm & Jone Crosier yᵉ daughter of [space for name] were marryed by Justice Mathewes yᵉ 3th of ffebruarie, 1653.

Stephen Banburie of this p'ish husbandman and Sarah Gabings of Stapleford yᵉ daughter of William Gabins had their certificate to be married yᵉ 31 March, 1654.

John Pateson and an butcher both single maryed January the 3th, 1660.

Henry Samuell of this parish, widdower and Margaret Statham, widdow, were married the 30ᵗʰ day of June, 1661.

Thomas Daken & Elezbeth Osban marryed June 22, 1662.

Augustion Scott was maried unto Elizabath Gill the 13 of november, 1662.

John Carpenter & Margerye Mournenills was married December the 27ᵗʰ 1663.

John Choppin and Mary Marshbend married March 25, 1666.

Here the entries break off abruptly. They commence again in register No. 3, which has been missing since 1859. Copies had, fortunately, been made of them by Mr. E. J. Sage, which are here subjoined.

Andrew ffuller, singleman and Abigall Oures, widd. marryed March the 29, 1668.

Hunfry Tooker, Single man of London & Elizabeth Comyn, Single woeman, were maryed August yᵉ 13, 1668.

John Marlow, Single and Sarah Comins, Single, were maryed Februarie yᵉ 9, 1670.

Mr. Michaell Wells & Prudence White, August the 24th, 1676.

Edward Gillett & Sarah Petchey, married 7th January, 1676.

Miles Tyler and Dorothy Wilson were maryed in March yᵉ 7, 1677.

John Emerton and Susannah Cumins married Decembʳ ye 19, 1679.

John Choate & Hester Meade maryed Octobʳ yᵉ 7, 1680.

Michaell Thompson of London, Merchant and ffrances Jones of Valence, Dagenham, were maryed Aprill 18, 1682.

Edmond Fremont & Sarah Goare, Octobʳ yᵉ 5, 1682.

Here the entries break off till 1695, from which year till 1704 they are found in the "Book of Parish Accomptes" already referred to.

Peter Cooze Gent of yᵉ Parish of Dagenham & Ruth Levit of yᵉ same

Parish were married according to the Rights and usages of yᵉ Church of England upon the 12ᵗʰ of September, 1695.

Mr. John Emerson of yᵉ Parish of Dagenham and Mrs. Rebecca Hinley of yᵉ Parish of Stepney were married the 23 of July, 1696.[1]

Williā Downes & Mary Paris were married the 30 of September, 1696.

Richard Effield & Susanna Hoods were married yᵉ 5 of Novemb. 1696.

William Bridges & Jane Whalseby were married yᵉ 3ᵈ of Octob. 1697.

Thomas Godfrey of yᵉ Parish of Rumford & Joan Little of yᵉ Parish of Dagenham were married yᵉ 25 of Jan. 1697.

John Raidon and Mary Smyth married at Little Ilford by me Williā Lamplugh ; both of yᵉ parish of Dagenham upon yᵉ   of April 1698 by a Licence.

John Warren & Elizabeth Brewster were married 6 of June, 1698.

Michael Reeks of Barking & Ann Hawkkins of Dagenham were married yᵉ 29 of September, 1699.

John Slemaker & Mary Wilkingson were married the 18th of December, 1700.

John Armstrong & Sarah Eve were married yᵉ 21 of April 1701.

John Spatchurst & Mary Taylor were married 11ᵗʰ of August 1702.

Samuel Ramsden & Mary Weed marryed yᵉ 19 of October, 1703.

George Reeve & Jane Evens were married yᵉ 19 of Octob. 1704.

Thomas Jenkinson & Friswith [no name] marr. yᵉ 2ᵈ of Nov. 1704.

Edward Osbourn & Mary lamplugh married 170⁴⁄₅ the 10 ffebruary.

The marriage entries copied into the parish accounts book stop here, and we are referred to the now missing register, No. 3. The following are the entries preserved by Mr. Sage, not already given :—

Henry Osborn of this Parish & Mary Jury of Barking married February 2, 170²⁄₃.

Daniell Evens & Ann Willmore yᵉ 26 of January, 170³⁄₄.

John Combers & Mary Bruster, married by banns, yᵉ 25th of May, 1711.

Thomas Taylour & Mary Bruister of Hornchurch, married by Licence, December yᵉ 11, 1713.

Joseph Fosster of yᵉ Parish of Shadwell, London & Francis Porter of yᵉ Parish of Barking, married by Licence, January 1, 172⁰⁄₁.

Richard Turner & Elizabeth Samuell both of this Parish by banns, October 21, 1720.

The entries are here re-continued in duplicate as before, and are much more numerous. No details are given as to the *status* of those married—whether bachelor, spinster, etc. Over 50 per cent.

[1] John Emerson the elder was, in 1681, granted the administration to a cottage at Aberry Hatch (Barking Manor Court Rolls).

of the bridegrooms were non-parishioners.   In fourteen cases
neither of the parties lived in Dagenham parish.   The highest
record is seven in 1733, and the lowest is one in 1724 and 1743.
The following are selections :—

John Warren and Susanna Soalmes, 1730, April 2.

William Pitt, of St. Mary le Bone, London, and Elizabeth Burnaby of
Kensington, by licence, April 16, 1730.

Charles Coulson and Elizabeth Read, July 29, 1733.

John Rudwell and Avice Keyley, both of this parish, Aug. 7, 1733.

Francis Nevill of East Ham and Sarah Harris, of West Ham, Oct. 6,
1734.

Edmund Scott, of Barking and Grace Fryer of Romford, Oct. 7, 1737.

Benjamin Fuller, of St. Dunstan's, Stepney, and Hannah Stead of St.
Botolph's, Aldgate, by licence, May 19, 1740.

George Seabrook and Ann Raydon, both of Dagenham, Feb. 3, 1746.

Robert Bird, of Coventry, Esq. and Mary Merttins of this Parish,
March 26, 1747.

Henry Dines and Anne Ford, both of Dagenham,   1748.

John Burridge Leigh, Esq. of Rushall, Staffordshire and Olympia
Houghton, of St. Mary, Aldermanbury, London, by licence, June 6, 1751.

John Ferard, of the Liberty of the Tower of London, Bachelor and
Ann Pilon, of Christ Church, Middlesex, spinster, by licence, June 10,
1753.

The following note is appended :—

After this time the Marriage Act took place and every marriage
hereafter is registered in another book provided by the Parish.

Abraham Blackbourne, Vicar.

The Act referred to is Lord Hardwick's Marriage Act, which
was passed in 1753.   It prescribed a special form of the entry of
banns and of marriages, similar to that now in use, with the exception of the ages of the bridegroom and bride, and of the names and
occupation of the fathers of the married pair, which are now provided for in the printed forms.   The terms "batchelor" and
"spinster" now came into use, and the custom commenced of the
wedded couple signing their names, and of witnesses attesting by
their signatures their presence at the marriage.   The signing of
the register shows us that education in Dagenham was then in a
backward state, inasmuch as nearly one-third of those who
signed from 1750 to 1803 merely made their mark instead of their
full signature.   On the whole the weddings during the eighteenth
century were less numerous than those in the previous one ; the

average being eight per annum, the highest number, fifteen in 1767, and the lowest, three in 1755.

Bound up with this marriage register is a " Register Book for the Publication of Banns of Marriage, according to Act of Parliament of the Twenty-sixth (1753) of King George II. by Joseph Fox, Parish Clerk to the Honourable the House of Commons. Printed for Joseph Fox, Bookseller in Westminster Hall, and Benjamin Dod, Bookseller to the Society for promoting Christian Knowledge, at the Bible & Key in Ave-Mary Lane, near St. Paul's, MDCCLIV."

This banns book contains several interesting items. It would appear that Mr. Abraham Blackborne, vicar, himself published the various banns for six years without a break (1754–60). Also, that on Sunday, June 15, 1760, a certain " John Lambert stood up and openly before the church forbade the banns of his son John and Ann Dorington." A fortnight later, however, the irate father withdrew his opposition, and desired the minister to " proceed with the banns." A month afterwards, his son and daughter-in-law had the pleasure of seeing him attesting his presence at, and approval of, the marriage, by his mark.

On another page we are informed that certain banns were not published for two Sundays because " there was no service." This was in 1771. On June 14, 1793, the banns of marriage between John Milborn and Abigail Astridge were publicly forbidden by both parents. Unlike the former objector, the parents did not relent ; consequently the lovers were not married, at least not at Dagenham.

In 1764 another marriage register was procured by the vicar and churchwardens. It is described as, " A Register Book for Marriages in all Parish Churches & Chapels, Conformable to the Act of the Twenty-sixth of King George II. Intitled, An Act for the better preventing of Clandestine Marriages."

There is not much matter for comment in this register. Nearly all the marriages were after banns ; less than 10 per cent. by licence. An entry in 1764 says that a " Thomas Vinten married Sarah Ives, a minor, with consent of Mary Ives her naturall & lawfull mother." Another, that on " May 5, 1770, Joseph Baden Newdick, of the Parish of St. Michael's, Cornhill and Frances Tyler of this Parish " were married by licence. The bridegroom's Christian name is the first *double* one in this or any previous marriage register. The next one is in the entry of the marriage of Thomas Littel to Hester Britton Willey on August 30, 1773. Another one is that of Anne Wilhelmina Seabrook, married to William Whitchurch, June 29, 1780.   On July 25, 1782, "William Haws, Batchelor, of the Chapelry of Romford, was married to Elizabeth Waters, Spinster & a Minor by & with the consent of Samuel Waters and Thomas Graves, her lawfull Guardians."   Here and there is inserted the marginal note, "Settled with the tax collector," referring to the tax on marriages, bachelors, and widowers.

CHAPTER XIV

THE PARISH REGISTERS (BURIALS)

"The annals of the human race,
    Their ruins since the world began,
Of him afford no other trace
    Than this—there lived a man!"

MONTGOMERY.

THE entries in the register of "Buryalls" are interesting, and afford much information concerning the history of the parish. They are far more numerous than the baptisms, which is accounted for by the fact that many Londoners lie buried in the churchyard. Here and there the cause of death is stated, from which it would seem that small-pox and ague, the products of the undrained marshes, were the most prevalent fatal diseases ; also that the former scourge counted far more victims among females than among males. The "plague" years were 1603, 1625, 1645, 1665, and 1666, when the rate of mortality was nearly trebled.[1] It is worthy of note that the suicides for the period of one hundred and fifty years (1598–1747) number six only—a commendable paucity which was doubtless due to the strong feeling of abhorrence with which our forefathers rightly regarded the act of self-murder. Nothing is said as to *where* suicides were interred, whether on the north side of the churchyard, which was the usual custom, or elsewhere.[2] Judging from appearances, the north side of Dagenham churchyard was *not* thus used, inasmuch as a large percentage of the most respectable

---

[1] The aggregate number of burials at Barking during those years of terrible fatality was 1119, giving an average of 224 deaths a year. The population could not have then been more than 3000. Possibly some of these deaths took place in Dagenham.

[2] Thus in the register of Little Clacton—"Prudence ffew, now the wife of Clem^nt ffew and late the wife of Nicholas lambert was buried out of the compas of Christian buryall in ye furthest syde of the churchyard northwards uppon the 17th daye of August 1592 for that shee most accursedlie hanged herself." The north side of the churchyard was objected to as being that part on which the sun never shone, and as the reputed abode of evil spirits.

inhabitants of the parish were interred on that side.   No ages are given, though here and there we are told that the "buryall" was that of an "infant" or "child," or "old man," etc.   Very few of the better class (yeomen and tradesmen) lived to see their "three score and ten."   Funerals took place on any day of the week, with the probable exception of *Thursday*, which we find sometimes mentioned whenever there was an interment on that day.   From a few entries in the parish register, it would seem that the Burial Office was sometimes read some days after the actual interment had taken place, which may be explained by the absence or illness of the minister at the time.   The "nurse" children of Londoners constitute a rather large class.   Eight entries refer to persons who died of the plague in 1644 and 1666.   We find no mention of the burial of "chrysom" children, although they are referred to occasionally in the Barking register, *e.g.* "A chrysom child of Andreu ffuller of Little Heath buryed the 21 of December, 1591." [1]

The following entries, taken from the Barking register, refer to persons belonging to Dagenham and Chadwell :—

Elizabeth, daughter of Iohn Green of Chawdwell buryed the 19th of Iuly, 1571.

Iohn the son of William Wells not baptized buryed the 13 Sept. 1571.

A poore man who dyed in Chawdwell ward buried the 14 October, 1576.

Isabell daughter of One Thomas Allen a Travailer out of the Grene Lane buried the 3 of ffeb. 1593.

Michael Grigson out of the Greene Lane buryed 7 Iulye, 1596.

These entries bring us to the time when the Dagenham register of burials begins, from which a selection is appended—

William Stevens was Buried the xxix[th] of march, 1598.

Rebecca the daughter of Peter Pindre of Ratcliffe beinge nursed at Owin Waithers (?) of marshe ffoote buried the xxvij[th] of Aprill.

Alice the Wife of Richard Witham was buried the first day of Maic.

Alice the daughter of Iohn Waddisworth, Clerk was buried the xxvij[th] of Iune 1598.

Seth Basingbourne the sonne of Mr. Basingbourne, corinner dwellinge

---

[1] A "chrysom," or chrisom, child was so called because it was wrapped in a white vesture anointed with chrism-oil at the time of its baptism.   It retained this name for one month after its christening, and was usually shrouded in its chrisom-robe if it died within that period.

in St. Lawrence lane in London nursed at Thomas Skinners was buried the xx[th] daye of Iulie.

Thomas the sonne of Steven Taylour cytyzen and letherseller dwellinge in the P'ishe of St. Marie Wolner within Lombard Street in the cytye of London was buryed the viij[th] daye of october, 1598.

Agnes the daughter of Mr. Lawrence Pike was buryed the xij[th] of december.

Andrew the sonne of Thomas Moore, gent. was buried the xxv[th] daie of Iune, 1599.

Pretiza the daughter of Richard Hill, cytizen and Ironmonger of London was buried the iiij[th] daie of Iulie, 1599.

Anne Culverhowsse the wife of Gyles Culverhowsse buryed the 5th of Aprill, 1600.

Iohn the sonne of Iohn Parke dwellinge in Castle Allie beinge nursed at Ieffraye Huggssons was buried the vij[th] of Aprill, 1600.

Ioice the daughter of Albone Coxe was buried the vi[th] of August.

Elizabeth the daughter of xxofer (*i.e.* Christopher) Jackson buried the xth Aprill, 1601.

Ioseph the sonn of Peter Balden of Bshopgate in London nurse childe of Widowe Skinner buried the vii of Aprill.

Rachell the daughter of Richard White cytyzen of London buryed the xvij[th] of Maie, 1601.

Anthony a nurse childe of w[m] woodcocks of this p'ish was buryed the first Daye of October, 1601.

Christylin the wife of Peter Smyth buried the xxi[th] of October, 1601.

W[m] Lake the elder was buryed the xxvi[th] of ffebruarie.

Annie Snoakes of the p'ish of Eastham and her lytle infant were buryed the 5th of Julie, 1602.

Mrs. Mary Morgan the Lady Stundley's gentlewoman buryed the vij[th] of August, 1603.

Henry osborne the yonger was buryed the xth daye of ffebruarie, 1603.

A wandring youth depted at Sir Nicholas Cootes[1] buryed the xv[th] daie of ffeb.

Sarah daughter to James Harvye Esquier[2] sepult, Dec. 12, 1605.

Frances, maide-servant to John Cooke, Esquire, was buryed 8th of September, 1606.

Thomas, master servant to Paul Pearson, buryed 25th February 1607.

Mr. William Harvye, Gent. buryed y[e] 9th March 1610.

Annie, wife of William Griffin, of Hornchurch, buried April 27th 1610.

Anna, daughter of Thomas Grove, of London, joiner, 25th May, 1610.

Alice, daughter of Guye Woode, of London, Cooper, buried 17th June, 1610.

[1] Of Valence.
[2] Of Wangey ; she was one of seventeen children.

William, sonn of ffrancis Capper of London, Skinner, buryed September 1, 1610.

Agnes, daughter of James Stubbs of Bednal Greene, buried 11th September, 1612.

John, sonn of Adam Bowles, of Westminster, buried 22nd of Aprill, 1615.[1]

Francisca-Katharina, daughter of James Pike, buried 19th September, 1615.

John sonne of Edward Agate of London buryed ye 31th of Decemb.

Ann Tiptapp buryed ye 20 of Januarye.

1616. Andrye Cuttford buryed ye 3 of Marche.

John Collopp Buryed ye 13 of March.

Katherine weife of Thomas Siggins Buryed ye 20 of March.

1617. Ann weife of Thomas ffoxe Buryed ye 27 of ffebruarye.[2]

Joane ye weife of Thomas Manninge, Vicar, Buryed ye sixe and Twentieth daye of Januarye, 1618.

Jeames Benson one yt was drowned at ye marsh worke Buryed 9 of Decemb.

Agnes Pearson daughter in law to John Birde Buryed ye 19 of January.

Jeames sonne of Edward Jackson Gent Buryed ye 9 of Decemb.

1622. Christopher sonne of Sr ffrancis Needā Buryed ye 17 of Decemb. 1624.

An old man from ye new howse in ye fforest ye 19 of Aug. 1625.

A man from Mar ffoxes ye 12 of Sept.

A poore woeman yt dyed at Richard Poole's buryed ye 11 of ffebruary, 1626.

Mar Jeames Hervy Esq. Buryed ye 3 of Aprill, 1627.[3]

Daughter of Aderin Vanderbiste Buryed ye 10 of Novber.

1636. Mary A Nursling in Cutmores house Buryed ye 28 of May.

The Widd Starbrooke Buryed ye 23th of Julye 1636.

Richard servante of Thomas Wittam Buryed ye 8 of Septem.

ffountaine sonne of William Coulstone buried November 11, 1637.

Mary servante to the Wido Nash buried January 17th.

John a yorkshire man wass buried October 27th 1638.

(Ye) servante of Tho. Newport buryed ye 17 of July, 1640.

Esster daughter of Jo : Meller of london buried februarie 26.

dority wyfe of Rich. Gull, July 28, 1643.

Will sonne of will douty buried of the plague Octob. 2, 1644.

Three more entries of a similar kind.

John sonne of Tho Charuell that was killed with a plow at mr. whites buried March the 6th 1644.

[1] There were forty burials in 1615, and forty-one in 1616, the highest numbers during the seventeenth century.

[2] A marginal note says that her gravestone lies in the chancel, before the communion table (a black stone). This note is in Mr. Manninge's handwriting.

[3] " His monument in the corner of ye vestry " (marginal note).

Simon Sturgine of north hamtone 1 of maye.

Mary daughter of one Marke of londone, May 2th, 1646.

Ann the wyffe of John Starkiss eodem die.[1]

Mr. Dennham Mrs. Hungat's father buried August 3th.

Mary daughter of Mr. Roger Morice, august 8, 1647.

Mrs. burges of london was buried august 17th.

Elizabeth wyfe of John Pricklove October 6th.

Izhak sonne of Mr. abraham ballard febr. 23th.

Noah, son of Mr. John bowyer, minister, buried Novr. 24, 1647.

hoope & charity twinns of Tho turner, buryed Feb. 23th, 1647.

A nurse child from Chadwell Heath, Aug. 3, 1648.

Anthony Pearce and his wife were buryed in one grave, November 9, 1648.

A poore woeman from goodman Garrod, bur. Dec. 19, 1648.

John Higens that hanged himself, March 10, 1649.

Mr. Hunting More, buried April 4, 1650.[2]

John wright son-in-law to Matthew Speller, on the same day.

Richard Gyver, clerk of the parish, Sept. 26, 1652.

Anne the wife of Jonathan Lloyd, minister of Dagenham was buried Dec. 5, 1652.

Richard Hills of Bentree Heath, Feb. 16, 1653.

John Foster, farmer, Dec. 8, 1653.

Thomas Platt, a butcher of Chadwell Heath buried a wife and child March 23, 1653.

A mayd of Hornchurch, Dec. 30, 1653.

The wife of Steven Dore buried August 15, 1657.

Goodman fflood of Ripple side, buried April 6, 1658.

The mother of Goodman ffrignall of Southend buried Sept. 21, 1658.

Goody Wright buryed ffeb. 18th.

The wife & child of John Walker of the wood were buried Jan. 31, 1660.

George Southerne, buried Nov. 28, 1663, being a Thursday.

A poore man brought with a cart from George Joyner's was buried Nov. 28, 1663, being a Thursday.

John Ranlison a butcher was buried Nov. 14, 1664.

Dec. 15, 1664. An infant of Edward Games unbaptized was buried a male child.

Dec. 27. Simon a journyman shoemaker of Henry Osburne's burried.

Jan. 19, 1664. John Pe ry of Cattswick a stranger and labourer buried.

---

[1] *i.e.* on the same day.

[2] In his will he bequeaths his house and land in Orsett to his brother Samuel, with reversion, failing issue of said brother, to Richard Broome his nephew. He also bequeaths him his houses and lands in Dagenham. To the poor of Dagenham he leaves 40*s*., and to Messrs. Thos. Aylett, John White, and Stephen Porter 20*s*. each for a mourning ring. Proved January 26, 1651.

Richard, son of Richard Bartholomew, Tuler's son-in-law, Feb. 20, 1664.

Ould Mr. Robert Comyns, June 24, 1665, memoria justi beata.

Elizabeth Savage, a wayfaring woeman at Valentine's buried August 12, 1665.[1]

The wife of John Chopping of yᵉ plague, buried Sept. 1, 1665.

A poore wench from East Hall buried Dec. ye 1th, 1665.

Mrs. Elborough, Mrs. Elliston's mother, July 4, 1666.

Rebecca daughter of William Walker, goldsmyth of London, July 24, 1666.

William Peacock's kinswoeman burried Octob. 3.

The wife of Meekin the smyth of Chardwell in Barking-parish, buryed Oct. 13, 1666.

Mary, daughter of Peter Mayburn the younger, bur. March 3, 1666.

Katherine a wayfaring woeman, wife to a sayler out by passe buried March 9, 1666.

Old ffrancis Cuttman, buried March 17.

Mary Comyn, daughter of John Comyn, Gent. buried, June 16, 1667.

Mrs. Uphill, buried, July 7, 1667.

The entries conclude here and are continued from Mr. Sage's transcript of the contents of Register No. 3.

Aprill 3th, 1668. Thomas Wittham buried. Vir sobrius ac bonae famae.

Robert Greene, servaunt to John Fanshaw, Esq. was buryed Aprill yᵉ 22.

Timothye Crowe yᵉ Taylour, May yᵉ 4, 1668.

Frances Daughter of Mr. John Blythman of Chappell Henolt bury'd August ye 4th.

John, sonn of Jeames Harvey, Esq. bury'd Oct. 4, 1668.

Thomas Harvye bury'd Octobʳ ye 5th, 1668.

Bathsheba, Daughter of Mr. John Blytheman of Chappell Henalt, buryed yᵉ 3th off Novemʳ.

John eldest sone of Mr. John Comins, Decembʳ yᵉ 23, 1668.

William Elliston, gent. was buriedd March yᵉ 24 he died 22 daye of Marche.

Sarah wyfe of Mr. John Comyns bury'd July yᵉ 23, 1669.

John yᵉ sonn of Walke in yᵉ truth Ayliff burried Octobʳ yᵉ 4th, 1669.

Jame sonn of Mr. Thomas Wittham deceased buried February 28, 1670.

Margery Commyns, Widdow, Februarie yᵉ 24th 1670.

Thomas Trueloue, Gent. Marche yᵉ 3.

—— daughter of Mr. Upphill of Barking Parrish bury'd May yᵉ 6, 1670.

[1] The Essex way of writing Valentine House; so, *e.g.* Dagnam's for Dagnam House, Rochett's for Rochett House.

William sonn of Willm Mayer buryed July 23, 1670, aetatis 7 yeares allmost.

> As carefull nurses in there cradles lay
> those babes which would too longe wanton play,
> So nature his nurse for to prevent his sins in living crimes
> hath laid him in his bed of dust betimes.

Thomas Sidgwick, Septemb. 2.

John sonn of John Jolley, Octob^r 6.

Ann daught^r of Mr. Harvey, Esq., Novemb^r 8.

The Widdow of Goodman Harvey Dec. 3, 1671.

Robert Harvey was burried February 6.

Jeames Sedgwick, February 26.

James Wittam, Gent. Aprill ye 20th.

Mary wife of Nathaniell Wright of ye fforest.

Nathaniell Wright, Decemb. ye 30th, 1671.

Mark Cooze, bury'd March 11, 1672.

A Major Deringham from Mr. Harvies was bury'd Januarie ye 21th, 1672.

Mrs. Whittcombe, widdowe, May ye 1.

Ann, wife of Jeames Harvey, Esq., June ye 12, 1672.

Judith Daughter of Mr. Bonham eodem die.

Job Allibon, Gentellman was buryed July ye 12, 1672.[1]

A sone of Mr. Blitheman, Octob^r ye 6.

Elzabeth daughter of Mr. Blithman buried Decemb^r 6, 1672.

A nurse from Mr. Blithman, Decemb^r ye 15.

Willm sone of Willyam Eaton, Decemb^r ye 9, 1673

John White, Senr gent. whoe hathe given to the Poor viz. 7 poor widdowes twoe pence per week in bread for ever, Februarie ye 2th, 1673.

Elizabeth careless servaunt to Mrs. Allibond, widdowe, burried March y^e 12, 1673.

Sarah weife of Thomas Berry y^e 18 of June, 1674.

William Mayers, Clerk of this Place foure yeares died at Stoke, June 23, 1674.

Henery sonn of Thomas Bonham, Esq. buryed August 14, 1674 whose burial not paid yet.

Mary y^e wife of Richard Uphill buryed y^e 5th of Febru. 167$\frac{4}{5}$.

Jane Daughter of Samuele More,[2] May y^e 30, 1675.

Thomas Bonham, Esquier was buryed May 18, 1676.

Widdow Botler buryed y^e 28 March, 1677.

An abortive of John Crampins Septemb^r y^e 9.

Mrs. Christian Ellistone, Decemb^r 17, 1677.

Mr. Homfroy Allabon was buryed Decemb^r y^e 31, 1678.

---

[1] Father of the judge.

[2] " Samuel More, gent. holdeth 21 acres of land at Dagenham called ' Colliers ' & at Eastbrook End & Dagenham Marsh " (Barking Manor Rent Roll, 1663).

James Harvey, Gent. Januarie y° 21, 1678.

Mrs. Ann Bonham, Widd. Octob' 29.

Ann y° Daughter of Thomas Bonham, buryed y° 28 of Decemb' 1678.

John y° sone of Richerd Uphill of Barkin was burried Septemb' 18, 1679.

William the sonn of Mr. Thomas Bonham January y° 9.

Jeane y° weife of Willm Eaton Sen' bury'd y° 18 of February, 1679.

Thomasin daughter of Peter Tyler, March y° 25, 1680.

Thomas Jolley, Gent. Febru. 4, 1681.

Robert Comings was buried Sep' y° 27.

John the sonn of John Hammond, March y° 10, 1682.

Rebeccah Daughter of Mrs. Elizabeth Commyns Widdowe, buryed y° 14 of May 1682. Affidavit certified by Justice Mildmay [1] 17 of May.

Robert Hungate, gent. burried Jan. 15.

Alice the Daughter of Mr. Pickitt of lobbard (Lombard?) street, jeweller, July y° 7.

Elioner Upphill buryed, affidavit certified by Mr. Peck [2] of Rumford, 7 of Februarie 1682.

Charles Collett, June y° 9, 1683.

John Bruster, 16 Aprill, 1684

There are no further entries till 1695.

The "affidavits" refer to an Act called the Woollen Act, which was passed in 1678, reaffirming with penalties an ineffective one of 1666. The purpose of this Act was to aid a struggling home industry. It ordered that—

For the encouragement of the woollen manufacturers and preventing of the exportation of money for the importing of linen, no corpse shall be buried but in woollen, after the first of August & not in any shirt, sheet, shift or shroud or anything soever made or mingled with flax, hemp, hair, gold or silver or any stuff or thing other than what is made of sheep wool only, under a penalty of five pounds.

A register was to be kept in every parish of all burials there, and an affidavit made within eight days after each burial that the corpse was buried in woollen. It was directed that the Act should be publicly read in church upon the first Sunday after St. Bartholomew's Day every year for seven years next following. At the conclusion of the Burial Service it was customary for the parish clerk to call out, "Who makes the affidavit?" when the nearest relative to the deceased came forward and took the necessary oath, which was duly noted in the register.

[1] Of Marks. [2] Curate of Romford.

The Woollen Act was a drastic, if somewhat gruesome piece
of legislation, and notwithstanding its design, was very unpopular.[1]
Those who did not like it, and could afford to do so, ignored it and
paid the penalty of their disobedience ; others again tried to evade
it by burying their dead in unconsecrated ground, an evasion which
the law would not overlook. Thus in the burial register of Little
Clacton is the entry—"Buryed Timothy Nooth's wife in his garden
but not according to Law. A certificate given & a warrant taken
to distrayne him for the 5ˡⁱ March 8, 1689." On the next page is
this note—" Mem. Tim. Nooth buryed his wife contrary to the Act
of Parliament & he payd the Five Pounds accg to the sd Act of
Parlⁿᵗ burying in woollin and twas disposed of according to law,
Aprill 10, 1690." All such fines were handed to the overseers and
appeared in their accounts, consequently it was their business from
time to time to inspect the certificates and affidavits which were
brought to the officiating minister by those who had charge of the
various funerals. There are references in the parish book to the
"settlements with the tax-collector." The references to the affidavits are, however, few in number, and it seems probable that they
were carefully noted in a special book which is also missing. The
Woollen Act was repealed in 1814, but long before that time it
had become a dead [2] letter.

The following selections are taken from the list copied in the
parish book—

Sarah daughter of Jona: Hawthorn was buried yᵉ 21 of July 1695.
Margaret wife of John Prentice was buried yᵉ 15 of November 1695.
John son of John Chams junʳ was buried yᵉ 24 of November 1695.
1696. A child of Thomas Stapler of yᵉ parish of Barking wᶜʰ dyed
unbaptized was buried yᵉ 8 of May, 1696.
Mary Belsham lately yᵉ wife of Francis Belsham was buried yᵉ 14 of
August, 1696.
Francis Belsham lately yᵉ housband of yᵉ aforesaid Mary was buried yᵉ
15 of August 1696.
Mr. John Marlow of London in yᵉ Parish of Sᵗ Lawrence Jury was buried
yᵉ 24 of October 1696.[3]

[1] See Pope's lines—

" Odious ! in woollen ! 'twould a saint provoke,
Were the last words that poor Narcessa spoke."
(Mrs. Ann Oldfield, an actress, 1730.)

[2] The custom of shrouding the dead in woollen still survives in some parts of the
country, *e.g.* Gloucestershire. A woman once alleged to me as a reason for it, that it was
not only proper and decent to do this, but that "it helped to keep the body warm."
[3] See his will in Appendix B.

Abigail daughter of mr. John Colcot was buried y⁰ 23 of April 1697.

Edward Foster a Strainger was buried y⁰ 10 of July 1698.

William son of Michael Marloe of stepney was buried y⁰ 12 of July 1698.

Mr. Oliver Buteler of Barking was buried ye 5 of September 1698.

Thomas Rogers, yeoman, buried June 8 (1699).

John Fanshaw, Gent. buried at Barking y⁰ 22 of December 1699.

Mr. John Newcome of St. Lawrence Parish, London, buried y⁰ 13 of March 1699.[1]

Edward Soames was buried at Sandon in Essex 1ˢᵗ of March, 1700.

1701. June 5. Willᵐ Housden, Labourer, buried.

George son of Wᵐ Kilpatrick a strainger yᵗ came by a loss, buried 31 of August 1701.

Elizabeth wife of Mr. Robert Hamon, joiner of Hornchurch buried y⁰ 9 of October 1701.

Ann Gun a travilling woman buried 4 Novemb. 1701.

Mr. Thomas Hungate buried y⁰ 16 of February, 1701.

1702. May 22. Mr. Robᵗ Hammond of Raynham.

July y⁰ 1ˢᵗ buried Thomas Carp of Whitechapel a child.

Sarah late wife of Richard Dyer of y⁰ Parish of Sᵗ Ann Blackfryers in y⁰ city of London was buried y⁰ 18 of August, 1702.

Thomas Slinnger who died in Hornchurch was buried ye 22 of January.

Dame Barbara widow to Sʳ Richard Alibon, Knight, buried y⁰ 22 of June 1703.

Frances Cramphor buried 3 Novem. 1704.

The entries terminate here, and only commence again in the "new burial register" of 1722. The interval is, fortunately, bridged over by Mr. Sage's transcription from Register No. 3, which contains the following entries—

Mary Benton buryed 2 of February, 1705.

George sone of Mr. ffrancis Eaton & Ann his wife of y⁰ Parish of Raynham, February 22 170⅞.

ffreckleton son of y⁰ Above, Feb. 29, 170⅞.

Mr. James Smyth, buried July y⁰ 12, 1707.

Peter sone of Peter Cooes August 20.

John Tiler of Hornchurch p'ish, buryed y⁰ 15 of Septembʳ 1709.

Rebekoh Eaton of Raynham, Novembʳ 30.

Elizabeth Merttins, Decembʳ 4, 1710.

Dorothy Eaton was burried Feb. 1, 1711.

Penelope Eaton, March 17, 1711.

Bartholomew Hungate, March 22, 1711.

George Eaton, April 14, 1711.

John Eaton of Raynham, 18 of June 1712.

[1] Referred to, probably, in the will on previous page.

James Nodes, ffebruary 26, 1713.

Richard Eaton, June 5, 1714.

Susannah Daughter of Mr. Robert Austen, y 7 of Novemb 1716.

A Daught' of Mr. Willm Eaton, April y° 8.

Sarah Daughter of Dame Loveday, June 21.

Alexander sone of Mr. Bennet in London was burried y° 30 of August 1717.

Elizabeth Hammond from London, Septemb' 2, 1718.

Penelope the wife of Mr. Will™ Eaton (aged 46) y° 25 of June, 1719.

Mary Eaton, Octob' 9, 1719.

Mrs. Woolaston, Octob' 10, 1719.

Mr. Eve one of y° Society of Rumford buryed y° 18 Octob' 1719, a sermon.

Mrs. Wilson wife to y° Presbyterian Minister buryed y° 18 Octob' 1719.

Mr. Ward of Dagenham.

Mrs. Stuart of y° Towne, March y° 18, 17$\frac{10}{20}$.

John sonn of George & Rebecca Harvey y° 29 of March, 1720.

Mary Daughter of Charles Stuart, infant, y° 11 of Aprill, 1720.

Charles sonn of Charles & Elzabeth Stuart, y° 25 of Aprill, 1720.

Mr. Stock from Rippleside, May 8, 1720.

Mrs. Watts from Mr. William Eatons, June 8, 1720.

Mrs. Walker of the Towne, 17 of July, 1720.

Mr. Baker from y° fforest, June 20, 1721.

Mrs. Clarke from Rippleside, y° 18 of July, 1721.

Mr. Hand from Chadwell Heath, y° 18 of August 1721.

Mrs. Lamb from Mrs. Waters, y° 11 Decemb', 1721.

Mr. Lincoln buried Decemb' 30.

John Bruister, infant January 22, 1722.

Mrs. French, March 13, 1722.

A child of Mrs. Peal, 16 of Aprill, 1722.

Robert Eyles, June y° 29, 1722.

Mrs. Hall from Chadwell Heath, June ye 27 or 29 1722.

Mrs. Bedle, Januarie 10, 172$\frac{2}{3}$.

John Crawforde, y° 10 of March 1722.

We now come to the register for burials, 1723. This is more methodically arranged. Sometimes the ages are given, or we are informed that such and such persons were infants, youths, girls, etc. Those who were buried at the charge of the parish have the initials P. P., *i.e.* parish pauper, appended to the entry. The fatal months of the year were January, March, April, and May, during which three-fourths of the funerals of the whole year took place. The yearly average from 1723 to 1773 was 47 ; the highest number in any one year being 73 in 1729 (one-twentieth of the then population of the

parish), and the lowest, 21 in 1773. The mortality among children
under the age of seven was very high, comprising half the total
number of burials (in 1723 it exceeded even this abnormal proportion). Between 1754 and 1760 a large number of children were
interred in Dagenham churchyard from the Foundling Hospital,
London. Three, four, and sometimes even five were buried on one
day. The record was made in 1757, when the bodies of forty-four
foundlings were laid to rest here. In this respect the churchyard
was used as a sort of "akeldama"—not in the primary sense of
having been bought with the price of blood, but as a "field to bury
strangers in." These foundlings were, as a rule, illegitimate children
sent from London to be boarded or farmed in the various cottages in
the villages round the metropolis, and were not too kindly treated
by their foster-parents. In the large number of them we have sad
evidence of the deplorable state of morals that prevailed in this
country during the eighteenth century. The Christian names of the
foundlings were of a classical character, e.g. Polydore, Cassandra,
Penelope, Rosamund, in curious and significant contrast to the
scriptural names found elsewhere.

The frequent occurrence of "a Sermon" or (S.) in the register
shows how common and cheap funeral sermons had become in the
eighteenth century. They averaged six a year, the highest number
being fourteen in 1729. The preaching of such sermons was advantageous to the minister, as he probably received some reward for
his pains, and also because he could make one or two of his old
sermons appropriate to the "solemn occasion." But it must have
been disadvantageous to his flock in that it deprived them of being
properly instructed in the doctrines and duties suggested for their
consideration during the Church's year.

The following is a selected list of names in this register :—

Captain John Moon (S.) August ye 19th 1723.
William Raynolds ye Clark (a Sermon) buried Aprill 1st 1724.
Thomas Palmy from ye Breach, buried ye April 12, 1724.
Edward Whistons, Schoolmaster, a Sermon, buryed ye 27th of August,
1724.
Mr. Christopher Tyler, a Sermon, buried ye 19 of March, 1724.
Mrs. Susannah Uphill, buried ye 24 Jan. 1724.
George Mildmay buried Dec. ye 11 1725.
Mrs. Foster (S.) buried ye 31 May, 1726.
John Samuel (S.) buried ye 16 March, 1728.
James Belciom (S.) buryed March ye 25, 1730.

Mr. Thomas Eve (S.) buried y⁰ 3 Feb. 1732.

Jonathan Belsham, Clerk, buried June y⁰ 4th, 1731.

Mrs. Clarke, from y⁰ Sheepe Cote, Dec. y⁰ 19, 1733.

Mr. Grace, Schoolmaster, buried y⁰ 1 August, 1736.

An Irish reaper, buried y⁰ 20 August, 1741.

Rebecca Barnard aged 94, buried y⁰ 27 June 1742.

A stranger found dead in y⁰ high road by virtue of an order from Brown Combers coroner, Oct. 11th 1742.

Mr. Thomas Whittham, buried from London, y⁰ 23 Dec. 1743.

Mrs. Dorothy Radcliffe, from James Street, Westminster, buried y⁰ 17 January, 1743.

Samuel Simpson and William Hitchin, both from Feeton's buried y⁰ 2th of May, 1744.

Mrs. Abigail Turner from great Ilford, buried y⁰ 18th April, 1745.

John & Elizabeth Blackwell, both from London, buried March y⁰ 15, 1745.

Capt. John Comyns buried y⁰ 20 March, 1745.

Ann Green & William her son, buried in one coffin, April 1, 1746.

Mrs. Eaton from Rainham parish, June 6, 1747.

Mrs. Forty, from Padnall Corner, buried Nov. 11, 1747.

Joseph Rawker from the Forest buried Dec. 4, 1747.

Mr. Thomas Beal (from Rumford) buried in the church, Aug. 8, 1749. A Sermon.

Thomas Robinson from Chadwell Heath, March 12, 1749.

Mrs. Elizabeth Merttins in their vault, Nov. 8, 1749.

John Bodkin drowned by accident, buried, July 8, 1751.

A traveling woman's female child died in its mother's arms in the towne, buried April 13, 1751.

A stranger found dead on Bentry Heath buried by y⁰ Coroner's warrant, May 13, 1751.

George Joyner who hanged himself, being deem'd a lunatic by Coroner's inquest, Dec. 18, 1752.

Edward Jenner, the parish clerk, buried March 13, 1755.

Samuel Fenn & Thomas Pratt, strangers from Mark's Gate.

Mrs. Sarah Cantrell of Coleman Street, London, Feb. 27, 1757.

Mrs. Dorothy Comyns from Sion College, London, buried March 17, 1757.

Mrs. Rebecca Mildmay, in the Vicar's chancel, March 21, 1757.

Thomas Fanshawe, of Parslows, Esq. died Aug. 21, 1758 and lyes buried in Barking Church.

George Whitby & Elizabeth his daughter, buried in one coffin, Sept. 16, 1758.

The burials from the Foundling Hospital this year were twenty-six.

Robert Banton from Mark's Gate buried July 12, 1759.

Alexander Bennet, Esq. from London, Oct. 6, 1759.

Mrs. Mary White from East Ham buried in yᵉ Vicar's chancel, Oct. 14, 1759.

Willᵐ Robinson, farmer (vir honestus) Dec. 7, 1759.

From the Foundling Hospital, sixteen burials this year.

John Potter, a farmer, buried June 25, 1760.

Mr. Willᵐ Johnson, from St. George's, Queen's Square, London, buried Nov. 12, 1760.

Mary Wood, yᵉ Tanner's wife, buried Dec. 7, 1760.

Jeremiah Young, killed at Ilford Bridge, Sept. 11, 1761.

Mrs. Hannah Witham, from High Ongar, Dec. 28, 1761.

Esther Star from Brentwood Weeld, buried Aug. 10, 1762.

John Allice, from St. George's in the East, Dec. 30, 1762.

Mary Mack Longhlin (a soldier's wife) & her infant daughter, P.P., buried Oct. 28, 1762, by virtue of yᵉ Coroner's warrant, they being killed by the baggage wagon on their march.

John Harwood & his infant son John, died of small-pox and were buried in the same coffin, March 10, 1763.

Isabella Flowers, daughter of the late Capt. Comyns, buried April 12, 1763.[1]

Mr. Henry Spence, from Hoxton, London, buried in Dagenham Church, Jan. 12, 1765.

John Lang, a Scotsman, buried Oct. 2, 1768.

Mrs. Sarah Spence, buried in yᵉ church, Dec 19, 1768.

Robert Collet, from Mr. Sumpner's, buried Nov. 1, 1769.

Mr. George Goffe, from Rippleside, buried Nov. 6, 1769.

Mrs. Sarah Ingrave, from London, buried Nov. 30, 1769.

Mrs. Frances, wife of Peter Pilon in the vault from London, buried Oct. 12, 1770.

Andrew Palmer, from Chadwell Heath, Oct. 28, 1770.

Mrs. Elizabeth Leech, Schoolmistress, aged 70, buried Dec. 16, 1770.

Stephen Champ, a Tanner, of small-pox, buried April 23, 1772.

Eleven burials from small-pox this year, out of a total of thirty-five.

Mrs. Elizabeth Ripley, from Little Heath in Barking Parish, buried May 5, 1772.

Thomas Creswell (a Sermon) buried Feb. 16, 1773.

Four burials from London out of a total of twenty-one.

John Robinson, from Chadwell Heath, Feb. 25, 1774.

Seven burials from small-pox this year.

---

[1] Out of fifty-four burials this year, ten were from small-pox.

Hannah Meredith, from Hog-hill house, Oct. 14, 1776.

Mary Dossiter, from the White Horse, Chadwell Heath buried March 20, 1777.

Thomas Starr from Bentry Heath, March 30, 1777.

Robert Butterfield, killed on the High Road and buried by Coroner's warrant, April 7, 1777.

Thomas Elmore, from St. George's, Hanover Square, buried Jan. 4, 1778.

Mrs. Catherine White, from London in the Vicar's chancel.

Mrs. Mary Butterfield in Capt. Comyn's vault, April 8, 1778.

Mr. Thomas Waters, Coroner's Warrant, by fall from his horse, June 21, 1778.

Maria the wife of Francis Burrel Massingberd, Esq. buried in a new vault in the rector's chancel & by her desire the relics of her three children buried in 1751, 1757, 1759, taken up & putt in a shell & laid by her in a vault. She was daughter to Thos. Fanshawe, Esq. April 16, 1778.

Sarah Hammond, submersa, buried by Coroner's warrant from West Thurrock, Feb. 10, 1779.

Richd Kemp, buried by Coroner's warrant, by a fall from his horse, March 12, 1779.

Joseph Ramsden, a Whitsler, June 13, 1779.

Frances Holmes, from Layton Stone, Aug. 13, 1779.

Between November 4 and December 29 there were eighteen burials, of which eleven were from small-pox.

1780.   Elizabeth Oakley, from Mr. Argent's, aged 84.

Marget Handson, dropped down dead in ye street by Coroner's warrant, Dec. 28.

Dame Hoy, from ye Workhouse, P.P. Oct. 4, 1780.

1781. Henry Allen hanged himself at ye Checker, P.P. by coroner's warrant, March 19.

John Dare, Esq. carried away to be buried, Oct. 8.

Abraham Davy a soldier's child, P.P.

1782.   Noah Haws from Chadwell Heath, Aug. 14.

James Harris, a soldier, Dec. 14.

1785.   Elizabeth Ashbolt, mistress of the workhouse, Feb. 4.

Thomas Crussel, a poor boy killed by a fall from his horse, by coroner's warrant, May 3.

George Merttins, Esq. from London in a new vault made for the Bennet family, Jan. 2.

Mrs. Susan Pouchett, sister to Mrs. Pilon.

Willm Smith from ye Cross Keys, June 11. A sermon at the charge of the Benefit Club.

1787.   Willm Green, a farmer (a Sermon) March 11.

Mary Chapman from Chadwell Heath, Feb. 13.

Elizabeth Hogeney, aged 99, widow, P.P. Nov. 4.

Only twenty-two burials this year, the smallest number during the century.

1788.   Daniel Huckaby, master of the Workhouse, July 1.

1789.   Thomas Kettle, from the Bull, March 1.

1790.   John Whitehead from yᵉ White Horse, Chadwell Heath.

Willᵐ Cannon, from Lambeth (the Tanner's brother) buried Nov. 5.

John Unwin, farmer, of Romford Almshouse, Dec. 26.

1791.   Mary Myers, from yᵉ Green Lane near Heavywaters, July 27.

1792.   Mrs. the wife of R. Tomkyns, Esq. of Cornhill & daughter of Joseph Chitty, Esq. Sept. 4.

Sarah, daughter to Thomas Smith, niece to the Countess of Exeter, aged 8 years, June 14, 1796.

1797.   Goodall & Perry drowned at the Breach House.

Thos. Mitchel, butcher, killed by a fall from his horse.   Sermon at charge of the Club.

1798.   Isabella Moss from the Whalebone, an infant, July 4.

The widow of Martin Orridge, of Bentry Heath, aged 100, buried Oct. 3.

1805.   John Hopkins Dare, Esq. aged 23, buried in the Vicar's chancel, Jan. 17, by Coroner's warrant through a fall from his horse.

Mr. Christopher Tyler, aged 31 in the Family vault, Feb. 2.

Mrs. Catherine Shakespeare, wife of David Shakespeare, Esq. of Hodges in the Island of Jamaica, was buried (from Parsloes) in the Fanshawe vault, April 16.

CHAPTER XV

THE PARISH REGISTERS—*continued*

" We scrutinize the dates
Of long-past human things,
The bounds of effaced states,
The lines of deceased kings ;
We search out dead men's words and works of dead men's hands."
MATTHEW ARNOLD.

IN addition to the parochial records of baptisms, marriages, and burials described in the preceding chapters, there is another one, which contains much interesting matter and throws many side-lights on the internal affairs relating to the parish. This is the "Dagenham Regester Book," a large folio volume, with brown paper back, and a hundred thin leaves. It bears the date "Ann. Dmi. 1675." This book was originally intended to contain the minutes of vestry meetings, lists of churchwardens, overseers, etc., church and parish accounts, the names of apprentices bound at the charges of the parish, and sundry other matters. Besides these items it contains entries of "Baptizins," "Marriages," and "Buryalls," from 1693 to 1706. Probably these entries were inserted in this book because the proper register ("y⁰ Vellum Book") was then missing. A few leaves are in a tattered condition, and the writing in consequence difficult to decipher.

The minutes on the first page are as follows :—

At a vestory this 27th [the date is entirely effaced, but the month was probably March] 1673, the several names hereunder written gave their hands for John Davis for Church clark, viz.—

Thomas Bonham.	Hen. Hungate.
John Emerson.	John Comyns.
Willm. Wittham.	John Foster.
	his mark.
	Armiger ✕ Mann.

Willm. Stockdale.   Samuell ffayers.
                              Richard Matheson.
                              William Woodroffe.
                              Henery Osborne.
                              John White.
                              John Remsden.

On the next page we have the names of " Officers chosen by a vestery for this present yeare 1674," viz.—

William Hadden } Churchwardens.
Thomas Elkin   }

Richard Mathyson } Overseers.
Willia^m Anger   }

Immediately below are the officers chosen for 1675, the church-wardens being re-elected, but—

Richard Mathyson chosen Overseer for the poore by the consent of the vestery this yeare also with this condison that the said parish shall excuse him from being a Constable herafter and there consent herunto.

John White, overseer this year also with him.

Then follows :—

Officers chosen by a Vestery for this present yeare 1676 this 27th of March, viz.—

John Nevell } Churchwardens.
John Soanes }

Henery Hook } Overseers.
Robt. Woolston }

James Blott   } Sirveyors.
Samuell ffayres }

Here follows a list of "Apprentices put forth by Richard Mathyson & John White, overseers for the present year 1675." A few samples are given.

William Herrington, bound to George Russell of Barking, ffisherman from the 12th of Aprill 1675 untill he shall accomplish the Age of 24 yeares. And a bond from the said George Russell to save the parish harmles of 20 shillings.[1]

Ann Nicholds bound to Thomas Elkin from the 12th of Aprill 1675 untill she shall accomplish the Age of 21 yeares.

Philip Mole and Thomas Everitt, bound in a bond of 5£ to save the Churchwardens and overseers & all the Inhabitants of the parish aforesaid

---

[1] This means that, if the said apprentice turned out an unprofitable servant, George Russell could only come upon the overseers for £1, as compensation for a bad bargain.

harmless from the said Philip his now wife Martha & all the children he shall have by her or any other during his abode.

Next follow several accounts presented to the "Vestery" by the churchwardens. The utter absence of any arrangement in the tabulating of the various items caused them to be all mixed up together in rather an amusing fashion. The first statement of accounts was "presented by Thomas Elkin & William Haddon, beginning May 10th 1673, as followeth."

	£	s.	d.
ffor a sumons to the Courte [1]	00	02	06
ffor charges at the Courte	00	04	00
ffor charges at the prambulation [2]	01	00	00
To the Ringers on the Corronation Day [3]	00	03	00
Releved 6 woemen by Cirtificate [4]	00	05	06
For a Lock for Jonathan Walker's doare [5]	00	00	10
To William Mayes [6] for halfe a yeare's wages	00	13	00
For repayring the Almshouses	02	11	08
For an assessment for the Churchlands	00	09	00
For goeing to y[e] quarter sessions to Chelmsford	00	05	06
To 4 woemen & children by Cirtificate	00	02	06
To 2 poore men by Cirtificate	00	01	06
To 10 men & women by cirtificate	00	04	00
To Mr. Bonham's worriner for 4 fox heads [7]	00	10	00
To y[e] High Cunstable for Charitable use money [8]	07	00	00
ffor 3 bell ropes	00	13	04

[1] The Archdeacon's Court, held probably at Romford.

[2] Originally, this was a solemn procession, with the singing of Litanies, round the parish on the Rogation Days. An injunction of Queen Elizabeth bids the "curate and the substantial men of the parish" to walk about the parishes as they were accustomed, and at their return to church make their common prayers. During the perambulation the people were to be reminded of the duty of thanksgiving to God, and of respecting parish boundaries and neighbours' landmarks. This observance gradually degenerated into the custom of merely "beating the bounds," when a few officials perambulated the parish with thick sticks, with which they beat the ancient landmarks and broke down unauthorized fences.

[3] Charles II. entered London as king on May 29, 1660, his thirtieth birthday.

[4] The "certificate" was a passport signed by the vicar and churchwardens or by a justice of the peace, certifying that the bearer of it was known to them, and was a *bonâ fide* traveller in search of work and deserving of relief. The various sums show to what amount the several bearers of it received relief.

[5] He lived in one of the almshouses.

[6] The parish clerk.

[7] Mr. Bonham lived at the Manor of Valence. His warrener answered to the modern gamekeeper.

[8] The high constable of the Becontree Hundred, who had authority to relieve the destitute.

	£	s.	d.
For 12 hundred of barens for yᵉ Church wall [1]	03	00	00
For 3 hundred of eathers [2]	00	18	00
For carrying yᵉ materialls to yᵉ wall	01	10	00
For 3/4 of Timber & carriage	01	14	03
To yᵉ marshmen for work at the wall [3]	01	05	06
To Nehemiah Payne as appears by bill	00	15	11
For setling the Churchland to yᵉ steward	00	07	00
To Mr. Tayler's for yᵉ ffeofees oaths	00	02	00
For ringing 3 severall days by comand [4]	00	09	00
To Holland for glazeing yᵉ Church	00	19	00
For Comunion wine to the wid ffeild [5]	00	08	00
For confirming the rate [6]	00	03	04
For a warrant for Aldridge	00	00	06
For an order to send away Aldridge	00	01	00
To Stapler as appears by bill	01	13	01
To Greenwood as appears by bill	01	00	03
For another sumons	00	01	00
For Comunion wine	00	14	00
For a fine for the Church land	05	00	00
ffor one acre & halfe of Marshland two yeares	04	10	00
Recᵈ of Mr. Eaton for a buryall	00	06	08
Recᵈ of Mr. White for a buryall	00	06	06
Of Thomas Estbrooke for a buryall	00	06	08
Of Mr. Uphill for a buryall	00	06	08
Recᵈ of the rate	40	10	11
Disbursed	46	03	00
due to the Churchwardens of yᵉ old account	05	13	11
Lost money more due to yᵉ Churchwardens	03	05	06

Another "accompte" is also given, of which we subjoin an abstract. It is for the year 1675.

	£	s.	d.
Imprimis. To 6 seamen by Cirtificate [7]	00	01	00
To 4 woemen by Cirtificate	00	00	06

[1] Broken pieces of flint-stone (?).

[2] For warming the church. Stoves and other heating apparatuses were not then in use, so heather, bracken, and straw were laid in the aisles and seats to lessen the cold and damp in the church.

[3] The wall or embankment to keep out the tide at the Dagenham Breach.

[4] April 23, May 29, November 5.

[5] Port wine was in much request as a cure for ague.

[6] After the churchwardens and overseers had ascertained what rate should be levied to meet their liabilities, they obtained the signature of a justice of the peace to make the demand legal. The sum mentioned was paid to his clerk.

[7] At this period there was great distress among seamen through their wages being in

	£	s.	d.
To John Davis for halfe a yeare's wages [1]	00	13	00
To Mr. Smithyes for Comunion wine [2]	00	15	00
To a Church booke for accounts [3]	00	04	00
For 3 Locks for the Church Chest	00	03	00
To 12 men by Cirtificate	00	04	00
To 4 women & 3 children by Cirtificate	00	01	00
For a rope for the great bell [4]	00	04	06
To John Cluirton in sicknes	00	05	00
For bread & wine for a Comunion	00	05	04
To yᵉ Ringers on Two severall dayes	00	06	00
For charges at the Preambulation	00	06	00
To a poor Minister by order	00	03	00
For mending the Churchwall to yᵉ Marshmen	01	06	00
For Charitable use money to yᵉ high Cunstable	03	18	00
Towards yᵉ loss of Deluge in yᵉ fenns	00	04	06
For mending yᵉ bells & stooles	00	06	00
To yᵉ glasier for mending yᵉ church windows	00	13	04
For a Cirtificate to discharge yᵉ poor from paying Hearth money [5]	00	04	00
For 8 old & 3 young foxes heads to John Gill	01	04	00
For work done by Stephen Doare at Church	00	09	09
For thatching yᵉ almshouses & straw	00	08	00
For Carryage of yᵉ Church lead	00	05	00
For yᵉ preambulation at yᵉ fforrest spent	02	09	06
For Charges in carrying away Ellis his guirl	00	03	06
For mending the Clock	00	11	00
For makeing the rate	00	03	06
For an Article booke	00	01	00

The "accomptes" of Thomas Elkin and William Haddon given up to "yᵉ p'rish the 24ᵗʰ of Aprill, 1676," are as followeth :—

	£	s.	d.
They stand charged with	34	10	10
Theire disbursements amount to	36	17	07
Soe upon this account theire is due to these Churchwardns from the prish	02	14	03
And due to them from the prish upon the other accounts before	08	19	05
In all due to them from yᵉ prish	11	13	08

arrears. They complained, too, that they could not get cash for the tickets they received from the Government. This grievance is referred to in Pepys' "Diary."

[1] The parish clerk.   [2] The Rev. Isaac Smythies, vicar.

[3] This book has, unfortunately, been lost.

[4] The tenor bell ; it was broken when the tower collapsed in 1800.

[5] The hearth or chimney tax was imposed in 1661–62 ; every hearth being taxed at 2s., "as a constant Revenue for ever to the Crowne" (Pepys' "Diary ").

Another "accompte" is that of Stephen Dore, churchwarden, "Begining Aprill the 15, 1680 and alsoe for the yeare 1681." It contains, *inter alia*, the following :—

	£	s.	d.
Impr: payd to Mr. Vaughan[1] at the Visitation & my oath & the booke	00	06	00
paid to eight seamen by Certificate	00	02	06
pᵈ at whitsontide for Comunion Bread & wyne	00	05	06
June 20. pᵈ to Thre women by Cirtificatt	00	01	06
July 13. pᵈ for mowing & makeing and Bringing home yᵉ broken acre of hay	00	08	06
Aug. 4. pᵈ for a payre of Rayles & mending the penn at the Theames wall	00	02	06
— 7. pᵈ to eight passengers by certificatt	00	02	00
pᵈ for quitt rentt	00	06	06
— 14. pᵈ at the Visitation at Brenttwood	00	11	06
Oct. 10. pᵈ for two Ringing days, May 29 & No. the 5ᵗʰ	00	06	00
No. 5. pᵈ to Tho. Osburne for mending the Bells	00	01	00
Dec. 3. pᵈ for a glass for the pullpitt[2]	00	00	06
for plateing a shovell	00	00	04
Dec. 12. pᵈ to Mr. Smith for of the Church Lands	00	01	00
pᵈ to 5 pooore persons by Certif.	00	01	06
pᵈ at Christmas for Bread & wyne	00	05	06
Jan. 23. pᵈ for cutting weeds in yᵉ churchyard	co	01	00
Mar. 24. pᵈ to Mr. Vaughan for a booke for yᵉ fast[3]	00	01	00

[1] Mr. Vaughan was the minister of St. Edward's, Romford. On the outbreak of the Civil War he sympathized with the Parliamentarians, who nominated him "preaching minister" of Romford. At the Restoration of the monarchy, Mr. Vaughan, like the vicar of Bray, threw off his Puritanism and declared for Charles II. He was an intimate friend of Joachim Matthews, who left him £5 to preach his funeral sermon. The inference is that Mr. Vaughan acted as the archdeacon's deputy at this visitation. The archdeacon at that time was Master Edward Layfield, A.M., Prebendary of Harleston in St. Paul's Cathedral. He was collated to the Archdeaconry of Essex by the Archbishop of Canterbury (Laud), *fro hac vice;* buried, 1680, at All Hallows, Barking, of which he was vicar.

[2] Not a glass for water or some other cordial, but an "hour-glass," to enable the preacher to measure and limit the length of his sermon. In Hogarth's "Sleeping Congregation" we see an hour-glass in an iron bracketed stand. Sometimes the preacher would turn the glass, remarking, "My brethren, we will have another glass." Some of the Puritan divines were reproached with being four, five, and even six glass men. Erasmus, in his "Praise of Folly," pithily remarks, "If what is delivered from the pullpitt be grave, solid, and rational, all the congregation grow weary and fall asleep, till their patience be released ; whereas if the preacher (pardon the impropriety of the word, the 'prater' I would have said) be zealous in his thumps on the cushion, antic gestures, and spend his glass in the telling of pleasant stories, his beloved then stand up, tuck their hair behind their ears and be very devoutly attentive.'

[3] A fast was appointed for the plague (1665).

1681.		£ s. d.
Apr. 10.	pᵈ for halfe a Load & 3 Trusses of straw in mending the Almshouses	00 . 04 . 06
	pᵈ for Bread & Wyne ffor two comunions at Christmas	00 . 16 . 00
	pᵈ for two Badger's heads	00 . 02 . 00
	pᵈ to Davis for Clark's wages & Looking to the Clock for one yeare	01 . 06 . 00
	pᵈ for a comunion Cloath	00 . 18 . 00
	pᵈ to Brewster & Mowle for 2 days worke a piece and thatching	00 . 07 . 11
	pᵈ for yᵉ king's declaration which shewed his reason for dissolving his Pliamᵗ & a smͦns to Rumford ¹	00 . 02 . 00
May 10.	pᵈ to Cock for mending yᵉ pulpitt cushing ..	00 . 00 . 06
	pᵈ for Comunion bread & wyne at Easter ..	00 . 05 . 06
— 25.	pᵈ for 3 ffox heads	00 . 03 . 00
June 10.	pᵈ chardges going perambulation	00 . 19 . 06
Aug. 17.	pᵈ for setting up the monement in yᵉ chancell ² ..	00 . 03 . 06
Oct. 4.	pᵈ chardges at yᵉ Bishops Court at Rumford & Sumͦns	00 . 03 . 06
No. 5.	pᵈ for 3 ringing Days. St. Geo day the 29 May & 5 of Novembr	00 . 09 . 00
Feb. 20.	pᵈ for a dyall ³	00 . 02 . 06
Mar. 26.	pᵈ for a sett of bell Roapes	00 . 08 . 03
	pᵈ Will Gibson Locksmith by a bill	00 . 10 . 00
	pᵈ Tho. Osburne by a bill	00 . 08 . 04
	pᵈ Mr. Witham by marsh tax	00 . 09 . 00
	pᵈ Abra. King Glasier by a bill	00 . 12 . 00
	pᵈ Edw. Stapler Bricklayer by a bill	00 . 08 . 02
	pᵈ Ino Crampton by a bill	00 . 10 . 03
	pᵈ Steph. dore by a bill	05 . 05 . 00
	Outting the weeds	00 . 01 . 06
	Mending the marsh wall	00 . 01 . 06

The accounts are briefly summed up thus—

brought over	04 . 18 . 11
more	05 . 00 . 02
more	03 . 08 . 07
This side	09 . 02 . 09
addiconall disburseˡˢ	00 . 04 . 00
disburseˡˢ totale	22 . 15 . 05

---

¹ Charles II. dissolved Parliament March 28, 1681. He issued a declaration in defence of this proceeding, and ordered it to be read in all the churches.

² To Thomas Bonham, armiger, Lord of Valence, who died in 1676.

³ *i.e.* a clock face.

	£	s.	d.
Rec^d by Rate	19	16	02
Rec^d by Rents	04	10	00
Made of broken acre in ye comon 15/- the first yeare & 9/- the last yeare	01	04	00
Rec^d in totale	25	10	02

I Stephen Dore doe hereby promise to pay Two pounds ffifteene shillings & three pence, ye lawful money to William Eaton & Robert Woolston, Churchwardens on the first day of June next. Witnes my hand ye day & yeare abovesaid,

STEPHEN DORE.

Witnes,
J. Smith,
John Emerson,

1 day of May, 1682.

As in the previous accounts, there are some score of payments by certificate to seamen, women and children, poor persons and single persons.

On the next page we have the account of the churchwardens referred to in the above. As it is not a very long one we give it in full.

The Accompt of William Eaton one of the Churchwardens of the Parish of Dagenham in the County of Essex, as followeth—

	£	s.	d.
May 16th. Charges at a Visitation Court	00	09	09
Paid Mr. Clent for an assessm^t	00	02	00
To Mr. Gillman for a surplice	02	05	07
Releived by Certificat	00	04	00
The like	00	03	00
Octob. 10. Charges at a visitation	00	11	00
Paid to Mr. Taylor charged on Dagenham ..	01	15	08
Releived by Certificat	00	01	00
for Comunion wine	00	15	00
To Hannah Reeves	05	19	08
1682.			
May 3^d. At a visitation	00	05	06
To David church clerk for washing the surplice	00	02	00
Releife by certificate	00	04	00
for Comunion wine	00	05	00
To Mr. Smith for a rate making	00	04	00
for drink for ringers	00	03	00

1862.

		£	s.	d.
Releife by Certificate	.. ..	oo	o2	o6
The like	..	oo	oo	o6
The like	..	oo	o1	oo
Paid to Mr. Smith	..	oo	13	o9
To Mr. ffanshaw for Armsteads will[1]	..	oo	1o	oo
Releife by Certificat	..	oo	o1	o6
p^d to Mr. Smith	..	o1	oo	oo
Oct. 3. At a visitation	..	oo	o9	o4
Bridgemony to Mr. Poulton[2]	..	o1	17	oo
Releife by Certificat	..	oo	o1	o6
To Gibson for cleansing the clock ..	..	oo	1o	oo
for Comunion wine	..	oo	o5	oo
Releife by Certificate	..	oo	o1	oo
To Davis for wages	..	o1	o6	oo
for Comunion wine	..	oo	1o	oo
to Mr. Hungate for heades of vermine ..	..	oo	o2	oo
To Mr. Smith	..	oo	o1	o3
To Goodman Hayle for repairing the church ..		oo	o3	o4
for beer for Ringers	..	oo	o3	oo
To Winter carpenter for 1 dayes work ..	..	oo	o2	oo

1683.

Aprill 23. Att a visitation	..	oo	o3	o6
		16	13	o4

From the foregoing accounts it would seem that the church-wardens in the olden time found it as difficult to pay their way as their modern successors do, notwithstanding the fact that they could draw upon the rates.   There is no mention of "church ales," formerly a common though unedifying method of raising money to swell the churchwardens' funds; in all probability they happily never survived the Puritan *régime*.   We notice the absence of various items of expenditure which frequently appear in similar financial statements at the present day, *e.g.* coal, gas, electric light, oil, insurance premiums, salaries of organist, sacristan, verger, etc. The large sums expended on communion wine are accounted for by the fact that the parishioners made their communion in con-siderable numbers at the chief festivals, and also that this wine was given to the sick poor of the parish.   The period comprised in the "accomptes" was that which followed the Restoration.

[1] William Armstead died 1657. He left money to the deserving poor of Dagenham and Hornchurch.

[2] The bridge was that over the marsh on the road to Rainham.

The following are brief summaries of accounts in the later parish book (1785–1815):—"John Biggs, late churchwarden, said his whole disbursements came to £106 18s. 8d., and his rate to £79 18s. 0d." He had obviously under-estimated the parochial expenditure, the result being that the parish owed him £25 17s. 9d., which the vestry requested his successor to pay to him, September, 1789.

"Robert Brittain, late churchwarden, presented his account and said his whole disbursements had amounted to £121 0s. 6d. He had received per rate £81 15s. 6d., and five guineas from Thos. Fanshawe, Esq., for going the Bounds of the Parish." The vestry ordered the balance to be repaid to Robert Brittain, August, 1791.

CHAPTER XVI

THE MANOR OF PARSLOES

"Hushed are the voices, that in years gone by,
    Have mourn'd, exulted, menaced, through thy towers ;
Within thy pillar'd courts the grass waves high,
    And all uncultured bloom thy fairy bowers."
                                        HEMANS.

THE manor-house of Parseloes, Passelowes, or Passelewes is a large, noble-looking, and substantially built house, standing about one mile to the west of Dagenham church, and north of the London and Tilbury road. It was separated from the adjoining manor of Jenkins by a lane, known as Gale Street. The manor belonged to Barking Abbey, and probably derived its name from one Simon Passelewe, who is mentioned in an old will as an inhabitant of Dagenham, and as having sold land in the time of Edward III. to a Cecilia de Lancastr, 1327–77. At a later date it came into the possession of Martin Bowes, Esq.,[1] citizen and goldsmith of London, Lord Mayor 1545–49, and afterwards knighted by Queen Elizabeth. He sold it to Rowland Hayward, an alderman of the city, and Thomas Wilbraham, Esq. The estate then comprised "10 messuages, 1 cottage, 10 gardens, 2 orchards, 100 acres of arable land, 20 of meadow, 50 of pasture, 30 of forest and 40 shillings in Dagenham, Berkyng & Upmenstre."

After the manor had been in the possession of R. Hayward and T. Wilbraham, Esquires, only a few years, it was acquired by Edward Osborne, Esq., who was Lord Mayor in 1583. He probably built the house, which, with the Parsloes estate, descended

---

[1] This Martin Bowes was suspected of being a buyer and seller of goods not always honestly acquired, especially church plate and ornaments. Stow accuses him of even removing brasses and marble tombs and gravestones from the churchyard of Christ Church, Newgate Street, and selling them for what they would fetch. He was butler at Queen Elizabeth's coronation, and bequeathed to the Goldsmith's Company his gold cup, out of which she drank. His portrait is in the great hall of that company. He was buried (1566) in the church of St. Mary, Woolnoth.

to his son Hewett. The latter died in 1599, having been knighted between the date of making his will and that of his death. Sir Hewett Osborne left Parsloes to his wife Joyce during her widow-hood, and his land to his sons Edward and William when twenty-one. Twenty years later, Edward Osborne, Esq., of Yorkshire, sold Parsloes to William Fanshawe, the deed of conveyance being dated February 16, 16th James I., and made between Edward Osbourne, Esq., of Keeton, Yorkshire, and Margaret, his wife, of the one part, and William Fanshawe, Esq., of London, and Katherine, his wife, of the other part. The "consideration money" was £1150, and the lands are described as follows :—

The manor & manor-house called Passelowes, & three acres of land lying about the house. An arable field called Barnfield, 22 acres; Kitchen-Field, arable, 8 acres; Stable-Field, arable, 5 acres; Mawlands, arable, 20 acres; Shortcrofts, arable, 8 acres; Ivye Lands, 6 acres; The Brokes, 8 acres; One Broke called Newlars broke, 1 acre; One grove adjoining, 2 acres.

All lying in Dagenham & Barking. Also Eylands & Heathy-Field, both in Barking. Also parcel of ground of Yvye Lands & a cottage & 8 acres in Dagenham, in the occupation of Thomas Grigson.

Edward Osborne covenants to deliver all deeds, etc., to Wm. Fanshawe at his dwelling-house in St. Sepulchre's, in London, and to give possession to Powl Waldegrave, Gent., of Barking, on behalf of William Fanshawe. Formal possession was accordingly given on February 22, following, in the presence of Thomas Fanshawe, of Jenkins, Thomas Fanshawe, of Ware, Henry Throckmorton, Thomas Truelove, and others.

This William Fanshawe, the founder of the Fanshawes of Parsloes, was the second son of Thomas Fanshawe and Ioan Smyth, and was baptized May 4, 1583, at Christ Church, London (Newgate Street). He was appointed one of the auditors of " His Majestie's Revenues of the Duchy of Lancaster." The purchase of Parsloes in 1619 brought him to Barking, and, twelve years later, he bought the site of the abbey there from one Matthew Stilts. His name is among those who signed the visitation of London, 1633–34. During his residence at Parsloes he added a large room to this mansion, panelled with oak, and enriched with handsome carving. He married, in 1615, Katherine, second daughter of Sir John Wolstenholme, Knt., of London ; she was buried May 18, 1642, at Barking. He predeceased her at St. Sepulchre's, London,

March 4, 1634, and was buried in the chancel of Barking church.[1] He left issue—John, his eldest son and heir; Thomas,[2] of London; William; Katherine, married Henry Ayloffe, Esq., of Brittens, Hornchurch, whom she survived; Alice and Elizabeth, died in infancy.

A description of Parsloes, as it was when Mr. Fanshawe purchased it, was written by the late Mr. H. W. King, which is so graphic and instructive that we reproduce it [3]—

During the two centuries and a half that it has been in the possession of the Fanshawes the manor-house has, as might be supposed, undergone much alteration, and at three very distinctly marked periods, the latest and most extensive of these took place in the year 1814, when the mansion was somewhat enlarged, the walls were faced with new brick and finished throughout with battlements, and many windows of pointed form were inserted. Its plan now consists of a central hall and two transverse wings. It is approached on the west by an avenue, which formerly swept round the north end of the house, giving access also upon the east front, over-looking the gardens and park, though the principal entrance, as now, was upon the west. Notwithstanding the successive changes which have either destroyed or concealed the more ancient architectural features and details, both externally and internally, it is still possible to define the original plan with considerable accuracy, and to trace the most important alterations and additions. It was one of the smaller class of manor-houses erected in the reign of Elizabeth, and then comprised a hall, with a single private apartment—perhaps that usually occupied by the family—at the north end, and kitchens at the south. A short passage from the north-west corner gave access to the great staircase, projected westward beyond the line of the hall, and also to the parlour on the right hand. Usually, especially in halls of earlier date, the doorway was towards the end, and visitors entered what was called "the screens," a passage at the lower end screened off by wainscot. No trace, however, exists of such an arrangement here, and, in all probability, the entrance was in the centre, as at present, and as we find in other examples of this date. The habits of society had changed before this time, and the upper classes had gradually abandoned the custom of eating with their retainers in the hall; and in some more ancient examples, the space which would usually have been allotted for the daïs and the high table is parted off from the rest of the hall by a solid screen. Here, although the hall is retained, a separate room was built at the upper end contemporaneously. The upper floor

[1] Will dated March 1, 1634; proved, 1650.

[2] Baptized at Dagenham, 1627; matriculated at Queen's College, Oxford, April 9, 1647; admͦon, January, 1665-66, to his brother John; was of St. Bride's, Fleet Street.

[3] *Fanshawe Wills* (from the collection of E. J. Sage, Esq.). Note appended to that of Wm. Fanshawe by Mr. H. W. King in 1872.

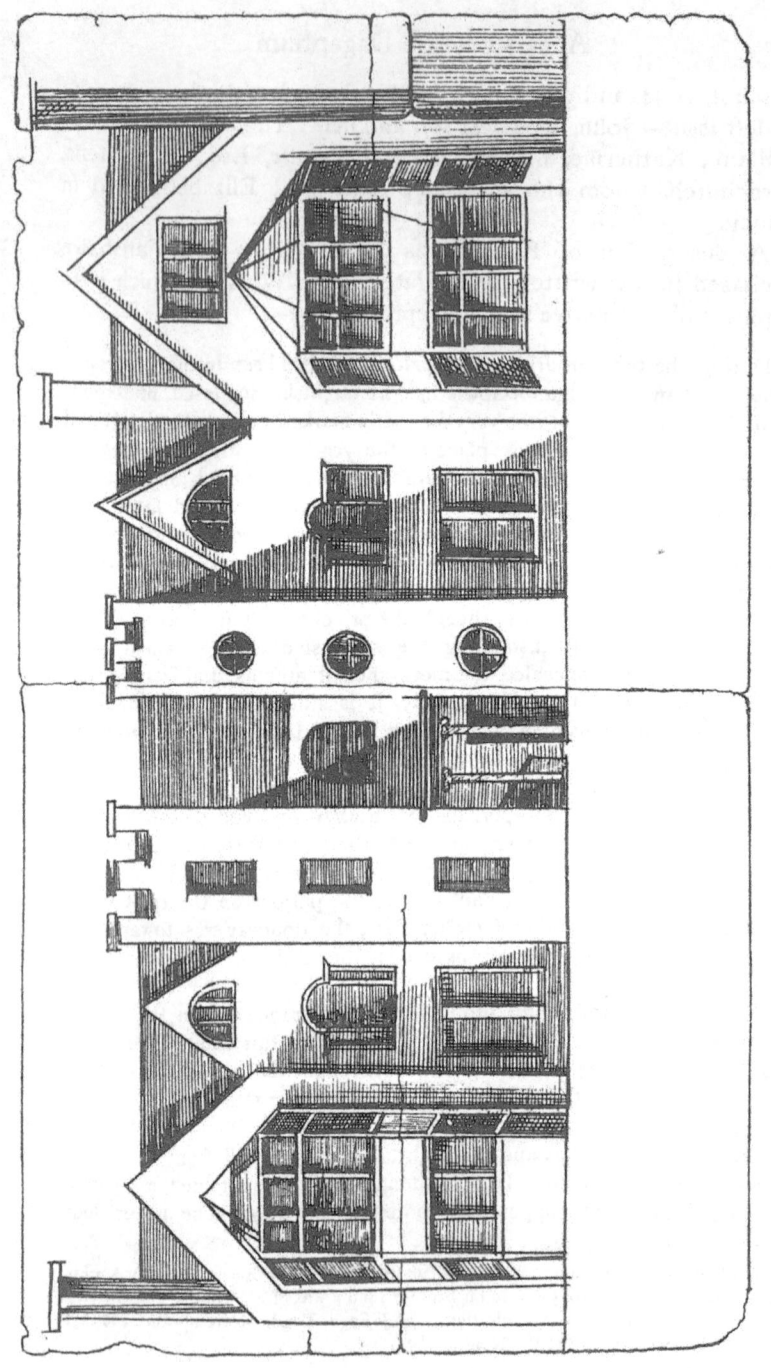

PARSLOES
(EAST FRONT)
as it appeared before the alterations made in 1814

contained the sleeping-rooms of the family and domestics. The hall is lighted upon the west, and panelled throughout with small square panelling. The ceiling is modern. The stone fireplace is on the east side, near the lower end; but this, as well as those in the servants' hall, kitchen, and library, were brought from the more stately Elizabethan mansion of Eastbury House. All are enriched with carving. Between the years 1619 and 1634, William Fanshawe appears to have added a large apartment at the north end of the house (now the drawing-room), also panelled with oak, and the fine Jacobean carving over the mantelpiece is, doubtless, part of the original decoration of the room; it is entered from the passage at the foot of the great staircase, which, with its massive hand-rail and spiral balusters, must be ascribed to the same period, having probably replaced one of Elizabethan date. In further proof that the drawing-room was a later addition to the fabric, Mr. J. G. Fanshawe states that on removing a portion of the panelling some years ago, nails in the brickwork behind it clearly denoted that trees had been trained against the wall. Prior to this addition, the ground-plan of the house may be described as a parallelogram, with at least one slightly advanced gable on the west front, and perhaps a second corresponding. The floors of the hall, drawing-room, and library, are of oak, and the two first were, no doubt, laid when the respective rooms were built; but that in the library came from Eastbury House. The library was erected by the Rev. John Fanshawe, about 1814, on the site of the south gable.

The accompanying lithograph, from an original drawing of the east elevation in the possession of Mr. Fanshawe, will, however, help us to understand somewhat better the external character of the edifice as it appeared in the latter part of the sixteenth century. It obviously represents an Elizabethan structure of brick, which had been greatly altered in the early part of the last century, chiefly by the insertion of modern windows. The square turrets which flank the entrance were probably very late additions; for although an external stair-turret is not altogether an unusual feature in a house of this date, yet, considering all the structural arrangements, these can hardly have formed part of the original design; that to the right still exists, and has a modern staircase. Sweep away these and other incongruous insertions of the eighteenth century, and substitute square-headed mullioned windows, with diamond quarries, the original character of the east front will then, in some degree, be realized, and the archæologist, with a slight effort of imagination, will restore a picturesque old manor-house of the Elizabethan age. The gable to the extreme left is probably in advance; there are the apartments of the domestics. The hall extends to the tower upon the right; the gabled portion beyond contains, on the ground-floor, the parlour at the north end of the hall; opposite, on the western side, is the staircase. The gable on the extreme right is the addition by William Fanshawe, in the reign of James I.; and, if we have not entirely failed in the description, the reader will easily comprehend the original plan of the structure. It may be added that the ancestral portraits remaining in the mansion are numerous.

John Fanshawe, of Parsloes, Wyersdale, Great Singleton, Lancashire, graduated at Trinity College, Oxford, in 1637-38. He became, three years later, auditor of the Duchy of Lancaster. He married, first, Katherine, daughter of Sir William Kingsmill, of Sidmanton, Hants, by whom he had one child, William ;[1] secondly (1659), Alice, eldest daughter of Thomas Fanshawe, Esq., of Jenkyns, by whom he had issue—John (his heir at Parsloes), and Susannah, who died in infancy.

When the Civil War broke out, Mr. Fanshawe actively interested himself in the king's behalf, with the result that he was called upon, in 1646-47, to " make a composition on the Barnstaple Articles for his delinquency in bearing arms for the King." He was ordered to pay a fine of £430 for his recusant conduct, but was allowed to compound for the lease of Dagenham parsonage for twenty-one years, held of the Master of Brentwood Free School, and now void. Permission was also given to " compound for the office of Auditor for the north parts of the Duchy of Lancaster, and to refer the ' Rectory ' matter to the House of Commons " (" Calendar of State Papers "). He was ordered, too, tc pay an annuity to the vicar of West Thurrock (Thomas Swinnerton), as granted to that benefice by the Commissioners for Plundered Ministers.

John Fanshawe died April 6, 1689, and was buried at Barking in the Fanshawe vault. (Will dated September 27, 1683 ; proved, April, 1689.)

John Fanshawe, Esq., of Parsloes, succeeded on the death of his father. He was baptized at Dagenham in 1662, matriculated at Trinity College, Oxford, in 1678, and was afterwards auditor of the Duchy of Lancaster. He married at Barking, November 21,

---

[1] William Fanshawe, Esq., of St. Martin's in the Fields, was disinherited by his father for some reason or other. He was appointed Master of Requests to Charles II. He married Mary, daughter of Lucy Walters, and sister of the unfortunate Duke of Monmouth. He had issue—Thomas Edward, who succeeded to the estate of his cousin Simon, Viscount Fanshawe, and died in 1726 ; Ann, married — Matthews, Esq. ; Dorothy ; Mary, married Mark Newdigate, Esq.

The above Thomas Edward Fanshawe married Elizabeth, daughter of William Snelling, Esq., of Bromley, Kent, by whom he had one son and four daughters. The son, Simon Fanshawe, of Fanshawe Gate, and of Saville Row, London, became clerk to the Board of Green Cloth and M.P. for Old Sarum. His eldest son, Henry, was a general in the Russian army, and died 1828, leaving five sons, four of whom were also in the Russian service.

1695, Mary, eldest daughter of John Coke, of Melbourne, Derby-shire,[1] and sister of Thomas Coke, Vice-Chamberlain of the King's Household. He died the 19th, and was buried December 22, 1699, in the family vault at Barking. He had issue—Thomas, his heir; John, afterwards Regius Professor of Divinity at Oxford, and Canon of Christ Church; Charles, born posthumous, afterwards admiral, Royal Navy; Susannah, died, unmarried, 1759.

Thomas Fanshawe, of Parsloes, was born in 1696, and, like his father, was baptized at Dagenham church. He was educated at Westminster and Jesus College, Oxford, taking his degree 1715–16, after which he became a student at Lincoln's Inn. He married Frances, daughter of the Rev. William Clarke, vicar of Thame, Oxon., and was buried at Barking in 1758, surviving his wife thirty-three years. He had issue—Thomas; Alice, died in infancy, 1719; John, died in infancy, 1725; Frances, married the Rev. Abraham Blackborne, vicar of Dagenham, died 1795, aged seventy-four, buried at Richmond; Maria, married Frances Burrell Massing-berd, of St. Michael's Cornhill, died 1777, buried in Dagenham church.

Thomas Fanshawe, Esq., of Parsloes, succeeded to the manor at the age of thirty-seven. He married, at the Ilford Hospital Chapel,[2] June, 1745, Anne, eldest daughter of Sir Crisp Gascoigne, Knt., of Bifrons, Barking.[3] The marriage licence describes him as of St. Dunstans in the East, and the bride as of Barking. The latter died August, 1762, and was buried in the Gascoigne vault at Barking. Thomas Fanshawe died in 1797, and was buried with his wife.[4] He had issue—John Gascoigne; Susanna, died 1764, aged seventeen; Ann, died 1791, aged forty-three; Mary, died 1770, aged eight.

John Gascoigne Fanshawe, Esq., of Parsloes, was born in 1746;

---

[1] Called Madame Fanshawe in the deeds; buried at Barking, June 9, 1713, as "Mary Fanshawe, spinster."

[2] Founded in 1189 by Adelicia, Abbess of Barking, as an asylum for their leprous tenants and servants. It was endowed with property in Barking, East Ham, and Great and Little Ilford, and had on its foundation a master, thirteen brother lepers, two priests, and a clerk. After the dissolution of the abbey, it was refounded in 1572 by Queen Elizabeth, the charity to support a master, a chaplain, and six aged poor men. It was bestowed upon Thomas Fanshawe, Esq., his heirs and assigns.

[3] There is in Barking church a mural tablet in memory of "Sir Crisp Gascoigne, knight, alderman, sheriff & lord mayor of London, who died Decr 28, 1761, aged 61."

[4] It was through the marriage, in 1821, of Mrs. Fanshawe's great niece, Frances Mary Gascoigne, with the second Marquis of Salisbury, that the latter family became possessed of the property they held till recently in Barking and Ilford, and assumed under the will of Bamber Gascoigne, Esq., the name of Gascoigne before that of Cecil.

was educated at Westminster and Christ Church, Oxford, taking his B.A. in 1767. He subsequently proceeded to Lincoln's Inn. He married Mary, daughter of Christopher Parkinson, of Prescott, Lancashire, who survived him. He died December 23, 1803, and was buried in the new family vault at Dagenham. He left three sons—John, Henry, and Thomas Lewis.

John Fanshawe, of Parsloes and Wyersdale, the last to be so described, was born in 1773, and baptized at St. Andrew's church, Holborn. Like his father, he was educated at Westminster and Christ Church, of which he became a senior student. He was ordained deacon in 1796, and priest the following year, to the curacy of Rainham and Winnington, two parishes adjoining Dagenham. Later on, he was appointed chaplain to the Bishop of Sodor and Man (Dr. Claudius Crigan), vicar of Torrington (Devon.), and vicar of Frodsham (Chester), no objection being raised to his holding these preferments conjointly, or to his still continuing to reside at Parsloes while holding them. In addition to being a " squarson " and a " pluralist," he was something of an architect too, as he considerably altered and enlarged his ancestral home, and made it the finest mansion in the neighbourhood. The walls were faced with new brick, and battlements and turrets were added. Additional rooms were also built, bringing the total number up to twenty-four. Mr. Fanshawe died October, 1843, and was buried in the family vault at Dagenham church. He was never married.

Henry, brother to the above, also unmarried, now became the head of the Fanshawe family at Parsloes, where he had lived some years. He did not, however, succeed to the estate. After holding an appointment in the Sun Fire Office, he was nominated one of the Commissioners of the Levels of Havering, Dagenham, Barking, East and West Ham, Leyton, and Walthamstow Marsh. He died in October, 1854, at the age of eighty, and was buried in the family vault at Dagenham.

John Gaspard Fanshawe, the eldest son of the then vicar of Dagenham, the Rev. Thomas Lewis Fanshawe, succeeded his uncle at Parsloes. He was born in 1824, and after being educated at Eton, went into his uncle's, H. Lefevre, bank. Subsequently he was appointed a clerk in the Board of Trade, and acted as private secretary to several cabinet ministers. He married, in 1853, Barbara Frederica Beaujolois, third daughter of the Hon. William James Coventry, a son of the seventh Earl of Coventry, of Earl's

PARSLOES

Croome Court, Worcestershire, and a major in the Worcestershire Yeomanry. Their children are—(1) Evelyn John, educated at Eton, and afterwards captain in the West Essex Militia ; (2) Basil Thomas, of Holywell, Bratton Fleming, Devonshire, and Lunugala, Ceylon ; (3) Lionel ; (4) Beaujolois Mabel, who married A. G. Ridout, Esq.; (5) Violet, who married the Hon. Huntly Douglas Gordon, son of Lord Gordon, of Drumcarn. Mr. J. G. Fanshawe continued to reside at Parsloes until 1855, since which time no one of this family has lived there. He died in December, 1903, in London.

After the departure of Mr. Fanshawe from Parsloes, this fine old mansion was dismantled, and its choice collection of portraits dispersed among the various members of the family. The most valuable picture was one attributed, though wrongly,[1] to Velasquez, or Vandyck, of Sir Richard Fanshawe, gentleman-in-waiting to Charles I., who was deputed to take the letter and picture of Charles II. to Katherine Braganza at Lisbon. He was subsequently ambassador to the Courts of Spain and Portugal, and died in 1666 from grief at being recalled by the King. Another interesting picture was one of Sir Thomas Fanshawe, of Jenkins, and his lady, by Sir Peter Lely. Another portrait, said—but with doubtful reason—to be by Vandyck, was of Sir Simon Fanshawe, with a view of the battle of Naseby in the background.

This Sir Simon, son of Sir Henry Fanshawe, of ffanshawe Gate, was knighted by Charles I. in recognition of his services. He suffered terribly for his allegiance, and, besides having to compound for his estates, was imprisoned and exiled. He married Catherine, daughter and co-heiress of Sir William Walter, Knt., of Wimbledon, and widow of Knighton Ferrers, Esq., of Beyford, Herts. Sir Simon died 1679–80.

There was also a fine portrait of Anne, Lady Fanshawe, by Teniers.

The manor-house has been without a tenant for some years, and is fast falling into decay. The oak wainscoting has been torn from the walls, the ceilings are disfigured with unsightly holes, and the walls and floors are bedewed with damp and moisture most visibly. The fine spacious library is, however, tolerably well preserved. The old bell still hangs in its turret. A ghost is said to wander around this gloomy, massive pile of brickwork, having

---

[1] It was the work of William Dobson, whose early death cut short a career of great promise.

been driven from the room he was supposed to haunt by the irrepressible though pardonable curiosity of visitors to Parsloes. And the once noble park has been of recent years converted into a racecourse, and is now the headquarters of the Essex Amateur Trotting Club.

We are glad to hear that there is a happy prospect of this ancient mansion being put into repair by a member of the family with which it has been for nearly four centuries associated.

CHAPTER XVII

THE MANOR OF JENKINS

" ' O then,' the grieving man replied,
No further, lassie, let me stray ;
Here's nothing left of ancient pride,
Of what was grand, of what was gay :
But,all is changed, is lost, is sold,
All, all that's left, is chilling cold."
CRABBE.

THIS, the oldest of the manors in Dagenham, stood three-quarters of a mile to the north of Parsloes Park, from which it was separated by a lane called Gale Street. On Norden's map of Essex it is marked as belonging partly to Dagenham and partly to Barking. The estate consisted of "three tofts, a garden, five oxgangs of land, 203 acres of arable, 3 of meadow, 40 of pasture, 5 of wood, and £2 13s. 4d. rent in Barking and Dagenham " (*Inquis.*, 12th Henry VII.). Jenkins is described in a MS. account of ancient houses in Ilford and Barking as "a very large Old Timber House," and was surrounded on three sides by an unusually deep moat. The grounds, covering seven acres, were magnificently laid out, and contained two large fishponds and several beautiful garden terraces. Attached to the manor was a chapel, which contained some rich stained glass, and in particular a window with the figure of one of the abbesses of Barking.

The manor of Jenkins was for various reasons one of more than ordinary importance. It was regarded as the true manor-house of Barking, and especially during the *régime* of the Fanshawes, and in virtue of his rights its owner possessed certain burial privileges in the chancel of Barking church.

The origin of the name Jenkins is obscure. Probably the manor took its name from one Jenkyns, a vassal of the abbess who lived there. Be this as it may, the manor is one of un-doubted antiquity, and belonged to Barking Abbey. We hear of it being held by one Ralph Fitz-Stephen so early as the time of King John (1199–1216), since when we do not know of any other lord until we come to 1496, when Sir Hugh Brice, or Bryce, held the manor under a lease from the Abbess and Convent of Barking. Sir Hugh died seised of it in 1496, Jenkins being then valued at £13 6s. 8d., and held at a quit-rent of 4s. 4d. (The latter had been £1 6s. 8d., but was reduced by an agreement between the abbess and Ralph Fitz-Stephen aforesaid.) Subsequently, his grandson, Hugh, succeeded to the manor and held it till his death, when it passed to his only sister, who married Robert Amidas; he died in 1531. This Robert Amidas afterwards left Jenkins and lived in a house called Amidas Place, which he had built in Barking opposite the abbey gate. Twenty years later the manor was purchased by Sir William Hewett, Lord Mayor of London in 1559.[1] A touch of romance comes into the history of the manor here, as Sir William subsequently gave his daughter in marriage to one Edward Osborne as a reward for saving her from being drowned in the river Thames at London Bridge, on which his house stood. This Edward Osborne, who was a citizen, clothworker, and Lord Mayor of London (1583), was the great-grandfather of the first Duke of Leeds. Sir William only retained the manor of Jenkins five years, as he accepted a good offer for it from Martin (afterwards Sir Martin) Bowes, Esq., who sold the estate in 1567 to Henry ffanshaw, Esq.

Henry Fanshawe was the second son of Robert Fanshawe, Esq., of Fanshawe Gate, in Dronfield, Derbyshire. He was appointed the Queen's Majesties Remembrancer in the High Court of Exchequer in 1560–61, and held this office till his death in 1568.[2] He lived first at the office in Bread Street, afterwards in Ivy Lane, and subsequently at a house in Warwick Lane. A year or so before his death he purchased the manor of Jenkins, and also that of Fulkys. He also held Clay Hall on lease, all of which manors were in Barking parish. He married, first, Thomazin, daughter of William Hopkins, of Carswell,[3] in Barking. She died in 1562, and was buried in St. Olave Church, Bread Street, as appears from the following reference in Henry Machyn's "Diary":—"The sam day at after-none was bered in Sant Nicolas Oliffe parryche good

---

[1] He belonged to the Clothworkers, and was said to have an income of £6000 a-year.
[2] This post remained in the Fanshawe family until the death of the fifth and last Viscount Fanshawe in 1716, nine succeeding to it in turn.
[3] Carswell was near Clay Hall.

masteres Fanshaw the good gentyll woman & wyff unto Master
Pfanthawe, on of the cheycker with no armes." This last
note implies that she was of humble origin, the daughter perhaps
of a yeoman.

Henry Fanshaw married, secondly, Dorothy, daughter of
George Stonard, of Loughton, by whom he had issue—Ann,
died unmarried, buried in Barking church, 1584; Susanna,
baptized at Christ Church, Newgate, 1567, married Timothy
Lucy, Esq., of Valence, younger brother of Sir Thomas Lucy,
Knt., of Charlecote, Warwickshire; she inherited Valence from her
father.

In a draft will of 1566 he mentions the value of his property
(amounting to £400 per annum), exclusive of Vallance, Gallance,
Clayhall, and his house in Warwick Lane. He died at his town
residence October 28, 1568, and was buried at Barking church.
In his will he left instructions to his executors to expend the four
years' profits out of the parsonage of Dronfield, of which he held
the lease, in founding and endowing a school in that town, to be
known as "The School of Henry Fanshawe, Esq., of Dronfield."
He also left lands and tenements in Chesterfield, Dronfield, etc., in
county Derby in trust to keep and maintain the said school. His
nephew, Thomas Fanshawe, inherited Jenkins.

On the death of Thomas Fanshawe, in 1600, the manor of
Jenkins descended to Thomas, his eldest son by his second wife,
Jane, or Joan, third daughter of Thomas Smith, of Ostenhanger,
Kent. The new lord of Jenkins was Clerk of the Crown in
the King's Bench and Surveyor-General of his Majesty's lands,
and was knighted at Theobalds in 1624. He sat in Parliament
for county Essex for several years. He married Anne, daughter of
Urias Babington, Esq. of St. Stephen's, Coleman Street, London,
who died in 1638. Sir Thomas Fanshawe died at his chambers at
the Inner Temple in his fifty-second year, on the 17th, and was
buried the 29th of December, 1631, at Barking. He had issue—
Thomas; Richard and John, who died in infancy.

Thomas Fanshawe, the only surviving son of the above,
succeeded to the paternal estates. He married, when only
nineteen, Susan, younger daughter and co-heir of Matthias Otten,
Esq., of Walthamstow, Essex, and Putney, Surrey, by whom he
had twelve children. He succeeded his father as Clerk of the
Crown in the King's Bench. Lady Fanshawe, in her "Memoirs,"
describes him as "a worthie honest gentleman & a grate sufferer

for yᵉ Crowne, wholly ingaging his estate for yᵉ maintenance thereoff."

By an ordinance of Parliament passed September, 1645, it was directed that the annuity of £5000 which had been granted to the Earl of Essex in recognition of his zeal against the king should be made up out of the properties of various individuals, among them being Thomas Fanshawe, who was required to contribute £600 per annum out of his manors and estates. He was charged with the accusation, that "being a member of the Honᵇˡᵉ House of Comons he deserted the p'liament & satt in yᵉ assembly at Oxford & was in Barnstaple at the surrender thereof" ("Royal Compo. Papers"). Also, that "he hath neither taken yᵉ Covenant nor negative oath." [1] Thomas died in 1651, and was buried, probably, in the family vault at Barking. His widow lived at Jenkins, with her son and daughter, Thomas and Margaret, both unmarried, until her death in 1668.

Sir Thomas Fanshawe succeeded to the manor in 165½, being then in his twenty-fourth year. Eight years later he was knighted, partly on account of his social position and his generous interest in the affairs of the county, and partly in recognition of his services and those of his family to the Royalist cause. He married (1656–57) Margaret, daughter of Sir Edward Heath, Knt., of Cotesmore, in the county of Rutland, who is described by Lady Fanshawe in her "Memoirs" as a "pretty Lady & a goode woman." By her he had an only daughter, Susanna. Being an only child and an heiress, and withal beautiful and accomplished, her parents and maiden aunt were desirous that she should make a good match, which she did in the person of the Hon. Baptist Noel, eldest son of Viscount Campden, of Exton and Luggenham, Rutland, and an M.P. for his county. The young man himself does not appear to have been of an amatory disposition, judging from his mother's comment upon him in a letter—"Bab will never breacke his harte with beinge in love." However, at a later period, she was able to write more hopefully—"The mach goes on with Mrs. Fanshawe & your brother," and again—"I heare Bab likes his mistress mightly." A few months afterwards we read of a visit to Jenkins by the viscountess, who thus writes to

---

[1] The "Covenant" was "The solemn League and Covenant" to abolish Episcopacy, drawn up in 1637 ; the "negative oath" was a sworn declaration required from suspected loyalists that they would be "true and faithful to the Government established, without king and House of Peers." The latter was proposed as a substitute for the former, to the great annoyance of the Presbyterians.

her husband—"I and my Uncle Robert & Brother Peregrine all went out of towne to Essex yesterday, first to my Uncle Robert's house, wheare we had a breakfaste of all cold things & good wine, and so from thence to diner to Sir Thomas Fanshawe's ; wheare your son Bab looked varly well & very fine & mightly pleased, & she very good & humble as cane bee that I think we could not a had Bab mached anywheare to a pleased you more & mine as she will due, for I due not see the least of pride or gallantrie in her." The viscountess was a good judge of what was suitable and adequate in matrimony in high life, as she had already married her daughters into some of the noblest families in England. The preparations for the wedding followed in due course, and Charles Bertie writes thus to his niece—"Your new sister-in-law has bespoke all her wedding favours & rich night clothes & everything is prepared on her side." Unfortunately, a hitch occurred, which shows that ladies then were as much in the hands of their dressmakers as they are at the present day, for, writing to a friend, Miss Bridget Noel says—"My sister Pen's gown is not sent nor mine, so we shall not have them until the week after the wedding." The calm patience with which the bride and her sister thus resigned themselves to the inevitable is indeed worthy of praise. Sir Thomas was, however, more successful with *his* preparations, for Miss Bridget continues—"I bleve we shall have a great weden for Sir Tomes Fansher is laying in a grat dell of wine and bruing a bundane of strong drink." The "weden" took place at Barking church in June, 1682, and a handsome marriage settlement was made by Sir Thomas. A son was born in the following year, who became the third Earl of Gainsborough, but died before his mother, as also did her husband. She died January 17, 1714, and was buried at Exton, Rutland. A daughter survived her.

Sir Thomas was a splendid specimen of the "fine old English gentleman," and was known for miles round for his kindness to the poor and genial hospitality. Lady Fanshawe says of him— "I confess I owe to Sir Thomas as good a carracter as I can express, for he fully deserves it, both for his true honour & most excellent and acquired natural parts."

Sir Thomas Fanshawe gave the rents arising out of the annual fair at Barking on St. Ethelburgh's Day (October 22), and the Saturday weekly market, together with five acres of land, called Cotlands, in trust to the vicar and churchwardens of Barking, for

the use of the poor.[1]   He, however, stipulated that his right to
hold his courts in the market court-house should remain intact,
and that the trustees in question should keep the court in repair.

Among the distinguished visitors to Jenkins in those days was
the vicar of Barking, the well-known Dr. Thomas Cartwright.   He
was educated at Christ Church, Oxford, where he took his B.D.
in 1660.   He was elected Warden of All Souls by a mandamus
from James II. in 1686, in which year he was also nominated to
the see of Chester.   He held these offices with the vicarage of
Barking.   He married Sarah, daughter of Henry Wight, Esq., of
Gaysham Hall, Barking.   We are indebted to Bishop Cartwright
for a diary full of interesting matter, which has been published by
the Camden society.   He frequently mentions the Fanshawes—
e.g. "I supped & lay at Jenkins;" "I preached at Barking &
dined at Jenkins with Serjeant Winter & Mr. Tison & Mr. Fanshawe & his son;" "I visited Sir Thomas Fanshaw & his lady
& my Lord Fanshaw at Mr. Charles Fanshaw's lodgings."   He
was an obsequious supporter of James II. and a friend of Sir
Richard Alibone.   He died at Dublin in 1689.

Besides being a lover of hospitality, Sir Thomas was a patron
of the drama in London, and took care that his guests should see
the best plays then on the stage.   Miss Bridget Noel writes—
"Lady Fanshaw tells us that it is very esey to goe up to town &
see a play & come down at night."   Later on she says—"We go
to town from here (Jenkins) three or four times a week & come
down so late that I am forced to lie in bed all the next day."
And again—"Last Tuesday I went to the musek meeting at York
Bildens & it was very late before it was don & my brother per-
swaded us to stay in town all night & to go to a play the next
day which was a Commity.[2]   The king & queen was at it & the
house as full as ever I saw it."   Dice and card-playing, not for
pleasure only but for money, were indulged in, as Miss Bridget
writes—"Sister Pen has won you a crowen and I plad at dice and
won you half a giney & a crown at cribedge, so if you ples I will
play till all the money is gon or more wone or if you will not
venter any more I will return the money."   And again—"We had

---

[1] The fair was abolished in 1875, by an order of the Home Secretary, at the request
of the local justices of the peace, and with the concurrence of the trustees of the charity.

[2] *The Committee, or the Faithful Irishman*, was written by Sir Robert Howard
shortly after the Restoration.   The play, with its two Cavalier colonels, was a great
favourite with the Royalists.   Sir Roger de Coverley went to see it because "it was a
good Church of England comedy."—*Vide* Addison's *Spectator*, No. 335.

iell luck at cards the last time we plad, for we lost 40 pound."
The Hon. C. Bertie, writing from Jenkins in 1685, says—"We were
so kindly entertained by my Lady & Sir Thomas that we played
at cards all night & are but just now returned home, scarce able to
hold up our eyes for want of sleep." One of the nieces writes—
"My uncle Charles and Lady Anne Cook dined here on Friday
last & played at cards till eight o'clock next morning & indeed I
think I have not had three hours sleep these three nights."

In 1677 Sir Thomas, who had become a widower in 1674,
married the Hon. Elizabeth Fanshawe, daughter of Viscount
Fanshawe, of ffanshawe Gate and Ware Park,[1] who survived her
husband twenty-four years, and died without issue. He died in
1705, and was buried by the side of his first wife in Barking
church. With his death this branch of the family became
extinct. He left a will, in which he stated that, having amply
provided for his married daughter, he bequeathed the manor of
Jenkins and the whole of his property at Barking to his great
nephew, Thomas Fanshawe, of Parsloes. But the will, written in
his own hand, was not attested as required by an Act recently
passed ; consequently, the two estates came into the possession of
the Hon. Mrs. Noel, despite the entreaties made to her to carry
out the testator's wishes. This misfortune was the beginning of
the decline of the Fanshawe family.

On the death of the Hon. Mrs. Noel in 1714, the manor of
Jenkins was sold to Sir William Humfreys, Lord Mayor of
London. He was the second son of Nathanael Humfreys, a
Welshman, who was a drysalter in the Poultry. Sir William was
knighted in 1704, and created a baronet by George I. in 1714, the
year of his mayoralty.[2] He was Master of the Ironmongers
Company, and for some years M.P. for Marlborough. After his

---

[1] Sir Thomas Fanshawe was created Viscount Fanshawe of Donomore, in Ireland,
September, 1661. He had represented Hertford in six Parliaments, and been fined
£1310 for his "delinquency" in having borne arms for the King at Edgehill. He
married, (1) Ann, daughter of Sir Giles Alington, Knt. of the Horse, of Leath, Cambs,
and Gt. Wymondley, Herts, by his wife, Lady Dorothy Cecil ; (2) (1629) Elizabeth,
daughter of Sir Wm. Cockayne, Knt., Lord Mayor of London. He died 1665, and
was succeeded by his son Thomas.

[2] "Of his lady mayoress an old story is told relative to the custom of the sovereign
kissing the lady mayoress upon visiting the Guildhall. Queen Anne broke down this
observance ; but upon the accession of George I., on his first visit to the City, from his
known character of gallantry it was expected that once again a lady mayoress was to
be kissed by the king on the steps of the Guildhall. But he had no feeling of admira-
tion for English beauty, and the kiss was withheld." (Thornbury's "Old and New
London," vol. i. chap. xxxiv).

purchase of Jenkins, he pulled down the ancient Tudor house and rebuilt it in the Queen Anne style of architecture, laying out the gardens in Dutch fashion, with fishponds, terraces, vistas, and avenues. One of these terraces was composed of four rows of walnut-trees. New gates were erected, which are now the church-yard gates of St. Botolph, Aldgate.

Sir William was twice married, his second wife being the daughter of Robert Lancashire, Esq. He entailed his estate on his grandson, Robert Humfreys, and his heirs for ever. He died October 26, 1735, in his eighty-fifth year. The funeral took place in the night of November 6, and is thus described—

> Last night the corpse of Sir Wᵐ Humfreys, Bart., was buried in great state, having all the trophies of honour suitable to his dignity carried before him. The City Marshal preceded the hearse which was drawn by six horses, followed by a coach & six (the horses belonging to his son Orlando) & fourteen other coaches & six & near two hundred lights & so passed from his house in Bloomsbury Square, through Holborn, down Chancery Lane, to St. Mildred's Church in the Poultry. The pall was supported by Sir Gerrard Conyers, Sir Edward Bellamy, Sir Willᵐ Billers, Sir Richard Hopkins, Sir Harcourt Masters, & Sir John Thompson, Knights & Aldermen in their gowns.

On the demolition of St. Mildred's church in 1875, his remains were conveyed, with those of others, to the City of London Cemetery at Ilford, where they rest in shell No. 20, among the unknown and unhonoured dead.

Sir Orlando Humfreys succeeded to Jenkins on the death of his father. He married Ellen, the only child of Colonel Robert Lancashire, by whom he had three sons and two daughters. The sons died young; Mary, the eldest daughter, had three husbands, the last being Thomas Gore, Esq., M.P. for Bedford, and uncle to Charles Gore, Esq., who had married her younger sister, Ellen, Sir Orlando died in 1737, and was buried in the south aisle of Barking church, where there is a monument to his memory.[1]

Robert Humfreys, on whom Jenkins had been entailed by his

---

[1] It has this inscription—"Sir Orlando Humfreys of Jenkins in this Parish, died June 14, 1737, aged 59 years. He had issue 3 sons & 2 daughters; two of his sons died young; Robert the 2ᵈ at 28 years of age died 1736. Mary the eldest daughter married Willᵐ Ball Waring of Dunston in Berks, by whom he has as yet no surviving issue. Ellen Wintour Humfreys the youngest daughter is unmarried." The survey of Barking Manor, made in 1737, describes William Ball Waring, Esq., and Mary, his wife, and Dame Ellen Humfreys and Ellen Wintour Humfreys, as the "lords and ladies of Barking Manor."

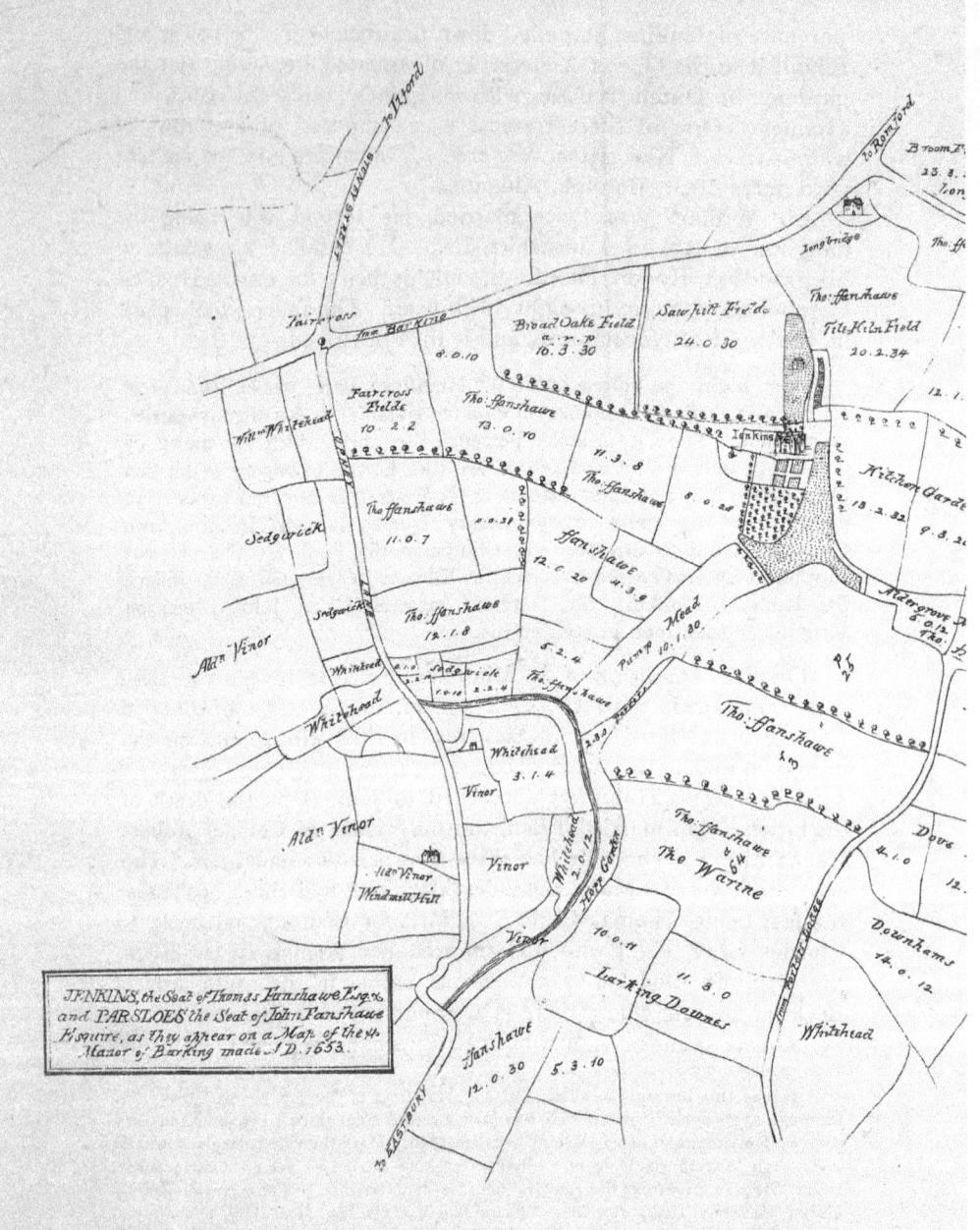

JENKINS, the Seat of Thomas Fanshawe Esqr. and PARSLOES the Seat of John Fanshawe Esquire, as they appear on a Map of the 4. Manor of Barking made A.D. 1653.

grandfather, died in 1736, unmarried. The manor lapsed consequently to Thomas and Charles Gore, Esqs., who sold it in 1760 to Smart Lethieullier, Esq., of Aldersbrook Manor.[1] The latter dying without issue, the estate, now no longer called Jenkins, but Barking Manor, was inherited by his niece, Mary, the daughter and heir of his brother Charles, who had married Edward (afterwards Sir Edward) Hulse, Esq. Mr. Hulse pulled down the mansion built by Sir William Humfreys, and worked up the materials into a good-sized farmhouse. Only the fishponds and traces of the terraces now remain to mark the spot of this once important manor, and even the very name Jenkins is all but forgotten. Its present owner is Sir Edward H. W. Hulse, a minor, whose father died a year ago in South Africa under tragic circumstances. Its tenant till recently was Mr. W. K. Marriott.

[1] Now the site of the City of London Cemetery.

CHAPTER XVIII

THE MANOR OF COCKERMOUTH

" Mirror of life ! the glories thus depart
  Of all that Youth and Love and Fancy frame,
When painful Anguish speeds the piercing dart,
  Or Envy blasts the blooming flowers of Fame.

" Nurse of wild wishes and of fond desires
  The prophetess of Fortune, false and vain
To scenes where Peace in Ruin's arms expires
  Fallacious Hope deludes her hapless train."

JOHN LANGHORNE
(curate of Dagenham, 1762).

THE manor of Cockermouth may be described, on account of its position, as the "Manor of the Marshes." It stood about a mile to the south-west of the village proper, and fronted the present London and Tilbury road. The mansion itself was a fine and commodious building, with extensive grounds attached to it, the whole being enclosed on three sides by a moat. Norden describes it in 1594 as a "fayre howse buylte of bricke near to Berkyng." This manor was, if not the largest, by far the most important of all the manors of Dagenham. A court was held here at stated periods for the settlement of civil cases, disputes, trespasses, and debts, at which the lord of Cockermouth presided. This right was exercised right down to the end of the seventeenth century, and was regarded as a valuable appanage to the manor. Another fact that added considerably to the *prestige* of the manor was the right of its owner to nominate to the vicarage of Dagenham, a privilege which was obtained under the will of John de Cokermouth, who bequeathed a large portion of this manorial estate to the Abbey of Barking for the endowment of a priest at Dagenham.

The estate consisted of a rectangular piece of land lying between the main road and the river Thames, and was about six hundred acres in extent. Of this nearly two-thirds was marsh (terra in marisco). We find references to it in ancient charters. Thus—

A grant from Robert, son of Simon Godefrey, to William, son of Humphris, of land in the parish of Dakenham and in marisco de Dakenham in Rugevill" *i.e.* Dakenham Marsh] for the yearly rent of 26^{d}.

Witnesses,—William Dun Godfrey, Fleccarius,[1]

Gervase Halward & others.

The date of this deed is uncertain, but somewhere between 1250 and 1280 (MS. Cart. 27363).

So again—

A Release by Iohn Godefrey & Richard Godefrey of Berkyngg to Iohn Ouhtred[2] and Agnes his wife of Land in villa de Berkynge in parochiâ de Dakenham, formerly the dower land of Amicia Godefreyes, sometime wife of Robert Godefrey.

Witnesses,—Thomas de Dakenham,

Richard Le May,

Stephen Bysshop & others.

Given at Berkyng, Tuesday after the Feast of the Nativity of Saint Iohn Baptist in the sixth year of Edward the Second (MS. Cart. 27366).

The date of this deed would be June 25—July 1, 1313–14.

Another charter is—

A Grant from Iohn Good, of Dakenham to William & Emma Outred of one acre of Land in Dakenham Marsh, with a portion of wall against the flood [*i.e.* the river Thames or the Dagenham Breach].

Witnesses,—Iohn Michel, Steward,

Iohn Beyntre.

Given at Dakenham, the Sunday after the Feast of Saint Nicholas the Bishop [December 6] in the second year of Edward the Third (MS. Cart. 27368).

And again—

The Grant from Iohn Fuller and Iuliana his wife, daughter & heiress of the late William Druewy of Dakenham & Thomas Spakeman of Upmenstre, of Land to William Outred in Dakenham Marsh.

Witnesses,—Iohn Baunton, Steward,

Iohn Estebrok.

---

[1] Probably from the Anglo-Saxon fleax (flax) or fleece—a weaver or woolman.

[2] An old epitaph in Romford church, preserved by Weever, an Essex antiquary, says—

Here lye Iohn Outred & Ione his wyff,
Who liuyd long togeddyr withouten stryff,
Iohn left this world & passyd to heuen—
On thousand fyue hundred yere & eleuen.

Possibly a descendant of the above Iohn.

Given at Dakenham, the Sunday after the Feast of Saint Matthias, in the 30ᵗʰ year of Edward the Third (MS. Cart 27370).

There is also an undated grant of land in Dakenham Marsh from Agnes, widow of John Estbrok, inherited from her father, Henry Albard (MS. Cart. 27372).

Judging from the references we frequently meet with to the appointment of special tithe-collectors for the purpose, the tithes of Cockermouth must have produced a very substantial sum, whether in kind or cash. Two and sometimes three tythers were appointed to collect them. Thus, at a court held on the Saturday next after the Feast of Thomas the Martyr (December 29), in the twenty-second year of Edward III. (1348–49), William Sherlock and John Hamonds were elected tythers (decimarii) of Dakenham. And again, at a court held on the Saturday after the Feast of Peter and Paul, Apostles (June 29), in the forty-second year of Edward III., John Spurling was elected to collect the tithe of hay (feni) of Dakenham Marsh, and William Godebolt and Benjamin Edwold, clerk, were elected to collect the tithe of corn at Dakenham.

Another court roll informs us that at a court held on the Saturday in the Feast of Thomas, archbishop, in the ninth year of Richard II. (1386–87), John Cory, Simon Jerkyn, of Cokermouth, John Swete, and Thomas Wodeward, were elected to collect the tithes of Dakenham, and took oaths for the proper execution of their office in time of autumn.

So again, at a court held on the Saturday next after the Feast of Apostles, Peter and Paul, in the thirteenth year of King Richard II., Simon Jerkyn and John Cory, of Cory in Cokermouth, and John Jacob, were elected to collect the tithe of hay in Dakenham.

And later, at a court held on the Saturday next after the translation of Thomas the Martyr in the twenty-second year of Richard II., John Hooke and John Sparwe were chosen to be tythers of Cokermouth, and were sworn to discharge their office.

And again, at a court held on the Saturday next after the Nativity of Saint John Baptist, in the second year of Henry IV., John Edwold and Richard Noleherst and John Hooke were elected tythers at Cokermouth, and took oath to execute their office.

A few years later, at a court held on the Saturday just before the Feast of the translation of Thomas the Martyr, in the sixth year of Henry IV., Henry Perryman was elected to collect tithe at Cokermouth, and took his oath.

And again, at a court held on the Saturday next before the feast of the translation of Thomas the Martyr, in the tenth year of Henry IV., John Cory, of Cory Hall, and John Hooke were appointed tythers at Cokermouth.

And once more, at a court held on the Saturday next after the Feast of the Apostles, Peter and Paul, in the twenty-ninth year of Henry VI., John Nattocke was chosen to collect tithes for Eastbury and Dakenham Marsh in time of autumn.

In all probability the manor took its name from John de Coker-muthe,[1] king's clerk, who in the reign of Edward II. was appointed to the office of Remembrancer to the Exchequer, in succession to John de Merkynfeld. Whether he purchased the estate or it was granted by its original owner, Bishop de Sandale of Winchester, for services rendered to him or to the king, we cannot now say, but John de Cokermuth is mentioned in a subsidy roll made in 1320 as occupying this manor, and as being assessed at 9s. 1½d. (equal to £30 of present money), which is the highest assessment on this roll of the taxpayers of Dagenham. It is possible that he acquired this estate with a view to founding and endowing a vicarage at Dagenham; at any rate, an ancient roll states that in December, 1330, he applied to Edward III. for leave to give and bequeath by will, to the Abbess and Convent of Barking in perpetuity, certain lands, viz. " 1 messuage [dwelling-house], 140 acres of arable land, 30 acres of meadow, 25 acres of pasture, 8 acres of wood, & 70 shillings in rent at Dakenham, Berkyng & Illeford." The application was granted, and on December 21, 1331, a commission was issued at Glastonbury for an enrolment of release by John de Cokermuth, clerk, to Iolenta, Abbess of Berkyng, of his right of certain lands, over two hundred acres in all. Witnesses—Sir Iohn de Suttone, Sir Thos. Gobioun, knights; Iohn de Dovere, Henry Gernet; Iohn de Haveryng; Edward de Northtoft, Iohn de Dakenham; Robert William de Haveryng; Samannus atte Walle, Iohn le Porter, Richard Malemayns; Iohn Samkyn; Iohn Chaumpioun; Nicolas Forester. Dated at Dakenham, December 9, 1331, 4th Edward III. (" Calendar of Close Rolls ").

After the will had been proved, doubts were raised as to the legality and validity of the gift, which resulted in a grant being given at Westminster on April 5, 1337, " for the security of the Abbess and Convent of Berkynge." It states that—

---

[1] See Appendix A, Chapter VI.

Whereas Ioan [1] the present abbess, with the king's license, has acquired in mortmain from Iohn de Cokermuth, now deceased, 140 acres of land, 30 of meadow, 25 of pasture, 8 of wood and 70/-. in rent in Dakenham, Berkyng and Illeford, Co. Essex, these shall not be liable in respect of a security given at the Exchequer of Edward II. by the said Iohn & Iohn de Heydon, as executors of the will of Iohn de Sandale, Bishop of Winchester, for payment of all debts due to the king by the bishop at his death.

The manor remained a part of the abbey estate for over two hundred years, until the dissolution of the abbey in 1537–38, when it was seized by legal process by the Crown. No charges of a grave nature seem to have been brought against the abbey by the commissioners whose business it was to get up a case against them. It simply shared in the general fate of the abbeys. The last abbess, Dorothy Barley, surrendered November 14, 1539, and was pensioned, with thirty nuns, her own annuity amounting to £133 6s. 8d.

In 1564 Queen Elizabeth sold the manor of Cockermouth and the vicarage of Dagenham to Sir Anthony Brown for the sum of £1265 6s. 8d. Sir Anthony was the son of Sir Weston Browne, of Abbesroding, by Elizabeth his wife. He was educated at Oxford, and after taking his B.A. degree, with honours, in due course was entered as a student in the Middle Temple, and became a serjeant-at-law in 1554. Being a strong Romanist and a supporter of Queen Mary, he was appointed serjeant to their Majesties Philip and Mary, and in the year following (1558) was made Lord Chief Justice of the Common Pleas. On the accession of Queen Elizabeth he was deposed from being Chief Justice to the position of a justice of that court. In 1566 he was knighted, but only enjoyed this honour a few months, as he shortly afterwards died at his house at South Weald.

Sir Anthony was a stern lawyer, and took a prominent part in the stirring and burning questions of his time. He was suspected of being the author of "Arguments for Mary, Queen of Scots, her right of succession to the Crown of England," a treatise published under the name of John Lesley, Bishop of Rosse. This accusation caused him to be regarded with much disfavour by Queen Elizabeth, all the more so, as a pamphlet appeared about the same time entitled, "A discourse upon certain points touching the inheritance of the Crown, conceived by Sir Anth. Browne, justice." This was answered by Sir Nicholas Bacon, Lord Keeper of England.

[1] Joan de Gillton ; she was buried before the Altar of the Resurrection in Barking Abbey. So an old MS. Her name is not given in Lyson's list of the abbesses.

Sir Anthony is remembered partly because he built the Free School at Brentwood, and endowed it with a portion of the tithes belonging to the vicarage of Dagenham, and partly because he was responsible for the burning of William Hunter in Brentwood market-place in 1555, and of blind Christopher Lister of Dagenham at Stratford, both for heresy.

As Sir Anthony Browne had no issue, he bequeathed the manor of Cockermouth to his great-nephew, Wistan Browne, Esq., but the latter had no sooner proved the will than he applied for a royal licence to sell the manor and advowson to one John Buttrell, Esq. Two years later (1574-75) they were purchased by William Nutbrowne, Esq., of Stanway Hall, Essex, who died in 1588. In his will he bequeaths Wakering Place and other properties to his wife Anne for life, £30 to the poor of Barking, the "Mannor of Cockermouth in Dagenham & Rectory there," and other lands to his executors for five years to pay debts and legacies. He gives "Gibbes' fields neere the Lands of Jenkins to Thomas ffanshaw, Esq., for life & his son & heirs."

To carry out the testator's wishes the executors sold Cockermouth and the rectory to one William Megges, of Whitechapel, a draper. He died in 1598, and was buried in Whitechapel church, which points to his having been a person of some consequence in that parish. In his will he gives his son William the third part of his manor of Cokermoth.[1] Three years later the manor and rectory were purchased by John Swinnerton,[2] sen., and John Swinnerton, jun., who disposed of them to John Darcy, from whom they descended to Sir Thomas Darcy, Bart., of Gt. Brackstead, who held the last court here June 8, 1685.

Down to this period the manor of Cockermouth and the advowson of Dagenham vicarage would seem to have been always sold jointly. In 1690 Sir Thomas disjoined them by selling the manor only to one William Clark. The latter gave it by will to his wife Anne for life, the remainder to Thomas Page and others in trust, by whom it was conveyed to William Watkins and Thomas Johnson, and passed to Miss Mary Page, Thomas Chippendale, and George

---

[1] In the Barking Manor Rent Roll (1663) a William Megges is described as holding a cottage at Bunting Bridge.

[2] "Mr. John Swinnerton holdeth one close called Cockermore" (Barking Manor Survey, 1616). He was Lord Mayor in 1612. He was ridiculed in a comedy called "The Hogge [Swine-ton] hath lost his pearle, publikely acted by certaine London prentices at the White Friars." The actors were interrupted during the play, and "six or seven of them were carryed off to finish the laste act at Bridgewell."

Evans. Edward Evans was the last of the lords of Cockermouth (1750–65), as the estate was at his death divided and sold in separate plots. It was probably in 1766–67 that the manor-house was shorn of its manorial dignity, as Muilmant, in his "History of Essex" (published in 1770), describes Cockermouth as a farmhouse. Shortly afterwards, it was pulled down and rebuilt nearer to the main road. In 1823 Rowland Stephenson, known as the "Fugitive Banker," owned it, but subsequently went off to America to escape his pecuniary liabilities. At the sale of Cockermouth farm, under a commission of bankruptcy, Mr. Thomas Hankey, of Mincing Lane, purchased it, but resold it to Charles Hulse, Esq. Meanwhile the name of the house had been changed to America Farm, which it retained until Mr. W. Varco Williams gave it the more jocund designation, "Merrielands."

To the south of Cockermouth lies Dagenham Marsh, or Level, alongside the Thames. We find mention of Sir William Humphrey purchasing land in Marsh Green from Lady Noel (1705), of John Henry Merttins holding a farm there in 1738, and of a Mr. Ind holding a marsh called Pear Tree. Thomas Pearson held land in that locality about 1666.

EXCHEQUER OF PLEAS. PLEA ROLL.

Easter 8 *Iames* I. *Membrane* 3.

Pleas before the Barons of the Exchequer at Westminster, Easter 8 Iames I.

Abstract.

Essex.

In Hilary term last past, Iohn Harvey, the King's debtor, came by Robert Ball his attorney and proffered his bill against Ioseph Haynes, esquire, and Christopher Wilson of a plea of trespass and ejection, to wit, that whereas Ieremiah Plomtree, schoolmaster of the grammar school, Anthony Browne, serjeant at law in Brentwood, and Edward Marwood and Iohn Wright of Southweald, gentleman, guardians of the lands of the said school, on 16th Ianuary 7 Iames I [16$\frac{09}{10}$] by indenture between the said schoolmaster and guardians on the one part, and Iohn Harvey citizen of London on the other part, dated 10 Nov. 7 Iames I [1609] and first delivered as the deed of the said parties at Dagenham on 16th Ianuary aforesaid, leased to the said Iohn Harvey the rectory of Dagenham with the tithes and appurtenances from Michaelmas then last past for 21 years ; on 18th Ianuary 7 Iames I the said Ioseph Haynes and Christopher Wilson wrongfully entered upon the possession of the said Iohn Harvey and ejected the said Harvey, to his damage to the value of £40. Hence the said Iohn Harvey cannot pay his debts to the King.

And now, 15 days after Easter, until which day the said Ioseph and Christopher had licence to parley apart, the said Iohn came by his attorney aforesaid, and the said Ioseph and Christopher by their attorney Abraham Baylie, and the latter pleading not guilty, both parties put themselves on the country. Moreover the said Ioseph and Christopher say that long before the said lease a certain Iohn Greenewood, schoolmaster of the grammar school, Anthony Browne, serjeant at law in Brentwood, Iohn Wright and Thomas Churche, guardians of the said lands, were seised of the rectory, tithes and appurtenances aforesaid in their demesne as of fee in right of the school, and on 19th November 1 Iames I [1603], at Dagenham, by indenture between the said schoolmaster and guardians on the one part, and the said Ioseph Haynes on the other, leased the said rectory, tithes and appurtenances to the said Ioseph from Michaelmas then last past for 21 years, and the said Ioseph enjoyed peaceable possession until ejected by the said Ieremiah Plomtree, Edward Marwood and Iohn Wright 16 Ian, 7 Iames I [16$\frac{09}{10}$]; hence said Ioseph and his servant Christopher Wilson were justified in re-entering upon the same.

Iohn Harvey asserts that the lease to Ioseph Haynes called the lands by another name ;—was not properly sealed, &c.

A day is given on the morrow of Trinity next to come.

There is no further reference to this case ; probably it was settled out of court. But it does not seem that John Harvey had a shred of right to his claim.

CHAPTER XIX

THE MANOR OF VALENCE

> " The stately homes of England,
> How beautiful they stand !
> Amid their tall ancestral trees,
> O'er all the pleasant land."
> HEMANS.

THE manor of Valence is a pleasant and elegant residence, situated about two miles to the north-west of Dagenham church. It is enclosed by spacious grounds, with a moat, now partly filled up, on its west side and another on the east boundary. Formerly there was a wood, known as Valence Wood, on the south side ; this has disappeared, and the only reminiscence of its existence is in the name of the lane, Wood Lane, which separated this manorial estate from that of Parsloes. Local tradition has it that the manor-house of Valence was connected by a subterranean passage with Barking Abbey, to which it belonged, but no trace of such a passage, if there ever was one, has come to light as yet.

This manor consisted of one messuage, with garden and dovecote, of the yearly rent of 2s., 128 acres of land, at 4d. an acre, 4 acres of meadow at 6d. an acre, and rent of assize, 7s. 3½d. from 6 free tenants there. The earliest tenant of whom we have any record was Margery de Moese, sometime wife of Thomas Weylond, who sub-let the manor to Agnes de Valence, about the end of the thirteenth century. In an *Inquisition post mortem*[1] held in 1309, it is stated that Agnes de Valence had recently died possessed of certain lands and tenements belonging to the Abbess of Barking, at a yearly rent of 17s. 4d., and "suit of court to the said Abbess every 3 weeks." Also that the "tenants were to ride with the said Abbess with two horses at the costs of the Abbess when rightfully forewarned." She was succeeded by her brother,

[1] See Appendix A, Chapter XIX.

VALENCE

Adomar de Valence, Earl of Pembroke, son of William de Valence, half brother of Henry III.[1] Adomar met with his death by being foully murdered while in attendance on Queen Isabella in France, in revenge for the part he had taken in beheading the Earl of Lancaster at Pontefract in 1319. He was thrice married, but had no issue, so was succeeded by his brother, or nephew, as we read of an Aylmer de Valence, Earl of Pembroke, holding in 1324 his Court of Common Pleas for the Forest of Hainault, at Stratford. This does not, however, necessarily imply that he lived at Valence, though he may have stayed here, it being only six miles east of Stratford.[2]

In the Close Rolls we find an order issued on July 19, 1325, from the Tower to John de Blomvill, escheator, to cause a rent of 17s. 4d. yearly to be paid to the Abbess of Berkyng for so long as certain lands in Dakenham are in the king's hands by reason of the death of Aymer de Valencia, late Earl of Pembroke. Another roll informs us that this, with the earl's other property, was assigned to David de Strabolgi, Earl of Athole, and Joan his wife, kinswoman and co-heiress of the said Aymer, in 1326. We learn, further, from another membrane, that an application was made to the king's court for the division of the Earl of Pembroke's land between Davide de Strabolgi, Earl of Athole, son and heir of Joan, lately the wife of Davide de Strabolgi, late Earl of Athole, kinswoman and co-heiress of the said Aymer, and Elizabeth, the wife of Richard Talbot, Knt., also kinswoman and co-heiress of Aymer. The bulk of the property was, by an order of the court, assigned to the earl. Whether this last order had reference to the manor of Valence (among other estates) is doubtful ; it is possible, at any rate. A later roll, dated 1332, is more explicit, as it gives an account of a petition made on behalf of the Earl of Pembroke, tenant-in-chief of the late king (Edward II.), re Aymer de Valencia, deceased, owner of certain lands in Dakenham, of the value of 37s. 8d., occupied by John de Nevill.

At the dissolution of Barking Abbey, the manor of Valence came into the possession of the Crown, and was afterwards bestowed upon the Dean and Canons of Windsor.

---

[1] There is a very fine recumbent monument of William de Valence in St. Edmund's Chapel, Westminster Abbey. He was murdered at Bayone in 1296—"His whole tomb is French, its enamels from Limoge, his birthplace Valence, on the Rhone, represented on his coat of arms " (Dean Stanley).

[2] There is also a similar tomb there to Aylmer, or Aymer de Valence, north of that of Edward the Confessor.

Norden, in his " History of Essex," mentions one Timothye Lucye as living at Valence in the latter part of the sixteenth century.[1] Elsewhere he is described as holding the leases of the manors of Wolves, Valence, Gallance, and East Hall. Mr. Lucye married, in 1584, Susanna, daughter and co-heiress of Henry Fanshawe, armiger, of Jenkyns. He left Valence about 1596, and went to his estate of Hugford, Middleton, where he died in 1616.

Sir Nicholas Coote, Knt., of Wyfeilds,[2] in Barking, occupied the manor, probably from 1596–1610. Judging from the frequent occurrence of his name in the subsidy rolls of Queen Elizabeth and James I. as a " commissioner," it would seem that he was a man of some political standing. He married, first, Eleanor, daughter of Sir Michael Stanhope, Knt., and widow of Thomas Cooper, Esq., of Thurgarton, Notts. ; second, Elizabeth, sixth daughter of Sir George Hervey, of Marks, Romford. He died in 1633, in his sixty-first year. His five children all pre-deceased him. In his will he bequeaths 20s. for a funeral sermon at Barking church, and to the men and women of that parish, who should, at the time of his death, be of the same age as himself, 12d. each.

The Survey of Barking Manor of 1616 states that Mr. Nathanael Henshawe then held Valence and various lands at the Marsh. He was the son of a Thomas Henshawe, a silk mercer and merchant tailor of London, and married Mary, daughter of —— Harbin, of Great Warley. He died some time before 1644, and was buried in Stoke Poges church. His children were—Charles, Mary, Flowre, Nathanael, Hercules.

From the Henshawe family the manor of Valence passed to that of Bonham, with which it was connected by marriage, Mr. Benjamin Henshawe, a younger brother, having married Anne, daughter of William Bonham, bookseller, of Paternoster Row, and of the Vintners Company. Thomas Bonham, son of William Bonham, by a daughter of —— Babington, of county Chester,

---

[1] He was baptized at Charlecote, near Stratford-on-Avon. He was the brother of Sir Thomas Lucy, Knt., of Charlecote, whose prosecution of Shakespeare for deer-stealing in Fulbroke Park has been the chief cause of his celebrity. The prosecution was conducted with some bitterness, in consequence of a lampoon said to have been written by the dramatist on Sir Thomas, who retaliated by compelling Shakespeare to leave his native place. This was in 1585. The immortal bard avenged himself subsequently by describing his prosecutor under the character of " Justice Shallow " (*Henry IV.*, Part II.). It is within the bounds of possibility that " Justice Shallow " paid a visit at some time or other to Valence. See Washington Irving's essay on Stratford-on-Avon in the " Sketch Book."

[2] Wyfeilds was near Cranbrook Manor. It was pulled down in 1806.

became the lord of Valence in 1647–48. He held a commission as "Captain of the Trained Band," 1634. He married Ann, daughter of Edward Manning, Esq., of St. Mary Cray, Kent, by whom he had twelve or thirteen children, of whom several died young. He himself "gave way to fate" in 1676, and was buried in Dagenham church, where an effusive Latin inscription bears witness to his great powers of mind. In his will he bequeaths his lands in Ashbocking and Hemington, Suffolk, to his son Thomas; to his wife Ann, his lands and tenements called Vallence-Gallance, leased of the Dean and Canons of Windsor and East Hall, for life; also his house in Hart Street, Crutched Friars, over against St. Olave's church. To his daughter Margaret £500, and "£500 more if she marries with the consent of her mother." To his sons-in-law, William Dagger and Thomas Ashby, £5 each, and to his daughter, Diana Dagger, £50, and Diana Ashby, his grandchild, £100 each, and sums of £100 and £50 to his other grandchildren, "And whereas my son-in-law James Hervey owes me £200, I bequeath £100 of same to his eldest son Thomas, and £50 to Anne Harvye." To his brother, Edward Bonham, Esq., £10 "good money;" to his brother-in-law, Edward Manning, Esq., £10; to his kinsman, Thos. Henshawe, £10; to his "cosen," Henry Adderley, Esq., living in London nigh Founders Hall, £10 for mourning; to his friend, Robert Thompson, of the Prerogative Court, and to Mr. Norton, 50s. each for a ring.

Thomas Bonham, the only surviving son and heir, succeeded to Valence, being then in his fortieth year. He was of the Inner Temple, and married Elizabeth, daughter of one Micklethwaite, by whom, he had issue—William, died in infancy; Frances; Elizabeth, married Daniel Skinner, of London, a linen draper; Ann; Rebecca married George Mildmay, Esq., of Corbet's Tye, a son of Francis Harvey Mildmay, of Marks, Romford.

Thomas Bonham does not seem to have remained long at Valence, as a Survey of Barking Manor of 1680 mentions one Henry Merttins as the "lord of Valence" on the surrender of Eleanor Robinson. Henry Merttins was the son of —— Merttins, citizen and jeweller, of London, and married Elizabeth, daughter of Sir Edward Wood, Knt., by whom he had six children—John Henry; Mary, who married Alexander Bennett, of London, merchant; Hester, who married the Rev. Dr. Wright, rector of Spitalfields; Edward, died 1709; and Elizabeth and Clara. Henry Merttins died at Valence, March 28, 1725. Among his bequests was one to his daughter Hester, of Butlers Panyers Grove, and other lands near Bentry Heath.

John Henry Merttins succeeded his father at Valence, where he resided till his death in 1776. He was buried in the family vault at Dagenham. His son, John Henry, died in April, 1740, aged thirteen.

At the close of the eighteenth century, John Hopkins Dare was the tenant of Valence. He was the son of John Dare, of Bentrye Heath, by Elizabeth, widow of John Marmaduke Grafton, Esq., of Cranbrook.

From particulars of a sale at Valence in 1843, we learn that Vallence-Gallance Manor Farm, consisting of 135 acres, was held by Mr. Samuel Seabrook ; and that "the present highly respectable tenant" also farmed "judiciously and liberally" the Warren House Farm of 158 acres. The total rental was £538 per annum, with a quit-rent of £2 1s. 4d., and an acquittance of 8d. to the manor of Barking. Since 1850 the farm has been occupied successively by John Geary Cholmondeley, George Winmill, Charles Cathie, and Thomas May, its present tenant. In 1863 a portion of the house, which included several rooms supposed to be haunted, was taken down, and the drawbridge over the moat was removed. Though no longer the mansion it once was, it is a pleasing, well-preserved residence, and happily still retains its old name. It is vested in the Ecclesiastical Commissioners on behalf of the Dean and Chapter of Windsor.

A quarter of a mile due west of Valence stands a large modern house, called Bennett's Castle House. This was built about twenty years ago, and replaced an older "messuage," which had stood there time out of mind. The Barking Manor Survey, made in 1663, mentions a Stephen Porter as holding land in Bennett's Castle which formerly belonged to Barking Abbey, and was held at a quit-rent of 14s. 2d. per annum. We hear of a Mr. James Hunsdon holding Bennett's Castle Farm (71 acres) in 1802. "Bennett" was, no doubt, the name of the tenant of the original house here, but there is no evidence or trace of any castle having ever existed here. In the north aisle of Barking church there is a monument in memory of Captain Bennet, of Pool, died 1706, and of his son, John, died 1716; possibly they may have given the name to the house, which by some fancy was termed a "castle."

CHAPTER XX

THE MANOR OF WANGEY

" Round this old-fashioned, quaint abode
Deep silence reigned, save when a gust
Went rushing down the country road,
And skeletons of leaves, and dust
A moment quickened by its breath,
Shuddered and danced their dance of death,
And through the ancient oaks o'erhead
Mysterious voices moaned and fled."

LONGFELLOW.

THE manor of Wangey, Wangye, or Wangay was situated on the south side of Chadwell Heath. In old wills it is described as being in "Grove Streat in the parish of Barking." It comprised about 150 acres of land, chiefly arable, together with a small coppice outside the Forest of Hainault, and a stretch of land by the highway known as the "King's Waste." As the lord of Wangey was supposed to protect the forest on its south side, he was allowed certain rights to timber and pannage. The manor was an ancient one, and derived its name, doubtless, from one of its earliest tenants. In common with the other manors it was the property of the Abbey of Barking, to which it was charged to pay an annual rent of £4 10s. 0d. The earliest tenant of whom we have any record was one John Humphreys, who held the lease in 1539, and various lands in the Marsh.

After the dissolution of the abbey the manor of Wangey was re-leased by the royal grant of Edward VI. to Edward Fynes, Lord Clinton, who shortly afterwards sold it to Thomas Barnes, Esq., or Barons, of Aldborough Hatch. On his death in 1573 it passed to his son Thomas. In 1601, the manor of Wangey was granted by Queen Elizabeth to a Joseph Heynes, and held by him twenty years. His son Simon sold it to Francis Fuller, Esq., Clerk of the Escheats in the Exchequer. An Essex historian (Salmon) says that "Francis Fuller was embroiderer to James I." As Mr. Fuller died (March 10, 1636) without issue, the estate was inherited by his nephew, Francis Osbaston, or Osbaldeston, the son of his sister Barbara, wife of Henry Osbaston, Esq., of Stanton, Herts. Its new owner had possession of it twelve years, and died in 1648, at Beehive, near Ilford. He was buried in Barking church, where there is a tomb to his memory.[1] He had no children. His widow, Alice, married the Hon. Robert Bertie, fifth son of Robert, Earl of Lindsay. At her decease in 1677, Wangey Manor reverted to her brother-in-law, Henry Osbaston, and afterwards to his son Francis. On the death of Francis Osbaston, all his manors, lands, and tenements whatsoever came to his brother Henry, subject to the payment of annuities to his wife and daughter Mary, and £10,000 to the latter when sixteen years of age. He was buried in Little Ilford church. His monument states that he "deceased high sheriff of the County, April 22, 1678, aged 32."

In 1694 the Osbastons sold the estate to John Lethieullier, Esq., from whom it descended (1760) to Mary, the only daughter of Charles Lethieullier,[2] Esq., and wife of Edward (afterwards Sir Edward) Hulse, Esq. The manor is now virtually extinct.

The lords of Wangey held the manor of the king *in capite*, but none of those whom we have mentioned resided at it. They preferred to sell the lease (usually for three lives) to the highest bidder, who in turn often resold it. Thus we hear of Sir James Hervey, Knt., citizen and ironmonger of London, purchasing Wangey and other estates about 1570 from Mr. Clement Cysley,

---

[1] It has the following quaint if not complimentary inscription :—

> " He that hath built alive by his deserts
> Himself a tomb within the best men's hearts,
> Might justly claim a charitable stone,
> To sign his dust with some inscription,
> His brother, who succeeds in his estate,
> Thinks that were but to supererogate,
> And death's and his joint purchase to secure
> Huddles him up in common sepulture,
> But his surviving half, his wife, who feared
> Lest with his corpse his name should be interr'd
> Devoted this, oblivion to prevent,
> He's twice buried who wants a monument."

[2] The Lethieulliers lived at Aldersbrook Manor, where they succeeded the Osbastons. Charles Lethieullier, Esq., was buried in Little Ilford church, where there is a monument to his memory.

of Eastbury House, and others. It is certain that Sir James lived at Wangey at intervals from 1570 to his death in 1583. His wife, Ann, was a daughter of Sebastyan Geans, of Antwerp. She died at Wangey, and was buried in St. Dionis church, London, 1580. Sir James (who was Lord Mayor in 1581) had three sons—

1. Sir Sebastian, Knt., of Mardike, citizen and ironmonger of London; Lord Mayor, 1618; married Mary, daughter of Peter Tryon, of St. Christopher-the-less, London; lived at Lyme Street in the city; died, 1621. On his death his widow remarried, thus— " Sʳ Thomas Hynton of Chilton Foliot, knight and the Lady Mary Harvie, late wife of Sir Sebastian Harvie, knight, married Octobʳ 1, 1622 " (Entry in Stratford-le-Bow register).

2. James Hervey, of Wangey.

3. William Hervey, Gent., of Dagenham.[1]

In his will, Sir James bequeaths the lands and hereditaments " which I own in right of my wife Ann deceased beyond the seas to be divided among my children excepting the house called the Golden Plowe in the city of Antwarpe." His lands at Marditch, in Hornchurch, his " great messuage " in Lyme Street, London, and and the " house south-east " of it, he leaves to Sebastian. Also his manor of Winterbourne, Mountjoy, Wilts. To his son James he leaves a house in Lyme Street; all his lands in Dagenham purchased of Richard Charwell of Romford; all his " freehold & copyhold lands, woods, & underwoods in the village of Wangey, Chawdwell,[2] & thereabouts, bought of Richard Bookie, Mr. Clement Cyslye, Esq. & of John Snaggs, John Thacker, John Humfrey, Willᵐ Clerk & Wᵐ Nutbrowne, with groves and new house at Bentrye Hethe."

The will contains the following bequests, a few of which are peculiar, and throw a sidelight on the history of those times :—

I wish 36 sermons to be preached on the occasion of my death one each month untill all are preached. For each sermon 6/-. To the Poor of Antwarpe 20 pounds Flemish. To the St. Bartholomew Hospital, £20; likewise to the St. Thomas Hospital & Christ's Hospital; To the prisoners in the Two Compters[3] and other Prisons in London,

---

[1] Buried at Dagenham, March 9, 1610.

[2] In a subsidy roll, made in the tenth year of Queen Elizabeth, " James Hervey, Gent., in the Chaldewell Warde," is assessed at £20.

[3] *i.e.* Two counters, or prisons, probably the Poultry and the Wood Street " comptes," where debtors were confined.

£20; To 50 of my poor kinsfolk dwelling within the parish of Stone, 3s. 4d. a peece; to 60 others in the sᵈ parish, 12d.; To the poor of Dagenham, 20 marks; To those attending the Dutch church, £30 5s. 8d.; To those attending the French church, £6 13s. 4d.;[1] To the Ironmongers Company, £100, and £10 for a dinner; To Melchar Hervye for learning, £40; To the Ironmongers, £10 for a dinner; To my cosen Thomas Harvye, £40 to stock his grounds and I forgyve him all his ffather my brother Thomas oweth me; To the Children of Christ's Hospital 20s. for a dinner on the day of my buryall.

The will concludes with bequests of rings to Master ffleminge and others,

James Hervey of "Grove Streat" succeeded to Wangey Manor on the death of his father, 1583. He married Elizabeth, second daughter of Anthony Radcliffe, Alderman of London, by whom he had issue—John, of Wangey; Samuel, married (1) Constance, daughter of Dr. John Donne,[2] and widow of Edward Alleyn, actor-manager of the Fortune Playhouse, lord of the manor of Dulwich, and founder of "the College of God's gift;" (2) Susanna, daughter of Robert Hungate, of Dagenham; Frances, married Edward Osborne, Esq.;[3] Isabella, married Thomas Barnes, Esq., of Aldborough Hatch; Joyce; Martha; Elizabeth.[4] James Hervey died at Wangey in 1627, and was buried in Dagenham church, where there is a stately monument to his memory.

In his will he leaves to his wife his mansion house and lands in Grove Street (Wangey), and lands in Dagenham, Barking, Cranham, and Chawdwell. He bequeaths Marditch, in the parish of Hornchurch, to Samuel, and divides his lands at Bentrye Hethe between his sons John and Samuel. To his daughters Joyce and Martha he leaves £1000 each on their marriage; to Marie and Rebecca £50 a year for life. To his eldest son John "my lease for 1000 years of the Marsh in East Ham, which I bought of ffrancis Bacon, Esq., since Viscount St. Albans."

[1] These were congregations of Huguenots, who had sought refuge in this country from the persecution of the Protestants by Philip II. of Spain (1565-75) in the Netherlands, and by Catherine de Medici in France.

[2] Dean of St. Paul's, 1623-31. He was a frequent visitor to Abury Hatch, where his son-in-law lived; was buried in St. Paul's Cathedral, where there is, in the south choir aisle, a tablet to his memory. See Izaak Walton's "Life of Dr. John Donne."

[3] Of the Inner Temple; died 1625. In his will he bequeaths his lands to his wife and his sons, Edward and William; his "stock in the East India Co." to his daughters and son William. He mentions a "guilte bowl given me by my Aunte ffanshaw, of Jenkins, at my marriage." He was brother to Sir Hewett Osborne, of Parsloes.

[4] She married Richard Heigham, Esq.; there is a brass effigy to her memory in East Ham Church.

WANGEY

John Hervey was lord of Wangey for nearly thirty years. During his long residence at the manor occurred the violent upheaval of Puritanism which shook the land. It was doubtless on account of his Huguenot descent that we find him taking an active though not obtrusive part in supporting the efforts made to firmly establish it in this neighbourhood. He married Anne, daughter of Anthony Haydon, Alderman of London, and died childless in 1656. In his will he desires to be " buried in the night under my Pue in the church of Daggenham with this inscription on the wall and coat of arms." He bequeaths the third part of his estate to his wife, and his "lands at Pondmans & Richards *alias* Mowbray at Collyer Rowe, & lands and houses at Rumford occupied by Tendell the bucher & Soles & others to my nephew James Herveye." Also his lands in Dagenham and Barking, with a charge of £20 per annum, to his nephew Edward Kightley [1] and to his sister Elizabeth. To the parish of Dagenham £5 to apprentice two children at the "charge of the nowe minister & John Sherman ;" and £5 to the poor of the said parish. To Mr. Tillney "to take some funeral next after the Lord's Day after my death to urge my neighbours to prepare for death, £5." Will proved, 1656.

Soon after the death of John Hervey, Wangey was occupied by Thomas Waldegrave, Esq., who had purchased the lease from James Hervey, Esq., who was heir to his uncle John. It is not known how long he remained here. In the Rent Roll of Barking Manor of 1734, Mr. Thomas Chitty is said to be the owner and occupier of Wangey. He was a citizen and salter of London, and Lord Mayor in 1760, in which year he was also knighted. It was from him that Grove Street took the name of Chitty's Lane, by which, with Rose Lane as a modern alternative, it is now known. He was succeeded in this estate, and in the tenancy of certain lands at Goodmayes, by his son Joseph, who died in 1799. Forty years later Wangey was purchased by Henry Bosanquet, Esq., in his capacity as chairman of the Eastern Counties Railway,[2] then being constructed between Shoreditch and Colchester. The old mansion

---

[1] Minister of Aldborough Hatch ; inhibited by Archbishop Laud from preaching on account of his Puritanism. In 1654–55 Mr. Keightley was appointed minister of a new chapel built at Barkingside. It stood opposite the Maypole inn, but fell into decay in the next century.

[2] It was called "The Eastern Union and Eastern Counties Railways." This was altered to "The Eastern Counties Railways" in 1854, and to the present title, "The Great Eastern Railway," in 1862.

came perilously near to extinction at this period, as the new line was laid right through its beautiful gardens, and necessitated the pulling down of part, unfortunately the Elizabethan, of the house itself. The tenant then was a Major Field. A further portion was removed in 1901, for the enlargement of the station. The embanking of the old "Grove Streat" to make the railway-bridge has destroyed the picturesqueness of Wangey, and given it the appearance of being in a hollow; in a few more years, doubtless, we shall look for it in vain, and another link in our parochial annals will have been entirely destroyed.

MARKS
(From a drawing by S.PROUT about 1800)

CHAPTER XXI

THE MANOR OF MARKS

> " O, the sad, the frail condition
> Of the pride of Nature's glory !
> How infirm his composition,
> And at best how transitory !
> When his riot doth impair
> Nature's weakness, then his care
> Adds more ruin by repair."
>
> FRANCIS QUARLES (of Romford).[1]

THE manor of Marks, or Marks Hall, or Marks,[2] as it is usually termed, stood at the north summit of Whalebone Lane, to the south-east of Hainault Forest. Part of the estate was in Dagenham, but the mansion stood in Romford parish, in the Liberty of Havering-atte-Bower. The manor of Marks was one mile west of Romford. It derived its name probably from some former owner. This manor had a much more elevated situation than any of the other manors which we have already described, as it was built on the crest of the hill looking eastward towards Romford and Warley. At the foot of the hill flowed a stream called Marks' Dyke, but now known as the river Rom.

The manor-house was a large "framed house," built of lath and plaster. It was in the form of a square, in the middle of which was the courtyard. It had two embattled brick towers. The mansion was surrounded by a deep moat, and was approached by a drawbridge. East and west of it were the gardens, the stables and brewhouse lay on the south, and the bowling-green to the east of the house. Part of a high red-brick wall, strongly

---

[1] " Hieroglyphics of the Life of Man," published 1638–40. Born at Romford, 1592 ; died, 1644 ; a prose writer and religious poet.

[2] There are several other houses in Essex with this name, viz. Marks Manor, Leyton ; Marks Hall, near Coggeshall ; Marks Manor, Great Dunmow ; this last after Adelof de Merc.

buttressed, as also of the moat, still remains. At some distance east of Marks were the kennels, and to the north the gate leading into the Forest of Hainault; the latter disappeared in 1854, at the "disafforestation."

The manor of Marks comprised originally two messuages, 100 acres of pasture-land, 100 of meadow, 60 of wood, and a wind-mill (called Marks' Mill). This mill was pulled down about 1760, and was set up some years later where it now stands.

The earliest owner or occupant of Marks of whom we have any record was one Henry Knollys, who owned it about 1420,[1] but little is known of it until it came into the possession of Sir Thomas Ursewyk, Knt., and was held by him till his death at a quit-rent of £5 10s. 0d. per annum.

Thomas Urswyk, who was by far the most distinguished of the lords of Marks, came of a Westmoreland family. He was a student of law, and was elected Common Serjeant to the Corporation of London in 1453, and Recorder in the year following. An old writer describes him as a "man remarkable for prudence, affability, and eloquence," but another says, "Urswick was neither wise, great, nor good." Putting together what we know of him, we do his memory no injustice in believing that he was a learned and able lawyer, but an ambitious and unscrupulous time-server as well. He played a leading part in the final deposition of Henry VI. from the throne, and in firmly establishing his young rival, Edward IV., Duke of York, in his place. It would seem that Henry was, early in 1470, placed for safety in the Bishop of London's palace in Aldersgate Street, and put under the care of Nevile, Archbishop of York, brother of the celebrated Warwick, the "king-maker." In response to his appeal to the people to be "trew unto hym," Urswick assured King Henry of the loyalty of the citizens and himself; but subsequently informed Edward of Henry's place of residence, the result being that that ill-fated monarch was re-captured and the archbishop imprisoned. This was on Maundy Thursday, 1471. According to Stow, it was Thomas Urswick "whose persuasions were forcible with the citizens" to support the claims of Edward. For his services in this matter, and also for his aid in quelling an insurrection led by Bastard Falconbridge, Urswick was knighted by King Edward on May 5, 1471, and created Chief Baron of the Exchequer. When Sir Thomas resigned the recordership, the Corporation voted him

---

[1] See Appendix B, *Inquis. post mortem*, Thos. Ursewyk.

two pipes of wine "by way of reward," and another one every year for the rest of his life. He died at Marks in 1479, and was buried in Dagenham church, where he had for many years, doubtless, worshipped. A tomb, once a work of great beauty, perpetuates his memory with a brass representing the knight and his lady with their children. The inscription has disappeared, but Weever has preserved the following:—"Here lieth Sir Thomas Urswycke, knight, Recorder of London, who died. . . ." Over the tomb hang the knight's helmet, tabard, and gauntlets.[1]

Sir Thomas married a daughter of Richard Riche, a London merchant, by whom he had four sons and nine daughters. All his sons and four of his daughters died in their youth; he was succeeded therefore by his five daughters as co-heiresses, viz. Katherine, wife of Henry Langley; Ann, wife of John Doreward; Elizabeth; Joan; Mary, wife of Thomas Scott, of Stapleford Tawney, who were all in their girlhood at their father's death. In addition to Marks, Sir Thomas owned also Uphavering Manor and Lalee Hall (Hatfield Broad Oaks) with three hundred acres of land. Whether his daughters continued to live at Marks after his death is doubtful. The *Inquisition* above mentioned states that Marks lapsed on the death of Urswyk to Guy Fairfax, and is "held of Elizabeth, Queen of England" (daughter of Sir Richard Woodville).

William Eton, a citizen and mercer of London, was the next lord of Marks. He died in 1503. In his will he desires to be buried in the parish church of the Blessed Lady atte-Bowe in London. He leaves to his wife Johana his "lands and appurtenances called Marks for life, but directs that this be sold if his personal estate is not enough to pay his debts, in which case Richard Grey, his son-in-law, is "to have the bargain and sale thereof before any other person." He leaves the residue to be divided between his wife and children "according to the order and custom of the City of London."[2] He appoints Richard Grey and William Ussher, citizen and mercer, his executors.

The next recorded owner was Sir George Hervey, who was a man of some distinction. He was nominated High Sheriff of Essex

---

[1] In Hackney church there is an old brass in memory of a Christopher Urswick, a priest. It bears no date, but the name is so peculiar that we cannot but imagine he was of the same family. In the visitation of 1612 occurs the name of Sir Nicholas Urswick, Knt.

[2] This was in three parts: (1) for debts, (2) for wife, (3) for children.

in 1596, and soon afterwards knighted and appointed Lieutenant of the Tower. Dugdale says that "Queen Elizabeth granted in 1602 to Sir George Hervey the right of cutting twelve loads of forest wood, twelve loads of rushes, a buck and a doe, yearly; and free warren for this manor in lieu of an extensive sheep walk in the Forest."[1] Sir George married Frances, daughter of Sir Leonard Beckwith, by whom he had five sons and six daughters. Of the sons the four eldest predeceased their father; of the daughters, Margaret married William, the eldest son of Sir Thomas Mildmay, of Springfield Barnes, and Elizabeth married Sir Nicholas Coote, of Valence, Dagenham. The others were unmarried. Sir George died August 10, 1605, and was buried in the Marks's vault at St. Edward the Confessor's Church, Romford. A handsome monument was erected to his memory on the south wall of the chancel, which at the rebuilding of the church in 1850 was removed to the south porch, where it now stands. Sir George and his lady are represented kneeling at a *prie-dieu*, with the sons behind their father and the daughters behind their mother, all in an attitude of devotion. The epitaph is as follows :—

Here lieth sir George Harvey, knight, fourth son of sir Nicholas Harvey, knight, and dame Bridget his wife, daughter and sole heir of sir John Wiltshier, knight. This sir George had to wife, dame Frances, daughter & co-heir of sir Leonard Beckwith, knight, and of dame Elisabeth, his wife, daughter & co-heir of sir Robert Cholmley, knight; he had by dame Frances his wife 5 sonnes, whereof 4 died yong; the fyft, sir Gawen Harvey, married to Mary, daughter of sir Thomas Edmonds, knight; by whom he had issue 6 daughters, whereof 4 died yong; the 5th named Margaret married to William Mildemaye, squire, son & heir apparent of sir Thomas Mildmay, of Barnes, knight; by whom she had 3 sonnes, Thomas, Carew and Henry, and one daughter named Frances; the sixth daughter, named Elisabeth, was marryed to sir Nicholas Coote, of Dagenham, knight. The said sir George Harvey died the 10 day of August, being then lieutenant of the Tower of London; & was buried the 4 day of September in the year of our Lord God, 1605; and Roger Harvey, third son of sir George, dyed a commander in the wars of Ireland XIX November, 1603, aetatis suæ 34.

On the opposite side is a monument (also removed from the chancel) to the memory of Sir George's sister, Anne, wife of George Carew, third son of Sir Edmond Carew (*alias* Montgomery), Baron of Carew.[2] She died at Marks, where she resided with her

---

[1] " Antiquities of Essex," vol. ii.

[2] She was the daughter of Sir Nicholas Hervey, by Bridget, daughter of Sir John

brother after the death of her husband, who was successively Archdeacon of Totnes, Dean of Bristol, and then of Exeter.

Sir Gawen, or Gawin, Harvey succeeded his father in the manor at the age of thirty. From the above epitaph we learn that he married a daughter of Sir Thomas Edmonds ; his second wife was Mary, daughter of Sir Thomas Lucas, by whom he had a daughter Mary, who died before her father. He thereupon adopted as his heir Carew Hervey, the second son of his sister, Margaret Mildmay. Sir Gawen died in February, 162$\frac{6}{7}$, and was buried in the family vault. In his will he bequeaths to his "deerlie beloved Daughter Marye Herveye" the whole of his property, together with his "Coppihould Lands at Hackney," and asks her guardian, Lord Hervye, to "take the care of bestowing her in marriage either to Sr William Hervye's sonne & Heyre, of Ickworth, or to some honest gentleman of my name that will love her . . . & to se her brought vpp vertuouslie and in the fear of God." The will concludes—"I give unto my Lord Hervye my black courser mare & her coult. I give unto my Lord Buchopp of Norwich[1] my kennell of Beagles all but Nancy, which I give to Sr Henry Mildmaie, of Wanstead." The will is dated June 22, 1622. Mary Hervey, the intended heiress, died in September of that year, and hence the estates passed to Carew Mildmay, his adopted heir.

Carew Harvey, or Carew Mildmay (he was known by both names), the lord of Marks, married Dorothy, daughter of William Gerrard, Esq., by whom he had Gawen and Francis, and two daughters. For several years he served as High Sheriff of Essex. When the Civil War broke out in 1642, Carew Mildmay, notwithstanding the fact that he then held office under Charles I. as Yeoman of the Jewel House, took the side of the Parliamentarians and received the command of a colonel. A troop of Royalist horse on the way to Colchester in 1648 attempted to take him prisoner, but the owner of Marks was forewarned in time, and escaped by swimming the moat, and subsequently raised a regiment to aid the Cromwellian forces. In recognition of his

Wiltshier, Knt. She was christened Anne, in honour of Queen Anne Boleyn, to whom her mother was lady-in-waiting. The celebrated George Carew, Earl of Totnes, was her son.

[1] This was Dr. Samuel Harsnett, the son of a baker in Colchester. After a brilliant career at Cambridge, he subsequently became Bishop of Chichester, 1609 ; then of Norwich, 1619 ; and Archbishop of York, 1629. He founded and endowed the Grammar School at Chigwell. He was buried at Chigwell, 1631 of which parish he was at one time vicar.

services and social position in the county he was appointed, in 1654, one of the Commissioners for Essex, "for the more effectuall propagation of the Gospell by the removal of scandalous and insufficient Ministers." In this capacity he was probably responsible for the ejection of Mr. Percy Hill from the vicarage of Dagenham. The following year the House of Commons, by way of acknowledging his "godly zeal," and also to secure his continued support, nominated him to be one of the " Two Elders of Hornchurch," for the arrangement of the Presbyterian *classes* in Essex.[1] These offices he held till the death of Cromwell in 1658, when he suddenly veered round and declared for the Royalist cause. Firmly convinced that with the restoration of the monarchy there was for him much to lose and little to gain if he still adhered to the Puritan party, Carew went in the garb of a humble suppliant to Charles II. (1600–1), and petitioned to be restored to his former position at the Jewel House. He stoutly maintained that he had " never been a bitter opponent of the Royalist cause ;" that he had served the last two kings (James I. and Charles I.) thirty-six years at the Jewel House; that he was the only officer left there when the late king went to York ; that he delivered plate and chains to ambassadors according to royal warrants ; that he refused, in 1649, entrance to the trustees for the sale of the king's goods, whereon they broke open the office and took plate worth £7000, besides what was in the Jewel House, where the crowns and jewels were kept" ("Calendar of State Papers"). Whether the "Merry Monarch" believed in Carew's protestations of innocence is uncertain, but as his chief anxiety was to make as many friends as possible, and, moreover, as one member of this family had supported the Royalists and aided in securing honourable burial for the remains of Charles I., with the reading of the Burial Office of the Church, he graciously granted the petitioner his humble request. Possibly it was out of gratitude for this undeserved favour that Carew presented a silver chalice to St. Edward's Church, Romford. It bears the inscription—" The guift of Carew Hervey alias Mildmay. 1661," and his coat of arms. He died in 1676 at the age of eighty, and was buried in the chancel of Romford church. He had two sons, only one of whom, Francis,

---

[1] The other elder was Thomas Witheringe, Esq., of Nelmes, Hornchurch, who was Chief Postmaster of England. He died at Hornchurch, where he is buried. A mural tablet in the church enumerates at length his virtues and gifts, which were unequalled.

survived him, and one daughter, Elizabeth,[1] who was alive in 1701; the other daughter, Amy, died in 1664, and was buried at Romford.

Francis Mildmay was, in point of character, unlike his father, being unambitious, good-natured, and but little interested in politics, though reputed to be a staunch Royalist. He married Matthew (*sic*), daughter of Matthew Honeywood, Esq., and died in 1703 in his seventy-fourth year.[2] His will is as follows :—

> I desire my bodie to have a decent Buryall in saint Edw. chappell in Romforde, in y⁰ vaulte belongynge to Marks among my dear relations there and to rest and sleep untill my Lord and Saviour Jesus Christ shall awake it at His moste glorious appearinge.

He divides his estate between his wife and his children: Carew, Walter, John, George,[3] Frank, Philidelphia, Judith, Mary, and Anne, and his son-in-law, John Eldred. To George he also bequeaths the manor of Dourncourt, Kent, held of St. John's College, Cambridge ; to Carew, among other fields, one called "Barley Field," near Marks. To the poor of Collyer Row ward and Rumford Town ward he gives £5 to be divided between ten poor persons in each ward. He adds—

> To my dear sister Elisabeth Mildmay I give £50 a year & I desire my dear wife & son & all the rest of my children to be very carefull of her & kind to her, as they will answer it at the great Daye of Judgement ; let her allways live with one of you ; trust her not alone nor with strangers ; provide allways a kind & carefull maid, one that may please her. I give her allso the furniture of her Chamber at Marks during her life.[4] I give her a Diamond Ring of Tenn Pounds value to wear in remembrance of me.

---

[1] Entry in Little Ilford register: "1706. Dec. 17. Dr. John Searle a minister and Mrs. Judith Mildmay, of Marks with a Licence from y⁰ Bishop of London by Mr. Hopkins, minister of Romford."

[2] She was niece to Sir Thomas Honeywood. Sir Thomas warmly espoused the Cromwellian cause, and led a regiment of Essex men in 1651 to fight against Charles II. at Worcester, where the latter was utterly defeated. He subsequently sat in Parliament as one of the (two) knights of Essex. Sir Thomas was cousin to Sir William Honeywood (Sheriff of London in 1639), whose son Edward was created a baronet by Charles II. for having lent him £3000 when in exile.

[3] In the Dagenham register there are entries of the burial of George Mildmay, February 22, 1750, and of his wife, Rebecca, March 21, 1757 ; both in the vicar's chancel. This George Mildmay belonged to Corbetts Tye, Essex, and had married the daughter of Thomas Bonham, of Valence ; their only child, Elizabeth, married Henry Eaton, Esq., of North Lodge, Rainham.

[4] She was deaf and dumb, which accounts for her brother's touching solicitude for her.

On the death of his father, Carew Hervey Mildmaye succeeded to the manor. He married Ann, daughter of Richard Barrett Lennard, Esq., and had issue. Shortly after his marriage (1686) he inherited, under the will of Humphrey Mildmay, Esq., Hazel Grove, and other estates in Somerset. The will runs thus—

I give & deliver unto my loving cosin, Carew Hervey, als Mildmay of Markes, in the parish of Hornchurch in the county of Essex, esquire & to his heirs, all my Mannors, Lands, Tenements and Hereditaments whatsoever, with the appurtenances, situate lying and being in the counties of Somerset, Essex and elswhere.

Carew Hervey held the office of High Sheriff in 1713, and was also one of the four verderers of Hainault Forest.[1] He "gave way to fate" in 1743, at the ripe age of eighty-five.

Carew Hervey Mildmay, the elder son of the above, had the melancholy honour of being the last of the lords of Marks. He married, first, Dorothy Eastmont, of Sherborne, by whom he had four sons, who died young, and a daughter, Anne, who died, unmarried, 1789. He was a strong, hale man, and a keen politician. Horace Walpole refers to him in one of his letters to George Montague (April 3, 1765)—"Mr. Chute has quitted his bed. . . . He was near relapsing, for old Mildmay, whose lungs & memory & tongue will never wear out, talked to him tother night from 8 till half an hour after 10 on the Poor bill." But Mr. Mildmay was not only a great talker, he was an ideal host as well. General Oglethorpe, writing to Dr. George Scott, of Cranham, says— "We are to dine by invitation at Mr. Mildmays on Thursday & see Old England; for Marks is what England was three hundred years ago & most worthy the contemplation of an antiquarian."

Carew Mildmay was, during his annual visit to Marks, very regular in his worship on Sunday mornings at St. Edward's Church, Romford, and was known by his portly, handsome figure, noble mien, and the snuff-coloured suit which he usually wore. He occupied the Marks pew, which was in the chancel, a square loose box, richly carved and curtained, with lock and key, and capable of holding twenty persons. An old Romfordian, who died in 1854, used to relate that he often saw as many as half a dozen coaches

---

[1] The other three were Sir Thomas Webster, Bart., Sir John Eyles, Bart., and William Hervey, Esq. The Rt. Hon. Earl Tilney was the hereditary ranger, and John Goodeere deputy-ranger. A court was held every forty days at Chigwell, before two verderers.

come from Marks on a Sunday morning, bringing to the church old Carew Mildmay and his numerous guests.

In his younger days Carew Mildmay was private secretary to Henry St. John, Lord Bolingbroke. He used to relate how that, when he waited on him to learn when he was to commence his duties, Bolingbroke, having named a day, called him back with the remark—" By-the-by, I mean to be drunk on that day ; you had better come the day after ! "

Mr. Mildmay maintained the Marks traditions of longevity by living till 1784, when he passed away in his ninety-fourth year. He was buried at Sherborne. Failing heirs of his daughter Anne, he left his estate to Jane, granddaughter of his brother Humphrey, who married, in 1786, Sir Henry Paulet St. John, of Dogmersfield, Hants. Under the terms of the will, Sir Henry, on taking possession of Marks, assumed the name and arms of Mildmay. Lady Jane Mildmay does not appear to have resided at Marks ; she died in 1857, aged ninety-three, being the last of that family. Thus the halo of historic romance that had hung over Marks for nearly four centuries entirely vanished, never to return, as the mansion, after falling into decay, was pulled down in 1808 and the materials sold. The only traces now remaining of the manor are a large barn, which is sometimes mistaken for a tithe-barn, a piece of the western garden wall, the moat, which is deep and usually full of water, and the west brick wall. In the north corner of Beansland Lane, at south-west corner of Marks estate, is the old Marks stone, on which was the date, "Sept. 1642," which has been copied on another stone near it.

A good-sized house has recently been built to the south of the site of Marks, which goes by the name of the Warren Farm. It is the property of the Commissioners of Woods and Forests, and is tenanted by Mr. Isaac Gay.

CHAPTER XXII

THE MANOR OF DAGENHAM

"A new house would be to me as intolerable as a new world. Even in restless and changeful days like these, the most powerful influence in the Present is the influence of the Past, just as the influence of our thoughts, actions, and decisions will be felt more a hundred years hence than they are to-day."—ALFRED AUSTIN.

THERE is a good deal of uncertainty in regard to this manor, both as to its exact situation and its various owners and occupiers. Some antiquarians confuse it with Dagnams in the parish of Romford; others identify it with the manor of Jenkins; others again with that of Cockermouth. The manor of Dagenham was, however, quite distinct from all these. It stood in all probability at the top of the village street, known afterwards as Church Street, which it faced, looking westward. If so, it was the most accessible of all the manors. It is not clear when it was built, or by whom, or when it was pulled down. The large house near Eastbrook End, marked on all maps so late as 1774 as Dagenham Hall, was not the manor of Dagenham, but a different house altogether.

According to Morant, the manor of Dagenham was holden of the abbess in the time of Edward III. by one Edmond de North-toft, who was succeeded by his two granddaughters, Emma and Florence, as his co-heiresses. This covers the greater part of the fourteenth century. From a post mortem inquiry held in the 6th year Henry V. (1419-20), we learn that the jury adjudged one "Robert Burford to have legal tenancy of the manor."[1]

In the "Calendar of State Papers" there is a grant (August, 1637) of the disafforestation of the manor of Dagenham to one Lawrence Wright, M.D.; also of free warren in the same, and a pardon for all offences committed within the same manor contrary to the Forest Laws (vol. xlv.).

---

[1] See Appendix B, *Inquis. post mortem*, Robert Burford.

Morant says that Sir Richard Alibone, Knt., had this manor in the seventeenth century, and sold it to Thomas, eldest son of Sir Henry Audeley, who died intestate and without issue in 1697. Also that this estate, with that of Gosebecks in Stanway, was decreed to his sister Katherine's son, Henry Barker, Esq.

The registers contain entries relating to the Scott family, which seems to have been one of some position in the parish. As we have been unable to locate it, it is possible that this family, at some time or other, resided at this manor. Or " Mr. Hunting More, Gent.," may have inhabited it.

THE QUASI-MANOR OF GREAT PORTERS.

The manor of Great Porters, as it was termed by courtesy, stood in Gale Street on the boundary between Dagenham and Barking. It consisted of one messuage, 200 acres of arable land, 40 of meadow, 100 of pasture, 6 of wood, 40 of marsh, 40s. rent, and Covent Croft, Perry-field, and West Marshe. It belonged to the Abbey of Barking, and was held at a quit-rent of £1 9s. 1½d. It took its name from John le Porter, mentioned in a subsidy roll (14th Edward III.) as occupying land " in Berkyngg "—probably this manor.

In the time of Henry V. (1413–22) it was held by one Philip Malpas, citizen and draper of London. In 1439 he was Sheriff of London, and M.P. for the City in 1441. He is said to have suffered at the hands of Jack Cade and his followers. He bequeathed the manor at his death to his daughter and heir, Elizabeth, wife of Sir Thomas Coke, Knt., from whom it descended to their son, John Coke, whose death is recorded in August, 1485. Under the will of John Coke, the manor passed to his brother Philip. The rent was now £4 a year. At the close of the fifteenth century one Richard Pygot, Esq., held the manor, perhaps for fifteen years or so, but not longer, as we learn from an old will that Joan, daughter and heir of John Malmeynes, brought Porters in marriage to her husband, John Rugby, in 1515 or thereabouts. On the death of John Rugby the manor was held jointly by Sir Henry and Toby Paravincini, Sir Charles Montagu, and Sir William Bernan. We find it in the possession of John Lucas, Esq., in 1556, and of Sir Thomas Lucas in 1611; the latter sold it to Thomas Fanshawe, Esq., in 1635. From various court rolls it would seem that one Stephen Porter held it in 1625, and that the same person also held land at St. Bennett's Castle in 1660 ; that Arthur Porter held land called Beechcroft, and Thomas land called Parkfield, both in Dagenham.

In 1690, or thereabouts, Great Porters was sold to Godfrey Woodward, Esq., whose only child married Walter Vane, Esq. It was inherited by their son, Godfrey Woodward Vane, whose son William Walter sold it in 1790 to Abraham Newman, Esq. Its owner in 1814 was William Thoyts, Esq., of Reading, from whom it was purchased by James Scratton, Esq., in 1830.

On Norden's map of Dagenham the manor of Porters is placed two miles south of Dagenham church ; this is a mistake, as it lies one and a half miles to the west of the church. He adds, that "the Brownes live at Porters." We have been unable to find any record of this family.

Morant says that this house is called Porters, otherwise Hedgmans. This is inaccurate ; Hedgmans was opposite to Great Porters, not identical with it. It was pulled down about fifty years ago.

THE QUASI-MANOR OF FRISLINGS.

The nominal manor of Frislings, or Firstlings, lies one mile to the north of the village of Dagenham and immediately to the south of Beacontree Heath. It derived its name, doubtless, from a Godfrey de Frislinge, one of its earliest occupiers. His name occurs in a subsidy roll made in the 13th Edward II. (1319–20), where he is assessed at 3s. 0¼d. (£7 8s. present money). In common with the other manors it was the property of Barking Abbey. In the middle of the fifteenth century it was held by St. Anthony's Hospital, London, from which it passed to the Dean and Canons of Windsor. In 1545 we find it leased to Thomas Hutton, Esq. ; in 1620 to Timothy Truelove, Esq., an intimate friend of William Fanshawe, Esq., of Parsloes. We next hear of it being held by Sir Robert Quarles (1650–60), who, was succeeded by John Truelove, Gent. The Survey of Barking Manor of 1680 states that "John Truelove holdeth Firstlings ; also Surmans & lands near Valence & Porters ; also Sawyers & lands at the Marsh." From this family Frislings came into the possession of Dr. Hugh Smith about 1740, and fifty years later into that of Joseph Joyner, Esq., of West Thurrock, Essex. The parish register has a note that "Colonel Wilson having taken Frislings as a

mansion only objects to being rated on the lands attached to it."
A further note states that the vestry allowed the objection (1830),
and altered the rate, assessing the house at £21, and the land, 45
acres, at £55. An old bill of sale describes it as " Frislings &
Jordans Lands," let to a Mr. Henry Gray (1837) at an annual
rental of £300, and as lying between Bentry Heath and Ockslough
Lane.

Immediately to the south of Frislings is the Four Wants
(Wonts and Wantz) cross-road. Tradition has it that suicides
were buried here, but there is no evidence of it, though such may
have been the case. This tradition throws light on the belief
current among the old inhabitants of the place that ghosts and
unnatural spectres have been seen at different times at this spot,
and that a coach drawn by four headless horses has been seen
there at least twice at midnight, to the great horror of those who
witnessed it.

Near this road a small arms factory has been recently built by
the Government on land often broken by the peaceful plough in
the days of old. *Cedant aratra armis* would seem to be the
modern rendering of the famous Ciceronian metaphor—*Cedant
arma togæ.*

CHAPTER XXIII

THE PARISH WORKHOUSE

" The interests of the rich man and the poor
Are one and same, inseparable evermore ;
And, when scant wage or labour fail to give
Food, shelter, raiment, wherewithal to live,
Need has its rights, necessity its claim.
Yea, even self-wrought misery and shame
Test well the charity suffering long and kind."

WHITTIER.

DOWN to the sixteenth century the relief and maintenance of the poor were chargeable to the various lords of the manors, whose jurisdiction practically covered the whole country. This relief was largely supplemented by free meals, which could always be had by vagrants and hungry suppliants at the monasteries which, to the number of eleven hundred, were scattered over the land. When, however, the manors lost their ancient privileges and rights, and became no more than private, unofficial residences, and when, moreover, the religious houses, by being confiscated to the king's use, ceased to be centres of hospitality, a serious problem was forced upon the country—how to provide for its poor. The bishops for a time sought to relieve the general distress by setting aside a portion of tithe for the poor, and by requesting their clergy to have frequent collections in their churches on their behalf.[1] But these remedies proved inadequate on account of the gigantic character of the evil they were meant to cure.

Under these circumstances there was no alternative but for the State to devise ways and means to solve the problem. Two Acts of Parliament were accordingly passed (1597 and 1601), ordering a poor-rate to be levied on all owners and occupiers of land, and authorizing the churchwardens and overseers to disburse the money

[1] The last rubric in the Communion Office, and another one in the Office for the Visitation of the Sick, throw light on this matter.

thus raised among the poor in their respective parishes. But these Acts were either disregarded or badly worked, and but little aid came from church collections, if we may judge from a pamphlet, printed in 1632, entitled, "Grievous Grones for the Poor." Eight years later Charles I. began his contentions with Parliament, with his "Orders and Directions, with a Commission for the better administration and more perfect information of His Majesty how and by whom the Laws and Statutes tending to the relief of the Poor were executed throughout the kingdom."[1] In 1662 the Settlement Act was passed, requiring the poor, under penalties, to keep to their own parishes, for the better distribution of relief. Some years later (1685) it was enacted that all persons moving from one parish to another should acquaint the authorities with the fact ; this was followed (1691) by an Act requiring the overseers to draw up, from time to time, a list of the poor in their respective parishes who were entitled to relief, and to post it upon the door of their parish church.

The first Act relating to the establishment of workhouses was passed in 1670. It was intended to check the exceptional poverty and distress caused by the recent Great Fire of London, whereby 100,000 people had been rendered homeless. The various parochial authorities were empowered to set apart houses where work was to be given to able-bodied poor, and to pay the latter partly out of the products of their own labour, and partly out of a special rate to be levied. This Act was for the metropolis alone. Fifty years later (1722) another similar Act was passed, to apply to the country at large. The churchwardens and overseers of each parish were to procure and maintain one or more houses where the sick and aged poor might have a refuge, and widows, orphans, and destitute persons a lodging. In 1782, owing to complaints of extravagance and favouritism on the part of the overseers, it was enacted that boards of guardians should be appointed to control the management of the various workhouses. These boards could either be the ratepayers generally assembled in open vestry, *or* a body of not less than four persons chosen by the ratepayers to act on their behalf.

It was in compliance with the Act of 1722 that the ratepayers of Dagenham provided a workhouse for their parish (1730–40), the house in question being the Comyns Almshouses, in the village,

[1] *Vide* Miss Leonard's "Early History of English Poor Relief." The authoress proves conclusively that this "Direction" initiated our English Poor Law.

which were utilized for the purpose. The rent of these was remitted by the committee out of the rates, and spent in bread for the poor. Attached to the poorhouse was a good-sized garden and twenty acres of land, which found work for the men who were able to dig, and kept the inmates supplied with vegetables. There was also a "poorhouse allotment," abutting on a lane now known as Workhouse Lane, which was let to a farmer, and marked off by four stones inscribed D. W. L.

The house was managed by a committee, which met for some time every alternate Sunday morning before Divine service, but afterwards every Tuesday, either at the workhouse or in the vestry.[1] Theoretically, this committee consisted of all the rate-payers of the parish; practically, it comprised those — usually fourteen in number—who took the trouble to attend the meetings regularly. They took a humane and charitable view of their duties, and endeavoured to discharge them conscientiously. Not having to satisfy a Local Government Board, or any other authority outside their own parish, they passed or rescinded resolutions, adapted them or qualified them, permitted technical irregularities, with considerable freedom of discretion. All they desired was to guard the rights of their poorer brethren, whom they treated as human beings, and not as "cases," to keep down the rates, and be on friendly terms with the neighbouring parishes.

In dealing with the distress of the parish, the committee preferred giving outdoor relief wherever possible, reserving admission into the house for the aged and infirm. Those who received outdoor relief were euphemistically called "pensioners." To be entitled to a pension it was necessary to live within the bounds of the parish for twelve months, to work for one and the same employer for the same period, to pay the rent regularly, and to bear a character of honesty, sobriety, and industry. Having thus duly qualified, the applicant had to attend the petty sessions at Barking or Ilford, and there produce a certificate of baptism, and, if married, of marriage also, together with a "vouching paper," from his employer, before the magistrate. If the application was deemed satisfactory, the bench granted a "certificate of settlement," which the recipient was to exhibit to the parish authorities,

---

[1] The Act of 1601 (43 Elizabeth) directs that the "persons charged with the administration [of the Poor Law] were to meet together at least once a month in the parish church, after Divine service on the Sunday, to consider of some good course to be taken, and of some meet order to be set down in the premises" (*vide* T. Mackay's "Lectures on the Poor Law").

when required. To prevent any possible fraud, the intending applicant had to signify his intention to the churchwardens and overseers, who thereupon put a notice on the church door, requesting all who objected to the application to appear before the justices and dispute the claim in their and the applicant's presence.[1]

A "settlement" could also be obtained by inhabiting certain houses in the parish, a list of which is given in the parish book, as follows :—"John Little's cottages at Chadwell Heath ; Shacklady's at Marks Gate ; Murray's at Bentry Heath ; Isaac Lake's at Mill Yard ; the Green Lane cottages ; White's cottages in the lane south of Vallance Wood ; Rick's cottages ; Mr. Smitherman's cottages." A tenancy of not less than four years was required to qualify for a "settlement" in this way.

When once gained, the rights of the settler were held as sacred. Thus, one Sarah Cornhill, having obtained her "settlement," went to Clare, Suffolk, where she had a serious illness, and on recovery desired to return to Dagenham. The committee [July, 1813] thereupon instructed the clerk [Mr. Cutler] to "forward £13 8s. 0d. to Mr. Sam. Stevens, attorney, Clare, for her maintenance, medical attendance, coach-hire, and other expences." Again, when John Barrington, then living at Purleigh, asked the Dagenham vestry to assist him in his illness, the latter caused inquiries to be made, which proved that the "applicant belonged to Dagenham by right of servitude with Mr. John Miller, near the White Horse, Chadwell Heath." The authorities of Purleigh were asked, therefore, "to relieve him till he is able to be remov'd to where he belongs" [January, 1814]. Again, one George Chasson, a "settler," removed to Louth, where, "in consequence of a severe indisposition, he apply'd to the committee at Dagenham for help." In response to this they arranged with the vestry at Louth to have medical attendance and food supplied to him, and on his recovery set him up as an "itinerant seller of booksellers' publications," and now and then replenished his stock-in-trade. At another time [July, 1828], the committee instructed their clerk to write a "courteous letter" to the churchwardens and overseers of Berdon, Herts, to allow James Brett and family, now living in that parish, ten shillings per week, and charge the same to them. Two months later, the

---

[1] An Act [13 Richard II.] directed that "the poor should abide in cities and towns where they then were." A later one [13 Charles II.] allowed the poor to gain a settlement by a forty days' residence. *Vide* Dr. Burn's "History of the Poor Laws," published in 1764.

Q

Dagenham vestry forwarded the sum of £9 11s. 6d., including the doctor's bill for £6 1s. 6d., for attendance on James Brett during his seven weeks' illness [October, 1828]. At another meeting they instructed the clerk to send a remittance to Charles Ward, overseer of St. Giles' parish, Oxford, for Thomas Kittle, who had gained his "settlement" at Dagenham. On the other hand, he was to write to the overseers of Stamford Rivers, to dispute the alleged "settlement" of one William Garton, of this parish, who had "let himself to Mr. John Jackson, of Stamford Rivers, in Essex, for the service of husbandry at the yearly wages of £1 11s. 6d., a pair of high shoes, and board and lodging."

The Book of Workhouse Accounts affords us much interesting information concerning the condition of the poor, and the methods adopted to solve the unemployed and labour question "when George the Third was king." The great variety of purposes for which relief was granted is worthy of note. A selection of extracts is appended.

Mrs. Elmore asked for relief for Rent of Bush's House, her Husband being under confinement for Twelve months. Deferred. February, 1814.

Forster's Wife said she was threatened with a Distress for Rent by Mr. Laypold. Allowed one Pound. May, 1818.

Mrs. Woodfield occupies Mr. Smitherman's Cottage & is rated at £6. Prays to be releeved on accᵗ of the illness of husband for whom the cottage was taken on accᵗ of air. Refus'd as it could not consistently be allowed to become a Precedent. June, 1818.

Mrs. Laybank apply'd for Cloths for her child at Service at Mr. Wains at Barking. Allow'd 10/-. January, 1814.

Mrs. Bennitt, the soldier's wife apply'd for temporary relief in consequence of the Inclemency of the weather. Allow'd 6/-. March, 1814.

Long Willᵐ Smith asked for relief for his mother Wid. Smith. Allow'd 2/6 per week. April, 1814.

John Hobbs apply'd for assistance towards defraying the expence of his wife's Funeral. Allow'd £1. June, 1814.

Mrs. Wilkinson ask'd for a Bedstead to put into her Lodging. Granted. June, 1814.

Old Ramsay's wife to ask Shirt & Shift. Allow'd 8/-.

Thomas Milbon's wife said they were behind with the club-money through illness. Allowed 5/-.

The Widow Milbon asked for a trifle to discharge some obligations incur'd by her husband's long illness. Allowed £1 and 3/- per wk. October, 1814.

The Widow of Leonard Whitby for permanent Relief. Recommended to go to Service as more reputable than a young widow keeping house.

Willm Barratt asks for 25/- to get his things out of pawn; is going on board the *Minerva* with Captⁿ Herne to the East Indies. Allow'd.

Bates' wife apply'd for Relief, in consequence of her Husband being committed to Chelmsford for Deer Stealing. The constable was directed to go to Chelmsford to examine the man's settlement. Allow'd now 10/-. March, 1816.

Howjego ask'd to be assisted to prevent a seizure of his goods by lending him Three pounds which was agreed to on condition of his not making away with his horse & cart, which he on his Part promises.

Marven × Howjego mark. April, 1816.

Mr. Bolton ask'd for allowance for Damage done by destroying 16 Rod of wheat growing where they broke ground for Gravell. Allow'd.

Mrs. Harlick brought a Doctor's Bill of £1 7s. 0d. & ask'd the gentlemen for assistance. Allowed 12/-. The Clerk to write to Mr. Copeland, Surgeon, of Chigwell & report this to him & say the Committee cannot help the Poor who are dwelling out of the Parish. March, 1817.

Frances Oliver pray'd assistance. Her school was now closed. Recommended to try Chigwell Row if she can get a room to keep a school in. June, 1817.

George Jarratt's wife applied for relief, having received a hurt while taking down tiles from the Barracks.[1] Allowed 8/-. 1822.

Benjamin Heath asked the gentlemen for assistance having lost a hand. Allowed 30/- to purchase a donkey & goods to trade as huckster.

John Church a poor seaman asked for money to rejoin his ship at Southampton. Allowed 30/-.

Thomas Smith's wife of Chadwell Heath said her husband had lost a leg & her children were down with small-pox. Allowed 10/-. Five shillings were allowed to Hooper's wife in Green Lane, who is ill with St. Anthony's fire. At this vestry Edward Westwood said he had a job to go to in London at 14/- a week with Mr. Johnson a scavenger and would like the gentlemen to help his wife & six children while away. Allowed 5/- per wk.

Tho' Flavill Relev'd with 4 shillings. Ordered to meet the Constable on Saturday to be sworn to his settlement.

Willm Cook apply'd Having broke a blood-vessel to get his Doctor's bill paid amounting to £4 0s. 0d. Allow'd Two pound.

Mrs. Dean pray'd to go into the House. She has at Pitsea a Feather bed & Bedstead and Three chairs, one Pillow & one Bolster & covering 1 Round Table & a Deal Chamber Table.

John March's widow asked for a trifle to pay the woman who had laid out her husband's body. Allowed 2/-. April, 1822.

Mrs. Bennett asked to leave the House in order to get married. Leave granted & 2/6 given for good-luck.

---

[1] The barracks were at Purfleet, then an important military station.

William Barratt was allow'd 5/- on being wrecked on board the *Good Intent* off Scilly.

John Prior asks for help, as his ancles are very weak. Mr. Brittain tells him that he has heard that threshing the afflicted part with nettles will cure the rheumatism. Allowed 2/6. [It does not transpire whether the suggested remedy was tried !]

Sometimes the vestry granted relief in kind instead of in money, thus—

Dame Randal pray'd relief. Allow'd a shift & p^r of shoes. October, 1814.

John Meadowcroft complained of feeling the cold. Allowed a piece of flannell to make a waistcoat.

Old John Heath asked for some clothing. Allowed a pair of stockings & a shirt.

William Kemp applied for help, saying that he & his family were destitute. Allow'd a smock-frock, a piece of calico, a prittle of potatoes & four loaves.

James Cornel who has worked for Sir Thomas Lennard[1] asked for help. Allowed £1, but told to go for further help to his own parish. 1822.

Joseph Kemp was charged with running away from the House & refusing to work. He is 9 years old & christened. Mr. Ephraim Seabrook undertakes to employ him.

Among the various applications we find some for the A. B. C., viz. Armstead's Bread Charity.

With all their charitable anxiety to relieve the distress brought before their notice, the committee could on occasion refuse applications of a dubious character. Thus, " George Forster's wife prays for relief. Her husband works at Mr. Webb's, Mudd Island & is forced to lodge near his work. Application refus'd." Again, "William Barratt asked the Vestry to repay him the money he had spent on burying his wife. Refus'd." And again, " Hannah Perry asked for relief & said she had lost the money allowed her last time and could not find it. Refus'd." And so again, " Root's daughter asked for money to get her father out of jail, where he was to remain two months. Refus'd." " Edward Wren & Arthur Williams applied for relief, being out of work. Formerly they were servants to Mr. Beale at £9 a year [this was in 1825]. They were interrogated whether they had put something into the manger, whereby the horses were much disordered, but

[1] He lived at Aveley House.

denied having done so. Refus'd." "Mrs. Goodall to be releeved of the Church rate: refus'd." "Wᵐ Barratt appeared again & said he had had an offer to go out to the Spanish main on an eight months' voyage & to receive £2 15s. 0d. per month. But he had no money to buy clothes & go to the ship. Refus'd." And once more, "Mr. Dawkins of Bradford in Yorkshire asked that Sarah Palmer be sent down to him & be clothed at the cost of the parish. The Vestry caused inquiries to be made & refused the application, although the situation offered was a good one."

Now and then the vestry granted relief by remitting or reducing the rates. Thus—

Shacklady of Marks Gate attended to pay half the rates now due, if they let the land at £5 per year. He has 2½ acres. Agreed to. April, 1816.

Mrs. Farrance asked for relief from Poor and Church rates. Ordered that her assessment be reduced to £1 per acre.

John Little asked for relief from the rates. As he is lame & unable to work the Committee excused him.

The widow of James Wiseman pray'd relief. Says he gain'd a settlement in Mr. Ford's service. Not excused rates, but granted 3/- temporary help.

Richard Cornhill pray'd to be relieved from rate by lessening the Assessment. To be rated in Future £6 instead of £9.

Robert Gates the same. July, 1814.

Robert Harper to have his rate reduc'd to Twenty pounds.

Joseph Palmer of the Sheepcotes beerhouse ask'd his rates to be reduc'd. Said they never sold more than 3 gallons of Liquor per week. His rent is £35 per annum. Deferr'd.

Mr. Ind's clerk called with a Bill for Beer on the 7th of June deliver'd to Josʰ Palmer at the Sheepcotes, thinks Mr. Lake gave the Order. Mr. Lake to be apply'd to for Information on the subject. January, 1818.[1]

In the following August, "the Vestry refus'd to sign the License for the Sheepcotes as it appears that the Trade of the House is insufficient for the support of a Family, the present Family having been a Burthen to the parish, also the former occupier nam'd Price has been chargeable, also the Predecessor of Price."

The following extracts are interesting by reason of their peculiarity—

Mrs. Oliver to ask relief for her son who is afflicted with the Evil. Offer'd 2/6 each time he goes to London which is represented once per

---

[1] This beer was ordered for the dinner with which the parish authorities concluded the perambulation, or "beating the bounds," of the parish.

week to Burrel & his wife of Bethnal green who professes to cure cancers. February, 1815.

At a meeting held July, 1813, the clerk was instructed to write to Mr. Dyer, J.P., to

complain of James Black who will not submit either himself or Family to the anointing ordered by them for the extermination of the Itch; whether tis not highly expedient some example may be made of him to deter others who seem to be waiting only till he has carried his point. Mr. John Kittle, overseer and constable, undertook to watch Black's misconduct.

Widow Coackham states she has been Rob'd of all her cloathes. Allowed one pound.

Joe Gardener's wife ask'd for relief. The Vestry resolv'd that his punishment seem sufficient & that the Parish Officers endeavour to get his enlargement that he may have the Benefit of Harvest on his promise to reimburse the Parish £6 11s. 0d. & live with his wife. July, 1813.

The Vestry resolved to apply to Mr. Talbot for Pressing waggons for Baggage. 27th Decr 9 waggons. March, 1814.

Ambrose Thompson holding out a feasable tale of his being interupted in his Occupation as a Ticket porter this Vestry consent to Mr. Kittle going a day to London to assist in restoring him to his rights as a means of his future support. August, 1817.

To alleviate the exceptional distress that prevailed in the parish during the winter, the vestry issued to such applicants as were able-bodied "round" certificates. These certificates were to be taken to the various employers of labour in the parish, who were required to find work for the applicant at the rate of at least one shilling per day. If the "roundsman," as he was termed, earned more than the shilling, the excess amount was to be repaid to the employer out of the poor-rate. This arrangement was permitted under the Act 43 Elizabeth. In some cases relief was granted by providing work at a sliding scale of wages, according to the capability or poverty of the suppliant, and the circumstances of the case. Thus—

John Hobbs ordered to Shibb in the Rutts upon the Road & Mr. Hanson will pay him six shillings per wk. February, 1816.

William Bond was ordered to work on the road at 20 pence per day, as he had a family. But George Benbow was to work at a shilling a day; and James Ainsworth and Samuel Meadowcroft were set to clean the town, the surveyor to pay them as he thought fit.

James Ramsden, discharged from the 53rd Foot was ordered to cut down nettles on the high road at 9d. per day.

John Black wants employment. Sent to Mr. Joyner's to hoe Turnips, & be paid suitably. Says his Daughter lived one whole year with a washerwoman near Valentines.

To supplement these efforts to solve the labour question, the farmers and tradesmen entered into an agreement to take lads and girls as apprentices, or in default thereof to pay a fine of £10 to the poor-rates. Judging from the number of fines paid, it would seem that they found it cheaper or more convenient to pay the fine than take the apprentices. During 1813, fines were paid by the following: Messrs. S. Choate, T. Beal, J. Milner, J. Peacock, S. Seabrook, W. Smith, and G. Winmill. It was, however, decided that if a farmer had a man living in his house who would otherwise be in the workhouse, he should be excused the fine. Occasionally lads were apprenticed outside the parish. Thus—

Griffith Davis proposed his son Edward to be apprentic'd to Tho' North a Peterman[1] of Lambeth; expects £5 as an Apprentice Fee. Consented to if the character of North for Steadiness & Humanity be approv'd, as the gentlemen are very carefull who they intrust the children of their poor to. June, 1817.

Elizabeth Black's mother apply'd to have her girl apprentic'd in London. The Clerk was instructed to write to her employer that the Vestry are willing to allow £5 for clothes and will send her up to the Blue Boar, Aldgate where the Coach arrives a little before Ten o'clock every day.

Only one lunatic pauper is mentioned, viz.—

Francis Oliver, aged 33, who first showed symptoms of a wandering mind at the age of 18. He is only dangerous two or three times a month. He was for a short time in Plaistow Asylum, then one year in St. Luke's Asylum, then eight years in Plaistow with a private person. His mother wishing to take charge of him is to be allowed 8s. per week for his maintenance. His case comes under Act of Parliament, 9th George IV.

THE POORHOUSE.

As the accommodation was limited, admission was only granted to widows, widowers, old and infirm persons who had no one to look after them, and orphan children. It was furnished in part by the inmates themselves, who took their goods and chattels into the house, the committee eventually buying them in, or claiming them as a set-off to some outstanding debt. The men and boys, who

---

[1] That is, a fisherman, from the occupation of St. Peter.

were able to walk some distance to their work, found employment on the farms. The wages they earned were not, however, paid to them, but to the master of the house, who gave them back an occasional shilling for pocket-money. The women were employed in laundry-work and charing, etc., in the house, and sometimes at the manors and farmhouses. The inmates lived well, having bread, milk, bacon, vegetables, tea, and coffee every day, and hot dinners four times a week. Their maintenance was undertaken by a Mrs. Collier at the cost of 5s. 6d. a head, increased to 6s. 6d. in 1816, on account of the high price of bread. Mr. Vial, of Gravesend, contracted to clothe the inmates for £20 a year. Frequently they were the recipients of clothing, puddings, broth, tripe, quinine (for the ague), from the farmers' wives, who did not wish to forget their old faithful servants. We find, however, no mention of beer in the accounts, or of "tobacco and snuff" among the gifts. At Christmas a dinner of the usual fare was provided at the expense of the vestry. On Sundays the inmates attended the morning service at the church, a privilege they much appreciated, especially on "bread" Sundays.

The matron of the house was Lucy Chapple, an active and capable woman, who was generally in want of something or other. Sometimes it was a pair of shoes, or an apron, or petticoat, or bed-ticks, or a "cinder shovel," or a "hook for the chimney," or a "hand flour-mill," or a "wash-tub," or a "hard brush," etc. Her duties were of a multifarious character, for in addition to look-ing after the needs and comfort of the inmates, she was sent out to nurse a dying parishioner, or "poultice a poor lad's arm," or "wash and scrub little children," or lay out a corpse. Although she was strictly enjoined not to receive any gratuity, she was in the habit of broadly hinting that "she was not above being gratituded" for her trouble. This coming to the ears of the vestry, she was reprimanded, and finally threatened with legal proceedings if she persisted in her "unchristian conduct." Lucy retaliated by taking herself off for several days, leaving word with the master where she could be found if wanted ; and, unfortunately, her feminine vanity was flattered by the vestry having to entreat her to return to her place in the house, not finding any one willing to take on her liabilities [1814–27].

Thomas Price was the master of the house. He was appointed by the vestry to "farm the poor," that is, to superintend the cultivation of the garden and allotment, to keep an account of the

earnings of the men and boys employed on the various farms, to
see that no inmate was out after 7 p.m. in winter and 8 p.m. in
summer, and to look after the furniture and fittings of the place.
He was to call in the parish constable (George Terry) to any
refractory pauper or vagrant, and, if necessary, confine such in the
"watch-house" attached to the house, or in the stocks, which were
near the churchyard gates. Occasionally he had a complaint to
make, *e.g.* "of the unchristian conduct of William Edwards in
refusing to work, and not going to church on Sundays ; " of "John
Ramsden lying a-bed after 6 a.m. in summer," and again, of the
probable cause of it, " being out late at night, and especially on
Sundays, when he does not return from the meeting-house in the
town till after 10 p.m. ; " and, once more, of the aforesaid John
"having pinched his wife." At other times he would complain
that " rats, mice, frogs, and cockroaches had been seen in the
house," and was advised by the vestry to procure several cats to
keep down these intruders. Price was assisted in the discharge of
his duties by Benjamin Holgate, the parish clerk, carpenter, and
general *factotum* of the place [1816–28].

The clerk to the vestry was Thomas Cutler, the village schoolmaster [1805–25]. He received a salary of £10 a year, and an
allowance of three shillings for every special meeting he attended,
and for examining the master's books every month. He was a
kind and sensible man, and a courteous letter-writer. In July, 1826,
he was instructed, *inter alia*, to write to all the publicans of the
parish, and request them "not to allow skittles or four corners to
labourers on pain of its being taken notice of." In legal matters
he was advised by Mr. Sterry (Sterry & Tweed, Romford), who
lived at Eastbrook Farm, rented at £70 a year [1811–29].

Mr. Ireland was the medical officer. The Book of Accounts
does not tell us anything about him beyond the fact that the
vestry accepted his resignation on account of ill-health with regret,
and accepted Messrs. Moore & Parkin, whom he recommended,
as his successors [June, 1816]. The latter held office three years
only, when Mr. Carruthers, of Romford, was appointed, at a salary
of £25 per annum, and an allowance of £5 for "expensive journeys."
Though a hard-working and conscientious servant, he did not
always succeed in pleasing his poor patients, who grumbled at his
negligence and want of skill. The doctor's defence on one occasion
was that the patient " would not send for the physic, though he
promised to cup him if the physic did not relieve him." On

another occasion, he said that the patient was "devoid of Christian patience and endurance, and did not calmly bear her afflictions, which he was doing his best to diminish, and this to the husband's satisfaction." An instance of his interest in the helpless is seen in the case of a Robert Gales, a Dagenham boy, who was brought home dead from sea. Mr. Carruthers said he had made a *post-mortem* examination, and was "sure the lad had died from ill-usage and exposure, thereby suspending the animal heat, and therefore urged the Vestry to prosecute the captain of the vessel." There are several cases where Mr. Carruthers reported that he had done his best for the sufferers, but without avail, so had sent them, with a letter of recommendation, to Sir Astley Cooper.[1]

The medical officer did not regard the vaccinating of people as part of his duty. This office was discharged by a Mrs. Palmer, who received one shilling for each person she inoculated. In 1813 she was paid £6 2s. 0d. for inoculating one hundred and twenty-two persons. In 1820 the vestry paid a Mrs. Woolner £3 5s. 0d. for "thirteen deliveries of children."

Mr. Brittain was the road surveyor. He had authority to provide work for those sent to him by the vestry, and to send in his bill to the overseer every year. In 1831 he succeeded Mr. Ephraim Seabrook as "collector of assessed and land taxes," amounting altogether to £1400 a year. Among the rates levied, it would seem that there was one on *horses*, as a William Hall complained that he was rated for three horses, whereas he had only *two*. The vestry, however, decided against him, as he admitted having used three.

The following is a "Statement of the Expences of the Workhouse For the First Three months to 5th October, 1813":—

Expence.				*Stock and Income.*			
	£	s.	d.		£	s.	d.
First month	59	13	9½	Coals	12	7	6
Second month	36	9	4½	Potatoes	11	0	0
Third month	53	7	6	Stafford's Bill not being for			
Master's Sallary	5	0	0	Housekeeping	1	10	0
	154	10	8	Earnings	10	11	10
Deduct earnings	35	9	4		35	9	4
Total expence ..	119	1	4				

The average number of Persons has been 32 and the weekly expence of each 5/8½ Children included."

[1] Sir A. P. Cooper was "serjeant-surgeon" to Guy's Hospital, 1768–1842. There is a monument to his memory in the south transept of St. Paul's Cathedral.

The parish workhouse continued to exist till 1835, when the new poor law, passed in the previous year, came into operation. This Act was the result of the appointment of a Royal Commission to inquire into the working of the Poor Law system. The Commission, which included Dr. Blomfield, Bishop of London, and Dr. Sumner, Bishop of Chester, produced a volume of 8000 folio pages. Under the new Act the relief of the poor was taken out of the hands of the parochial authoities, and parishes were grouped together into district unions to enable larger and more sanitary workhouses to be erected for the poor. With nine other parishes Dagenham now forms the Romford Union, which has an area of fifty-nine square miles. The population of the Romford Union when formed was 21,000. The union workhouse was built in 1838, at a cost of £9500, and was designed to accommodate 460 inmates. It has been enlarged since, with wards for the sick and infirm.

CHAPTER XXIV

THE PAROCHIAL CHARITIES

" Beneath an humbler roof we place
　　This monumental stone,
　To names the poor shall ever bless
　　And charity shall own ;
　To soften human woe their care,
　To feel its sighs, to aid its prayer,
　Their work on earth—not to destroy ;
　And their reward—their Master's joy."
MONTGOMERY.

THE parish of Dagenham has, in the past, been richly endowed with charitable bequests, both of a temporary and permanent character. They are as follows :—

The REEDE Charity.—Roger Reede, in his will bearing date February 15, 1482, left his house in Ioyes Mead, *alias* Hoo Croft, to be an almshouse for five poor men belonging to Hornchurch, Romford, or Dagenham. They were to be no blasphemers or common beggars, but men whose only misfortune was their poverty ; and were to attend church every Sunday and holy day, and at such times to pray for the souls of the founder and his wife. None were to wed after their admission by the feoffees to the charity. Roger Reede also bequeaths his lands at Havering and Eastbrooke, in Dagenham, for the support of the almshouse and its inmates, with a gratuity to the priest who shall minister to them.

Owing to complaints as to the mismanagement of this charity, and of the unfitness of its beneficiaries, made from 1789-1815, the Court of Chancery ordered a revision of the scheme, and an increase in the number of the trustees.

It was stated, in the report of the Charities Commissioners in 1839, that the Roger Reede's charity land comprised, among other parcels and tenements, "one tenement called Eastbrook's with the messuage, barn, stable, 18 acres of land & one acre of marsh in

Dagenham," which was let to one Ann Palmer on a fourteen years' lease, expiring in 1841. Also that the almshouse had six occupants, of whom two belonged to Dagenham, viz. Archibald Dunbar, the ruler,[1] unmarried, formerly a farmer in Dagenham, and George Masterman and his wife, of Dagenham, a farmer.

The cost of maintenance of the almshouse was, in 1836, £388 6s. In that year the Rev. T. L. Fanshawe was one of the trustees of the charity.

The BENNETT Charity.—In March, 1589–90, died one Ioane Bennett, who left her estate " for the use of the poor of Dagenham." A document written in Latin states that the administration of her estate to Rychard Brown and Willm̄. Comyns was sworn on May 11, 1590, before one William King. [As this charity was simply the distribution of Ioane Bennett's effects among the poor of Dagenham, it had but a brief existence.][2]

The ARMSTEAD Charity.—William Armstead, of Hornchurch, left, in 1567, a rent-charge of £4 a year out of Hay Street Farm, in Hornchurch, to be distributed "among the most poor, aged & needy people " in Dagenham and Romford.

The WHITE Charity.—John White, Gent., left, in 1671, twenty shillings in money and twenty shillings in bread, to be distributed to the poor on the day of his burial (February 9).

Item. I give unto severn poor widdows within the parish of Dagenham & in case there be not severn found within the parish, then to some other of the poorest to make up the severn, One dozen of bread every week for ever, to be payd for by my Executrix during her natural life & after her decease to be pd or provided by the owners, possessors, couchants or tennants which after the decease of my wife, shall hold or possess the two parcels of land called Wright's afore bequeathed which I do give upon this condition & the said 12d. a week in bread shall be given & disposed of every Sunday in the forenoon after service, for ever, as aforesaid, by the minister, churchwardens & overseers of the said parish or the major of them, then in being. And so by their successors for ever provided always upon default & non-payment of the said 12d. a week, it shall & may be lawful to & for the said minister, churchwardens & overseers of the poor of the said parish of Dagenham or the major part of them to enter & come upon the said parcels of land called Wrights or any part thereof, destrain

---

[1] The ruler was the quasi-master, who kept the accounts and preserved order. He received a yearly salary of £48 15s. 0d., the other brethren £26, and the widows £16 each.

[2] Robert Green left, in 1668, and William Elliston in 1673 (both of Dagenham), £5 to the poor of Dagenham.

the goods & cattel of the said owners, possessors or tennants holding & possessing the lands and for them to keep or make seizure upon the lands until such money that is in arrears for the said bread be fully satisfied and paid & this my gift to continue for ever as aforesaid.

This will was proved at the office of the Archdeacon of Essex in 1673.

A note in the parish book informs us that this land was, in 1806, occupied by one Mitchell, and adjoined Camsey's land. In 1840 it was called the Two Acre Piece, and was then in the owner-ship of Mr. Henry Gray.

The FANSHAWE Charity.—John Fanshawe, Esq., of Parsloes and Wyersdale, left, in 1689, a bequest to provide a dozen of bread every week for the poor of Dagenham.

The WITHAM Charity.—William Witham, a wealthy clothier of Cloth-Fayre, Smithfield, and of Bushells, in Dagenham Street, left, in 1692, a piece of land rented at £5 per annum, to aid the education of the " decay'd poor of Dagenham." The piece of land was part of Wants Farm.

The UPHILL Charity.—Richard Uphill, by his will bearing date January 28, 1716, bequeathed two orders of the receipt of Exchequer, the one for an annuity of £50 per annum, for eighty-nine years, from January 25, 1702, and the other for an annuity of £40, for ninety-nine years, from Lady Day, 1704, to apprentice the children of poor inhabitants not taking alms. Six trustees were to be appointed, all members of the Church of England, two to be local justices, and the other four substantial householders in the parish. The annuities expired in 1803, but previous to that year the trustees had purchased Consols to the value of £5000 out of accumulated savings, the beneficiaries of the charity having been so few in number. The interest was expended in apprenticing youths and girls to some trade, with a premium of £15 each, and in gratuities of £3 each to those going out to service.[1] The trust, in 1805, stood in the names of Henry Merttins Bird, Esq., Christopher Tyler, Esq., and John Marmaduke Grafton, Esq., the other trustees being the Rev. Henry Morice, vicar, Messrs. Thomas Boulton and John Baker, churchwardens, and John Armstrong and John Biggs, over-seers. The treasurers, in 1815, were Thomas Mashiter and Edward Ind, Esquires, and Mr. Samuel Seabrook.

The annual dividends now amount to £150, and are applied as

[1] Among the beneficiaries of this charity in 1817 was one " Eliza Wood, servant at Mrs. Elizabeth Fry, Breach House."

above stated, except that £10 is the usual sum voted to an apprentice, and the gift to servants is £1 on the completion of six months' service, with another £1, together with a handsome Bible and Prayer-book, if the applicant stays a whole year with the same employer. The present trustees are the Revs. Dr. Moore and J. P. Shawcross, and Messrs. W. Varco Williams, J.P., Colson Parrish, R. Farrance, and C. West.

This worthy benefactor, whose name is a household word in the parish, was the son of Jacob Uphill, who held a small estate at Eastbrook End in Dagenham, called Wards. He derived his wealth, however, from his grandfather, Anthony Uphill, Gent., of the parish and precincts of the Trinity Minories, Without Aldgate, who died in 1636, leaving him £2300 when twenty-one. We hear of him mortgaging his lands in Dagenham in 1680, and entering into the service of William III. in 1695. He was made standard-bearer in 1699, and held that honourable position till his death in 1717.[1]

Philadelphia Uphill (mother of the above) left, in 1651, £5 to be distributed among the poor of Dagenham. She bequeathed to her husband, Sir Jacob, her house and garden in Goodmayes Field, and an "estate" in the East India Company.

The SYMONDS Charity.—The Rev. James Symonds, vicar, left, in 1719, £20 to the charity school in the village.

The MERTTINS Charity.—Henry Merttins, Esq., of the manor of Valence, left, in 1725, £10 to be distributed among the poor of the parish.

The WATERS Charity.—In 1756, Thomas Waters, of Dagenham, died, leaving the interest of £100 South Sea annuities to be expended by the minister and churchwardens in "placing out to school as many poor children of poor decayed parishioners as they shall think most deserving." Thomas Wincle and Frances French are appointed executors.

The COMYNS Charity.—At a court of the manor of Barking, held August 20, 1757, Richard Comyns surrendered two houses, with about twenty acres of land, in the village of Dagenham, to Messrs. Thomas Fanshawe, John Gascoigne Fanshawe, Thomas

---

[1] The late Mr. H. W. King suggested the following humorous epitaph for him—

> "Uphill I started on life's pilgrimage,
> Uphill I toil'd from youth to hoary age;
> Uphill I journey'd until life was ended,
> And still Uphill I to the grave descended."

Fanshawe, Jun., and John Tyler, their heirs and assigns, to pay out of the rents and profits of these premises the yearly sum of 40s. to the minister and churchwardens of Dagenham, to distribute to poor widows of the said parish not receiving alms. The distribution was to take place at Michaelmas and Christmas. One of these houses was called Wright's.

In 1801 these premises were converted into the parish workhouse. The trustees, in 1817, were the Rev. T. L. Fanshawe, G. Winmill, and T. W. Brittain. In 1835 the workhouse was abolished and the premises were let as dwelling-houses, the rent being distributed among poor widows. In 1847 the houses were thoroughly repaired at the cost of the parish, and turned into almshouses for several poor widows.

In 1820 the annuities stood in the names of the Rev. T. L. Fanshawe and Messrs. G. E. Pollett and S. Seabrook. The dividend—£3 per annum—was paid to Mary Shipton, the wife of the master of the Sunday School, for the gratuitous instruction of five girls, the children of poor parishioners, chosen by the vicar.

Richard Comyns was the last of an old family which had lived in Dagenham parish for two centuries at least. The elder branch had settled at Hare Street, Romford, where they owned a considerable estate, and exercised much influence, which, during the Great Rebellion, was on behalf of the Parliamentarians. The Comyns family of Dagenham were tanners, and lived at the tanyard, near the church. Subsequently they occupied a large house in Dagenham Street, opposite to the present Comyns' almshouses. There were other branches of this yeoman family, which was held in repute, as entitled to "arms and gentry." Richard Comyns died, in 1775, at the age of ninety-two, and was buried at Dagenham.[1]

The PILON Charity.—Mrs. Pilon, of Whalebone House, left, by will, £20, in 1788, to be distributed by the vicar and churchwardens to the deserving poor of the parish not receiving alms.

The MERTTINS Charity (2).—Mrs. Elizabeth Merttins, of Bedford Row, London, a frequent visitor to Valence, bequeathed, in 1803, £10 to be distributed to "poor who frequented Dagenham church, and were not common swearers."

The BENNETT Charity (2).—Alexander Bennett, Esq., of Valence, gave by will, in 1817, £432 12s. 11d. South Sea annuities,

---

[1] Richard Comyns was granted administration to Fox Lane End house under the will of his brother Henry, 1738.

the interest to be expended in "maintaining his family tomb, and the surplus to the poor who attend the parish Church and are not Drunkards or Common Swearers."

The COOMBES Charity.—John Coombes, a farm labourer, bequeathed, in 1818, "the remaining part of his property, amounting to £23 6s. 0d., to be doled out to the poor of the parish at the church every Sunday until the whole was distributed. The distribution commenced on Sunday, February 15, and finished April 5, 1818; it was undertaken by the executors of the will, William Scott and Benjamin Holgate.

The WHIPPLER, or WEPLER, Charity.—Mrs. Whippler, of Furze House, Marks Gate, bequeathed, in 1821, £30, the interest thereof to be distributed to the poor of Dagenham by the vicar and churchwardens every Easter Monday.

The FORD Charity.—William Ford left, in 1825, the sum of £10,000, Three-per-cent. Bank securities, to build and endow a school for the children of poor parents. The children were to be educated and also clothed out of the charity. The founder directed that the trustees of the bequest should be the lord bishop of the diocese and the churchwardens and overseers (not the *vicar*) of the parish of Dagenham. He also directed that the school should be conducted according to the principles of the Church of England, but not on the Bell, Lancasterian, or any other new system ; and further, that no person of the name of Fanshawe should act as trustee.

In 1828 the Court of Chancery established a scheme for the management of the charity. The Bishop of London (Dr. Blomfield) declined to act as a trustee, and Thomas Mashiter, Esq., and Digby Neave, Esq., justices, and Messrs. John Milner, Archer Moss, George Winmill, Ephraim Seabrook, and Thomas Waters Brittain were appointed trustees. The court ordered two rooms to be rented *pro tem.*, one for the boys and the other for the girls, and apartments for the master and mistress. The number of boys was to be thirty, of girls, twenty, to be increased or diminished at the discretion of the trustees. Each child was to be clothed at least once in two years, to attend school every day from 9 to 12 a.m., and 2 to 5 p.m. (2 to 4 p.m. in winter), except on Wednesdays and Saturdays, when there was to be no afternoon school. The salary of the master and mistress was fixed at £50 and £30 respectively, and £70 was allowed for the expenses of the school each year, excluding a gratuity of two guineas

R

to a clergyman to preach a sermon annually for the benefit of the charity.

After the lapse of twelve years, sufficient funds had accumulated to build the present schools, and the residences of the master and mistress. In 1851 the trustees decided to apply a portion of the large balance they had then in hand to build another "Ford's School," in Chadwell Heath, with a master's residence, thus bringing the total number of children benefited by the bequest up to one hundred and thirty.

In 1876 the Charity Commissioners revised the scheme, and made important alterations in it, under the Endowed Schools Acts of 1869, 1873, and 1874. In place of trustees, ten governors were to be appointed, thus—three *ex officio*, the vicar and churchwardens of Dagenham ; four representative governors (who were to be residents and ratepayers in the parish), nominated, two by the magistrates for the petty sessions for the Half-Hundred of Becontree, and two by the parish vestry, or present parish council, and three co-optative governors, to be appointed by the governors, and approved by the Charity Commissioners. The representative governors were to hold office for five years, and the co-optative for eight years. The scheme, however, specified that the first co-optative governors should be five, all appointed for life, viz. Henry Thompson, Archer Moss, Alexander Anderson, John Blott, William Reeve Mihill. Also that "whenever Charles Freeman shall cease to be an *ex officio* governor, he shall become a co-optative governor for life, whether there be a vacancy in that office or not."

It was also directed that the master of Ford's School, whether at Dagenham or Chadwell Heath, shall be a certificated teacher, and a member of the Church of England.

Under the new scheme the schools ceased to be "free" as intended by the founder. The governors were empowered to charge each child a "suitable fee," which was not, however, to exceed 9d. a week. The vested interests of the children then attending were secured by this proviso—"Any payment, or exemption from payment, or other benefit to which any boy or girl who was on the foundation on June 30, 1876, is legally entitled thereunder, shall be continued to him or her." The scheme came into force on January 1, 1877, when the schools were to be conducted under the terms of the Elementary Education Act of 1870 (sect. 7). In 1889 the governors decided to take advantage of the Free Education Act, and receive the fee-grant. Thus "Ford's Free Schools" became free again, and this time to all the children on the books, whether belonging to the parish or not. Owing to the fall of the Three-per-cents., and the increased requirements of the Education Department, as well as of the children attending the schools, it has of recent years only been with great effort that this "charity" has been kept up. Probably under the new Act (1902) its resources will be augmented, and its usefulness thereby increased.

The first master and mistress of Ford's School at Dagenham were Mr. Thomas Cutler and Miss Ann Bridge, respectively; at Chadwell Heath, Mr. J. W. Freshwater and Mrs. White. Mr. Freshwater resigned, in 1877, on a pension of £20 a year, paid out of the charity.

Besides the above bequest for educational purposes, William Ford left £1000 Three-per-cents. to be spent in clothing aged poor parishioners, and directed that the gifts of clothing should be given on December 16 every year (the anniversary of his death).

The individual who has laid the parish under such obligations to his benevolence was a sheep-farmer in the parish. For some years he was churchwarden, and was most assiduous in attending vestry meetings and doing what he could to promote the welfare of his native place. "Billy Ford" was regarded as "a bit of a character" in his day. Not only was he a bachelor, and a crusty one at that, but, because he was frugal in his habits and went about shabbily dressed, he was set down with good reason as a miser. He is remembered by tradition as a stern man, possessed of a disagreeable temper and a raucous voice. He used to drive to market and church in a "tumble-cart," *i.e.* a cart with a chair in it, on which he sat, which prevented him from offering, and others from asking for, a lift. On Sundays he was most regular in his worship at church, when he always wore a smock-frock, and sat at the back with the men who worked for him (also in smock-frocks) immediately in front of him. The bitter prejudice against the Fanshawe family shown in his will was due to a quarrel over a matter of tithe with the Rev. John Fanshawe, of Parsloes. There is a mural tablet to the memory of William Ford in the church.

The ARNOLD Charity.—Jonathan Arnold gave, in 1851, £100 Consols "to maintain his tomb and the surplus to the deserving Poor."

The STONE Charity.—Sarah Stone left, in 1852, £200 in the Three-per-cents., the interest to be spent in giving a dinner every Christmas Day to the children attending Ford's School. Eventually it was decided to spend the money in prizes for these school children. This benefactress was the niece of William Ford, and the wife of William Stone, a Dagenham farmer.

The WOODS Charity.—From time immemorial every poor widow in the parishes of Dagenham and Barking whose husband had been dead one year, and who was not in receipt of parochial relief, was entitled to a load of wood from Hainault Forest. The wood was to be hauled on Easter Monday; if the widow was unable to get a team to haul it, she was to receive, in lieu of it, eight shillings. When the forest disappeared, in 1855, a scheme was devised whereby pecuniary compensation was to be granted to needy widows in the aforesaid parishes. For this boon the beneficiaries are indebted to the late John Scrafton Thompson, Esq., of the mansion of Clements, Ilford, who procured a grant of £413 in Consols from the Board of Green Cloth, the interest to be expended annually in relieving poor widows. To those who are unacquainted with its origin, the charity is erroneously known as Widow Wood's Charity.

In addition to the foregoing benevolent bequests, a large number of small legacies to the poor of Dagenham have been left by the principal residents and vicars of the parish. It is, however, noteworthy, and at the same time significant, that no bequests have been left to the poor during the last fifty years. Is this due to the fact that the parishioners "as are of ability" have not been moved to "be liberal to the poor?"[1] Or is it the result of subsequent revisions by the Charity Commissioners of charitable bequests, whereby the charitably disposed have in these later days been disheartened? Or does it merely indicate the declining prosperity of the good folk of Dagenham?

The charitable bequests of Dagenham, as compared with those of many other parishes, are marked by several omissions. In none of them do we find any money left for the repair of the fabric of the church, or for keeping the churchyard in order; and in only two instances is anything said as to the maintenance of the family tomb of the testator. Nor is any special bequest made for the preaching of a sermon by the minister on a special occasion, e.g.,

---

[1] See rubric in the Visitation of the Sick.

Good Friday.[1] Nor, again, are there any peculiar conditions attached to the distribution of any of our parochial charities other than the exemption of drunkards, swearers, and the encouragement to the poor to "frequent" their parish church.

[1] The writer's father, who was rector of Hewelsfield, Gloucester, 1881–99, used to receive 5s. from an old bequest for preaching a sermon on Good Friday.

CHAPTER XXV

DAGENHAM BREACH.

> " Mighty river, oh, mighty river,
> Rolling in ebb and flow for ever,
> Through the city so vast and old ;
> Through massive bridges—by domes and spires
> Crown'd with the smoke of a myriad fires :—
> City of majesty, power and gold :—
> Thou lovest to float on thy waters dull
> The white-winged fleets so beautiful.
> And the lordly steamers speeding along
> Wind defying and swift and strong ;
> Thou bearest them all on thy motherly breast,
> Laden with riches, at Trade's behest."
>
> MACKAY.

THE parish of Dagenham is bounded on its south side by the
river Thames. Advantageous though the proximity of this river
has been, and still is, for navigation, commerce, shipping, and
fishing, the inhabitants, especially those dwelling on the river-side,
have had reason to regret it, on account of the numerous tidal inundations which have from time to time caused considerable damage
to land and property.[1] The earliest recorded inundation occurred
in 1376, when the bank, or sea-wall, alongside the river was swept
away by a conjunction of heavy tide and strong wind, and some
acres of land belonging to Barking Abbey completely submerged
and put out of cultivation. In their distress the abbess and
convent appealed to the king (Richard II.) to help them in their
calamity.[2] There were no Mansion House relief funds in those
days, or widely circulated journals in which they could themselves
make a direct appeal to a charitable British public ; so the sufferers
had no other source of help than the State. They petitioned that
they might be excused from contributing towards the cost of the

---

[1] See Appendix A.
[2] Katherine Sutton, abbess, 1358–76 ; Matilda de Montacute, 1376–94.

war with France, on account of the expenses they had incurred in repairing the damage done by the tide. The appeal was allowed.

Four years later another inundation took place, which made a second appeal to the king imperative. In this the abbess stated that the income of the abbey had decreased four hundred marks (equal to £3000 of present money), owing to recent tidal invasions and charges for repairs to land and property at Dagenham. She added, moreover, that the income of the abbey had fallen so low that there was scarcely enough money left to maintain the occupants of the nunnery. This appeal was also granted. Further inundations having occurred in the next year, it was determined, by the King's Council, to appoint a Commission *de walliis et fossatis* to supervise the breach walls or banks and report on their condition. They were to watch the marshlands also, and see that they were properly drained and "inned" (*i.e.* enclosed). At first only three commissioners, termed "sewers," were appointed (March, 1380), viz. Iohn de Dakenham, Richard Rolf, and Iohn Gale ; but in 1385 a fresh body of nine sewers replaced them, viz. Robert Bealknap, Willm Wanton, Iohn Gildesburg, Iohn Chanceux, knights, Willm Rikhull, Ivo Sandherst, Clement Spice & Thos. Sampkyn ("Patent Rolls," Rich. II.).

Notwithstanding the labours of these and other commissions, little progress was made either in checking damage by the tide or in reclaiming the "drowned" land. Matters, in short, went from bad to worse, and the abbess[1] and convent had no option but to present another petition to the Crown for relief (1409). They stated that they had spent the greater part of the income of the abbey for some years in repairing their banks, but all to no purpose, and that none of the ladies had more than fourteen shillings per annum for clothes and necessaries. The merits of the appeal were recognized by the king (Henry IV.), and a royal mandate was issued to exempt the abbey for seven years from taxes and other burdens. Writs were also issued to hire labourers to work at the sea-walls, and a licence was granted to appropriate the endowments of certain churches to the use of the Abbey of Barking, as on former[2] occasions.

[1] Sibilla de Fenton, 1394-1419.

[2] In the Hornchurch inventory of church goods, 1552, mention is made of damage done by " outrageous tides " being repaired out of part of the proceeds of the sale of its church goods. The money was paid to the marsh reeves of Hornchurch. On the temporary relief granted to Barking Abbey, see Appendix A, Chapter XXV.

DAGENHAM BREACH HOUSE
(from an old print)

The "Calendar of State Papers" contains occasional allusions to Dagenham Breach. Thus, under date January, 1540—

Commission of Sewers, Westminster.—Sir Richard Ryche, Sir Thos. Denys, Sir Edmund Walsyngham, Sir Humph. Browne, King's Sergeant at Law, Sir Roger Cholmeley, Sergeant at Law, Sir Richard Gressham, Sir Iohn Champneys, Clement Haslyston, Sir Edw⁴ Bowton, Thos. Pope, Martin Bowes, Rob' Southwell, Anth. Coke, Richard Stapylton, Iohn Poynes, William Harman, Barth. Prowse, for the district lying by the river & water-course that runneth from Bowbridge to Laymowth, from thence to Dagenham Beame as well for Kent as for Essex upon the north side of the Temys and from thence to Haveryngwell, Wysden Waterynges and the highway from Ilford to Rumford, as the bounds of Haveryng do lead within Essex.

From the same source we learn that in May, 1633, Charles I. wrote to Robert, Earl of Warwick, Lord Chancellor, Justice Richardson, Sir Nich. Coote,

recommending George Glanville, gentleman, servant to the Queen, for Clerk to the Sewers for the levels of Eastham, Westham, Dagenham & Havering. He was accordingly appointed. In the following July the King wrote, saying that as he now understood George Glanville was unfit for a post of that sort, they were to appoint Styward Trench, who has given good testimony of his ability to serve the King & his country in causing the repair of bridges between Stratford & Bow and in freeing the country of vagabonds.

A good deal of information on this subject is given in Sir William Dugdale's "History of Embanking and Draining" (London, 1662). Speaking of the dykes and breaches of the Thames, he remarks—

The first mention of the marshes in Essex is in King John's time. Roger de Crammervill being then attached to show cause why he did not stand to the determination made in the said King's court, by a fine betwixt himself and the Prior of St. John of Jerusalem, touching the banks, gutters and ditches in Renham (Rainham) marsh, at which time the said Prior produced the before-mentioned fine so made between them ; which testified that the said Roger did then agree that he and his heirs would make and repair those banks, etc., according to the proportion of his land in that marsh, so that every acre which the said Roger possessed should be taxed as those that belonged to the Prior. And the said Roger came and acknowledged the agreement, and justified that he had fully made those banks according to what belonged to his tenement, and thereupon put himself upon the view of those who knew the Laws of the Marsh.

The repair and proper maintenance of the dykes and sea-walls seems to have been a vexed question, and the cause of frequent litigations.[1] In the "Calendar of State Papers" we read of a dispute, in 1330, between the Prioress of Stratford and William de Masun, bailiff of the marsh of Westhamme, the latter having distrained her for one hundred shillings for repairing a marsh-bank called Prior's Wall. The prioress denied her liability, but was ordered by the jurors to pay the amount claimed, this being in their opinion " her just share." The foreman of the jury was Iohn de Dakenham, and one of the jurors Simon de Passelewe (or Passeloes).

In the work referred to, Dugdale tells us that,

touching the levels of Havering and Dagenham, at a session of Sewers held at Romford, 16th May, 36 Elizabeth [1594–95], before Sir Henry Gray, Knight, Sir John Peter, Knight, Richard Warren, Esqire & others ; where, for the recovery of Havering Marsh, then overflown and drowned and preventing the like to Dagenham Level, it was decreed that Dagenham Creek should be immediately inned ; and that whereas the said drowning had been occasioned by a breach in the wall of Will. Ayloff of Horn-church, esquire, he the said William to pay the sum of five hundred pounds, and the landholders of Dagenham certain rates by the acre for all their marsh grounds lying in the said level, viz. the lands on Dagenham side against the said creeks at £265 and the lands in Havering Level the sum of seven hundred pounds.

Notwithstanding the efforts made by the Sewers Commissioners to have the main water-courses of the Thames kept clean, to prevent the various rivulets from becoming stagnant, and to keep the marshes free from poisonous matter, and to prevent damage to property by keeping the sluices and river-walls effective and strong, the results were both inadequate and unsatisfactory. This was because they were kept short of funds. Those whose lands immediately adjoined the river complained of the loss they suffered through the high tides destroying the banks they constructed at considerable expense, and desired that steps should be taken to compel the owners of uplands, or lands away from the river, who escaped this inconvenience and pecuniary outlay, to contribute their share in this undertaking. They pleaded, with justice, that the owners and occupiers of lands away from the river derived benefit from the draining of the marshes and the repair of the

---

[1] Some interesting articles by Mr. W. W. Glenny, on "The Dykes of the Thames," appeared in the *Essex Review*, vols. x.-xi.

sea-walls. They pointed out, moreover, that in Holland free-holders who lived away from the sea were legally compelled to assist those whose lands suffered from inundations of the sea. The "uplanders," on the other hand, objected to the continual taxing of their lands for an uncertain and intangible benefit. Meanwhile, the tidal waves continued to work mischief, and the commissioners, becoming alarmed at this, engaged an eminent

Dagenham Breach.

Dutch engineer, Cornelius Vermuyden, in 1621, to stem a breach in the embankment of the Thames, near Dagenham. Smiles says of him—

> He was a person of good birth and education, a gentleman of some importance in his time. He had been trained as an engineer, and having been brought up in a country where embanking was studied as an art and afforded employment to a considerable proportion of its inhabitants, he was familiar with the most approved methods of defending land against the encroachments of the sea. He was so successful in his operations at Dagenham that when it was found necessary to drain the royal park at Windsor, he was employed to direct the labourers in that work, by which he became known to James I. He collected from different parts the skilled labour of Dutch and Flemish workmen to embank the lands at Dagenham and Canvey Island.[1]

Although Vermuyden was in matters of engineering ahead of his time, he found his task one of serious difficulty. The commissioners complained of his operations being ineffective, the inhabitants that the levels were as dangerous as ever, and the

[1] "Lives of the Engineers," vol. i. chap. ii.

workmen that their wages were withheld.[1] At a Council of State, held December 26, 1622, at Whitehall, it was decided to inform the Commission of Sewers for Essex, that—

On complaint of the labourers employed by Cornelius Vermuyden in recovering the surrounded ground in Essex called Havering and Dagenham marshes, that their wages are withheld, Vermuyden promises to pay them, but requests that as most of his work is done & he has expended £3600 thereon, he may receive the money due to him from the county for his charges. Recommended some course for the speedy payment thereof" ("Calendar of State Papers," 1619–23).

The recommendation of the council was not, however, followed, except perhaps partially, as we learn from the following entry—

Commissioners of Sewers to the Council.—Cornelius Vermuyden, who contracted for draining the levels of Havering & Dagenham, before Michaelmas last, for £2000, on pain of losing his money unless completed in time, not only has accomplished little hitherto, but by his delays & the want of durability in the work he has accomplished, the land is in a worse condition than it was before. On this account the county refuses to pay Vermuyden ; he urges for payment & his workpeople clamour for wages, while land holders complain of dangers to their property from the state of the levels. Request directions [February 2, 1623].

A further entry runs thus—

Commissioners of Sewers in Essex to the Archbishop of Canterbury and others.[2]

Are unable to mediate in the business of the levels of Havering & Dagenham & find Mr. Vermuyden's demands unreasonable, the loss & misery of the landowners great & the levels in a dangerous state ("Calendar of State Papers," 1625–26).

To solve this wearisome dispute, it was decided to grant Vermuyden a share in the enterprise he had undertaken. This solution was covered by an Act of Parliament, 13th Elizabeth, which recites that, " where any person should be assessed by the commissioners to any lot & refuse or neglect to pay the same, the land shall be leased or passed in fee simple in recompence to the undertaker." Certain lands, amounting to about one-third of

---

[1] The workmen, sixty-two in all, presented a petition to the Council at Whitehall twice. The second " prays for a summons against Justice Wright, one of the sewers, for refusing to pay them their wages according to promise, as they are in great distress and far from home" ("Calendar of State Papers," 1622–23).

[2] The archbishop at that time was Dr. George Abbot. The duties of his high office seem to have been of a diversified character.

those recovered, were "granted to Vermuyden & confirmed to him & his heirs, in recompence of his charges for work done in the repair of Dagenham Breach." The grant is dated from Windsor Castle, July 17, 1625.

While Cornelius Vermuyden was sedulously pressing his claims before the sewers, another engineer, named Edward Standen, of Sherborne, was doing the same, though for a much smaller amount. He stated that he was engaged to repair damage done by inundations between the levels of Dagenham and Havering, but afterwards resigned the undertaking to Sir Cornelius Vermuyden on promise of being paid £100, of which he received £20, the remainder to be paid when the next scot for the levels was collected ("Calendar of State Papers," 1631–32).

It seems incredible that the project for stopping the breach should have encountered any opposition, least of all in Dagenham. Such, however, was the case. The fishermen and poachers and lovers of sport saw with regret the disappearance of what had provided a rich harvest in the past. The labourers resented the importation of Dutch and Flemish workmen to execute the work. Ballads were composed full of ridicule at the enterprise, and insinuating that it "bod'ed more ill than good" to the parish. Take the following stanzas from "The Powte's Complaint" (published 1625)—

"Come, brethren of the water, and let us all assemble,
  To treat upon this matter, which makes us quake and tremble,
  For we shall rue it, if't be true, the Fens be undertaken,
  And where we feed in fen and reed, they'll feed both beef and bacon.

"They'll sow both beans and oats, where never man yet thought it,
  Where men did row in boats, 'ere undertakers bought it :
  But, Ceres, thou behold us now, let wild oats be their venture,
  Oh, let the frogs and miry bogs destroy where they do enter.

"Behold the great design, which they do now determine,
  Will make our bodies pine a prey to crows and vermin ;
  For they do mean all Fens to drain, and waters overmaster,
  All will be dry, and we must die—'cause Essex Calves want pasture.

"Away with boats and rudder, farewell both boots and sketches,
  No need of th'one nor t'other, men now make better matches ;
  Stilt-makers all, and tanners, shall complain of this disaster ;
  For they will make each muddy lake for Essex Calves a pasture.

"The feather'd fowls have wings to fly to other nations,
  But we have no such things to help our transportations ;
  We must give place, O ! grievous case, to hornèd beasts and cattle,
  Except that we can all agree to drive them out by battle.

" Wherefore let us intreat our antient water-nurses
    To show their power so great as to t'help us drain their purses ;
    And send us good old Captain Flood to lead us out to battle,
    Then two penny Jack with scales on's back, will drive out all the cattle.

" This noble Captain yet was never known to fail us,
    But did the conquest get of all that did assail us,
    His furious rage none could assuage ; but to the world's great wonder,
    He bears down banks, and breaks their cranks and whirligigs asunder.

" God Eolus, we do thee pray, that thou wilt not be wanting,
    Thou never said'st us nay, now listen to our canting :
    Do thou deride their hope and pride, that purpose our confusion ;
    And send a blast, that they in haste, may work no good conclusion.

" Great Neptune (God of Seas), this work must needs provoke thee ;
    They mean thee to disease, and with Fen water choke thee ;
    But, with thy mace, do thou deface, and quite confound this matter ;
    And send thy sands, to make dry lands, when they shall want fresh water."

And again—

THE DRAINING OF THE FENS.

" The upland people are full of thoughts,
        And do despair of after-rain ;
    Now the sun is rob'd of his morning draughts,
        They're afraid they shall never have shower again.

            Then apace, apace drink, drink deep, drink deep ;
                Whilst 'tis to be had, lets the liquor ply ;
                The drainers are up, and a coil they keep,
                And threaten to drain the kingdom dry.

" Our smaller rivers are now dry land,
        The eels are turned to serpents there ;
    And if old Father Thames play not the man
        Then farewell to all good English beer.
                Then apace, apace drink, etc.

" The Dutchman hath a thirsty soul,
        Our cellars are subject to his call,
    Let every man then lay hold on his bowl,
        'Tis a pity the German Sea should have all.
                Then apace, apace drink, etc.

" Our new Philosophers rob us of fire,
        And by reason do strive to maintain that theft
    And now that the water begins to retire
        We shall shortly have never an element left.
                Then apace, apace drink, etc.

" Why should we stay here then, and perish with thirst ?
        To th' New World in the moon away let us goe ;
    For if the Dutch Colony get thither first,
        'Tis a thousand to one that they'll drain that too.
                Then apace, apace drink, etc.

The tidal inundations which we have already noticed, destructive though they were, were not of such magnitude as the terrible overflow that occurred on December 17, 1707, which produced what is now known as Dagenham Breach. It would seem that this catastrophe was the result of neglect or indolence on the part of the marsh-bailiff at that time, one Edward Osborne, in allowing the sluice to get out of working order, with the result that it collapsed altogether. Although serious consequences were imminent, no great inrush of water took place till a fortnight afterwards, and had Sir Nicholas Garrett, a Commissioner of the Court of Sewers, shown promptitude and energy, further disaster might have been averted. He convened a meeting of the commissioners at Ilford, it is true, but the gravity of the situation not being realized, there was not a quorum present, and no business was done. Meanwhile, two labourers, John Cole, of Barking, and James Harvey, of Plaistow, were set to work on the marsh-wall, but with ineffective results. A Dutch engineer, John of Ghent, with Mr. Fleming, a farmer of Barking, and a marsh-bailiff named Thorne, succeeded in fixing a sluice, which proved too frail, and was dislodged by the first tide. Even thus it was not too late, and had the commissioners engaged a competent engineer at once, an outlay of £50 would probably have saved the country the later grant of £40,000, as well as the special Act of Parliament passed for the purpose. The gap grew wider and wider, and soil from the adjoining fields began to be washed into the Thames. A small island, called Hopes in the Marsh, in the possession of John Emerton, was also swept away. After the lapse of several months, Mr. John Ward, of Hackney, M.P. for the City, and a Mr. Jackson, took the matter up. Huge piles were driven in, backed with tons of earth, but the former were inadequately flanked, and could not resist the tidal inrush when there happened to be a high wind with it.

These ineffectual attempts caused much disappointment and discontent in the parish. A levy of as much as £28 per acre had been made on the land beside the Thames by the commissioners, and the owners and tenants naturally felt that they had done their share in raising funds to repair the sea-wall. They accordingly presented a humble petition to Parliament "to be relieved of land-tax for these said drowned lands, until they be regained." The Lord Mayor of London, Sir Samuel Stainer, Knt., thereupon, as conservator of the river Thames, requested his water-bailiff, Walter Bateller, to make a formal report on this subject, in 1713, which must have been very unpleasant reading when produced. It states that—

Sandy Creek, in the Level of Dagenham, hath done very great damage to the river, which visibly appears for four miles below & two miles above the breach. From the lower end of Bugsby's Hole to the uppermost ballast wharf by Woolwich, which is 1½ miles in length, ships before the breach, drawing twelve or fourteen feet of water, used to ride at ancher with safety, & now it is so choked up with sand and earth that in most places it is not above five feet at low water. About half-a-mile from the breach mouth down to Dagenham Jetty, a place where His Majesty's ships used to ride at anchor with the biggest merchant ships, is now almost choked up, & a great bank of sand & earth appears dry before low water; and although many thousand tons have been taken up yearly by the ballast men, yet it daily increases.

This report was followed by a complaint from the Thames pilots of the dangers of the breach at Sandy Creek, which endangered the navigation of the river. The landowners, too, presented a second petition, stating that, after raising £40,000, by direction of Her Majesty's (Queen Anne) Commission of Sewers, which they had spent in stopping the breach, a great storm had destroyed the walls (February 15, 1714), and again let in the tide. Three months later, the clerk to the Elder Brethren at Trinity House wrote to them, "If the breach be not quickly restored, it will in all probability force a passage into the adjoining Flete, called Rainham Creek, to the further prejudice of the river Thames." A committee of experts also reported that the ebb tides were doing great harm, to the detriment of trade and commerce in the country generally.

Realizing at last the serious state of things brought before their notice from all quarters, Parliament passed an Act, entitled, "An Act for the speedy and effectually preserving the navigation of the river Thames, by stopping the breach in the levels of Havering and Dagenham, in the county of Essex." The Act decreed that the cost of doing this should be defrayed by a small duty of three-pence per ton on the burden of every ship for every voyage inward, and that every coaster shall pay the duty of three shillings and no more for each voyage they shall make to the port of London. It was evidently a case of the preferential tariff, for the purpose of putting what was termed a "national river" into a thoroughly navigable condition. Colliers, fishing-vessels, ships or vessels in ballast only, and coasters were to be exempt; but vessels laden with coal or culm were to pay a duty of one penny for every chalder. The Act was to be in force for ten years, from July 18, 1714, and its operations supervised by a body of influential trustees. The latter body advertised in the *London Gazette* for tenders, and eventually accepted an estimate for £16,500 (the lowest), from Mr. William Boswell. Unfortunately Boswell broke down in his task, and abandoned the enterprise. This greatly alarmed the trustees, but having consulted several eminent engineers,[1] they again invited tenders, and accepted that of £24,000, from Captain John Perry, which they had previously rejected.

Perry proved himself to be more equal to his arduous undertaking than his predecessor, having had more experience in marsh-draining, both in this country and in Russia. He had, however, no sooner drawn up his plan of proceedings, than Boswell presented a petition to Parliament criticizing his methods as impracticable. Perry was, therefore, examined as to his scheme before a Parliamentary committee, but the ability which he displayed reassured the trustees, and the contract with him was signed in June, 1716. He found his task one of enormous labour and peril, owing to recent inundations and exceptionally strong tides, which he three times turned out of the Dagenham levels. After five years' assiduous effort he succeeded in constructing a wall which stood two feet above the highest tide. He received for his labours a grant from Parliament of £15,000,[2] and a testimonial of £1000 from the local landowners, over and above his contract, but nearly the whole of this sum was expended on the scheme. In his book on "Dagenham Breach," Captain Perry mildly censures the trustees for keeping him short of money, and adds, "had not my good friends, the Russia merchants, who knew me in the Czar's service, stood firmly by me, it is certain I should never have been able to go through with my undertaking."[3]

From this statement it would seem that the parish of Dagenham owes a debt of gratitude to Russia, and one which it can never hope to discharge, and so cannot ever ignore.

When Captain Perry found that his task was likely to be a

---

[1] Brigadier Richards, Surveyor-General of Ordnance; Colonel Armstrong; and Sir Jacob Ackworth, Chief Surveyor of the Royal Navy.

[2] This was raised by a special clause in "An Act for continuing the Malt Tax and for other purposes" (7 George II. c. 20), authorizing the trustees to pay Captain Perry this sum in consideration of his unexpected heavy outlay.

[3] "An Accounte of the Stopping of Daggenham Breach, with the Accidents that have attended the Same from the First Undertaking by Capt. John Perry." [1721.]

tedious affair, he built a suitable house for himself near the breach, and also cottages for his workmen.   For this he was assailed by his jealous rival for effeminate and selfish extravagance, in a book entitled, "An Impartial Account of the Frauds and Abuses at Dagenham Breach" (London, 1717)—a malicious treatise, which does its writer much discredit.   In 1724 Boswell followed up his slander by bringing an action against Perry for breach of contract in not paying him a specified sum for the materials taken over and for labour ; after hearing both sides at some length, the Lord Chancellor made an order for Perry to pay £1720 and costs, instead of the £10,000 which Boswell claimed.

Although Captain Perry succeeded in making an embankment strong enough to keep out tidal inundations, and thus prevent further sea-floods, there is no evidence that he ever attempted to reclaim the land which had been so long in the grip of the tide. A large sheet of water, covering forty acres of unreclaimed land, consequently remains as the memorial of the terrible storm of 1707 ; this is known as Dagenham Breach, Lake, or Gulf.

While the reclaiming operations were being carried on, a very extensive stratum of moor-logg, or rotten wood, of various kinds, was found a few feet from the surface.   This stratum was nearly four yards deep, and consisted of a mass of trees—oak, hornbeam, yew, willow, and brushwood.   A quantity of hazel-nuts were also found, and several stags' horns, lying above the moor-logg.

On the successful conclusion of Captain Perry's enterprise, the breach trustees ceased to exist in their official capacity, and the Commission of Sewers resumed their responsibilities as guardians of the marsh-walls of Dagenham.   They found the Breach House, which that able engineer had built that he might be on the spot to superintend operations, a convenient centre for transacting business, and also for social intercourse "across the walnuts and the wine."   As the commissioners were partly wealthy city merchants and partly country gentlemen, the dinners at the Breach House in the Dagenham marshes became a feature of city life in the country.

In 1792 a fishing club was formed, having its headquarters at the Breach House.[1]   Its founders were Sir Thos. Dundas, Bart., Sir Hugh Pallison (Governor of Greenwich Hospital), Sir Joseph Banks, F.R.S., Edward Hulse, Chas. Alex. Crickitt, M.P., and Bamber Gascoigne, Esquires.   The club flourished about twenty

[1] See Appendix A, Chapter XXV.

years. While it existed, it had a few distinguished visitors, the chiefest being Mr. William Pitt, the then Premier, and the Right Hon. George Rose, Secretary of the Treasury, and an Elder Brother of the Trinity House, who were intimate friends of Sir Robert Preston, Bart., M.P., who belonged to the club, and had a cottage at Dagenham Lake. For several years these statesmen were entertained by Sir Robert at Breach House, and dinners of a *recherché* description were given. This was the origin of the ministerial whitebait dinners, which were subsequently given at Greenwich, from being a more convenient centre than Dagenham.

Breach House was occupied for several years by Richard Broome, Esq., Gent., who is mentioned in an old deed as holding land near Little Heath on the surrender of John Cooper, of Whitechapel, sugar refiner (1737). He was brother to the Rev. William Broome, rector of Pulham, Norfolk, a poet and a friend of Pope, and included in Dr. Johnson's "Lives of the Poets."

Another illustrious resident was Mrs. Elizabeth Fry, "dove-like Betsy," who came here for retirement and rest, and occupied a cottage near the breach during the summer months of 1826–33. She was on intimate terms with the Rev. T. L. and Mrs. Fanshawe, and often drank tea at the vicarage. Breach House did not then exist, as it had been pulled down in 1812.

In 1856 a company was formed, and an Act of Parliament obtained, to purchase Dagenham Lake and convert it into a dock. Two skilled engineers, Sir John Rennie and Mr. J. Murray, were engaged for this purpose, and all went well for a year, when the work was stopped through lack of sufficient capital. According to the prospectus, this dock was to have been "one of the largest in the port of London, and capable of receiving the largest vessels afloat." It was an ambitious scheme, but the time for its accomplishment was not ripe.

On an old map of Dagenham a gallows is marked by the riverside near the breach. Here the Thames pirates, and those who had been guilty of smuggling and other "river crimes," suffered the extreme penalty of the law. The last execution took place so late as 1780.

The parish registers contain frequent references to the "Breach," the "marsh-lands," the "reed-shore," and the "marsh-walls." The occurrence of the entry, "drowned at yᵉ Breach," which is fairly common, indicates the perils of the Dagenham Lake. The number of deaths from ague is attributable to the marshes and "drowned" land at this end of the parish. The parish minutes' book informs us that the marsh was managed by a jury, which met twice a year ; that the Breach House Company were rated at £46 to the Poor and £30 to Highway or Statute duty from 1800–30 ; that on the dissolution of the company Mr. Sterry, of Romford, was appointed steward to the lord of the manor, and paid the Statute duty for the "Guelph." The lord of the manor was Mr. John Fanshawe, of Parsloes, who paid duty for the "reed-shore." At his death it came into the hands of Mr. John Wade, who appealed against it at the Ilford sessions on the

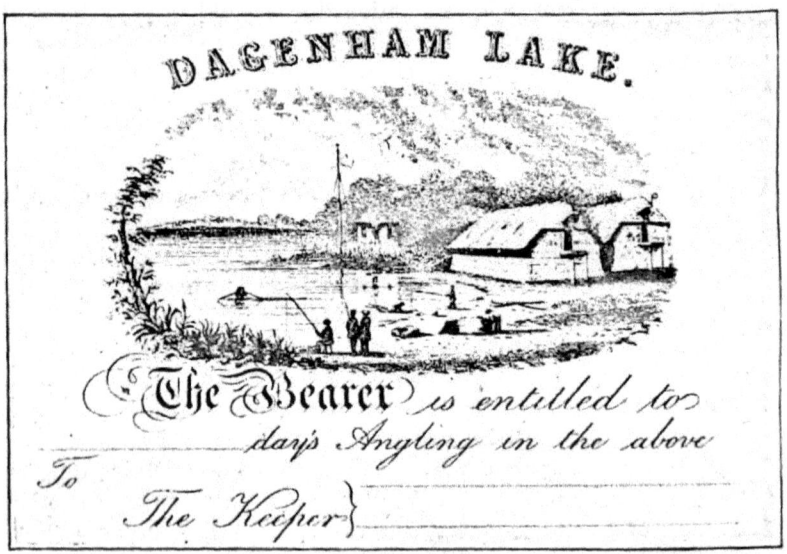

DAGENHAM LAKE.

The Bearer is entitled to ____ day's Angling in the above

To
The Keeper}

ground that he " sent all the reed away by barge on the Thames." The result was that the vestry eventually (1827) reduced the rate on the " reed-shore, comprising 2¼ acres of very inferior land," to £4 10s. 0d. A good trade used to be done in reed-marshes, as the tops of the reeds were useful, and in request for household decorative purposes. The marshes produce in some years a good crop of oysters, which find a ready sale, though they cannot compare with the well-known " Colchester natives."

The parish book gives also a brief account of a proposal to construct a canal between the river Thames and Romford, passing through Dagenham at Rippleside. A special vestry meeting was convened to protest against it, and a memorial was drawn up to be presented to Parliament (February 25, 1825). It states that the inhabitants are

"strongly apprehensive that if the scheme is accomplished the most imminent dangers will arise to the Proprietors as well as to the Occupiers of lands in the levels of Ripple, Dagenham & Havering; also to the great annoyance of Proprietors and occupiers of land in the Uplands, by dis-uniting their fields & bringing strangers that in a very extensive degree will become chargeable to the Poor-rates & permanent Paupers at a perpetual expense to the Parish.

"We are the more anxious to protest against the Scheme of the Canal & Embankment through the Marshes as it is so clearly known to us, the nature of the soil which is a few feet from the surface an entire Moorlog & quicksand, incapable of withstanding weight of earth or pressure of water; and we have every reason to fear that if the wall next the river is allowed to be cut through a breach will be the consequence."

The petition concludes with a reference to past inundations and the large sums of money expended in repairing the damage done by them. The Bill was eventually dropped, as the opposition to it was considered to be based on just and sound reasons, and has not been heard of since.

In 1864 the Dagenham Docks Company was floated, with a supposed capital of £300,000, comprising thirty thousand shares of £10 each. The inaugural ceremony of turning the first sod was performed in May of the following year by the Hon. Howe Browne. Owing to deficiency of funds the scheme was not, how-ever, carried through. In 1875 the lake was acquired by Messrs. S. Williams & Son, who erected commodious jetties, and de-veloped a large coal wharf there. Three years ago the Act of 1856 was renewed, and there is now a happy possibility of Dagen-ham Breach serving a useful purpose as Dagenham Docks in the world of trade and commerce.

CHAPTER XXVI

CHADWELL HEATH

"Much, was there not, in place and people both,
    To lend an eye to? And what eye like yours—
    The learned eye is still the loving one!
    Our land : its quietude, productiveness,
    Its length and breadth of grain-crop, meadow-ground,
    Its orchards in the pasture, farms a-field
    And hamlets on the road-edge, nought you missed
    Of one and all the sweet rusticities!"
                        R. BROWNING.

CHADWELL HEATH is the name by which the northern portion of the parish of Dagenham is known. It comprises the common or "heath" lying between the old Forest of Hainault and Beacontree Heath, which, until a few years ago, consisted of rough, boggy pasture, with an abundance of gorse and furzy bushes. In various old wills, even so recent as 1802, it is called "Blackheath," and sometimes, as an alternative, "Chadwell Common." With the exception of a few farmers and tradespeople, its inhabitants were a poor, thriftless set of people, who lived in small log cabins, thatched, one story high, much after the style of the Irish peasantry of to-day. They gained a precarious livelihood by cultivating patches of land, lopping trees, and breeding cattle, colts, donkeys, swine, and geese, which they turned into the forest to graze. This latter privilege they enjoyed in virtue of being bred and born in the parish, though it varied in extent according to the amount of rates they paid. Those who paid more than eight shillings a year in rates were at liberty to turn out five head of cattle, or as many colts, or a dozen pigs or geese, into the forest; those who paid less, grazed less in proportion. Some of the squatters imagined, in consequence, that if they kept their live-stock out of the forest altogether, they were exempt from the payment of rates. From the parish books it would seem that this erroneous impression

THE THREE MILLS, CHADWELL HEATH
(from an old painting made about 1810)

caused a good deal of friction with the parochial authorities, from time to time, inasmuch as the aggrieved defaulters made the non-payment of their rates a matter of "conscience," and offered a passive resistance. A few of the men found profitable employment in trapping vermin, such as foxes, stoats, and badgers, the heads of which they took to the churchwardens, who paid them two shillings for a fox's head, and one shilling for a badger's or weasel's head. Those who were dishonestly inclined indulged in poaching pursuits, even going so far as to steal the king's deer, whenever a suitable opportunity presented itself, or when they were able to outwit or outmatch by superior numbers the deer-keepers, or reeves. This was a daring proceeding, as, under the old game laws, no animals of the chase were so strictly protected as the deer in the royal forests. Notwithstanding, however, the heavy penalties, deer were stolen, and stolen frequently, and the quarry speedily carried off by cart to London. Once over Bow Bridge the deer-stealers were safe, as they were then beyond the operation of the forest laws, even supposing the keepers took the trouble and risk to follow them so far.

Chadwell Heath is bisected by the London and Colchester road, which is said to have been made by the Romans during their government of this country. It has been traversed by many historic personages. Edward the Confessor, William the Conqueror, Henry I., and John Lackland *may* have passed along it during their visits to the royal palace at Havering-atte-Bower. The inglorious Queen Mary certainly did in 1553–54, on her way to and from the ancient loyal borough of Colchester. Seven years later the Earl of Oxford and Lord Robert Dudley conducted the Duke of Finland in state from that town to London when he came as a suitor for the hand of Queen Elizabeth. In May, 1578, that illustrious queen herself passed through Romford, spending the night at Gidea Hall as the guest of Sir Antony Cooke, in her royal progress to Norwich. In 1599, William Kemp, the then famous comic actor, who answered, perhaps, to our Dan Leno, performed his "nine daies wonder" by dancing "the morrise to Norrige" (Norwich) from London. This William Kemp was a personal friend and colleague of the immortal William Shakespeare, and rendered him much assistance in the production of his plays on the stage, especially *Romeo and Juliet*, and *Much Ado about Nothing*. In October, 1637, the unpopular Queen Maria de Medici, widow of Henry IV. of France (Henry of Navarre) and mother of Henrietta Maria, wife of Charles I., landed at Harwich, and came by road to London. She stayed for a short time at Gidea Hall, from which her royal son-in-law escorted her (on the 31st), amid much display of hostile feeling, to his capital, where she resided three or four years. We do not after this hear of any more distinguished equipages until September, 1761, when Princess Charlotte of Mecklenburgh Strelitz passed through Chadwell Heath on her journey from Harwich to London, the king's coach and servants having met her at Romford. The next day (September 9) she was married to George III. by the Archbishop of Canterbury (Dr. Secker).[1] The next royal visitor was George, Prince of Wales (afterwards George IV.), who came in 1795 to review the troops locally raised to resist the threatened invasion by Napoleon Bonaparte. It was a time of thrilling excitement, and it is no wonder that the Prince's visit, with its object, left an impression on the neighbourhood. Yet another memorable though sad procession passed through the village in August, 1821, when the body of Queen Caroline (wife of George IV.) was conveyed in semi-state from London to Harwich, for interment at Brunswick. This was the last pageant which the dwellers on the heath witnessed. The introduction of railways, together with other changes in the county, has put an end to royal progresses and historic displays on the highways, which for seven centuries had kept a quiet rural hamlet in touch with some of the chief events of the political and social life of the nation.[2]

To these pageants may be added yet another one, which, for three centuries at least, took place every year. This was the progress of the Abbess of Barking on her way to the Grange, Ingatestone, which belonged to the abbey. This lady, on account of her position, as well also on account of her usual high rank, was perhaps the most influential personage in East Anglia, and her annual visits would cause considerable excitement on the " heath." Borne in a litter by her servants, and attended by her tenants on horseback (chief of whom was the lord of Valence), the abbess would travel with semi-regal retinue from Barking to Ingatestone, a fifteen miles' journey, reaching her destination before nightfall. Probably her stay at the Grange lasted five or six weeks, during

[1] This prelate had the, perhaps, unique distinction of baptizing, confirming, and crowning a king, viz. George III.

[2] On August 5, 1762, the great Dr. Samuel Johnson passed through Chadwell Heath in the stage-coach to Harwich, whither he accompanied his faithful biographer. See Boswell's " Life of Johnson," chapter xiv.

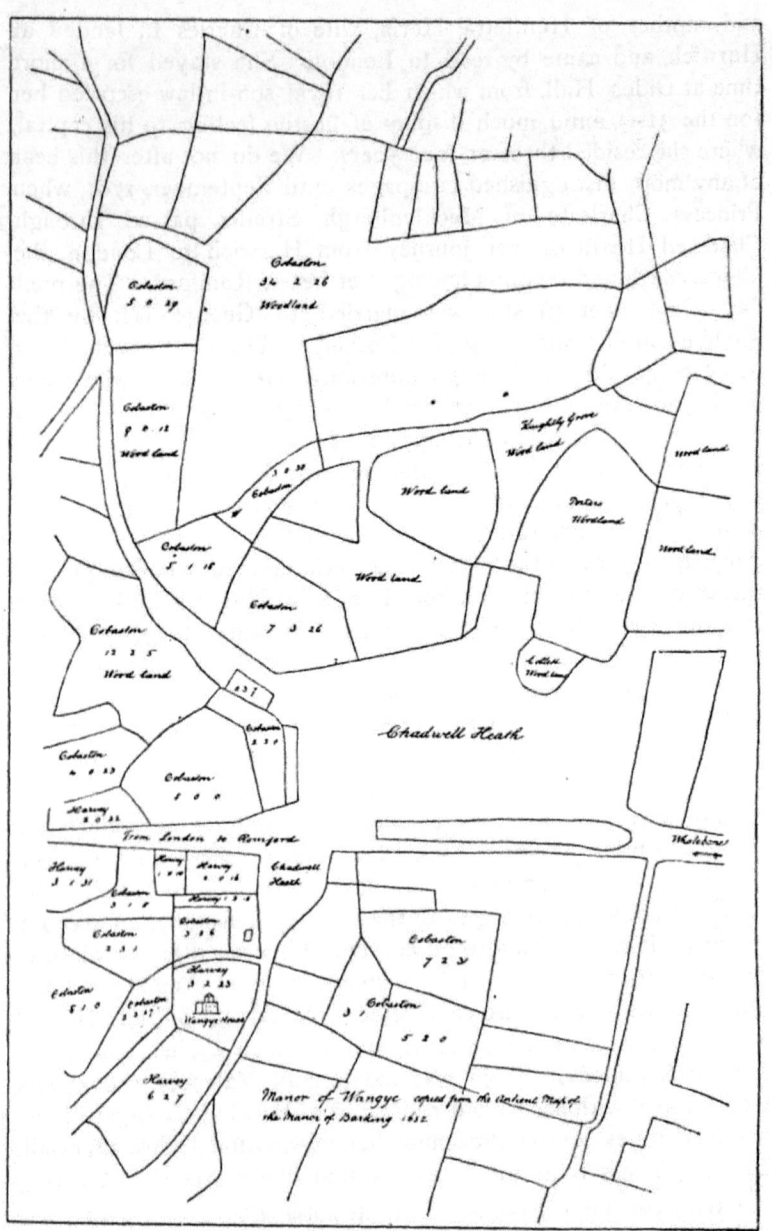

MAP OF CHADWELL HEATH (ABOUT 1750).

[To face p. 265.

which time she and her servants consumed the produce of the abbey lands at Ingatestone, to the value of the rents due to the Abbey of Barking. Assuming that these progresses were kept up to the spoliation of the abbey, the last one took place in 1537 or 1538.

The advantageous position which Chadwell Heath occupies on the king's highway caused it to be much infested in days gone by with footpads and highwaymen. Many a coach was stopped and robbed by the " gentlemen on the road," with crape-covered faces and pistols in holsters. Many a lonely pedestrian had cause to treasure in his breast unpleasant memories of Chadwell Heath. No wonder that travellers heaved a sigh of relief when they had passed the heath in safety. Sometimes the thieves were caught, but not often, as the large shrubs and the forest hard by afforded ample cover to these evil-doers, and aided their escape. An old chronicle tells of one Mary Richardson and Sarah Gibbs, spinsters, being sentenced to transportation by Lord Chief Baron Comyns and Baron Carter, at the Chelmsford Assizes, in July, 1740, for stealing a gown from a Margaret Rounce, at Chadwell Heath, in the Forest Lane (probably Whalebone Lane). A few other cases are recorded of people being convicted of sheep-stealing, goose-stealing, and small felonies on the heath, and being sentenced to be hanged, or whipped, or burnt in the hand for these offences, respectively. Richard Downes and another were also sentenced to death for robbing a coach not far from Romford. But there are not any notorious highway or other offences associated with Chadwell Heath in the criminal calendar, for the obvious reason that the culprits were not caught. Tradition, resting on some support, however, says that the notorious Dick Turpin was, at one period of his exciting career, a familiar figure on the heath. The Dick Turpin inn, which is a mile or so away, is either an historical reminiscence of that individual, or the result of a desire to immortalize his connection, real or fancied, with this locality.[1]

Before quitting the high road, let us glance for a moment at the picturesque scenery before us. On its northern side were the three windmills, all at work, grinding the corn brought from the productive fields of Dagenham. In the far distance was the Marks

[1] This "enemy of society" was a native of Hempstead, Essex, who, after a life of adventures on the road, was finally arrested at York, where he was hanged in 1739 at the age of twenty-eight. His wife, one Hester Palmer, belonged to East Ham. See additional note at the end.

windmill. Beyond these was the Forest of Hainault, extending far away to that of Epping, thickly wooded, and well stocked with deer. On either side of the road are fields, some pasture, and some arable, the products being cabbages, turnips, and potatoes. Here and there we see an orchard, covered with rich blossom. We notice that, instead of horses, oxen are used for hauling and plough-ing. At the corner of Wangye Lane,[1] where, by a curious coinci-dence the police-station now stands, were the village stocks, where the inebriated and the disorderly were afforded time for rest and reflection, while onlookers made merriment at their expense. Along the hard turnpike lumbered heavy-laden waggons going to Covent Garden, meeting and being overtaken by stage-coaches, which, to the number of seventy, ran daily between London and Colchester. These latter were a popular institution. The cheerful horn, the news brought by the coachman and guard, the work it brought to the smithy, the excitement produced at the inn (The Greyhound), while the horses were being changed or refreshed with water and provender, the adventures by the way, the pointing out to the passengers of the exact spot where noted highwaymen had done some daring deed of robbery, all lent a charm and an air of romance to the high road which, under the changed conditions of our modern life, can never be revived.

Chadwell Street lies to the west of, and is contiguous to, Chadwell Heath. Formerly it was part of the parish of Barking, but, since 1836, it has belonged to Ilford. It is frequently mentioned in the parish registers and in subsidy rolls, under the name of Chaldewell, Chawdwell, or Chardwell Ward.[2] It con-sisted of a cluster of some thirty cottages, which were inhabited by a colony of poor Irish, who were a terror to wayfarers. Several of the old inhabitants of the district remember quite well this annoyance, and how they were accustomed to make a *détour* in order to avoid them, on their way to and from Ilford.

In regard to its derivation, Chadwell Heath means the heath adjoining Chad's Well. This well is in Billett Lane, which marks the southern boundary of the forest. The spring was held in great veneration, partly because St. Chad was supposed to have baptized his Saxon converts to Christianity there, and partly because the

---

[1] This was changed into Station Road, after the railway-station was built. The lower part is called Chitty's Lane.

[2] This included not only Chadwell Street, but Aldborough Hatch, Barkingside, and Little Heath as well ; in short, that portion of Barking which was north of the London and Romford road.

COTTAGES ON CHADWELL HEATH (PULLED DOWN IN 1895), ON THE HIGH ROAD

water was believed to possess medicinal properties. We hear of two saints of this name—Ceadda, Cedd, or Chad, who according to Bede was Bishop of the East Saxons, and Chad, his brother, who was Bishop first of York and then of Mercia (Lichfield). It would appear that Oswy, King of Northumbria, sent Cedd, a priest, from Mid Anglia, with another to preach the Gospel in Essex, "where having gone through all parts they gathered a large church for the Lord." Encouraged by this success, Cedd returned in 654 to Lindisfarne, where he had been trained, to seek the advice of Bishop Finan, who, gratified at the labours of his pupil, made him bishop for the race of the East Saxons.[1] Returning to his work, Cedd carried it on with greater energy than before, "building churches and ordaining presbyters and deacons to assist him in preaching and baptizing, especially in that city which is called in the Saxon tongue Ythancaester,[2] and also in that which is called Tilabury" (*i.e.* Tilbury). Cedd died in 664 from the plague. His name lingers not only in Chadwell, but also in Chafford (Chad's Ford), by which this rural deanery is called. He is commemorated on January 7, his brother on March 2, the day of his death from pestilence in 673.

The general primitive character of Chadwell Heath remained unaltered until the latter part of the nineteenth century. First came the school in Whalebone Lane, built in 1857, out of the bequest of one William Ford, who died in 1825. It is a mixed school, and has places for one hundred and twenty children. Next followed a few villa residences, dotted along the main road and Whalebone Lane, which brought in a sprinkling of London denizens. In 1865 a railway-station was opened; this gave a slight impetus to building operations, and put up the price of land. As yet, however, there was no church, and the inhabitants had to walk to Dagenham, Romford,[3] Ilford,[4] or Little Heath.[5] Eventually, the present vicar of Dagenham arranged for services to be held every Sunday in Ford's School above-mentioned, which were

---

[1] Camden says he was Bishop of West Tilbury.

[2] This place cannot be identified. Was it Upminster?

[3] The parish church, dedicated to St. Edward the Confessor, was built about 1400; taken down and rebuilt in 1850.

[4] St. Mary's Church was built in 1831. In 1902 it ceased to be the parish church, and was made a district church.

[5] This church, or proprietary chapel, was built by Major Ibbetson in 1862. It is dedicated to St. James, and is in the ecclesiastical parish of St. Peter's, Aldborough Hatch.

conducted by Mr. J. W. Freshwater and the Rev. William Morris. So well were these attended that it was deemed imperative to take steps to build a church for this growing district, and a committee was formed for the purpose. At first it was proposed to build a church of wood or corrugated iron, at a cost of £600, but this project was abandoned in favour of one for building a permanent church of brick. After seven years' steady patient work, the com-mittee had the satisfaction of seeing the foundation-stone of the new church laid on May 28, 1884, by the Hon. Susanna Claughton, wife of the then Bishop of St. Albans. The church is of Early English architecture, and was designed by Mr. Fred Chancellor. Exclusive of the site, which was given by Mr. Richard Payze, the cost of the edifice was £3000. On St. Chad's Day, March 2, 1886, the church was dedicated and licensed for Divine service by Bishop Claughton, as a chapel-of-ease to the parish of Dagenham. Its consecration, however, did not take place till June 25, 1895, when the new church was constituted a parish church, with a consolidated district consisting of Chadwell Heath and Chadwell Street (less Aldborough Hatch and Little Heath) assigned to it. The officiat-ing bishop was the Right Rev. Dr. Johnson, Bishop-Suffragan of Colchester. The funds for the necessary endowment of the newly formed benefice were generously contributed by the late Colonel T. H. Sale (Bengal Engineers) and the Ecclesiastical Commissioners, with the addition of a fixed sum in tithes and pew-rents. The deed of separation was signed at Osborne House on August 13, 1895, and published in the *London Gazette* in the week following.[1] The patronage is vested in the vicar of Dagenham and the vicar of Great Ilford, each to present alternately. A few weeks later the Rev. J. P. Shawcross, who had been curate-in-charge the two years previous, was instituted to the perpetual curacy of St. Chad by the Bishop of the Diocese (Dr. Festing). The population of the new parish was then about sixteen hundred; it is now just under six thousand.[2]

The following additions have been made to the church since its consecration :—the vestry, dedicated 1895 ; the south-west porch, dedicated 1896 ; the patronal stained glass window, depicting SS.

[1] The "consenting parties" mentioned in the *Gazette* are "the Right Reverend John Wogan, Bishop of the diocese of St. Albans, Stewart Stevenson Moore, of No. 5, Pump Court, Temple, barrister-at-law, the patron of the parish of Dagenham, and the Warden and College of the Souls of all faithful people deceased, of Oxford, the patrons of Gt. Ilford." The schedule of separation is signed C. L. Peel.

[2] It was returned at 163 in 1811, and 388 in 1851.

ST CHAD'S PARISH CHURCH

Chad and Alban, in memory of the late Mr. Archer Moss ; the brass eagle lectern, both dedicated on St. Chad's Day, 1898 ; the tower, the cost of which (as also of the porch) was defrayed by Colonel Sale, dedicated August, 1898 (the clock was given by public subscription) ; the organ, in place of a smaller one, dedicated on Easter-eve, 1903, by the Bishop-Suffragan of Barking (Dr. Stevens).

The vicarage house was built in 1896 on a site given by Messrs. Ind, Coope & Co., Romford.

Other buildings of a public character in Chadwell Heath are the Baptist Chapel, " Ænon," erected in 1860 ; the Congregational Hall, 1887 ; the Plymouth Brethren Meeting-house, with small graveyard attached, built originally as a village school by Mr. F. Glenny in 1844 ; the Infants' School (Dagenham School Board), 1886, enlarged 1899 ; the police-station, built 1891, the headquarters of the local section of the metropolitan " K " division.

Immediately to the north of the London road is the recreation-ground, on either side of which are the allotments for the industrious poor, the whole covering seven acres. This valuable acquisition was the result of a vestry meeting held at Dagenham church on December 6, 1831, the Rev. T. L. Fanshawe in the chair ; when it was resolved to apply for fifty acres of waste-land belonging to the Crown, to be let out in allotments to the poor. A memorial was drawn up to be presented to the Lords Commissioners of Woods and Forests, together with a plan made by Mr. T. W. Twyford. The fifty acres were to comprise twenty acres in Chadwell Heath and thirty in the forest. From some cause or other only four acres were granted for allotments, to be divided between the people of Chadwell Heath and those of Chadwell Ward in Barking.[1] A few years after the disafforestation, the Crown granted seven acres of heath (1866) to be used as a recreation-ground by way of compensation on the enclosing of the heath. Small strips of land were granted at the same time to those who had by long residence here acquired rights of whatever sort. The recreation-ground is conveniently situated, and will, doubtless, in course of time supply a want to be yet more keenly felt.

On the passing of the Local Government Act (parish councils), an attempt was made, in 1894, to form Chadwell Heath proper into a separate civil parish, and a commission of inquiry was held to

[1] Formerly there were twenty acres of allotment north of St. Chad's, or " Wooden," Well. Also between Parsloes and Wood Lane, and at Five Elms. These have all disappeared.

report on this proposal to the Essex County Council. This scheme was, strange to say, opposed by some of the inhabitants of Chadwell Heath, with the result that it fell through, to the disappointment of many people in Dagenham, who were prepared to let the northern part of the parish develope in its own way. In lieu of this abortive scheme, Chadwell Heath and Beacontree Heath were united to form the Chadwell Heath Ward of Dagenham, and to elect six out of the thirteen councillors for the whole parish of Dagenham.

During the last four years, Chadwell Heath has shaken off some of its rural features, and bids fair to become an important suburb of Greater London. The primitive and comfortless railway-station has been replaced by one which augurs great things. The old quaint hovels have been pulled down, the narrow, leafy lanes have almost disappeared, the trees have bowed before the wood-man's sturdy stroke, and the hedges have been grubbed up, to allow for the making of new roads with rows of houses of a more or less monotonous appearance. Now, instead of the solitary, dreary trudge to Ilford, a quick and agreeable ride thither is afforded by the electric trams. The lamps once lit with oil are now illumi-nated with incandescent gas. The dangers of the once wild and unsafe heath have been exchanged for the "sweet security of the streets." The place, in short, is parting with the associations and traditions of its name ; and in a few years there will probably be as much or as little "heath" left here as there is of the "green" in the crowded neighbourhood of Bethnal Green. One solitary windmill remains as a connecting link with the past, but even this ancient landmark is threatened with extinction. "'Tis true, 'tis pity ; and pity 'tis, 'tis true." [1]

WHALEBONE HOUSE.

This is the oldest and most interesting house on the heath. It stands on the high road at the eastern extremity of the parish. Its curious name is derived from two huge jawbones of a whale, which overhang the iron gates adjoining the house. They are said to have belonged to a whale that was washed ashore on Dagenham Breach, during the terrific storm on September 3, 1658. The original length of these bones was twenty-eight feet, it is now half that measurement. Two other whalebones stood at the opposite corner of Whalebone Lane, near the mile-stone ; these

[1] Between 1870–90 no less than forty windmills were taken down within a radius of ten miles around Romford.

WHALEBONE HOUSE
(From a photo by Mr R.T. ALDOUS)

were removed and sold to Major Ibbetson, of Little Heath, in whose grounds they are preserved as a quaint relic of the past.[1]

Whalebone House is an imposing building, three-storied and with bell-turret. The fine trees around it give us a good idea of what this neighbourhood was like when Hainault Forest was still standing; they are over one hundred years old. This house was, however, never a manor, nor even termed such by courtesy. It was built during the Stuart period, probably in the time of James I. It contains some finely panelled rooms, an oak staircase, a fine kitchen with large firegrate and oven of curious pattern, and a long, massive oak bench. Several of the bedrooms have two doors to them (one has three), which are fitted with iron bars and staples. Over the firegrate in one of these there is a beautiful antique carving, representing the "Wealth of Autumn." At the top of the house are two attics, one with a large firegrate, as though it had been intended to serve as a kitchen or living room, the other with strong iron loops on the beams supporting the roof, from which hammocks were swung. The house was admirably suited as a place of shelter and concealment in times of unrest and danger. Some of the old inhabitants say that Oliver Cromwell spent a night here, but of this there is no evidence, though it is of course not impossible.

The earliest reference to Whalebone House is in the Rent Roll of Barking Manor, 1663, where it is stated that "Daniel Robinson holds a tenement near the Whalebone." Also that "Abigail Vanderbrook, widow, holdeth land near the Whalebone, called Butlers, late Clark's." Frequent allusion is made to it in the parish registers, though generally in connection with some gruesome discovery, e.g. "A travelling man found sick by ye Whalebone, buryed August 19, 1749;" "A stranger found dead at ye Whalebone, by a Coroner's order, buryed Oct. 20, 1750;" "Charles Bryan, a stranger who died near the Whalebone on the High Road, aged 64, buried Aug. 20, 1811."

Whalebone House is described in a few old deeds as Beansland. The Barking Manor Court Rolls speak of Thomas Teeton, who tenanted Withy House, Bentry Heath, as occupying Beneslands, which he surrendered in 1744 to "Daniel Pilon, of Christ Church, Spittlefields, weaver." Mr. Pilon is elsewhere described as the occupier of Whalebone House, and during the period he was at

---

[1] "On April 9th, 1677, a monstrous whale, being two and forty Foot in Length and of Bigness Proportionable, was killed near Colchester, having been brought up with the tide" (*The Intelligencer*).

Beansland. He was succeeded by his son Nicholas Peter Pilon, in 1783, who in turn was followed by Mr. John Pickering Peacock, who was for some years churchwarden, and kept a private school at his "gentlemanly residence."

At the opposite corner of Whalebone (formerly Marks) Lane, an octagon-shaped toll-house stood until 1877. Behind it was a weighbridge. The toll-gate faced towards Romford, and at right angles to it was a bar, which stretched across the Whalebone Lane on the south side. People driving to Dagenham from the forest used to evade the toll by turning off at the corner towards Romford and rejoining the main road at Beacontree Heath. At the south-east corner of Whalebone Lane there used to be a small inn, which has been converted into a private dwelling-house, and is now the property of Mr. F. Trafford.

In the garden wall attached to a cottage near Whalebone House there is an old boundary stone, two feet high, with an inscription, of which the only decipherable words are—"Sept. octavo, 1783." On the opposite side of the road is an iron post, containing the arms of the City of London and the words—"Act 24 & 25 Vict. cap. 42." There is another similar one in Whale-bone Lane, near Paulatim Lodge. These are the last metropolitan boundary marks found on the east side of London.

ADDITIONAL NOTES.

The subjoined list of taxpayers in the Chadwell Ward is taken from a subsidy roll made on February 2, in the fifth year of the reign of Edward VI.

CHALDEWELL WARDE.

				£		s.	d.
Richard Brown	..	..	..	..	12	..	12 . 0
Jefferey Brownynge	..	..	..	..	12	..	12 . 0
Nicholas Woollande		..	..	..	10	..	10 . 0
John Ffrancke	..	..	..	..	5	..	5 . 0
Richard Horne the elder	..	..	..	10	..	5 . 0

The king's majesties' natural subjects.

In another subsidy, made October 10, in the tenth year of the reign of Elizabeth, we have as follows :—

				£		s.	d.
	William Clarke, in lande	..	..	..	10	..	0 . 8
	James Harvey, Gent.	..	..	..	20	..	3 . 4
	James Bramston, Gent.	..	..	..	10	..	26 . 8
Goodes	Thos. Barnes, Gent.[1]	..	..	..	20	..	3 . 4
	John Hudsonne, Gent.	..	..	..	5	..	8 . 4
	Francis Lynnett	..	..	..	..	4	..	10 . 8
	Thomas Stephens	..	..	..	..	3	..	0 . 8

[1] Thomas Barnes lived at Aldborough Hatch, and frequently acted as collector.

						£		d.
Assessors	Thomas Upney, in lande	..	..	..		3	..	12
	William Humphrey	..	..	..	..	3	..	12
	Richard Hidde, in goode	..	..	..		6	..	16
	Andrewe Fuller, in goode	..	..	..		6	..	16

Another subsidy roll runs thus—

The Extracte & Certificate indented made the fifth day of September in the eighth year of the glorious reign of James the first, for the Liberty of Havering-atte-Bower.

CHADWELL WARD.

							s.	d.
Landes	Richard Westwood	..	..	..	40/-	..	5 .	4
	George Berner	..	..	..	20/-	..	2 .	8
Goodes	James Hervey, Esquire	..	..	..	20£	..	33 .	4
	Christopher Hammond, Gent.	..	..	5	..	8 .	4
	Thomas Barnes	..	..	..	4	..	6 .	8
	John Savage, Gent.	..	..	..	3	..	5 .	0
	Willm Clarke	..	..	..	3	..	5 .	0
	John Turnage	..	..	..	4	..	6 .	8
	Christopher Willson	..	..	..	3	..	5 .	0
	Nicholas Bennett	..	..	..	3	..	5 .	0
Assessores	Richard Johnson, in bon (i.e. in goods)	..	5	..	8 .	4
	Richard Hides, in terr	..	..	40/-	..	5 .	4
	John Ffrith, in terr	..	..	..	4£	..	10 .	8
	Thomas Pechye	..	..	..	3	..	5 .	0

The commissioners were Nicholas Coote, Thomas Fanshawe, Willm Heigham, who appointed Thomas Barnes, of Aldborough Hatch, Gent., to be high collector, " to demand, levie and receive the said subsedie."

An old deed records " an Acquittance to Henry Famynge & James Ashfield for fine of lands at Chaldewell in the Manor of Barking " (June 7, 1596). This was for rent due to the Crown. The "acquittance" was a receipt which would contain the words, " Quietus est," hence the term.

Baron Comyns was the son of William Comyns, of Writtle and Lincoln's Inn. He graduated at Queens' College, Cambridge; became Serjeant-at-law in 1705; burgess of Maldon, 1707-9; Baron of the Exchequer, 1726; Knight and Justice of the Common Pleas in 1735, and Chief Baron three years later. He died in 1740. He married Ann, daughter of Dr. Nathanael Gurdon, rector of Chelmsford. His country residence was Hylands, a fine mansion which he built not far from Widford Bridge.[1]

From the *Chelmsford Chronicle*, June 29, 1832—"John Filewood summoned George Palmer, driver of the Norwich Times, for unlawfully carrying more than twelve passengers. Robert Clark said he lived at Barking, and was returning thither from Braintree when the coach overtook him. He offered 6s. to be taken to Chadwell Heath. Clark was told to get under the luggage-box for a time, which he did. He rode to the Greyhound, where he alighted. Mr. Brassey and Major Anderson, the magistrates, fined the coachman £5 and costs."

On the same day the above justices attested the assessed taxes for the year ending April 5 for the Half-Hundred of Becontree at £19,897 2s. 10d.

The *Moderate Intelligencer* for Thursday, August 7, to Thursday, August 14, 1645, says—" There is still more and more robberies about London. The two Essex thieves are hanged, that's good newes; he in Hertfordshire is to go to the pot or gallowes also.

---

[1] See Appendix C—the Comyns family.

This is the way to make the country flexible to all good, when they may enjoy their estates and trade."

My friend, the Rev. J. H. Pemberton, has had the privilege, rarely enjoyed nowa-days, of hearing the story of a bold adventure from a highwayman's own lips. He says—

"We were talking of Collier Row. This old gentleman remarked that in his young days the way from Romford to Chigwell was through green lanes and forest rides. There were no hard roads. He then related the part he took, but only by way of a practical joke, in a highway robbery on Chadwell Heath. Omitting names of persons and places, his story was this. From time to time there used to come and stay with his father, an old man—let us call him Lord X. He would drive from town in a yellow chariot with four horses and postillions. The narrator of that story—we will call him Mr. Y.—said that on one occasion when Lord X. was stopping with his father, Lord X. boasted that never in his life had he been challenged by highwaymen, and he would like to see the man who dared to stop him. On the day of the return of Lord X. to London, Mr. Y. and another young man determined to put him to the test. They stole away on horseback and awaited the coming of Lord X. over Chadwell Heath. As the yellow chariot appeared in sight, the two mock highwaymen, with crape over their faces and pistols in their hands, rode up to the chariot, stopped the postillions, and bade Lord X. stand and deliver. They took from him his gold watch and also his money, and returned home unobserved. The next time Lord X. came to visit Mr. Y.'s father he again boasted of his defiance of all highwaymen, whereupon Mr. Y. placed before him his watch and purse of gold. Such practical joking is not to be commended, but the story is of interest, since it shows the state of the roads in those days. It is not every one who can claim to have spoken to a highwayman, who had committed a highway robbery on Chadwell Heath" (*Hainault Parish Magazine*).

St. Chad's Well, in Billett Lane.

CHAPTER XXVII

BEACONTREE HEATH

THE central portion of the parish of Dagenham is known as Beacontree Heath, a compact hamlet supposed to cover one hundred acres. The derivation of the name is either from the hundred in which it is situated, or, more probably, from that of an ancient resident on the "heath." We hear of a Iohn de Beyntree being one of "the King's natural subjects" and liable to the king's tax in 1340. By the middle of the fifteenth century, this locality had definitely acquired the description of "Byntre-heth," hence the variant "Bentry Heath" found in the parish registers and on old maps. If this be the true derivation, the term "Beacontree" is unhistorical and inaccurate; and, at any rate, quite modern. In the will of Sir James Harvie, Knt. (of Wangey), there is a reference to his "newe house at Bentrye Hethe" (1627). In the Barking Rent Roll of 1663, we read that "Charles Large hath a tenement at Bentrys," and in the Survey of Barking Manor that "Mary Alibone,[1] widowe, holdeth land called Bees or Bees Down, formerly Bairmans; also land called Bentrys alias Rowlands." Also that "Elizabeth Holderman holdeth land in Bentrye Hethe, near Wisdom Brook; also Withy House, bought of William Comyns & previously had by John Peachy & Richard Harwood."

Until a few years ago, Bentry Heath shared with Chadwell Heath an unenviable reputation by reason of the rough character of those who dwelt on it. The parish constable had anything but a pleasant time of it with these people, if we may judge from his complaints recorded in the annals of the parish. By way of assisting him, the Rev. T. L. Fanshawe procured, in 1819, a pair of stocks at his own expense, which the parish authorities gratefully accepted and ordered to be set up on the heath near the

---

[1] Mother of the judge. She also held lands called Mays and Osbornes.

Travellers' Inn. But they must have disappeared some years ago, as none of the old inhabitants remember seeing them.

In 1875 the Free Methodist meeting-house was opened ; two years later the first Board school in the parish was built here. In regard to the heath, it is satisfactory to note that the parish council are doing their best to preserve it from encroachments and disfigurements of whatever sort.

CHAPTER XXVIII

GOODMAYES

> " Meanwhile, at social Industry's command,
>   How quick, how vast an increase !   From the germ
>   Of some poor hamlet, rapidly produced,
>   Here a huge town, continuous and compact,
>   Hiding the face of earth for leagues—and there,
>   Where not a habitation stood before,
>   The abodes of men irregularly massed
>   Like trees in forests,—spread through spacious tracts,
>   O'er which the smoke of unremitting fires
>   Hangs permanent, and plentiful as wreaths
>   Of vapour glittering in the morning sun,
>   And, wheresoe'er the traveller turns his steps,
>   He sees the barren wilderness erased,
>   Or disappearing ; triumph that proclaims
>   How much the mild Directress of the plough
>   Owes to alliance with these new-born arts ! "
>   WORDSWORTH.

GOODMAYES is a large district, about six hundred acres in extent, lying partly on the north, but chiefly on the south, of the London road, midway between Great Ilford and Chadwell Heath, and eight miles from Aldgate. On the north it is bounded by the ecclesiastical parish of Aldborough Hatch, on the south by Barking, on the east by Chadwell Heath, and on the west by Ilford.[1] Down to 1836 it was in Barking parish, and formed the greater part of the Chadwell Ward, but in that year it was thrown into the newly formed ecclesiastical district of St. Mary, Great Ilford, which in 1888 was constituted a civil parish. Seven years later, when the consolidated chapelry of St. Chad, Chadwell Heath, was carved out of Dagenham and Ilford, Goodmayes found itself in a new district, with St. Chad's Church (one and a quarter miles away) as

---

[1] It is separated ecclesiastically from Ilford by the Seven Kings' Watering. Tradition has it that the seven kings of the Saxon Heptarchy met here for conference. The Heptarchy lasted from 580 to 830, when it was united under Egbert.

its parish church.   Yet even thus its separation from its venerable mother was not completely effected, as it so happened that Dagenham and Ilford were in different rural deaneries, viz. Chafford and South Barking, respectively ; consequently, whereas Chadwell Heath proper is in the former, Goodmayes is in the latter, deanery.[1]

Goodmayes derives its name from a large farm-house called Goodmayes Farm, which stands west of the Barking Lane, and is within the Ilford boundary.   It is a large and imposing house, three-storied, built (the west portion at any rate) about the end of the seventeenth century.   It is a brick and oak structure, and contains some twenty rooms, a few of which are unusually spacious, even for a farm-house.   Round it ran a moat, which, till a few years ago, was always full of water, when it was filled in by the present tenant, on account of a sad drowning accident to one of his family. This house was never a manor-house, like Valence or Wangey, but simply a fee-farm attached in all probability to the manor of Jenkins or Jenkyns, situated a mile due south.

Until last year a good-sized house stood at the north-east corner of Barking Lane, facing Stoup Lane.   This was Goodmayes Lodge, formerly known as Raveling.   A row of shops now stands here.

Goodmayes Farm probably took its name from that of one of its earliest tenants.   Or it may have been the name of one of the stewards of Barking Abbey.   As we perhaps have in Barley Lane the name of the last Abbess of Barking, Dorothy Barlye or Barleighe, so is there a probability that Goodmayes is but the modern form of Godmeys or Goodmeyes, to be yet deciphered in some ancient manuscript hitherto unnoticed in ancient records. In the Barking parish register it occurs as " Goodmaiz."   Thus, " Edward Snags[2] slaine at Nevill's house in Goodmaiz Streat, buryed the 13th of Maye, 1595."   And again, " Thomas Trevers ffrom Goodmaiz Streat, buryed 7th daye of Iulye, 1596."   The first of these entries looks like a case of murder, or manslaughter at least, but it is quite as likely to mean " killed accidentally," as in another place we read of an old man being " slaine by the fall of a gate post."   " Goodmaiz Streat " would be the lane from Good-mayes Farm to Barking, and now called Barking Lane.

An early mention of the name occurs in a Survey of

---

[1] The rural dean of Chafford is the Rev. R. T. Crawley, rector of North Ockendon ; of South Barking, the Rev. J. H. Ware, vicar of East Ham.

[2] A " Iohn Snags of Little Heath was baptized at Barking the 7th of Iune, 1593."

Barking Manor made in 1616, where we learn that "Mr. Thomas Palmer holdeth one close called Goodmayes & another called Stoney Croft." A rent-roll of the manor of 1663 says that "Bennett Sands has land near Goodmayes." An old map of 1774 has this district marked "Goodmath." It is also found as "Goodmay's."

Between the London road and Green Lane[1] is a large and well-stocked orchard which belonged to the farm. East of it is a short lane called Stoup or Stoop Lane, which connects Barley Lane with Goodmayes Lane. "Stoop" is said to mean a post driven in the ground as a boundary mark. In this case, it marked the dividing line between Barking and Ilford, or between Chadwell Ward and Ilford. It was the scene of a terrible tragedy on December 8, 1794, when one James Martin, "a king's messenger," was shot dead by five highwaymen, and robbed of all that was worth taking. An entry in the Romford register says—"1794, December 14th, James Martin, a king's messenger, shot near the Stoup, by five footpads, was buried." Unfortunately the murderers escaped, and were never brought to justice.

By a singular coincidence a murder was committed at the same spot in February, 1853, when a Mr. John Toller, of Chadwell Heath, was murdered by a tramp, who was, however, arrested, and subsequently executed at Chelmsford.

A great transformation has recently been effected at Goodmayes. The broad acres, which once produced some of the finest corn, potatoes, and cereals in Essex, have been covered with over one thousand houses, of varied size, to meet the requirements of the business men who earn their bread in the City, yet who either cannot or will not live in London itself. To quote and adapt an old rhyme—

> "The Goodmayes fields are fields no more,
> The trowel supersedes the plough ;
> Hovels inhabited of yore,
> Are changed to civic villas now."

The development of the estate is due to the enterprise of Mr. A. Cameron Corbett, M.P. The commodious railway-station there was opened in February, 1901.

Midway between Goodmayes and Little Heath is the lunatic asylum for the West Ham County Borough. It has an area of a hundred and ten acres, the buildings alone covering one-tenth

[1] "Green Lane," or "Green Way," is frequently found, but never Green "Lanes," as now locally known.

of this space. The foundation-stone was laid in August, 1898, and the asylum was opened three years later. The total cost was £210,000. There is accommodation for 800 inmates. The medical superintendent is Dr. David Hunter.

On the east of the asylum is the Ilford Isolation Fever Hospital, built in 1897, and enlarged in 1902.

With a view to providing for the spiritual needs of this new neighbourhood, a site was secured in Barley Lane by the Council of the Bishop of St. Albans' Fund, whereon to build a church. To this the adjoining piece of land was afterwards added, thus giving the proposed church a commanding position at the corner of Athol Road. A committee was appointed, and Messrs. Chancellor & Son were instructed to prepare plans for a church, consisting of nave, chancel, vestry, organ-chamber, morning chapel, and tower. The total accommodation will be 750 and the cost £8000. On the eve of the Conversion of St. Paul (to whom the church is dedicated), 1903, the foundation-stone was laid by Lady Florence Cecil, in the presence of the Bishop-Suffragan of Colchester (Dr. Johnson) and a large gathering of clergy and laity. On May 23 in the same year, the morning chapel was dedicated and licensed by the Bishop of St. Albans (Dr. Edgar Jacob).

The following is a list of the clergy who had the pastoral care of Goodmayes previous to its inclusion (1895) in the consolidated chapelry of St. Chad, Chadwell Heath.

VICARS OF NORTH BARKING.

Martinus	1315
Rad. de Ansi	1328
Hugo Smith	1373
Thomas Bene	1385
Iohn Sacome	1395

In 1398 the two parishes of North and South Barking were united, the patronage still remaining in the hands of the Abbess and Convent of Barking.

Iohn Makewye	1398
Stephen Chamberlayne	1403 (?)
Iohn Willougby	1438
Iohn Grening	1439
Robert Waleis	1462
Galf King	1486
Iohn Frothingham	1505

Iohn Long	..	..	..	..	1511 (?)
Iohn Gregylle	..	..	..	..	1534
Richard Tirwitt	..	..	..	..	1560
Edward Edworth	..	..	..	..	1584
Richard Wignall	..	..	..	..	1587
Richard Hall [1]	..	..	..	..	1620
Thomas Cartwright	..	..	..	..	1660
Leopold Finch	..	..	..	..	1689
John Chisenhale	..	..	..	..	1696
Thomas Macken Fiddes	..	..	..	..	1720
Lewis Owen	..	..	..	..	1734
William Stephens	..	..	..	..	1746
Savage Tyndal	..	..	..	..	1751
Christopher Musgrave	..	..	.	1762
Peter Rashleigh	..	..	..	..	1781

On June 9, 1831, St. Mary's Church, Ilford, was consecrated by the Right Rev. Chas. J. Blomfield, Lord Bishop of London.[2] On the death of Mr. Rashleigh in 1836, St. Mary's, Ilford, was formed into an ecclesiastical district, the patronage being vested (like that of Barking) in All Souls College, Oxford.

VICARS OF ILFORD.

Francis Knyvett Leighton	..	..	..	1836
Folliott Baugh	..	..	..	1841
Hon. Henry William Bertie	..	..	..	1844
Henry Broughton Barnes	..	..	..	1881
Henry William Elliott Molony	..	..	1892–95

As already stated, Goodmayes is now in the ecclesiastical district of Chadwell Heath, but it is not at all improbable that it will at some future time form a district of itself. Its distance from Chadwell Heath, as well also as its rapidly growing population, and the fact that it is part of the civil parish of Ilford (as consti- tuted in 1888) will make some such separation suitable, convenient, and imperative, if the Church on the fringe of London-over-the- Border is to keep pace with the spiritual needs of this expanding suburb.

[1] Richard Hall was ejected by the Puritans in 1645 for refusing to subscribe to the Solemn League and Covenant. He was succeeded by one Benjamin Way, a Presbyterian, who in turn was ousted by the Independents several years later.

[2] The appeal made in 1825 for the building of this church states that, "so far back as 1650 the then Ecclesiastical Commissioners recommended the division of Barking that all people might hear the Word of God, the population being nearly two thousand at that time."

CHAPTER XXIX

THE FOREST OF HAINAULT

"You shall true Liegeman be
    Unto the King's Majestie.
Unto the beasts of the Forest you shall no hurt do,
Nor to any thing that doth belong thereunto ;
The offences of others you shall not conceal
But to the utmost of your power you shall them reveal
Unto the officers of the Forest,
Or to them who may see them redrest ;
All these things you shall see done,
So help you God at His Holy Doom." [1]

UNTIL the disafforestation of the Forest of Hainault in 1853–54, the northern portion of the parish of Dagenham comprised a part of Hainault Forest. Originally this forest covered nearly 17,000 acres, of which over 1000 acres lay within the Dagenham boundary. With that of Epping, this forest was included in, and formed part of, the ancient Forest of Waltham, which, in turn, originally extended nearly over the whole county of Essex—from Bow Bridge to Colchester.

Hainault is found in various forms — Hineholt, Hyneholt, Inholt, Henholt, Heynault, and Hainault, the last-named not occurring earlier than 1720. Its exact derivation is obscure. "Holt" is the Saxon term for "wood," while "ing" is a common prefix and suffix of the names of places in Essex. Hainault would, therefore, be a corruption of "Ing-holt," the place of a wood. Another suggested derivation is that it was named after Hainault or Hainhault in Germany, the birthplace of Queen Philippa, the consort of Edward III. But against this theory is the fact that Henholt and Inholt are found in records previous to the time of the noble-hearted Queen Philippa, and also that

---

[1] The oath taken by the inhabitants of the Forest of Waltham, 1200-1600. See Fisher's " Forest of Essex."

no certain connection of that queen with Hainault Forest can be traced.

The Forest of Hainault being a royal forest was subject to "forest law." This special branch of English law may be traced so far back as the time of Canute (1017-35), when the keepers of the king's forest possessed the power of life and death over all unqualified persons who disturbed, hunted, maimed, or killed game. Those who lived within the area of a royal forest were unable to claim the protection of the common law of the land, inasmuch as it was superseded by forest law. The object of forest law was to preserve and protect, under severe penalties, the privileges and rights of the king within the limits of his forest, where the common law of the land was without authority and force. In short, the Forest of Hainault was the king's private pleasure-ground, stocked with wild beasts and fowl, which found cover and pasturage in the trees and rich vegetation of the forest, and were kept free from molestation by the strict laws which belonged exclusively to forests.

The supervision of Hainault Forest was in the hands of officers, who, with a few exceptions, were appointed by the king. These were verderers, foresters, regarders, agisters, and woodwards, who were all under the steward. The verderers were inspectors or overseers who were chosen by the freeholders, and were generally persons of some local standing. They were two in number, and held office for three years. The earliest mention of this office with reference to Hainault Forest occurs in a royal writ dated the 16th Edward II. (1323-24), wherein, on the nomination of Queen Isabella, the king appoints Henry Beaufytz to be an associate with Aymer de Valence, Earl of Pembroke, to supervise the forest and maintain its rights. It was at this time that the Liberty of Havering-atte-Bower, till then within the Forest of Waltham, was severed from it and given by the king to Queen Isabella in dower.

The foresters' duties were to look after the game; to see that during the "fence," or forbidden month, the deer were not disturbed in fawning; to keep count of the deer, and report losses from disease, accident, and depredation. They had authority to kill all dogs, and to destroy all guns, nets, and weapons found in the forest. They were to satisfy themselves that mastiffs or other dogs kept for purposes of defence had been properly "expeditated," i.e. had had the three claws of the forefoot struck off to incapacitate them from following the game. They were to see that all gates or "hatches" leading into the forest were kept in good repair, and that the hedge which enclosed the forest was never less than five feet in height.

The agisters or reeves were responsible for the pasturage or "agistment" of the forest.   People who lived near the boundaries of the forest were allowed by right of "vicinage" to agist their cattle and sheep in the forest on payment of a small charge per head of cattle and sheep.   Each village bordering on the forest had its own reeve to protect its interests.   These payments (varying from sixpence to threepence per head) were made to the agisters, who marked each animal with a distinctive mark, after which the cattle might roam at will anywhere in the forest.   The "marking" was done at some fixed point four times a year—May, July, September, and November—notice of the same having been given in the churches in the locality on the Sunday previous.   The "crooked billet" was the mark for horses and cattle belonging to Barking, and a three-pronged fork with short L-shaped handle that for Dagenham.   The former designation still lingers in the name of Billett Lane.   The mark was seven inches long.   Animals found in the forest unmarked were impounded by the reeves.   To prevent the latter from marking for persons who had no pasture rights, they were required to produce written evidence that each applicant for "marking" had paid the rental of pasturage laid down by the Court of Attachments at Stratford Langthorne.   The rental varied according to the circumstances of the commoner.   In 1754 it was not to exceed £4 per annum for two cows or one horse.

The regarders were a body of visitors whose duty it was to examine the accounts and decide all cases of trespass, breaches of forest law, and other offences on the part of people or officers. Their visitation of the forest took place once in three years.   Courts of inquiry were, however, held at intervals to hear complaints or deal with matters of urgency.   Thus we hear of a court being held in 1301 at Chelmsford, to fix the assessment of the Forest of Waltham for the cost of the war with France.[1]   And again, three centuries later, of a swainmote being held at Stratford Langthorne in 1630, when the regarders, after due inquiry, adjudged that, "time out of mind, all persons inhabiting within the Forest of Waltham, which have right of comoning bye theire lands, messuages or tenements, have had comon of Pasture upon the saide Forest and Wast Soyle with all comonable cattell."   It was at this court that the

[1] One of the members of the court was Thomas de Seven Springes, Hyleford.

regarders granted the request of Dame Joyce Carewe, of Marks, to
depasture eight hundred sheep in right of "vicinage."

The woodwards or woodmen were deputed to look after the
trees of the forest. This was an office of some difficulty, as the
people of the neighbourhood had certain rights to lopping wood,
though for fuel only. This fuel was known as *estovers*. The parish
of Barking had thirty-four assignments, *i.e.* private rights of lopping
wood in the waste lands or lawns on the west of the Forest of
Hainault. The parish of Dagenham had thirty-nine similar assignments on the south side. Each assignment consisted of five hundred
faggots of pollard trees only. The woodwards had to see that these
assignments were not abused by people cutting down wood for
trade or commerce. They were to take care, moreover, that they
were not exceeded by encroachments in the forest proper. This
was done by means of posts and marked trees. The assignments
were to be carried away between the Feast of Martinmas (November
11) and that of Candlemas (February 2), and the wood was to be
taken away each day by the "commoners," and not to be allowed
to accumulate. "Certificated" men who left their parish in search
of work were to be prohibited from lopping—so runs an instruction
to the keepers in 1761.

These assignments had their origin in the royal grants made
from time to time to the Abbess of Barking to cut down wood in
Henholt Forest for repairs and fuel. We find records of grants to
fell wood to the value of £30 (20th Edward I.) ; to cut down three
hundred oaks (12th Edward II.) ; and also to keep dogs for hunting
game. The lords of Marks and Wangey also claimed the right
to a "Christmas block and a midsummer bough," in virtue of
"vicinage." The assignments represent, doubtless, the compensation granted to the parishes of Barking and Dagenham on the
spoliation of Barking Abbey, and the deprivation of the manors
of various rights and privileges which had long been attached to
them.

Three courts were held for the proper administration of the
laws of the forest, viz. the woodmote, swainmote, and justice-seat.
At the woodmote all offences against the game were tried by the
chief foresters or master keepers. At the swainmote, presided over
by the verderers, rents were paid and cases of trespass gone into.
This was held usually at Stratford Langthorne. The justice-seat,
or Court of Attachments, held at Chelmsford, was the court at
which all great offences (deer-stealing, assaults on keepers, murder,

etc.) were tried and final sentence imposed. We hear of Lord Chief Justice Sir Thomas Fanshawe trying serious cases at Chelmsford, and declaring "alehouses to be nusans to the fforest." The foresters were ordered to inquire whether alehouses had proper licences, and whether deer-stealers were harboured in them. This direction, made in 1670, seems to point to an increase of the number of alehouses in the forest, as in the perambulation made in 1631 it was stated that there was only one alehouse-keeper there, viz. of the Marks Inn, which stood nearly opposite to the Marks Stone.

The trees of the forest were chiefly oak, hornbeam, and pollard. The beasts of the forest were the hart, the hind, the hare, the boar, the wolf[1]—these were the wild beasts of venery; the beasts of the park or chase were the buck, the doe, the marten, the wild cat, the fox, the badger, and the roe. The stag or red deer was the special forest deer. The red deer stood about four feet high at the shoulder, was of a grey-brown colour in winter, which he exchanged for a thinner red-brown coat in summer. Its antlers were rounded, and bore triple branches, the top spreading out, forming a crown of three points, increasing with age to twelve. A royal stag is one with twelve points. The red deer is a timid, shy animal, with a most acute sense of smell. While the forest afforded it a spacious and secluded retreat for it to roam in safety in its wild state, it was the stag of the forest. When, however, the population increased and forests were reduced in the fifteenth century, the red deer gradually disappeared, and is almost extinct in this country. James I. is generally credited with having introduced its successor, the fallow deer, from Norway. It is not so large or so shy as the red deer. If we may judge from later figures, there were probably not less than five hundred or even six hundred fallow deer from the period of the Stuarts to that of George I.

At an inquiry of perambulation held at Stratford Langthorne in 1641, before a court of verderers, it was stated incidentally that the Forest of Hainault was bounded at the south by the Romford and Colchester highway, where "near the Whale-Bone there are four wonds," and at the south-east by "Beamesland Lane." This lane ran alongside Beamsland, or Beansland, afterwards Whalebone, House, from the main road to Marks Stone,

---

[1] An old inhabitant, who died in 1894, once told me that his grandfather, when a boy, saw a young wolf killed in Hainault Forest. He could not give the precise date, except that it was "before George III. had become king." My informant also said that his father had in his time killed two wild cats in the said forest.

where the forest touched the ancient parish of Hornchurch. On the north the forest stretched to that of Epping, the two forests being, in fact, but different sections of the Forest of Waltham. On the west it was bounded by the river Lea, which separates Essex from Middlesex.

The Forest of Hainault had four gates or hatches, viz. Marks Gate, near the manor of Marks on the south; Collier Row (also Collyreaux) Gate, on the north-east; Aldborough, or Aldbury, or Abury, Gate, on the west; Billett Gate, on the south-west near Saint Chad's fount. These were. to prevent the deer and cattle straying from the forest. At an inquiry held in 1839 it was reported that only two of these were in good condition; also that the forest fences were below the required height and broken in places.

In the middle of the forest was a fine old Elizabethan house, called Chapel, or Chapple, Hainault Lodge. In the Barking Survey of 1616 it is described as the Garth. An old deed of 1701, signed by Thomas, Lord Wharton, Justice of the King's Forest, gives leave to John Lethieullier, Esq., to cut wood in Chappell Hainault. Round it was a waste known as the "Lawne," where sheep were pastured. The lodge was about two miles from the famous Maypole at Chigwell, and previous to its demolition, before 1830, had the distinction of being thus described by the graphic pen of Charles Dickens—

It was a dreary, silent building, with echoing courtyards, desolated turret-chambers, and whole suites of rooms shut up and mouldering to ruin. The terrace-garden, dark with the shade of overhanging trees, had an air of melancholy that was quite oppressive. Great iron gates, disused for many years and red with rust, drooping on their hinges and overgrown with long, rank grass, seemed as though they tried to sink into the ground and hide their fallen state among the friendly weeds. The fantastic monsters on the walls, green with age and damp, and covered here and there with moss, looked grim and desolate. There was a sombre aspect, even on that part of the mansion which was inhabited and kept in good repair, that struck the beholder with a sense of sadness. It would have been difficult to imagine a bright fire blazing in the dull and darkened rooms, or to picture any gaiety of heart or revelry that the frowning walls shut in. It seemed a place where such things had been, but could be no more—the very ghost of a house, haunting the old spot in its old outward form and that was all.[1]

The earliest known tenant of Chappell Hainault Lodge was a

---

[1] " Barnaby Rudge," chapter xiii.—" The Warren."

Mr. Blythman, of the baptism of whose children there are frequent records in the Dagenham register, 1660–80.

Hainault Lodge was another large house in the forest; it stood half a mile to the north of Chapel Hainault, and was the hunting lodge of the forest, where the verderers and other distinguished visitors used to stay.

The modern Hainault Lodge probably stands on the hill where there was a large swine-breeding farm, known as Hog's Hill. Near this were several cottages, occupied by the foresters. From a return made in 1630 it would seem that there were then thirty-five houses in Hainault Forest belonging to the parish of Barking, and seven to that of Dagenham. The oldest house now standing within the limits of the ancient forest is Sheepcotes, which may have been on " Chapple Henolt Lawne." It contains a good deal of fine oak, handsomely carved, and is in several details picturesque and interesting. This house was included in Barking Manor estate; as we hear of one " John Hubbard of Barking, mariner," being admitted as tenant of Sheepcotes in 1771.

The population of the forest varied from one hundred and fifty to two hundred. Persons wishing to live in the forest had to obtain permission to do so from the chief forester, and to take the oath to observe the forest laws. Each tenant had the privilege of pasturing his cattle, and having "pannage" for his pigs, which he could turn out to feed on the acorns, nuts, and products of the trees. This he could do throughout the year, with the exception of the " fence," or forbidden month, which began fifteen days before and ended fifteen days after July 6 (old Midsummer Day). He was not to build a house without leave under penalty of a heavy fine for the offence of " purpreste," or make a clearance on pain of being guilty of " assarting." [1]

On the western side of the forest lived a gipsy colony. The gipsies were an industrious, quiet-living set of people, and do not seem to have given much trouble to the forest officers. The women were held in some awe by the inhabitants on account of their reputed skill in fortune-telling. From these gipsies are probably descended the plebeian natives of Chadwell Heath, whose dark eyes, tawny complexion, and short, curly, black hair all point to foreign descent.[2]

---

[1] Forest land made cultivable is termed "assart," or "occation," land.

[2] On April 6, 1543, a passport was signed at St. James's Palace by the king, for twenty-four Egyptians, with their wives and children, to depart off the Realme wythin twenty days after the date thereof.

In the Barking register there is the following entry—" 1708, April 24, Buried the Queen of the Gipsies."

It is very possible that Mr. Langhorne, the curate-poet of Dagenham, visited the gipsies occasionally, and that their peaceful, contented life suggested his poem, "The Gipsy," which opens thus—

> " The gipsy race my pity rarely move ;
> Yet their strong thirst of liberty I love . . .
> For this in Norwood's patrimonial groves
> The tawny father with his offspring roves ;
> When summer suns lead slow the sultry day,
> In mossy caves, where welling waters play ;
> Fann'd by each gale that cools the fervid sky,
> With this in ragged luxury they lie.
> Oft at the sun the dusky elfins strain
> The sable eye, then snuggling, sleep again ;
> Oft as the dews of cooler evening fall,
> For their prophetic mother's mantle call,
> For other cares that wand'ring mother wait,
> The mouth and oft the minister of fate !
> From her to hear, in evening's friendly shade,
> Of future fortune, flies the village maid,
> Draws her long-hoarded copper from its hold,
> And rusty halfpence purchase hoards of gold."

All went well with Hainault Forest till the middle of the eighteenth century, and the laws relating to it were till then enforced without any great difficulty. By that time, however, the country, especially round London, had become infested with highwaymen and footpads, who found cover and shelter in the various forests. Chief of these was the Black Gang. Robberies and outrages became frequent, and the keepers found themselves unequal to their trust. Tree-lopping by the natives had been so extensively and wantonly carried on, that the verderers in 1761 recommended that the whole forest should be replanted with oak. This proposal fell through. Fifty years later they reported that not only were trees rapidly disappearing, but land-grabbing by the lords of the manors as well as by the householders and squatters in the forest was constantly going on. Mr. Long Wellesley, the warden of the forest, complained, in 1813, of the number of deer-stealers in the forest who kept lurchers and greyhounds for game ; also of the hundreds of acres which had been unlawfully enclosed. As an eminent novelist (Sir Walter Besant) puts it—

They (the dwellers in the forest) gave up their whole leisure time to carving bits out of the forest and adding them to their own gardens ;

U

sticking up palings round these bits; here a cantle and there a snippet; here a slab and there a slice; a round corner and a square corner; a bare piece of turf or a wooded clump, and all so neighbourly, encouraging each other the while, with a "Brother, will this be to your mind?" or, "Help yourself, neighbour;" and, "Let me recommend, sir, another slice;" or, "A piece of the woody part, dear friend." [1]

With a view to stopping these encroachments, a scheme was drawn up, in 1817, to allot two-thirds of Hainault Forest to the king, and the remaining third to the commoners. This liberal proposal was, however, resisted by the people, as well as by the lords of the manors, and petitions were presented to Parliament against it, with the result that it was withdrawn. In 1839 the Commissioners of the Forest reported that the deer had been considerably reduced in number through the organized depredations of the navvies then employed in constructing the Eastern Counties Railway. Nothing, however, was done for some time; the consequence being that the deer dwindled down in number to less than fifty, the trees were mercilessly lopped, and more encroachments took place. In 1850–51 an Act was passed to disafforest the Forest of Hainault, on the ground that the deer were scarcely worth preserving, and that, with the building of ironclads for the Navy, oak would no longer be required for England's "wooden walls," and, moreover, that the forest was of little profit to the State. The Act authorized the removal of the deer, the felling of the trees, and the conversion of the forest into arable and pasture land. Special commissioners [2] were appointed to award full compensation to the lords of manors, freeholders, and others in respect of their several ancient rights in the forest. Under their direction, the wild, spacious, and beautiful forest was cleared and converted into large farms, with fertile, productive soil, properly fenced and divided by good roads. The commissioners stated, in 1851, that about 7000 acres of wood, warren, and waste belonged to the Crown, and that over 9000 acres of the original forest had been enclosed by private persons. At the end of their labours in 1856, they reported that 100,000 trees had been cut down and sold for £21,000, which had covered all the expenses of disafforestation, drainage, fencing, and making new roads; that they had invested a sum of money to compensate the poor widows of

---

[1] "All in a Garden Fair," chapter ii.—"Forest of Hainault."
[2] These were Charles Gore, Thomas F. Kennedy, G. W. Cooke, Nathan Wetherell, Esquires.

Dagenham and Barking for the loss of fuel rights; that they had abolished the office of lord warden, and given him £5250 as compensation; that the Court of Attachments had been abolished, and a Commission of Woods and Forests formed; and that an annual rental of £4000 might be expected from the Crown farms and allotments carved out of the forest. Also that a score of the old inhabitants had been compensated with strips of land stretching from their cottages to the new road. With this report closes the history of the ancient and beautiful Forest of Hainault.

The parish registers contain a few, but not many, references to the forest. Thus, "For yᵉ preambulation at yᵉ fforest spent £02.09.06;" from which it would seem that the parish had to pay, in part at least, the charges of the verderers' inquiry. The burial register records the burial of persons found dead in the forest, and mentions Sheepcotes and Chapple Henault.

A public park for East Suburban London is now being laid out on the north side of the modern Hainault Lodge. The cost will be £20,000, and is being borne by the London County Council, the City Corporation, and the Essex County Council. Access to it will be by the new line from Ilford to Woodford, opened two years ago. The park comprises 800 acres. The credit for this scheme belongs chiefly to Mr. E. North Buxton, grandson of the famous abolitionist.

With the disafforestation of Hainault Forest, several romantic and time-honoured institutions disappeared too. The annual deer-hunt, which took place on Easter Monday amid an excited crowd of spectators, which included some of the city magnates, has become a thing of the past. It is only as a bygone memory that the surviving nestors of the village tell of the preparations made for that popular holiday, and how the deer, with a garland of flowers round his neck, was driven into the open heath, where he presently caught a glimpse of the hounds and huntsmen in wait for him, and how he usually gave the field several hours' sport before he was run to bay. Gone, too, is the venerable Fair-lop oak, the pride of the forest for its hugeness, and the scene of revels occasioned by people who came here from East London. It was under its spreading branches, near the new park, that an annual fair was held on the first Friday in July, which was considered the chief event of the season by East London denizens. It was originated by one Daniel Day, a pumpmaker of Wapping, who owned a small estate near the oak, where he was in the habit of inviting his friends and feasting them with beans and bacon. This enjoyable excursion was kept up after the death of its promoter, in 1767, by the pumpmakers of Wapping, until the famous tree collapsed, in 1820, and thus broke the spell of historic sentiment associated with it.

The following is a list of the verderers :—

HUNDRED OF CHAFFORD.

1250 { Dominus Henricus de Helehetone.
{ Dominus Willelmus Toral.

FOR THE FOREST.

1489 { Robert Plomer.
{ William Wything.
{ Edward Waren.
{ Thomas Broke of Berkyng.

1495 { Richard Barley.
{ Edward Waren.

1594 { Thomas Colshill.
{ Barnard Whelston.
{ Francis Stacye.

1620 { Clement Stonard.
{ Edward Elrington.
{ John Barfoote.

1630 { Sir Thomas Fanshawe.
{ Tobie Wood.
{ Carew Hervy, *alias* Mildmay.

1640 { Charles Hervey, *alias* Mildmay.
{ John Wood.
{ William Conyers.
{ John Goulding.
{ Charles Maynard.
{ Edward Keighley.

1670 { Carew Hervy, *alias* Mildmay.
{ George Scott.
{ Henry Wollaston.
{ William Maynard.
{ Sir Wm Holcroft.

1713 { William Scott.
{ William Nutt.
{ John Wroth.
{ Carew Hervey.

1718.   Sir Thos. Webster, Bart.
1721.   Sir John Eyles, Bart.
1725.   Sir Hen. Maynard.

1739. William Harvey.
1743. John Conyers.
1745. John Goodere.
1751. Sir Crisp Gascoigne.
1757. Richard Lockwood.
1762. Bamber Gascoigne.
1767. Sir Wm Wake, Bart.
1771. William Harvey.
1779. John Conyers.
1785. Sir Eliab Harvey, K.C.B.
1792. Sir Wm Smyth, Bart.
1798. Montagu Burgoyne.
1812. Wm Joseph Lockwood.
1830. Henry John Conyers.
1831. W^m St. Julien Arabin.
1837. J. P. Lockwood.
1838 { William Whitaker Maitland.
      { George Palmer.

(Appointed by the Epping Forest Act.)

1878 { Sir Thos. Fowell Buxton, Bart.
      { Sir Antonio Brady.
      { Thos. Chas. Baring.
      { Andrew Johnston.

Besides the foregoing, there were also foresters and chief foresters, or master keepers. The following were Master Keepers of East, or Chapple Hainault, Walk.

1590. Sir Henry Graye.
1625. Sir Gawin Hervy.
1630. Sir Henry Edmonds.
1641. Anthony Eyres.
1707. John Cross.
1713. William Graham.
1724. Sir John Eyles, Bart.
1726. Lord Castlemain (afterwards Earl of Tylney).
1749. John, Earl of Tylney.
1771. Andrew Moffat.
1785. Samuel Pole.
1788. John Moffatt.
1796. William Raikes.
1801. William Matthew Raikes.
1814. Jeremiah Harman.

This list is taken from Fisher's "Forest of Essex."

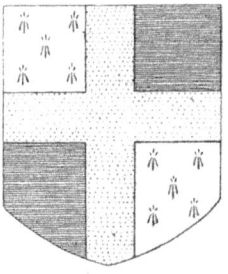

APPENDIX A

The following notes have reference to the contents of the preceding chapters.

Chapter I.

HUNDRED.—A division of a county; considered to have been fixed by King Alfred. Here lived a hundred free men, responsible for the king's peace. "Alfred the Great, to reduce anarchy and disorder, divided counties into hundreds and tithings, that every Englishman living under laws as a liege subject, should be within one hundred or another. And if a man were accused of any transgression, he should bring some one out of the hundred to be bound for his appearance to answer the law. If he could not find such security, then he had to abide the severity of such laws. In case the criminal fled, the hundred incurred a mulct or fine to the king. In this wise he brought such peace and fright to the country, that on highways where they crossed each other, he caused bracelets of gold to be hung up to tempt the greediness of the people, but none dare take them" (Camden).

HIDE.—Some derive it from the Saxon "hidden," and take it to mean lands belonging to a *covered* dwelling-place; hence hides is understood sometimes to mean homesteads. Others say that it is a land measure; " in the time of the Conqueror one hide was a hundred acres, a knight's fee. In Essex the inquisitors who aided in the compilation of Domesday Book, considered it a hundred and twenty acres" (Seebohm's "Village Community").

ENDOWMENT.—" In No. XXV. of the Excerptions of Archbishop Egbert (A.D. 735–66), it is ordained that 'to every church shall be allotted one complete holding (mansa), and that this shall be free from all but ecclesiastical services.' This was simply putting the priest in the position of a recognized village official, like the *præpositus* or the *gaber*. They held their virgates (holdings) free of service, and perhaps their strips were ploughed by the common ploughs in return for their services without their contributing oxen to the manorial plough team. The Doomsday

Survey proves that, in a great number of instances at least, room had, in fact, been made in the village community for the priest and his virgate" (Seebohm).

CHAPTER II.

"VILLENAGE was a tenure compounded of feudal Norman, Saxon, and Danish usages. Under Saxon rule the villeins or folkland were removable at the lord's pleasure; under the Normans they were raised to a condition slightly above downright slavery, but inferior to every other condition. This they called *villenage*, and the tenants *villeins*. Villein regardant was annexed to the manor or land. Villeins in gross, or at large, were transferable by deed under one owner to another. Villeins lived in the village under the lord—not under the lord's roof, as the serfs did" ("Encyclopædia Britannica").

SOCAGE (socagium).—Tenure in socage was where the tenant was bound to do work on the lord's land. It was of two kinds—

1. *Free socage*, where the services were commuted for a rent in money.
2. *Villein socage*, where the work was actually done.

A socage tenant was free from military service, but was bound to render homage to his lord, and assist him when required. He was liable to the taxes under *aids* and *reliefs*, but was excused the liabilities of trusteeship in wards and marriage settlements.

"KNIGHT'S FEES, as introduced by William the Conqueror, empowered the king, or even a great lord, to compel every holder of a certain extent of land, called a "knight's fee," to become a member of a knightly order; and, in time of war, each knight was bound to attend the king forty days, which was a full knight's service. Some lands were held for part of a knight's fee, and the holder performed half a knight's fee (twenty days)" (Camden).

This institution seems to have been peculiar to Normandy, from whence it came.

In reference to great outrages, the sheriffs and other wardens of the peace in each shire, are required to cause to come before them the four men and the provost of every parish, and to cause these to summon all the men themselves of the parish, when any wrong is done or threatened in any parish; and the "said men of the parishes are required, if need be, to raise the hue-and-cry, and follow the offenders from parish to parish, and from hundred to hundred, and from shire to shire, and arrest, keep, and safely guard them" (Toulmin Smith, "The Parish," quoting a statute of 6th Edward III.).

At a meeting held at the London Tavern, on January 19, 1803, it was stated that 40,000 persons died every year from small-pox. A resolution was carried recommending "a new species of inoculation lately providentially introduced by our countryman, Dr. Jenner."

At a poll for a knight of the shire of the county of Essex, taken at Chelmsford, December 13 and 14, 1763, the following voters attended from Dagenham:—John Hather, James Turnbull, Thos. Waters, John H. Merttins, John Bane, P. D. Muilman, Abraham Blackbourne, William Butterfield, Thos. Mitchell, Thos. Flower, Joseph Ford, Thos. Fanshawe.

CHAPTER VI.

September 12, 1330. Licence was granted at the King's Court at Nottingham "for the alienation in mortmain by Iohn de Cokermuth, clerk, in part satisfaction of a licence from the late king for the Abbess and Convent of Berkyng to acquire land & rent to the yearly value of £20 of a messuage, 140 acres of land, 30 acres of meadow, 25 acres of pasture, & 8 acres of wood, found by inquisition to be of the yearly value of 58/9 & of 70/- in rent, in Dakenham, Berkyng & Hilleford" (Patent Rolls, Edward III., p. vi.).

A grant was given at Westminster "for the security of the Abbess and Convent of Berkyng, that whereas Ioan the present abbess, with the king's licence, has acquired in mortmain from Iohn de Cokermuth, now deceased, 140 acres of land, 30 acres of meadow, 25 acres of pasture, 8 acres of wood and 70/- in rent in Dakenham, Berkyng and Illeford, Co. Essex, these shall not be liable in respect of a security given at the Exchequer of Edward II. by the said Iohn & Iohn de Heydon, as executors of the will of Iohn de Sandale, Bishop of Winchester, for payment of all debts due to the king by the bishop at his death" (Patent Rolls, April 5, 1337).

CHAPTER X.

TRINOBANTES.—This was the name of the tribe which inhabited the district north of the Thames, i.e. the modern county of Essex. Their capital was Camulodunum, not far from Colchester, where extensive earthworks still remain. In the Roman invasion by Julius Cæsar (B.C. 55), the Trinobantes and other tribes (Cantii, Iceni, etc.) were conquered, and Cassivellaunus (of the tribe of Cassi—the modern Herts), who led the Britons, had to yield and submit to the Roman tribute. Some authorities assert that in this invasion the Trinobantes joined forces with the Romans in revenge for their defeat some years previously by Cassivellaunus. Mandubratius is said to have been made king of the Trinobantes by Cæsar, and to have been expelled by Tascisvanus and his son Cunobelinus. All these names have been found on Essex coins, and also that of Dubnovellaunus.

"The lady's head-dress is the fashionable one of the fifteenth century, called the *great butterfly*, from having wings on each side of it, like that insect'; these were covered with fine lawn hanging down to the ground, part of which was generally worn tucked under the arm; one of the daughters is dressed in a religious habit; two of them appear in the same costume of the mother; the others have the steeple head-dress, which was at that period carried to such an extravagant length that they extended half and sometimes three-quarters of an ell in length. In the early part of this century, Isabel of Bavaria, wife of Charles VII., King of France, and her ladies, wore their head-dresses of such a preposterous size, that it became necessary to make all the doors of the Palace of Vincennes, where she kept her court, higher and wider to admit them" (Strutt's "Dresses," vol. ii.).

CHAPTER XIX.

The INQUISITION POST MORTEM was an inquiry held on oath by a local jury, before the county escheator, to ascertain of what lands a tenant *in capite* had died seized and by what rents and services they were held; who was his next heir, and of what age, etc. The verdict of the jury, together with the writ of inquiry, was sent to the King's Chancery. The Exchequer, in due course, levied the duties and services to be discharged by the heir. A tax, termed a "relief," was, on the death of a tenant *in capite*, due to the Crown, and the heir could not take possession till this death-duty was paid, and proper homage done. We append an abstract of the one referred to—

INQUISITION POST MORTEM.

Abstract.

3 *Edw.* II. *No.* 37. *Agnes de Valencia.*

Writ annexed dated at St. Alban's, 31 Dec. 1309.

Inquisition taken at Dakenham, Essex, 20 Ian. 13$\frac{09}{10}$. The jurors (named) say that Agnes de Valence held certain lands & tenements in Dakenham at her death of the Abbess of Berkyngg', for 17s. 4d. yearly, & suit of court to the said Abbess every 3 weeks. And the tenants of the lands ought to ride with the said Abbess with two horses at the costs of the said Abbess when rightfully forewarned, to wit [the tenants of] one messuage with a garden & dovecote, worth by the year 2s., 128 ac. of land, worth by the year 42s. 8d. at 4d. an acre; 4 acres of meadow, worth by the year 2s., at 6d. an acre. Also rent of assize 7s. 3$\frac{1}{2}$d., yearly from 6 free tenants there. Total 53s. 11$\frac{1}{2}$d.

Adomar de Valence, Earl of Pembroke, brother & heir, aged 30.
Also lands in Cambridge & Herts.

INQUISITION POST MORTEM.

Abstract.

18 *Edw.* II. *No.* 9. *Adomar de Valencia.*

Writ annexed dated at Westminster, 8 Nov. 1324.

Inquisition taken at Berkyng' 20 Nov. 1324. The jurors (named) say that Adomar de Valencia, late Earl of Pembroke, was not seised in his demesne as of fee of lands or tenements in Dakenham, co. Essex, but Margery de Moese, sometime wife of Thomas Weylond, was formerly seised thereof for life, and leased them to Agnes de Valence for life of said Margery; said Agnes dying before Margery, Adomar held the lands till his death. Said Margery is dead, and the reversion belongs to Iohn de Neville. Said lands are held of the Abbess of Berkyng' for 17s. 4d. yearly.

CHAPTER XXV.

"Licence for the alienation in mortmain by Gilbert de la Rye, parson of the church of Roding Abbots, to the Abbess & nuns of Barking of 200 acres of land & 40/- of rent in Barking & Dakenham" ("Calendar of Patent Rolls," Edw. II., 1308). Probably granted in relief on account of some inundation.

"October 24, 1313. A commission was issued at Westminster *de walliis et fossatis* to Willm. son of Robert Henry Gernet and Thomas Dakenham, for the coast of the sea and the adjacent parts of the county of Essex & also for the town of Wolewyck [Woolwich] in the Co. of Kent " ("Calendar of Patent Rolls," Edw. II.).

On June 26, 1339, Edward III. commissioned twelve jurors of the vicinage of Westhamme to inquire of defects in the marsh of Westhamme, to wit, Iohn de Dakenham, Thomas le Brewere, Iohn Samkyn, Iohn le Porter, Henry de Wynfeld, Iohn Galien the elder, Iohn Dannger, Iohn de Pellam, Gilbert le Dore, Willm. Oygor, Henry de Gaisham, Iohn Bone, Richard le Blake, Simon le Wynd, Iohn le Clerk of Leyton, and Geoffrey de Nottele. This was on the petition of the prioress of Stratford.

The fishes caught in Dagenham Gulf include the common carp, bream, white bream, tench, roach, rudd, perch, pike, eel, trout, and flounders. Of late years there has been a falling off both in quantity and quality, the result of the pollution of the Thames. Wild fowl (swans, geese, ducks, herons, gulls, moor-hens, and coot) are seen occasionally ; larks, starlings, and reed warblers frequently.

For further information the naturalist may be referred to "The Birds of Essex," by Miller Christie; "The Mammals, Reptiles, and Fishes of Essex," by Henry Laver; "The Flora of Essex," by G. S. Gibson.

APPENDIX B

The following are the wills of some of the persons mentioned in the foregoing chapters.

WILL of William Fanshawe, Esq., of Parsloes, proved at Westminster by John Fanshawe, eldest son of the testator, December 2, 1650.[1]

"In the Name of God, Amen. The first day of March in the tenth yeare of the raigne of our Soveraigne Lord Charles etc. A.D. 1634: I William ffanshawe of Parslowes in the Co. of Essex, Esquire, one of the Auditors of his Majesties Duchie of Lancaster, findeing myselfe sickly and infirme, but being of good and perfect memory thankes be to Almighty God and willing whilst I am of good memory soe to settle & dispose of my estate, as that I bee not neere the time of my Death distracted or diverted with the thought & care thereof from making my reconciliation and peace with Almighty God, Doe make this my last will & testament in manner following (viz) ffirst & principally I commend my soule unto the hands of the blessed Trinity, three persons and one God, Hopeing and undoubtedly beleiving by the only merritts Death and passion of my blessed Lord & Saviour Jesus Christ, to have remission of my sinnes & to enioy everlasting life ; And my body I commend unto the earth whereof it was made to be buried in a decent manner at the discretion of my Executors hereafter named. And for my worldly estate wherewith it hath pleased Almighty God to blesse me, I have lately by a declaration of trust vnder my hand & seale beareing date the eight and twentith day of ffebruary last past, directed certaine of Lands, tenements & hereditaments where with I trusted my wives brother Sr John Wolstenholme the younger of London, knight & my nephew Thomas ffanshawe to be disposed to the vse & for the benefitt of my children, as by the said Declaration may appear (which I hereby ratifie and confirm). And whereas Sr John Wolstenholme[2] the elder, of London, knight, by his indenture of bargaine

---

[1] Proved sixteen years after his death. Such delays were not uncommon where the disposition of land was concerned. Perhaps, too, the troublous times added to the delay.

[2] This Sir John was greatly interested in Arctic researches, and in 1616 he, with Sir Dudley Digges, chartered and fitted out a vessel, which they named the *Discovery*, and placed under Captain Baffin, the great Arctic voyager. She sailed on March 26, 1616, from Gravesend. In June she had passed Melville Bay, and on July 1 reached a deep

& sale beareing Date the twentith day of July 1622, in the twentith yeare of the raigne of our late king James etc, and enrolled in the hon^{ble} Court of Chancery, conveyed to me & Wm. Bromehall of London, gent. & my heires, divers Messuages, Lands, Tenements, Hereditaments in Haverford, Haverford West, Haverford Magna and Haverford Parva in the Co. of Pembrooke & in the Co. of the said Towne of Haverford, & in Molestone & other Townes, Hamletts, Villages & Places in the said Indentures menconed as thereby may appear. And whereas the name of the said William Bromehall was nominated by & in trust for me, of which premises soe conveyed to me & the said William Bromehall as aforesaid I have only sould to Sr James Perrott a Messuage & two Gardens thereunto annexed & a close compassed about with hedges thereunto adjoining lying within or neere Haverford Parva, sometime in the tenure of Richard Hoell. And by the particular therein mentioned to be of the yearely value of thirteen shillings & fourpence. And all that tenement called Molestone with the appurtenances whatsoever, situate lying & being in the Co. of Pembrooke, sometime in the tenure of Morgan Phillips or his assignes. And which by a particular thereof is menconed to be of the yearely rent of three pounds, two shillings & fourpence, sould to Edward Barlow, Esq. And the rest we stand still seized of. I doe give, Will & devise All & Singular the lands etc in the said Indenture menconed, except that sould to Sr James Perrott and Edward Barlow as aforesaid, to the said Sr John Wolstenholme the younger & Thomas ffanshawe their heires & assignes for ever. To the interest & purpose & vpon the speciall trust and confidence that they or the survivor of them or heire of the survivor of them shall sell with all convenient speed after my Death the same; And the monyes to be raised thereby to be for the benefitt of my daughter Katherine & to be ordered & disposed in such sort, manner & forme as I have directed other meanes intended to her by the Deed of Declaration hereinbefore menconed. And I direct the said Wm Bromhall to joyne with them in the said sale. And whereass I am interessed in the Rectory & Parsonage of Daggenham in the Co. of Essex in my owne name, for Divers yeares in revercon after a certaine terme therein to come now in the said Sr John Wolstenholme the younger, in trust for me, I doe give & bequeath the said Rectory & parsonage of Daggenham with all the rights, members and appurtenances thereof to my Dearly beloved wife Katherine for soe many yeares of the said severall termes as shee shall live. And after her decease in case she dye before the said severall termes shall be fully expired, I give the said remainder of the said termes to my eldest sonne John, And doe hereby direct my said brother Sr John Wolstenholme to see the same performed accordingly. And all that my Manno^r of Parslowes in the Co. of Essex, & all other my messuages, lands etc. in the

bay, which Captain Baffin named Wolstenholme Sound. Sir John fitted out another vessel in 1631, with Sir Thomas Roe. He was a staunch Royalist, and was heavily fined in 1645 by Parliament as a malignant.

said Countie & elsewhere, saveing & excepting a wood called Crickle wood in the said Co. of Essex & such other Lands as I have formerly directed by the declaration aforesaid, I give, will & devise to my said loveing wife for terme of her life.

"W. FANSHAWE.

"Sealed & delivered in the presence of Anthony Flintton, Peter Walden, William Rous.

"Registered Pembroke 197."

Abstract of the will of John Fanshawe, Esq., of Parsloes. Proved April 6, 1689, by John Fanshawe, youngest son and executor.

"I John Fanshawe of Parslowes in the Co. of Essex, Esq. this Twenty-seventh day of September, A.D. 1683 & in the 35th year of the Reign of our Sovereign Lord, Charles the Second by the grace of God King of England etc. in good health of body & of perfect memory & understanding (God be praised) Doe make & ordain this my last Will and Testament as follows (viz) I desire to be decently buried at the discretion of my executor hereinafter named. And my will is that all such debts as I shall owe vnto any person or persons at my death be fully satysfied. And whereas Henry Ayloff, Esq. by vertue of certain lres Pattents to him made by his said now Majesty at my nomination, is seized for his life of & in the office of Auditor of accounts of all his Majesties' Receivers, Sheriffs & other officers of all his Honours, Castles, Manors, Lands etc. of his Duchy of Lancaster . . . and of all fees, profits etc to the said office, to take effect in revercon immediately & soe soon as the said office (granted to me for my life by the same Letters Pattents) by my death or resignation or forfeiture or otherwise, should become voyd . . . I doe hereby direct & appoint that the said Henry Ayloffe do & shall permit my youngest sonne John ffanshaw, his heirs & assigns, to receive, take & enjoy all the benefitt & Profits of the said office, until my debts be fully satisfyed & paid. And the said Henry Ayloffe shall . . . surrender the said Letters Pattents & doe any other lawful act or thing to enable my said sonne John ffanshaw, his heirs & assigns, to renew the said Letters Pattents, or to take or procure a new grant of the said office to him. And I doe make my said sonn John ffanshaw the sole executor of this my will. And I do give & bequeath to him all my Leases,[1] ready money, debts, household stuff, goods & chattells whatsoever, as well reall as personall, for the better performance of this my will.

"JO. FFANSHAW.

"Signed, sealed, declared & published as his last will in the presence of Robert Bertie,[2] T. ffanshawe, Wm. Clent."

[1] His eldest son, William, had been amply provided for with the estate of Great Singleton, Lancashire.

[2] The Hon. Robert Bertie, fifth son of Robert, Earl of Lindsey, of Bee Hive and Valentines ; died 1701. A descendant of his was vicar of Ilford, 1844-81.

Will of Thomas Fanshawe, Esq., of Jenkins, A.D. 1651. Proved at Westminster 165½ by John Fanshawe, Esq., executor.

"I Thomas ffanshawe of Jenkins in the Co. of Essex, Esqr, being weak in body but of perfect memory, Doe make & ordayne this my last will in manner ffollowing. My soule I comend into the hands of Almighty God, my body to bee buried in such decent manner as my Executor shall think fitt. All my p'sonnell estate I will & devise for & towards the payment of my debts, of which I desire my Cozen Jo. ffanshawe's debt due to him of 200^{ll} & such other debts as my said Cozen ffanshawe doeth stand engaged for may bee first satisfied & after for the payment of such other debts as are my owne proper debts; for my younger children I have left itt in charge to my sone ; my wife is provided for by settlement in my lifetime. And of this my will I make my Cozen John ffanshawe of Parslowes, Esqr, my sole executor. In wittness whereof I have herevnto sett my hand the 22 daye of January, 1651.

"Tho. ffanshawe.

"Signed & published as the last Will & Testament of the said Thomas ffanshawe in the presence of Tho. ffanshawe, Ri. Benett, Hen. Sedgwicke."

In the will of William Fanshawe, of London, merchant, proved in 1683 (younger son of Sir Thomas Fanshawe, of Jenkins), is a bequest to Sir Thomas ffanshawe, of Jenkins, Knt., of "All those peices of Land called Hatfeild Hatchlands, Knighton Grove & ½ acre of Marsh which came p. Lott to me of those lands my mother left amongst her younger children. With all my horses & armes." The will concludes—"Lastly I appoint my sister Margaret ffanshawe my sole Executor to injoy the Remainder of my estate whatever it be, in goods, moneys or accompts where ever, with this my Desire onely, That in case she marry not, That she leave the same money att her decease to the ffamily of the ffanshawes att Jenkins."

This Margaret Fanshawe died unmarried at Islington in 1725, and was buried at Barking.

Will of Henry Upney ; buried at Dagenham, May 3, 1533.

"In the Name of God, Amen. Ande in the yere of our lorde God the twenty-thyrd yere of Henry VIII., I Henry Upney, senior of Dagenham being in whole mind & of good remembrance make my Testament & last will in forme following. ffirste I gyve and bequeth my soule to God Almyghty to his Mother Seynt Mary ande all the holly companie of hevyn and my bodie to be bured in the church yarde of Seynt Peter and paul of Dagenhm. I give to the hie aulter of Dagenham for my tythes and offerynges not don or negligently forgotten. Itm. I gyve to our lyght iiij$d$. Item. I gyve to the lyght of Seynt Iohn, Seynt Xopher (Christopher) and seynt Anne ij$d$. each to every one of them. Itm. I give 40s. to make a lofte over the belfrie, and if there be any part of the 40s. to be spared, I will that it go to the use of the Churche. I will that Rychard Stevyn of Dagenham shall have order and oversighte of same. I give 20s. to have two trentalls[1] of masses sayde for my soul and all Christen soles shortly after my departing. The Reste I give to my wyffe and I make Elizabeth and William my sonne the exors of this my will, and Rychard Stevyn of Dagenham supervisor with full powers to ordering my exors if they cannot agree.

> " These witnes,
>   " Sr Thomas Wagstaffe,
>   " William Clerke, Senior,
>   " Henry Upne, Iunior.
>   "cum alys (*i.e.* with others).   3 March, 1533."

Will of Iohn Bisshope ; buried at Dagenham, Ianuary, 1533.

" I, Iohn Bysshope of the p'ishe of Dagenhm̄ in the Countie of Essex beyng in good mynde and of perfecte remembrane makyth my last will & Testament in manner & forme following. ffirste I bequeth and comende my soule to Allmyghty God and his blessed Mother Ladie sainte Mary & to all the glorous seyntes in heyven : my bodie to be buried in the Church-yarde of the blessed apostles peter and paule of Dagenhm̄ aforesaide.

" Item. I gyve to the hyghe aulter of the same church for my tythes and oblattions negligently forgotten xii*d*.

" Item. I gyve and bequethe to the iiij lyghtes, that is to say, a lyghte to remite sinnes to our ladie, to seynt Ann, to seynt Xpher a lygthe, to seynt Iohn a lyghte to every one ii*d*. I gyve to common lyghte iid.[2]

" Item. I give and bequethe to Iohane my daughter a blake cow and x sheepe. I gyve of my goodes the matres and bolster & beste bedd and counterpan, a pr of sheetes and blankett and chest and a great panne ij dishes & lattyn candstick, pewter potte that was her mother's.

" Item. I bequethe to Iane my daughter ij bullockes the which ij bullocks I will that Christian my wyffe shall have the custodie & kepeing of them until the time that they be able to perfect & to increase and then I will that they be delyvered to the said Iane directly after with v ewes.

" I make Rychard Stevyn to be overseare of this my saide testament & last will & I gyve unto him for his labour & peyne xx*d*.

" In witnes of this the vicar Thomas Purtennte, Thomas Mill (or Hill ?), Thomas Estbroke at the ffieldes end & other moe (*i.e.* some more others)."

Will of John Marlow (1696).

" I John Marlow Citizen & Apothecary of London now in reasonable health make my last will. I desire to be decently buried at Dagenham by

---

[1] An office for the dead, consisting of thirty masses said on thirty consecutive days. From the French *trente.*

[2] The light of the patron saints of the church.

my late wife. To my only and well beloved daughter Elizabeth Marlow
I bequeath all my messuages, lands, etc., both freehold & copyhold in
the Co. of Midd⁵. Berks & Essex for her life & afterwards to my brother-
in-law Richard Commins, & to my kinsman Joshua Morris, attorney-at-
law and their heirs in trust for her sons & daughters in succession & in
default of her issue to my loving brother Michael Marlow & his heirs for
ever. To my said daughter Elizabeth I give my estate & term in three
houses, one in Grays Inn Lane, another in High Holborn & the other in
the parish of St. Anne's Soho, charged with £4 yearly to my sister Huldah
Lyford free from her husband. Also with 40/- yearly to my sister Ann
Andrews. Should my said daughter die without issue I give my said house
in the parish of St. Anne's Westminster to my said sister Huldah Lyford.
And the house in Grays Inn Lane to my sister Elizabeth Griffen & the
house in High Holborn to my sister Ann Andrews, widow. To my brother
Michael & his wife £5 each for mourning. To my brother & sister Griffen
£5 each for mourning to wear at my funeral. To my sisters Huldah
Lyford & Ann Andrews £5 each for mourning ; to my brother Commins
& his wife £5 each for mourning to wear at my funeral & the same to my
brother Davis & his wife. To my cousin Lydia Netham £5, to my cousin
Markman's wife living at London bridge £5 ; to my cousin Moore the
mid-wife £5 ; to my nephew John Marlow £30 when 21 ; to my nephew
Richard Lyford £5. I give unto my nephew Francis Emmerton all that
sum of £5 which I lent his mother, my sister Ann Andrews, the which I
desire may be applied towards putting him out an apprentice. The residue
to my daughter Elizabeth Marlow. The exors. to be my daughter Elizabeth, my brother Michael & my brother-in-law Richard Commins.

"Signed in the presence of Josiah Ragdale, Samuel Stone, Joshua Morris
& Thomas Jackson drawer att the King's head neare Guildhall. April 5,
1695.

"Whereas since the making of said will I have maried my said daughter
to John Newcome of whose integrity I am greatly satisfied & rely on, I
hereby authorize my said exors. if they think fit to sell all or any of the
three houses devised to my said three sisters, paying to my sister Ann
Andrews £10 towards putting her son Francis out an apprentice in lieu of
said 40/- per annum. And I appoint my said son-in-law John Newcome
one of my exors with the others. Signed in the presence of Sara Ann
Buttery, Walter Finch, Samuel Wingfield. Sept. 14, 1696. Proved Nov.
1696 by Elizabeth Newcome & John Newcome."

INQUISITION POST MORTEM.

49 *Edw.* III. *Pt.* 2. *No.* 19. *Edmund de Northtoft.*   Abstract.

Writ annexed dated at Westminster 5 Iune 1375.

Inquisition taken at F[*ynch*]yngfeld before Roger Keteryche, escheator,
18 Iune 1375. The jurors (named) say that Edmund de Northtoft

X

together with Anne his wife, likewise deceased, held the manor of North-toftes of Iohn de Nevill' as of his manor of Claverynges for ½ a knights' fee, worth by the year, clear, 18 marks :—Also of the church of St. Paul, London, as of the manor of Boytonhall, 18 acres of land, 1½ ac. of wood & 3 ac. pasture in Fynchingfeld', worth by the year, clear, 10ˢ :—1 ac. 1 rd. in Fynchingfeld' held of Roger Toly, worth by the year, clear, 12ᵈ :—3½ ac. in F. of said Roger, worth by the year, clear, 8ᵈ :—6 ac. in F. held of Iohn Repethon, worth by the year 18ᵈ :—53 ac. land, 3½ ac. meadow, 2 ac. pasture called Hildirshams & Shaldfordes held of the manor of North-toftes :—of the Abbess of Berkynges the manor of Dagenham, worth by

Monday,
Oct. 25,
1372.
Tuesday,
Oct. 31,
1374. the year 8 mark. Said Edmund died the Monday before All Saints 46 Edw. III. ; said Anna died the Tuesday before All Saints 48 Edw. III.— Emma & Florence, daughters of William son of said Edmund, heiresses, aged 10 & 6. The Abbess of Berkyng' & Nicholas Cumspol now occupy lands.

INQUISITION POST MORTEM.

Abstract.   19 *Ric.* II. *No.* 116. (*Ad quod damnum.*)

Writ annexed dated at Beverley 11 Sept. 1395.

Saturday,
Oct. 9,
1395. Inquisition taken at Reileigh before Clement Spyce, escheator of Essex, Saturday, the feast of St. Dennis 19 Ric. II. The jurors (named) say that it is not to the King's damage to allow Iohn Bray de Ipworthe & others to assign lands to the College of Plecy, to wit, the manor of South-fambregge ; and that there will remain to the said Iohn (among other lands) divers lands & tenements in Dagenham, worth by the year 100ˢ, held of the Abbess of Berkyng' by knight's service.

INQUISITION POST MORTEM.

Abstract.   6 *Hen.* V. *No.* 39. *Robert Burford.*

Writ annexed dated at Westminster 23 Nov. 1418.

Monday,
Dec. 12,
1418. Inquisition taken at Brendewode, Monday after the Conception of Blessed Virgin Mary 6 Hen. V. before Reginald Malyns, escheator.

The jurors (named) say that Robert Burford was seised of 1 acre in West Tillebery called le Mersh, worth by the year, clear, 18ᵈ, held of the King in chief by knight's service & ¾ᵈ yearly : one tenement next the church in Est Tillebery called Ganges, 1½ ac. there called Cherchefeld' ; 3 acres there between Iohn Sudbury's land on the west & Richard Frauncey's tenement in the east ; a marsh called Bakereshope, & a way under " le Downe Vicar' ; " also Deynes tenement with ½ ac. and barn, & ½ ac. in Cranemere Regoz :—1½ ac. in West Downe in Est Tillebery between Lewis Iohan's land on the north and William Berdefeld's on the south ; 2 ac. at the end of Bradewey, said Lewis's land on the north & said

William's on the south ; 3 ac. under the tenement of the College of Holle-
well towards the east ; 4 ac. under the tenement of Thos. Castell ; 3 ac. in
North feld', said Lewis's land on the south, Iohn Fyssh's land on the
north :—5 virgates of land, said Lewis's on the south ; Iohn Cook's on
the north ; 1 ac. under the tenem! late Nicholas Denys's ; ½ ac. under the
tenement late Ralph Halstede's ; ⅓ ar. under Thos. Castell's tenement ;
½ ac. lying beneath le Downe in Est Tillebery ; all held of Lewis Iohan,
esq. by homage, fealty, a rent of 6⁶ 8½ᵈ yearly and suit of court every 3
weeks, of the manor of Est Tillebery, & worth by the year, clear, 4 marks :
Also 2 " Hopes " called " Bachelereshopes," 1 ac. beneath le South
Downe, 1 ac. on le West Downe, & common of pasture for 52 sheep in
Est Tillebery, held of the manor of South Halle in Est Tillebery, yearly
rent 23ᵈ, worth by the year, clear, 26⁶ 8ᵈ :—Ravenesmersh in Est Tille-
bery held of Rich. Birle for 6ᵈ yearly ; 20 ac. marsh called Monshope in
West Tillebery held of said Richard for 6ᵈ yearly ; 1½ ac. in Cranemere in
Est Tillebery held of said Richard far [8ᵈ] yearly ; worth by the year, clear,
20⁶ :—1 ac. late Nicholas Denys on le West Downe held of the Manor of
Dagenham by 12ᵈ yearly, worth by the year, clear, 6ᵈ :—1 hope called le
Cornhope in le Mersh held of the tenement of Sencleres by 6ᵈ yearly,
worth by the year, clear, 2⁶ :—1 ac. on Broodwey held of Will. Baret by
5ᵈ yearly, worth by the year, clear, 6ᵈ :—1 ac. in le Goze held of the Prior
of St. Iohn of Ierusalem by 6ᵈ yearly, worth by the year, clear, 6ᵈ :—1 ac.
beneath the tenement of Stephen Bussh held of the rector of Est Tillebery
by 4ᵈ yearly, worth by the year, clear, 6ᵈ :—Said Robert Burford died on
Thursday, Michaelmas Day last past, without heirs.

INQUISITION POST MORTEM.

19 *Edw.* IV.   *No.* 75.   *Thomas Ursewyk.*   Abst

Writ annexed dated at " Oborn " 8 May 1479.

Inquisition taken at Rumford' 5 Nov. 1479 before Rich. Wurlich,
escheator. The jurors (named) say that long ago Thomas Haunsard was
seised of the manor of Markes, with 2 messuages, one windmill, 200 ac.
land, 100 ac. pasture, 100 ac. meadow, 60 ac. wood & 110⁶ rent in
Hauerynge atte Boure ; 15 messuages in Dagenham, Barkyng' & the new
town of Colchester in his demesne as of fee : So seised, he conveyed the
same to Katherine then wife of Bartholomew Seman' late citizen &
"Goldebeter" of London, for life, and then to Robert Knolles, esq., and
Elizabeth his wife, dau. of said Bartholomew, and the heirs of Elizabeth ;
with remainder to Thos. Stonys, esq., of Bernake, co. Northampton, Will.
Crowton, late rector of St. Anthony's, London, Iohn Savage, rector of
St. Andrew's, Cornhill ; Robert Couper, vicar of the church of Dagenham,
Will. Bouerton, vicar of the church of Northmymmes, Will. Saier, chaplain
in St. Brides's, Fleet Street, Iohn Stonys, chaplain living with the said

Katherine, Iohn Bonyngton, chaplain in St. Benedict's, Gracechurch, Iohn
Bryan of London, clerk, Thos. Pragill of Dagenham, Iohn Plum of
Dagenham, Iohn Pynchon, barber, & Thos. Fermory, scrivener, citizens
of London ;—Hence said Katherine was seised thereof in her demesne
as a free tenement :—Will. Crowton released his right to Robt. Knolles &
his heirs :—Elizabeth Knolles dying without heir, said Robert, by fine
levied at Michaelmas 39 Hen. VI. between Thos. Ursewyk, Iohn Say, Iohn
Grene, Will. Marowe, Iohn Walden, Thos. Coke, Rich. Riche, Guy Farr
fax, & Robt. Ursewyk, plaintiffs, & the said Robt. Knolles, esq., de-
forciant, agreed that the premises, then held by Katherine Otteley for life,
& which should be to said Robert (after her death) for life, & then to
Will. Crowton, Iohn Savage, Iohn Stonys, Thos. Pragils, Iohn Pynchon &
Thos. Fermory aforesaid,—should remain after the death of said Katherine
to the plaintiffs aforesaid during life of said Robt. Knolles; Hence the
said plaintiffs were thereof seised in their demesne as of free tenement :
and afterwards Will. Crowton, Iohn Stonys, Thos. Pragils, Iohn Pynchon
& Thos. Fermory died, & Iohn Savage surviving his co-feoffees was seised
of the premises in his demesne as of fee :—said Katherine died :—and
Iohn Savage by his deed released his right to Thomas Ursewyk, knt., &
his heirs; hence said Thomas was thereof seised in his demesne as of fee,
Iohn Say and the other plaintiffs being thereof seised in their demesne as
of a free tenement : Thos. Ursewyk and Guy Fairfax survived the other
plaintiffs : said Thos. died thereof seised in his demesne as of fee, and
Guy yet holds the premises as free tenement, and they are held of
Elizabeth Queen of England as of her manor of Haueryng atte Boure in
socage by service of 4^{ll} 5^s $1\frac{1}{2}^d$ yearly, worth by the year, clear, £6.

Also they say that said Thomas Ursewyk held divers other lands in
Essex (Dagenham not again named.) and they mention Anne his wife,
dau. of Richd Riche. Said Thomas died 19 Mar. $147\frac{3}{9}$. Daughters &
heiresses,—Katherine wife of Hen. Langley, esq., aged 21 ; Anne wife of
Iohn Doreward, esq., aged 19 ; Elizabeth, Ioan & Mary Ursewyk, aged
respectively 14 years, 8 years, and 9 months.

INQUISITION POST MORTEM.

2 *Ric.* 3.   *No.* 39.   *Elizabeth Coke.*

Writ annexed dated at Westminster 8 Ian. $148\frac{4}{5}$.

Abstract.

Inquisition taken at Stratford Langthorn 18 Ian. $148\frac{4}{5}$ before Roger
Philpot, Rich. Higham & Will. Nynge. The jurors (named) say that
Philip Malpas late citizen and clothier of London was seised of the manor
of Chaldewell and of the advowson of the parish church there; the manor
of Belhows in Stanford Ryvers; a tenement called Morrelles in Stanford;
another called Apultons in Chikwell ; £4 rent called porters fee in the
parish of Dagenham ; a tenement called Tylcherst in South Welde near
Brendewode ; 8 messuages, gardens, etc. in Westham ; & 40 ac. land in

the said parishes :—And had issue Elizabeth, late wife of Thomas Coke, knt., who inherited the same, and by her charter dated 27 Oct. 1484 granted the same to Iohn Coke, Iohn Vavesour, Iohn Forster & Iohn Vale for the fulfilment of her last will, namely, to the use of said Elizabeth during her life, and after her death to the said Iohn Coke and his heirs, with remainder to the said Iohn Forster & Ioan his wife, dau. of said Elizabeth, & heirs of said Ioan. (Tenure of lands given, but no further mention of Dagenham). Said Elizabeth died 17 Nov. 1484. Philip Coke, son & heir, aged 30, does not inherit by her will.

An old subsidy roll reads as follows :—

" The Extracte indented made the second daye of February in the fifth year of the reign of his most dread sovereign lorde Edward the Sixth (1552) by the grace of God, of England, Ffrance & also of Scotland king, Defender of the ffaith & of the Church of England and also of Ireland in earth, supreme heade, delivered to Iohn Carrowe of Romforde in the Countie of Essex, gent. named & appoynted high collector of the Hundred of Bekyntre and the Liberties off Barkynge and Havering-atte-Bower by Iohn Ga'e, knyght & underchamberlayne of the king's majestie's most honourable Household, Anthony Cooke, knyght, Peter Mawtis, knyght, Willm Ayloff, Iohn Ffreeman, Willim Pouncett, Iohn Cooke & Morgane Woollff, esquire, high commyfsioners assigned & dyvided to levie the said payments of the relief graunted to the sovereign lorde the king by acte of Parliement made in the third yeare of his most noble reign comprysing in the said extract the names & also the persons as were assigned to levie the particular sommes."

Under Dagenham occur these names with their assessments and the amounts paid.

	£ s. d.	s. d.
Henry Clarke	14 . 0 . 0	14 . 0
Winifryde Campe, widowe	20 . 0 . 0	10 . 0
Iohn Lyttle	15 . 0 . 0	15 . 0
William Grasbie	10 . 0 . 0	10 . 0
Iohn Money	10 . 0 . 0	10 . 0
Andrew Dowcett	15 . 0 . 0	15 . 0
Richard Sokes	10 . 0 . 0	10 . 0
Peter Clerke	10 . 0 . 0	10 . 0
Richard Barbor	10 . 0 . 0	10 . 0

The King's majestie's natural subjects.

Iohn Ga'e.   Peter Meantys.
Willm Ayloff.   Willm Pouncett.

A later subsidy roll was made October 10, in the tenth year of the reign of Elizabeth, the commissioners being Henry Gray, George Harvey, and Thomas Leggatte, who appointed Iohn Tedcastle, of Barkynge, to be high collector, to "collect for this first intire subsedie."

Dagenham Towne Ward.

		£		£	s.	d.
Land	Henry Osborne, Esq.	20		4 .	0 .	0
	Richard Blaksley	6			24 .	0
	William Litle ..	5			8 .	0
	Thomas Rogers	5			8 .	0
	Iohn Flaninge	20		4 .	0 .	0
	Iohn Truelove	10			8 .	0
	Christopher Curtis	20/-				4
	William Crane	20/-				4
Goodes	Albyon Cox, Gent.	5			20 .	8
	Lawrence Baker	3				8
	Iohn Harwoodd	3				8
	William Cummens	4			10 .	0
	Richard Wytham	4			10 .	8
	Henry Fetter ..	4			10 .	8
	William Stockdale	3				8
	Iohn Crowe ..	3				8
	William Bearde	4			10 .	8
Assessors	Thomas Cowx, in goode	10			26 .	8
	Henry Osborne, ,,	6			15 .	0
	Iohn Foster ,,	4			10 .	8
	Thomas Esbrooke, in land	5			20 .	0

APPENDIX C

THE Comyns family, although they did not at any time live at one of the manor-houses in Dagenham or neighbourhood, were occupying influential positions two hundred years ago, not only in Dagenham, but also in the adjoining parish of Barking, and by the middle of the seventeenth century were also established in Romford. The name of Comyns does not occur in the Dagenham registers until 1603, when "Thomas Comminges Widower & Elizabeth Nicholas marryed the xi daye of Sept^r;" but in Barking they are mentioned as early as 155$\frac{8}{9}$, when "Elizabeth Cumins, buried 8th Jany." We cannot follow the Barking branch, neither can we clear up whether Thomas Comyns of Dagenham, William of Barking, and Robert of Dagenham were brothers; the two last we know were nephews, and that John Comyns, the father of Robert, was brother of a William Comyn of Dagenham, yeoman, who was buried at Dagenham December 21, 1624, and whose will is dated October 1 of the same year, in which he leaves "to William Comyn of Barking, my nephew, all my Mannor and farme of Redden Court which I purchased of Thomas Legatt of Hornchurch, Esq$^{re.}$" with remainder to his sons and heirs male, and failing them, to the sons, in succession, of his nephew Robert Comyns of Dagenham.

This Robert Comyns of Dagenham, who married Margery Humfreys of the same parish in 1607, is the first named in the "Visitation of Essex" of 1664, which was signed by his eldest son, William Comyns, Esq., of Hare Street, in the parish of Romford in Essex, and though a tanner by trade, had his pedigree and arms (azure; a chevron ermine between three garbs or) duly recorded at this visitation. William Comyns, who died in 1668, had married Mary, daughter of Thomas Bennet, of North Weald, who died only nine months before him; they had three sons—William, of Writtle Lodge and of Queens' College, Cambridge, and Lincoln's Inn; John, who was alive in 1686; and Robert, who was buried at Romford in 1662, and seven daughters, two only of whom, Hannah and Clemence, survived their father. William Comyns, in his will, dated October 19, 1667, desires to be buried in Romford churchyard, and the flat stone, which is still there, though the inscription is nearly gone, testifies that his wishes were carried out. This inscription, and extracts from William Comyns' will, will be found in

"Memories of Old Romford" (by the Rev. Geo. Terry). William Comyns, of Writtle, Navestock, Romford, Dagenham, and Margaretting, all in Essex, succeeded his father; he married Elizabeth Freeman, widow, daughter of Matthew Rudd, of Little Baddow, by whom he had John, Richard, William, Robert, and Thomas—the last two died infants—and two daughters. John was the celebrated Sir John Comyns, of Hylands, in Essex, and, like his father, of Queens' College and Lincoln's Inn; he was Serjeant-at-Law, M.P. for Maldon 1693, and Chief Baron of the Exchequer 1738. Sir John was thrice married, but died without issue, November 13, 1740, and left Hylands to his nephew John Comyns, of Pettits, in Romford, son of his brother Richard by his second wife, Frances.

We must not, however, linger over this branch of the family, but return to Robert Comyns of Dagenham. Besides the above-mentioned William, he had Robert, who died in 1625, John, Bartholmew, Paul, and Thomas. John was baptized at Dagenham, October 10, 1613. Like his brother William, he signed the "Visitation of Essex" in 1664, and is described as of Dagenham, Gent., tanner. He married Sarah, daughter of Richard Marlow, of Barton, in Suffolk, and had four sons, John, who died at the age of twenty, in 1668; Robert, who was buried at Dagenham in 1648; another Robert, who was baptized at Dagenham, February 27, 165$\frac{4}{5}$; Richard, afterwards known as Captain Richard Comyns; William, Thomas, and Mary, who died in their infancy, and Elizabeth, Sarah, and Susan, who married and survived their father. Robert married, in 1676, Elizabeth, daughter of William Hinton, citizen and ironmonger of London; he is described in the marriage licence as then of Hare Street, Romford, tanner, bachelor, about twenty-four. He only enjoyed four years of married life, and was buried at Dagenham, September 27, 1681; he had a son, Robert, and two daughters, Elizabeth and Rebekah, the latter was probably posthumous, at any rate she was baptized at Romford five months after her father's death. Her brother Robert is mentioned in the will (dated October 14, 1687) of his grandfather, John Comyns of Dagenham, who being desirous that the house where he then lived, and the tanyards, which, by entail, would have descended to the said Robert, should be enjoyed by a Comyns that was a tanner, says, "have therefore out of the said entaile and by this my will amongst other lands given and devise the said house, Tann yard and lands . . . to my onely serviving sonne Richard Comyns & to his Heyres for ever & in lieu thereof I give and bequeath to my said grandchild Robert Comyns, if he arrive at his full age of 21 years, the sum of £200. My exors. to pay him £10 per ann. for use thereof until he is 21 as interest," etc. Robert grew to man's estate, and married in 1698, the marriage licence, dated July 20, 1698, says, "Robert Comins of Dagenham gent. Bach. 19 and Mary Henley of Ratcliffe Sp. 19. Consent of her guardian John Emerton gent. of Dagenham." The fourth son of Robert Comyns, the great-grandfather of the last-named Robert, was Bartholomew, who died before 1656, but left a son Robert;

the next, Paul, who was alive in 1624; and Thomas, of London and Lambeth, Doctor of Physic, who is first mentioned, not by name, as he was then unbaptized, in his great-uncle's will, October 1, 1624. He was baptized at Dagenham, October 7, 1624, and married Elizabeth, daughter of Sir Thos. Nightingale; he died August 17, 1656, at the early age of thirty-two, and was buried in Dagenham church, where, on the vicar's chancel floor, there is a slab to his memory.

Dr. Thomas Comyns, in his will, leaves to his brother William, "My lands, Woods & springs with a Tenement & appurt⁹ known by the name of Derrifalls in the parish of Hornchurch" (the house is still standing on the Upminster road, a little to the east of Hornchurch church). He also leaves lands and tenements at Hatfield Heath, and lands in Dagenham called "Butts ffields & Durrants Brookes," and other lands and property in Dagenham and London. "My studdie of Bookes vnto that sonne of either of my brothers that shall ffirst commence Doctor in Phisicke, either in Oxford or Camb. or in Padua in Italy. [He probably took his degree in Padua.] In the meantime I committ them to the safe custody of Dr. Thomas Croydon to be del⁴ to my Exors. 7 years hence."

As we have seen, John Comyns of Dagenham had only one son who survived him, Captain Richard Comyns, who succeeded his uncle William in the house and tanyards at Hare Street. The Comyns house at Hare Street was probably the low timber and plaster house which stood where "Balgores" now stands; it was in existence about forty years ago. The family mansion at Dagenham is shown in the map of Dagenham village, and stood on the same side of the street as the church, to the east of it; part remains, but is now divided into several cottages, and a stranger, in passing, would never think that at one time they had been part of the mansion of a well-known family. Richard Comyns is described as of Hare Street, Romford, and Dagenham. He married Dorothy Steevens, of Romford, on April 15, 1681, and had by her, John, Robert, and Thomas, who died in infancy; John, afterwards Captain John Comyns, Richard, Henry, and three daughters, Dorothy, Ann, and Sarah—the two last died infants, and Sarah was a posthumous child. Captain Richard Comyns died at the age of forty-five, at his house at Dagenham, on February 10, 1700, and was buried the following day. His widow survived him thirty-one years, and died at the age of seventy-one. Their youngest surviving son, Henry, died in 1736, and was buried at Dagenham; John, whom we shall have to notice presently, died in 1745, aged sixty. Richard, of Brakes,[1] county Essex and Grey's Inn, one of the six clerks, was the last male representative of this branch of the Comyns family; he died in 1775 at the age of ninety-two. His brother, Captain John Comyns, of Dagenham, had died thirty years before; he was

---

[1] Brakes, or Brakes Place, of which not a trace now remains, stood near Hare Hall in Romford, on the opposite side of the lane leading from the high road to Squirrel's Heath.

baptized at Romford, June 27, 1685, died March 15, 1745, and was buried at Dagenham five days after; his widow died in 1748, aged fifty-six, and was also buried at Dagenham. They lie with Captain Richard Comyns and Dorothy his wife in a decaying tomb in the north churchyard. John Comyns left no male issue, his only son, John, died when a few days old. Of the ten daughters, four died in infancy; Dorothy, the eldest daughter, died at the age of thirty-eight, and was buried at Dagenham, from Sion College, 1757; Anne died in 1752, aged thirty-seven; Mary, the second surviving daughter at the time of her father's death, was baptized at Dagenham, August 19, 1711, and married William Butterfield, she was buried at Dagenham, April 8, 1778, and her husband also, three years later—they left no family; Elizabeth, born April 2, 1718, and baptized at Dagenham two days later, married the eldest son of Sir John Holmes, and was buried at Dagenham, from Westminster, November 24, 1775, leaving no issue; Isabella, baptized at Dagenham, April 13, 1721, married — Flowers, and was buried at Dagenham, April 12, 1763; Sarah, the youngest daughter, born May 25, 1723, and baptized at Dagenham, June 6 following, married at St. Paul's, Covent Garden, October 20, 1763, the Rev. Thomas Cole, D.D., of the Manor House, Milbourne St. Andrew, Dorset. He was afterwards vicar of Dulverton, Somerset, where two sons were born, Richard Comyns in 1766, and Thomas Comyns in 1770. Richard Comyns Cole, of Milbourne St. Andrew and Bath, married Charlotte Ewing, by whom he had John, who died in 1896; Charlotte, who died young, and Mary Anne, who married W. H. Clifton, Esq., of Romford, and died 1889. She had William Comyns, of Romford, who, with his sister, Mary Frances, are the only representatives in this neighbourhood of the Comyns of Dagenham and Romford; there was another daughter, Julia Comyns, who died in 1882. Richard Comyns Cole died November 29, 1838. His brother, Thomas Comyns Cole, married, and had a son and daughter; both died unmarried.

NOTE.—The author is indebted for this article to A. Bennett Bamford, Esq.

APPENDIX D

The following is a list of the bishops who have had episcopal jurisdiction over the parish of Dagenham :—

ARCHBISHOPS OF LONDON.

Theanus	Theodwinus
Eluanus	Theodredus
Cadar	Hilarius
Obinus	Restitutus
Conanus	Guitelinus
Palladius	Fastidius
Stephanus	Vodinus
Iltutus	Theonus

BISHOPS OF LONDON.

Mellitus	604
Cedd	654
Wina	•666
Erkenwald	675
Waldhere	693
Ingwald	706
Egwulf	745
Sighaeh	772
Eadberht	774
Eadgar	789
Coenwalh	791
Eadbald	794
Heathoberht	794
Osmund	802
Æthilnoth	811
Coelberht	822
Deorwulf	839
Swithwulf	860
Heahstan	892
Wulfsige	898

Theodred	.. ..	926
Brithelm	.. ..	953
St. Dunstan	.. ..	959
Ælfstan	.. ..	961
Wulfstan	.. ..	996
Aelfhun	.. ..	1004
Aelfwig	.. ..	1014
Ælfward	.. .:	1035
Robert Champard	.. .. ..	1044
William	.. ..	1051
Hugh de Orval	.. .. ..	1075
Maurice	.. ..	1085
Richard de Beaumes I.	.. ..	1108
Gilbert (Universalis)	.. .. ..	1128
Robert de Sigillo	.. .. ..	1141
Richard de Beaumes II.	.. ..	1152
Gilbert Foliot	.. ..	1163
Richard FitzNeal	.. .. ..	1189
William of St. Mary's Church	..	1199
Eustace de Fauconberge	.. ..	1221
Roger le Noir	.. ..	1229
Fulk Basset	.. ..	1244
Henry de Wengham	.. .. ..	1259
Henry of Sandwich	.. .. ..	1263
Iohn de Chishul	.. .. ..	1274
Richard de Gravesend	.. ..	1280
Ralph de Baldock	.. .. ..	1306
Gilbert de Segrave	.. .. ..	1313
Richard de Newport	.. .. ..	1317
Stephen de Gravesend	.. ..	1319
Richard de Bentworth	.. ..	1338
Ralph de Stratford	.. .. ..	1340
Michael de Northburg	.. .. ..	1354
Simon of Sudbury	.. .. ..	1362
William Courtenay	.. .. ..	1375
Robert de Braybroke	.. .. ..	1382
Roger Walden	.. ..	1405
Nicholas Bubbewyth	.. .. ..	1406
Richard Clifford	.. .. ..	1407
Iohn Kempe	.. ..	1422
William Grey	.. ..	1426
Robert FitzHugh	.. .. ..	1431
Robert Gilbert	.. ..	1436
Thomas Kempe	.. .. ..	1450
Richard Hill	.. ..	1489

Thomas Savage	..	..	..	1496
William Wareham	..	..	..	1502
William Barons	..	..	..	1504
Richard Fitz-Iames	..	..	..	1506
Cuthbert Tunstall	..	..	..	1522
Iohn Stokesley ..	..	..	..	1530
Edmund Bonner	..	..	..	1539
Nicholas Ridley	..	..	..	1550
Edmund Bonner	..	..	..	1553
Edmund Grindal	..	..	..	1559
Edwin Sandys ..	..	..	..	1570
John Aylmer ..	..	..	..	1577
Richard Fletcher	..	..	..	1595
Richard Bancroft	..	..	..	1597
Richard Vaughan	..	..	..	1604
Thomas Ravis ..	..	..	..	1607
George Abbot ..	..	..	..	1610
John King ..	..	..	..	1611
George Monteigne	..	..	..	1621
William Laud ..	..	..	..	1628
William Juxon ..	..	..	..	1633
Gilbert Sheldon	..	..	..	1660
Humfrey Henchman	..	..	..	1663
Henry Compton	..	..	..	1675
John Robinson	..	..	..	1714
Edmund Gibson	..	..	..	1723
Thomas Sherlock	..	..	..	1748
Thomas Hayter	..	..	..	1761
Richard Osbaldeston	..	..	..	1762
Richard Terrick	..	..	..	1764
Robert Lowth ..	..	..	..	1777
Beilby Porteus	..	..	..	1787
John Randolph	..	..	..	1809
William Howley	..	..	..	1813
Charles James Blomfield	..	..	..	1828

In 1836 the diocese of London was relieved of the counties of Essex and Hertfordshire, which were transferred to the diocese of Rochester.

BISHOPS OF ROCHESTER.

George Murray	..	..	..	1827
Joseph Cotton Wigram	..	..	..	1860
Thomas Legh Claughton	..	..	..	1867

This arrangement, whereby two counties north of the Thames had their diocesan centre in a city south of that river, proved, however, both inconvenient and unsatisfactory.   Consequently, in 1876, Essex and Hertfordshire were formed into a new diocese, with the ancient town of St. Albans for its see.

BISHOPS OF ST. ALBANS.

Thomas Legh Claughton	..	..	1877
John Wogan Festing ..	..	..	1890
Edgar Jacob ..	..	..	1903

As the county of Essex has now a population of nearly a million souls, it is not unlikely that a further rearrangement may take place, giving this metropolitan county a bishop for itself, having his *cathedra* at Chelmsford or Colchester.

It should be added that there are two suffragan bishops in this diocese, viz. the Right Rev. H. F. Johnson, D.D., Bishop-Suffragan and Archdeacon of Colchester [1] (1894), and the Right Rev. Thomas Stevens, D.D., F.S.A., Bishop-Suffragan of Barking (1901) and Archdeacon of Essex.

[1] This title was revived in 1882, after having been in abeyance more than three centuries.   Dr. Wm. More was appointed, in 1536, Bishop-Suffragan of Colchester, to assist probably the Bishop of Ely, and Dr. John Stern in 1567.   The last bishop was Dr. Alfred Blomfield, Vicar of Barking and Archdeacon of Essex.

SUPPLEMENTARY APPENDIX TO THE FIRST EDITION

THE will of William de Burgoyne, March 12, 1258-9, mentions the "quit rents of land" held by William de Dagenham and others at Writtle, Co. Essex. (Calendar of Wills, Court of Husting, London.)

Among the MSS. Balliol Coll., Oxford, is a Latin deed on parchment dated "at Dakenham" the day before the Kalends of December, 1295, whereby Richard, Bishop of London, confirms the appropriation to Balliol College of the Church of Saint Laurence, Jewry. The Bishop's seal originally appendant by a silk cord, is in fragments.

Also a like deed by the Dean and Chapter of St. Paul's confirming that of the Bishop. Dated at London, January, 1295. The seal in good preservation. (From the 4th Report, Hist. Manuscript Commission.)

Among the MSS. of Westminster Abbey is a notarial instrument by a notary of Lincoln of proceedings in the Consistory Court of St. Paul's, London, as to the marriage between John Convers and Ann de Langton at Dagenham, December 26, 1347.

P. 5. A Thomas de Dagenham is mentioned as receiving a bequest of money in the will of William de Blith, son of Ralph de Blithe, saddler of the City of London, dated April 12, 1349. (Calendar of Wills, Court of Husting, London.)

P. 17 (note). The Act *Quia Emptores* was passed in 1290.

P. 20. A review in the *Athenæum* doubts whether the description here drawn of early manorial life would apply to the "unimportant manors in Dagenham parish," and adds, "We do not suppose that half a dozen high tables in the whole kingdom possessed silver plates at the time specified, whilst the general household would certainly dine off wooden trenchers; pewter was costly, and reserved for the more wealthy."

P. 22. The Records of Justice Seat, 1631, give under Dagenham—

> 1 alehouse keeper
> 1 victualler.

The "alehouse" was probably either the Cross Keys or the White Horse or the White Hart.

P. 23. There was also another inn, viz. the Sun. Mr. Blackborne writes, December 21, 1717, "Dined at the Sun at Dagenham on a haunch of venison. All agreed to give Col. Graham, the founder (*sic*) of the venison, a carting day for chalk next summer." Col. Graham lived in or near Ilford.

P. 30. In note read Hamo de Chiggewelle.

P. 34. Major-General Fleetwood was son-in-law to Cromwell, Commander-in-Chief of the Expedition to Ireland, and for a short time a Lord Deputy. He was a strong Baptist.

P. 38. The historical date of the inventory would be October 4, 1552.

P. 39 (*note* 1). The pyx for the reserved Sacrament was (according to the English use) a receptacle in the form of a dove, made of silver or gold. It was suspended over the Altar.

P. 40. In John Heywood's interlude "The Four P's," published in 1553, there is an allusion to the Holy Rood at Dagenham, as appears from the following :—

THE FOUR P's.

PALMER . . . .

I am a Palmer, as ye se,
Which of my lyfe much part have spent
In many a fayre and farre countrie,
As pilgrims do, of good intent.
Before Chryste's blessed sepulture :
The mount of Calvery have I sene,
A holy place, ye may be sure.
To Josaphat and Olyvete
On fote, god wote, I went right bare ;
Many a salt teare dyd I swete,
Before thys carke could come thare.
Yet have I been at Rome also,
And gone the statyons all arow :
Saynt Peter's shryne and many mo,
Than yf I told all ye do know,
Except that there be any suche
That hath ben there, and diligently
Hath taken hede, and marked muche,
Then can they speke as much as I.
Then at the Rodes also I was ;
And rounde about to Amias.
At Saynt Toncomberer and Saynt Tronion :
At Saynt Botolph and Saint Anne of Buckston,
On the hills of Armony where I see Nae's arke
With holy Job, and Saint George in Southwarke ;
At Waltam and at Walsingham
And at the good rood of Dagnam,
At Saint Cornely's ; at Saint James in Gales.
. . . .

P. 41 (*note* 6). The usual place for the organ was, in Pre-Reformation times, in the rood-loft.

P. 54. The following from "Church-lore Gleanings," by the Rev. T. F. Thiselton-Dyer, may perhaps throw fresh light on this discovery—

"Occasionally, the skulls of horses have been found in sacred buildings; the popular idea being that, like earthenware jars, they were built in for acoustic purposes; although it has been suggested that the remains of sheep and horses found under the floors of churches indicate the traces of heathen sacrifices on the spot in earlier times. Some years ago 'a horse's head was placed under the organ in a parish church at Munster, to give increased effect to the music; a superstition,' writes a correspondent of *Notes and Queries* (4th series, iii. 564), 'very prevalent in the county Clare.' Near the old mansion of R——, where I spent some of the years of my childhood, was a field in which there was a very fine echo. This was invariably attributed to the skull of a horse, which had lived on the estate for thirty years, and which was buried in that field. I remember well finding the skull, and carrying it away from the field, with no injury to the echo. In the bell turret of Elsdon Church, Northumberland, there were found, built into the masonry, three skulls of horses. Horses' skulls, too, have frequently been put into the sounding-boards over the heads of Presbyterian ministers in Scotland. . . ." (See *Notes and Queries*, 4th series, iv. 66; 6th series, i. 424; 8th series, viii. 351.)

P. 57. In 1595 a commission was granted to Anthony Cooke, armiger, of Haveringe-at-Bowre, Richard Elliott, and others, for dividing and separating the Manor of Dagenham from the Manor of Havering.

The Deed is dated 28 June, 37 Elizabeth, with seal affixed, probably the Court of Exchequer, with inscription. It is in Latin.

P. 58. Mr. William Blackborne was High Sheriff of Essex in 1709. In a letter to a friend he says he had the right to present Mr. Butler to the benefice of Dagenham in consequence of having held the above office.

Mr. Blackborne was robbed by highwaymen while on the Romford coach, on February 4, 1716, "between the Whalebone and Mr. Teaton's." Perhaps this took place between Whalebone House and another whalebone near the cross-roads. Mr. Blackborne, by the way, was utterly ruined in the South Sea Company, and had to sell (1725) all his landed property, including Brittens.

P. 67 (*note* 2). The "portose" was a portable breviary, as distinguished from the large and massive breviary which lay on the desk. It did not contain the antiphoner for the musical rendering of the Hours.

P. 70. For February or March, 1552, read November, 1554. Mary's reign began July 6, 1553, and her marriage with Philip took place at Winchester ·Cathedral, July 25, 1554. There was a William Smith, Rector of Wanstead, Essex, from July 10, 1542, till his ejection in 1554. Newcourt gives no indication that he was the same person as the Vicar of Dagenham.

P. 74. The Solemn League and Covenant. This should be the Scottish Covenant which was drawn up in 1638. The former was promulgated in 1643.

P. 75. Thomas Coleman was a native of Oxford. He held the rectory of Blyton, Lincs., which he exchanged for that of St. Peter's, Cornhill. Selden describes him as a learned man and an Erastian. He was buried March 30, 1647, at St. Peter's, Cornhill, all his fellow-members of the Westminster Assembly being present.

P. 76. Mr. John Bowyer: Certificate of the Assembly of Divines of John Bowyer to the rectory (*sic*) of Dagenham 1646-47. (Hist. MSS. Comm. 6th Report.)

P. 78. For "about 1630" read 1645.

P. 81. For (1674) Mr. Smythies bequeaths, etc., read (1673).

P. 81. A William Blackmore was curate of St. Peter's, Cornhill, of which he became rector May 13, 1656. Subsequently he became a presbyterian preacher at Hornchurch. Died at Hare Street, and was buried at Romford July 18, 1684.

P. 87. Abraham Blackborne was not the son, but perhaps the nephew of William Blackborne, who had two daughters only. The latter, however, had a brother called Abraham, a merchant in London, who may have had a son called after himself.

P. 90. The Rev. Dr. Moore died October 4, 1906, aged 77, and was buried in Dagenham Churchyard. He was succeeded by the Rev. Clement Charles Harrison, curate of Dagenham. Mr. Harrison graduated B.A. at St. John's College, Cambridge, in 1880, and M.A. in 1883. He was ordained by the Bishop of Worcester, in 1881, to the curacy of Temple Balsall, which he served for two years, when he became curate of Holy Trinity, Warrington, and subsequently curate at Cottisford, Oxon.

P. 90. The Rev. J. E. Stevenson Moore died suddenly in 1905.

P. 109. The coat of arms of Harvy of Wangey is given in *Notes and Queries*, 3rd series, 327, viz. : Or, a chevron between three leopard faces, gules (for Harvy) argent, two bends, engrailed sable, a label of points (qy. gules) (for Radcliffe) impaled at bottom.

P. 110. Job Allibone was the third and youngest son of Peter Allibone, rector of Chenies, Bucks. Joined the Church of Rome and was disinherited. Both he and his wife were buried at Dagenham.

P. 111. Sir Rich. Allibone died August 22, 1688, in Brownlow Street, Holborn, two months *before* the landing of William III.

P. 119 (*note*). Mr. Denman was made Lord Chief Justice in 1832; died September 22, 1854, buried at Stoke Albany. His wife (Theodosia) was a daughter of the Rev. Richard Vever, rector of Saxby, Melton Mowbray.

P. 127, line 17. This should read as follows: "It may not be out of place to mention here that until the year 1752, the civil and ecclesiastical year began on Lady Day (March 25) and ended on the eve of the following Lady Day. The beginning of the historical year was, however, January 1st, which was regarded as New Year's day."

P. 127, line 28. For 1752 read 1751 and in the next line 1752 for 1751. September 2, 1752, was a Wednesday, and the next day, Thursday, was reckoned September 14.

P. 133. By the Stamp Act all entries in registers were to be made upon stamped paper. But by section ii (23 Geo. III. c. 68) provision was made that in certain cases entry might be made without any stamp. To secure against penalties, a licence under the hands of three of the commissions was required for this to be done. At Little Waltham there are embossed stamps in the registers. At Broomfield (Essex) a note occurs: "Inspected by Chas. Frost, collector, December 10, 1784." The minister of the parish was to receive 2s. in the £ for his trouble. In many cases collectors granted printed licences for entries without stamps, such entries to be subject to inspection.

P. 140. During the Commonwealth it was ordered that civil marriages should be performed by a justice of the peace, but this did not necessarily exclude a religious ceremonial in the church. The justice or magistrate was not the same person as the registrar who was elected by the parish.

P. 140 (*note*). Joachim Matthewes sat in the House of Commons in 1653. He was a "moderate," and belonged to the party favourable to the "godly, learned ministry and universities."

P. 140. Sir Philip Matthews married Anne, daughter of Sir Thomas Wolstenholme; he died 1681.

P. 141. Mr. E. J. Sage died in 1904. He bequeathed his collection of Essex MSS. and prints to the Stoke Newington Library.

P. 143 (bottom). For 1750 read 1764.

P. 154. Read "Narcissa."

P. 172. Martin Bowes was Alderman of Aldgate, Farringdon Within and Langbourne in succession. Sheriff in 1540; Lord Mayor 1545–6. Died August 4, 1566. He left a bequest for the repair of the road between Yelford (Ilford) and Whitechapel. (Court of Husting. Cal. of Wills.)

P. 182. The Dict. Nat. Biog. states that Sir Wm. Hewett possessed the manor of Parsloes. Lysons is quoted. Environs iii. 64 (Parsloes is probably an error for Jenkins).

P. 182. Stow tells the story of the London Bridge incident in 1536, but as Sir W. Hewett only married November 7, 1536, it sounds improbable. The latter is said to have lived in Philpot Lane, and not on London Bridge.

P. 182. Clay Hall. Sir Christopher Hatton, 1st Baron, baptized at Barking, July 11, 1605, eldest son of Sir Christopher Hatton (died 1619), sometime of Clay Hall and afterwards of Kirkby, Northumberland. His mother was Alice, eldest daughter of Sir Thos. Fanshawe of Dronfield and Ware.

P. 184. The "negative oath" was the oath not to bear arms against the Parliament imposed on the defeated Royalists by an ordinance dated April 5, 1645. By a second ordinance dated November 1, 1655, all persons compounding for their delinquency had to take the oath.

P. 184. The "engagement" was a sworn declaration drawn up in October, 1649, to be faithful to the Commonwealth as established without King or House of Lords. It was imposed on all members of Parliament, State, and other officials, and afterwards (January, 1650) on the whole male population. Persons refusing to take it were to be debarred from seeking legal remedy for wrongs to which they had been subjected. This injustice was removed by the Nominated Parliament, and on January 19, 1654, the whole ordinance was repealed by the Protector, who declared that "such general and promissory oaths and engagements had proved burdens and snares to tender consciences." From henceforth no man was to be counted disloyal to the existing Government who did not assail it by his acts. (See S. R. Gardiner's "History of Commonwealth," Vol. III.)

P. 185 (bottom). St. Ethelburgh's Day was October 11, which remained unaltered, but the fair was probably kept up on the corresponding day of the old style.

P. 188. Sir Wm. Humfreys married, first, Margaret, daughter of William Wintone of Dymock, Glos., Esq.; and secondly, Ellen, relict of Robert Lancashire, of London, merchant. Orlando was his son and heir by his first marriage.

P. 196. The Exchequer of Pleas was supposed to be devoted to litigation arising directly or indirectly from debts due to the Crown, but of late years jurisdiction in general matters was obtained by a fiction, by which the plaintiff alleged that *he* was a debtor to the Crown, and through the defendant not paying him, he in turn was "the less able to settle with the King,"—a fiction technically known as "quo minus." (Rye's Record Searching.)

P. 199. Adomar (or Aymer) de Valence, Earl of Pembroke, son of William de Valence, half-brother of Henry III. by Joan, sister and heir of William, Baron Munchensi. Aymer was slain at a tournament or, according to Dugdale, murdered June 23. 17 Edward II. (1323-24). His third marriage was July 5, 1321. His widow, Mary de St. Paul, was foundress of Pembroke Hall, Camb., and benefactress of Grey Friars. He had no issue, and at his death all his dignities became extinct (will enrolled Court of Husting, London, October 28, 1324). The Court of

Common Pleas must have been early in 1324, as there was no other Aymer de Valence than the above.

P. 204. Little Ilford Register (Burials). " 1678. April 30. Francis Osbaston of Aldersbrook, Esq., and High Sheriff of Essex, who died upon 22nd, at the Angel and Star in Cheapside."

His daughter, Mary, married Sir Thomas Wroth, fourth and last Baronet, who died June 27, 1722.

For 1694 read 1684. Henry Osbaston died in June, 1684, his will being proved in the following month.

P. 205. Sir Sebastian Harvey, Sheriff, 1609 ; died Feb. 21, 1621. A Court (Ironmongers Company) held March 12, 1620–21, records that " whereas the lady Harvey hath paid to the Warders XX^{li} for a dynner for the Company the 21st of this month being the funeral day of Sir Sebastian Harvey deceased ; it is ordered that Mr. Thomas Large & Mr. John Wilson shall join with the Wardens for the provisions of that dynner to husband the same to the Company's best profit."

P. 205. Peter Tryon. " Peter Trioen born at Wulvergem, Flanders, now dwelling in the psh. of St. Christopher, near the Stocks, being a free denizen of England." Will dated June 20, 1608. Court of Husting, London.

Among other legacies, £4000 to Mary, his daughter, wife of Mr. Sebastian Harvey.

Hornchurch Register (Marriage). " 1599. Sebastian Harvey, gent., & Mary Tryon of the parish of St. Christopher in London were married April 23."

P. 210. Thomas Urswyk was son of Thomas Urswick, of Bedsworth and Uprawcliff. His first wife's name was Needham, by whom he had one daughter, who became a nun.

P. 211. Richard Riche was great-grandfather of Richard, first Baron Rich (*vide* p. 38 and note). Thomas Urswyck's widow re-married, in 1482, John Palmer, of Otford, Kent.

P. 211 (*note*). There is little doubt as to this relationship. Christopher Urswick died March 24, 1521–2. He was Dean of Windsor. Buried in St. Augustine's Church, Hackney, and when that church was demolished his memorial was removed to the neighbouring church of St. John's.

P. 212. Sir George Harvey. " As Lieutenant of the Tower he had the custody of Sir Walter Raleigh, whom he indulged in a variety of ways. He frequently invited him to his table, and finding ' the prisoner was engaged in ' various chemical experiments, he lent him his private garden to set up his still." (Gosse's " Raleigh.")

P. 214. Line 14. For 1600–1 read 1660–1.

P. 218. For Henry V. (1419–20) read (1418).

P. 218. Was Lawrence Wright father to Henry Wright, of Dagenham, Co. Essex ? Courthope says that the latter was created a baronet June 11, 1660, married Anne, daughter of John, Lord Crewe, and died Feb. 5, 1663, and that his son and heir (Henry) died a minor and unmarried in 1681, when the title became extinct. ("Extinct Baronetage.")

P. 263. John Lackland was at Havering September 23, 1212, and at Colchester on September 28.   Edward II. was at Romford November 18, 1321, and at Ilford a few days afterwards, where there were said to be supporters of one Bartholomew de Badlesmere, then a rebel.

P. 265. The windmills have now all disappeared, the last one being taken down in 1906.

P. 267 (*footnote*). This church, together with the adjoining house and grounds, is now the property of the West Ham County Borough. Major Ibbetson died in February, 1908.

P. 268. The Rev. J. P. Shawcross resigned the benefice in October, 1904, on his appointment to the chaplaincy of Winchester Union, with a general licence to officiate in the Diocese of Winchester. He was succeeded by the Rev. Elson Isaac Colnett, formerly curate of Loughton. Mr. Colnett graduated B.A. at Cambridge in 1888, M.A. in 1893; ordained by the Bishop of Rochester in 1890.

P. 268. Mr. J. W. Freshwater died in 1908, and the Rev. W. Morris (Chaplain to the Romford Union) in 1907.

P. 280. The second portion of St. Paul's was dedicated in July, 1905. The third section will shortly be in hand; when completed, the whole edifice will be consecrated and constituted the parish church of a new ecclesiastical district.

P. 284. Under the Forest system each parish in the Forest appointed a reeve and four assistants, who were duly sworn at the Forest courts, and whose duty it was to mark all cattle (horses and horned stock, not sheep) turned out by the inhabitants of the parish.   Each branding-iron bore a U-shaped trefoiled crown, impaled on a letter of the alphabet, not the initial letter of the parish, but one of a series.   The one alphabetical series from A to R ran over both sides of the Roding, *i.e.*, Epping and Hainault Forests.   The letter for Dagenham was L; for Barking K.

P. 300 (*note*). This Sir John was born in 1562 and died 1639 (November 25).   Buried in Great Stanmore Church.   Married Catherine Fanshawe and had issue, two sons and two daughters.   Of the latter, the eldest married Sir Robt. Knollys ; the other (Catherine) married William Fanshawe a nephew of Sir Thos. Smythe, a half-brother or son of Sir Henry Fanshawe. (Dict. Nat. Biog. lxii.)

The staunch Royalist referred to in the note was not the above Sir John.

INDEX

For technical terms, *e.g.* "Hide," "Villenage," etc., see Appendix A.

PRINTED BY WILLIAM CLOWES AND SONS, LIMITED, LONDON AND BECCLES.

Lightning Source UK Ltd.
Milton Keynes UK
UKHW02f2041180218
318060UK00003B/81/P